MW01069242

THE DEVIL'S MUSIC

THE DEVIL'S MUSIC

How Christians Inspired, Condemned, and Embraced Rock 'n' Roll

Randall J. Stephens

Harvard University Press
Cambridge, Massachusetts
London, England
2018

Printed in the United States of America

First printing

Library of Congress Cataloging-in-Publication Data

Names: Stephens, Randall J., 1973– author.
Title: The devil's music : how Christians inspired, condemned, and embraced rock 'n' roll / Randall J. Stephens.
Description: Cambridge, Massachusetts : Harvard University Press, 2018. | Includes bibliographical references and index.
Identifiers: LCCN 2017038288 | ISBN 9780674980846 (cloth)
Subjects: LCSH: Rock music—Religious aspects—Christianity. | Rock music—History and criticism. | Rock music—United States—History and criticism. | Christian rock music—United States—History and criticism. | Fundamentalism—United States—History.
Classification: LCC ML3921.8.R63 S74 2018 | DDC 306.4/84260973—dc23
LC record available at https://lccn.loc.gov/2017038288

CONTENTS

INTRODUCTION

In 2014, the rock 'n' roll and country music legend Jerry Lee Lewis was seventy-nine years old. He had entered a quiet, more reflective phase of his life. And he was ready to talk a little about it. Somehow, he had survived, whereas other first-generation dynamos like Elvis Presley, Roy Orbison, Carl Perkins, Johnny Cash, and so many others had passed away. The Ferriday, Louisiana, native's sensational career, starting in the mid-1950s, had been marked by a frenetic stage show, wild pounding on the piano, and songs that rose to a blistering crescendo. His 1957 hit song "Whole Lotta Shakin' Goin' On" rose to number three on the pop chart and topped both the country and the rhythm and blues charts. The follow-up, "Great Balls of Fire," scored similar success. But in the harsh glare of the public spotlight, Lewis also suffered the indignities of marital scandal, came under the watchful eye of the Internal Revenue Service, had run-ins with the law, and succumbed to drugs and alcohol. One of his sons drowned in a swimming pool. Another died in a jeep accident.[1]

His career suffered a particularly strange blow on November 23, 1976. The Killer, a nickname that stuck, showed up at the gates of Elvis Presley's Graceland mansion in the middle of the night, waving a gun and shouting obscenities. He wanted to see the hermit King. Elvis did not go out to meet the maniacal Lewis. Instead, police came to arrest him at three in the morning. "Talk about rock-and-roll depravados," cracked the critic Nick Tosches, "Jerry Lee makes them all look like Wayne Newton." He dubbed the performer a "Baptist Dionysos aflame with glorious cowardice and self-killing guilt."[2]

Late in life, however, it seemed as though Jerry Lee wanted to set things right. "I put God first now, always," an older, chastened Jerry Lee told Patrick Doyle of *Rolling Stone* magazine. "I pray all the time, really. I do a lot of what's required," he confessed. "I pay my tithe offerings at the Church of God, in Cleveland, Tennessee. That's how I was raised." That pentecostal denomination, headquartered in the hills west of the Blue Ridge mountains, had once counted the young Johnny Cash among its faithful.[3]

Try as he might, Lewis could not keep the hounds of guilt at bay. "I was always worried whether I was going to heaven or hell," he confided to a *Guardian* journalist in 2015. "I still am. I worry about it before I go to bed; it's a very serious situation. I mean you worry, when you breathe your last breath, where are you going to go?" He regularly hinted that he felt torn between good and evil, God and the devil. His pentecostal roots ran deep. So in 1979, when *Rolling Stone* magazine's Robert Palmer asked him, "[Is it true] that you believe you're a sinner and going to hell for playing rock & roll," Lewis fired back, "Yep." "I *know* the right way," he replied emphatically. "I was raised a good Christian. But I couldn't make it. . . . Too weak, I guess."[4]

Conservative Christians found the Killer's life and actions objectionable, to say the least; however, they certainly agreed with him on some counts. Rock 'n' roll *was* the devil's music. Indeed, Jerry Lee's cousin, the pentecostal televangelist Jimmy Lee Swaggart, said as much from the pulpit. The two were close in their youth, along with another cousin, the future country singer Mickey Gilley. Swaggart liked to say that he and Jimmy Lee were almost like twin brothers. They took in the music and the message of pentecostalism, the religion of the spirit, of signs and wonders. Neither completed high school. But what they lacked in formal training they more than made up for in charisma and stage presence. As Jerry Lee made it big as a rock 'n' roller, Jimmy Lee embarked on his preaching and music ministry career. In the 1970s and 1980s, the high-profile Assemblies of God minister was using his rock 'n' roll cousin as a sermon illustration and a stern warning to youngsters and their parents.[5]

At a summer 1985 service in New Haven, Connecticut, Swaggart made direct links between the satanic scourge of rock music and pentecostalism. He was ashamed to admit that his own religious tradition had helped produce the horrid music, he said as he paced furiously back and forth on a long stage. He was wearing his trademark large, square-framed glasses, and his blonde hair was styled into a conservative coif.

To dramatize his points, he spoke with a loud, staccato voice, elongating words like "pul-pit" with his southern drawl. Sweating under the harsh, bright stage lights he waved his open Bible high above his head. "My family started rock and roll!" he shouted to the quiet assembly of thousands and then paused for emphasis. "I don't say that with any glee! I don't say it with any pomp or pride! I say it with shame and sadness, because I've seen the death and the destruction. I've seen the unmitigated misery and the pain. I've seen it!" His voice cracked with emotion. "I speak of experience," he warned, pointing his index finger into the air. "My family—Jerry Lee Lewis, with Elvis Presley, with Chuck Berry . . . started rock and roll!"[6] Such claims served a rhetorical point. And they worked well. The congregation clapped with approval while some wiped away tears, moved by his convincing words. Finally, the well-known evangelist concluded the event with an emotional call to repentance and an invitation to the altar.[7] In these years other forms of repentance would be worked out in public rituals. A popular record-burning craze in the late 1970s and early 1980s had already made the moral outrage of Swaggart and other crusaders the stuff of national headlines.

In early December 1980, Pastor LeRoy Peters, a Catholic-turned-fundamentalist Christian, organized an anti-rock-'n'-roll rally. It was a quarter of a century since Jerry Lee and a host of other performers had fired the imagination of the country's teenagers and sparked a moral panic. One hundred evangelicals gathered with the minister on a chilly night in Saint Paul, Minnesota, at Zion Christian Life Center. They came to smash and burn rock records. The red-carpeted chapel was soon littered with their night's work. Shouts of "Hallelujah" and "Praise the Lord" rang out over the ruckus. They pulled the black vinyl records out of their sleeves and snapped and cracked them with excitement. Scattered around their feet lay thousands of LP covers by American and English bands and artists like the Eagles, Donna Summer, Chicago, the Electric Light Orchestra, the Bee Gees, Led Zeppelin, John Denver, and the Beach Boys.[8]

The glam metal band KISS was a favorite target of such holy rage. The group, decked out with its outlandish makeup and costumes, embodied all sorts of devilish tropes for evangelicals and fundamentalists. The band licensed plenty of kitschy merchandise, including trading cards, a board game, T-shirts, and action figures, all ready-made for the purging flames. Youth ministers and traveling speakers liked to warn young people that the band's name stood for "Knights In the Service of Satan."[9]

Pastor Peters addressed his enthusiastic crowd. His listeners, like many other conservative Christians—whether Catholic, Protestant fundamentalists, or their more moderate evangelical cousins—thought God was near them. God was close as well as personal. He answered prayer, redeemed sinners, healed the sick and performed other miracles, heard the prayers of the faithful, came alive in the pages of the Bible, and was a real and powerful force in the modern world. Many of them believed America was meant to play a critical role in the moral cleansing of the world. "Almighty God, we thank you for bringing us together tonight," Peters proclaimed. "God, we thank you for helping us to release ourselves from these graven images and, Lord, we thank you for America, which lets us give witness to You in the way we do." That rang even more true when reports of such crusades made their way into large-circulation newspapers and magazines and then onto national television and radio news. For example, the *Washington Post* ran a feature story on LeRoy Peters and his campaign against rock. The reporter who witnessed the affair wrote, "Outside, on this cold, crisp Minnesota night, a fire burns for Jesus, waiting to reduce to ashes the album jackets that now lie in repose on the chapel floor."[10]

Other well-publicized, church-sponsored public burnings, youth group record-smashing parties, and seminars condemning rock occurred around the country in the late 1970s and early 1980s. Such bonfires of the vulgarities coincided with a much broader conservative turn in America. They took place in church parking lots and at Christian schools and colleges in the years that Jerry Falwell's Moral Majority, Phyllis Schlafly's Eagle Forum, Beverly LaHaye's Concerned Women for America, and similar advocacy groups formed and drew millions of Americans together in a conservative, "pro-family" battle. America's largest Protestant denomination, the Southern Baptist Convention, with approximately fourteen million members in the 1980s, lurched to the right. Fundamentalism gained ground in its colleges and seminaries. Liberal mainline denominations had been in decline since the 1960s. The sociologist Ellen Rosenberg labeled Southern Baptists "hyper-Americans." Patriotism, biblical literalism, and conservative positions on gender and sexuality shaped the denomination's new, strident outlook.[11]

The intense reaction against rock 'n' roll music, which reached a new crescendo with the enthusiastic rallies and public record burnings of the early 1980s, reveals much about conservative American Christianity. Similarly, the long and complex relationship between believers and pop culture has been a dynamic story of how the faithful encountered and reacted to the perceived moral chaos surrounding them. Recent scholarship has focused on evangelical, fundamentalist, or Catholic political engagement. Attention has seldom been paid to the fascinating world of Christianity, rock music, and pop culture.[12] Scholarly accounts of Christian rock and the Jesus people tend to focus mostly on the Christian rock genre but do not look at other intersections of rock music and religion or at the prevalence of the distaste for rock among American religious groups.[13] Some have zeroed in on the culture or the materiality of evangelicalism.[14] But here, too, little focus has been on music and the social and cultural revolutions rock inspired.

In 2012, the music critic and journalist Greil Marcus reflected on the seismic cultural changes the music brought to youth and pop culture. These new, bizarre, and even threatening songs were intelligible to young listeners. That was one of the many reasons rock 'n' roll struck befuddled parents, pastors, and teachers with such force.

> As a seemingly newly discovered form of speech, rock 'n' roll proclaimed its novelty in the way in which it became instantly self-referential, a world that, even as it was being built, was complete in itself, a Tower of Babel where whatever was said, however unlikely, no matter how close it was to speaking in tongues, regardless of whether it was babble and meant to be, was instantly understood.[15]

But even if parents and church leaders thought the music was cacophonic and its lyrics were an incomprehensible, moronic babble, they still took them quite seriously. They did not shut out the teeming culture and the wider world around them. The historian Joel Carpenter fittingly observes that "fundamentalists at turns could be deeply alienated from the mainstream of American culture while still yearning to engage that culture for the sake of the gospel."[16] Their pendulum swung from an inward-focused sectarianism to an outward-moving exploration of the secular, political arena, or the realm of pop culture. Evangelicals and fundamentalists always had a hot and cold relationship with entertainment phenomena and the worldly society around them. Few attractions brought out this tension as rock 'n' roll music did.[17] Conservative Christians from the mid-1950s onward wanted to understand rock 'n' roll music's appeal and power. Evangelicals were certainly not the insulated, Bible-thumping troglodytes that hostile critics often claimed they were. The image of the sectarian, cutoff believer persists, though. As one observer put it, in the eyes of many of their determined opponents, fundamentalists were "arrogant, blinkered, and culturally illiterate."[18]

Stalwarts engaged with the pop culture, just as they lashed out at trends in music and youth fads that they thought were dangerous or sinful. Rock 'n' roll actually made believers think long and hard about race, gender, the limits of freedom of expression, music and decorum, and much more. And when hyper-American evangelicals and like-minded conservatives began to explore popular and rock music they did so by thinking through how their churches and denominations could or could not relate to the larger culture and to a secular society.

Whether shouting down heavy metal or borrowing the rhythms and fashions of rock music, evangelicals won few allies. In 2005, a critic in *Pop Matters* wondered how it was that God's "omnipotent creativity does not extend to the music."[19] For decades, critics and the cognoscenti had labeled "Christian rock" a hopeless oxymoron. The genre was tragically uncool. Jesus rock bands had committed the cardinal sin of substituting evangelism and sincerity for artistry and craftsmanship, said doubters.

In some ways the battle over music, values, and taste was a proxy war for control over the nation and for the hearts and minds of teens. In 1980, it looked to many as if the conservatives were winning the war. There was some worry within the music industry about the chilling effect that the Religious Right and the Reagan Revolution would have on a lucrative, multibillion-dollar industry.[20] Artists and performers fretted, too, about freedom of expression. So hostile were the two camps in the early 1980s that punk rock outfits and even progressive rock groups targeted intolerance, censorship, and political conservatism in their songs with greater frequency and vigor. Television preachers and the Republican president were favorite objects of scorn and ridicule. A singer and keyboard player for the progressive rock band Styx felt that he needed to clear things up with the press. Their 1983 album *Kilroy Was Here,* which went platinum, "is *not* about Jerry Falwell," said Dennis DeYoung. DeYoung, who went on to play Pontius Pilate in the 1995 Broadway revival of the rock opera *Jesus Christ Superstar,* claimed *Kilroy* was "a statement about extremism—in this case, the extreme censorship of rock and roll."[21] Two veteran managers (for AC/DC, Ted Nugent, and Aerosmith) commented on the conservative ascendancy in the pages of *Billboard* magazine. "The biggest threat to [the rock] industry in the next 10 years will come from the . . . Moral Majority," they speculated, adding sarcastically that Jerry Falwell's mass movement would try to "shut down the 'devil's trilateral commission' of sex, drugs, and rock 'n' roll."[22]

Presidential candidate Ronald Reagan rallied believers who were fed up with the hold that Satan seemed to have on youth. They were frustrated with the direction in which their country was heading. In early August 1986, a group of political commentators and journalists interviewed President Reagan about the troubles of modern youth and drug abuse in America. Asked about how his sunny optimism squared with darker social realities, Reagan admitted that there was much work to be done. He also pointed the finger squarely at rock celebrities and the entertainment industry.[23] The former California governor had already risen to national fame in the 1960s for targeting the counterculture and denouncing, as he put it, "that mess in Berkeley."[24] Now he went after other Pied Pipers of teenagers. If the president "described America as upbeat, optimistic—why are drugs such a problem now?" the reporters asked. "Well, how do you relate that?" said Reagan in his typical off-the-cuff and somewhat disjointed, rambling style. "For one thing," he continued,

> we've had some of our modern day things of interest to young people in the music world that has stimulated this, that it made it sound as if it's right there and the thing to

> do, and rock and roll concerts and so forth, musicians that the young people like and that make no secret of the fact that they are users, and many times, when they're performing, the lyrics of songs, show business, itself.[25]

Record company executives, music chain stores, and others in the industry felt unfairly targeted. The president grossly mischaracterized their business, they replied. Yet Jerry Falwell, Jimmy Swaggart, LeRoy Peters, and similar anti-rock-music evangelists would have nodded in confident agreement.

The Reagan-era crusade against drug-pushing and immoral performers found a handful of young, high-profile enthusiasts. Peters's sons, Jim and Steve, toured the Midwest, hosting events featuring condemnations of rock, and claimed to have destroyed $500,000 worth of magazines, records, and tapes. The Peterses spelled out the decadence of pop stars in lurid detail. Top musicians, the two warned, championed not only drug use, they also promoted bestiality, incest, and a host of other depravities. The Beatles were dead, said Jim, "but I know personally that Jesus is still alive."[26] Teens who attended the brothers' rallies ripped tape out of eight-track cartridges and cassettes. Young men and women stood around bonfires, the flames reflected in their joyful faces. They were happy to have broken the bonds of hell that the music had fastened on them. ABC television's *Good Morning America* and CBS's *Morning News* reported on these celebrated record burnings, and United Press International picked up the story as well. At one of the Peters brothers' mass meetings in Lafayette, Louisiana, 1,700 youths attended. Those assembled burned an estimated $50,000 worth of rock memorabilia and records. Public spectacles like these more often occurred in fundamentalist and pentecostal churches, which paid greater attention to the work of the devil in the world.[27] But seminars, rallies, and other events denouncing rock had widespread appeal.

Record and tape burnings spread across North Carolina and South Carolina as well. At a 1983 meeting at Ocean View Baptist Church in North Carolina, teens threw their records into a fire in an old rusty barrel. They pitched in copies of albums by relatively harmless FM radio standards like Bread, Glen Campbell, Chicago, and Blood, Sweat, and Tears. Such public rituals divided opinion in small communities around the United States. Did not these public burnings look like what happened in Nazi Germany? asked unsettled onlookers. A pastor of a local Pentecostal Holiness Church thundered that rock music "is definitely poisonous, disruptive," and bad for society. Still, it seemed a little too drastic, he thought, to start torching records and stirring up youth. The *Wilmington Morning Star* contacted an expert to make sense of it all. A psychology professor at a branch campus of the University of North Carolina responded that record burning was strange but completely acceptable in a free society.[28]

Of course, these angry, public protests and ideological battles were nothing new. Record and rock 'n' roll paraphernalia pyres had been kindled by youth pastors, Sunday school teachers, parents, and their teenage children since the 1950s. From the days when the music first made national news in the mid-1950s, concerned Americans had been demonizing rock 'n' roll's shouting and shaking performers. For them it not only represented a threat to their schools and to their children but also seemed to show that the church was losing its influence on the nation. Young men and women, who should have been content to sing hymns or peppy gospel songs, became enthralled with rock 'n' roll celebrities and films, and spent their disposable income on records and dance tickets. In 1958, radio DJs and station managers responded to the clamor against rock 'n' roll by Christian listeners. A number of stations banned the music outright. A station in San Francisco came up with the slogan "I Kicked the Junk Music Habit by Listening to KSFR." At the Milwaukee-based WISN a DJ burned two hundred rock records in the courtyard of the station. Denver's WDEN launched a civic improvement campaign that targeted rock 'n' roll. "Help stamp out rock and roll," proclaimed a regular spot that the station aired. *Billboard* magazine called these "sneer campaigns." Such stunts especially appealed to the more conservative Protestants, anxious about rock 'n' roll's hold on their children.[29]

When Congress held hearings on the music business and rock 'n' roll in 1958, Americans took greater notice. Letters flooded into senators' offices and to the committee chairman. Writing in March 1958, one Philadelphia businessman urged action. "Sir, please believe us when we say we beg of you and your committee to give us immediate relief from those nasty, filthy types of music and songs that is [*sic*] being forced into our homes against our will and is doing more to create juvenile delinquency." It was all "very harmful to the morals of our children, even those too young to know what they are trying to imitate." What he called "lewd and suggestive songs" were particularly troubling.[30] Anxious parents had plenty of examples, from jukebox singles to chart-topping radio hits. Early 1950s rhythm and blues songs set the tone. Jackie Brenston and His Delta Cats' "Rocket 88" (1951) employed a double entendre about sexual prowess and a stylish, fast car. The titles of other numbers—the Swallows' "It Ain't the Meat (It's the Motion)" (1951); the Toppers' "Baby, Let Me Bang Your Box" (1954); Dinah Washington's "Big Long Slidin' Thing" (1954)—produced similar outrage. Later rock 'n' roll hits added to the moral panic. Songs such as Little Richard's "Long Tall Sally" (1956), Gene Vincent's "Woman Love" (1956), and Jerry Lee Lewis's "Big Legged Woman" (1958) provoked religious and secular leaders' righteous indignation.[31]

Even President Dwight Eisenhower added his voice to the chorus of censure. A little more than two years out of office, Eisenhower delivered a scathing critique of rock 'n' roll. His speech, given at the opening of his new presidential library in Abilene, Kansas, took a decidedly contemporary tone. Modern, abstract art and the dance craze called the twist irked the former commander in chief. The dance that rock 'n' roll star Chubby Checker made an international sensation was anything but innocent, said Eisenhower. The fad seemed a sure sign that the nation's spiritual development had not kept up with its scientific and industrial progress. Twenty-five thousand listeners on the Kansas plains heard the seventy-two-year-old Ike venerate the hardy pioneers of his home state, who battled Indians and suffered through innumerable floods and droughts. They were strong, self-possessed, and God fearing, he said. "Now, I wonder if some of those people could come back today and see us doing the twist instead of the minuet—whether they would be particularly struck by the beauty of the dance?" It represented a decline in the nation's morality and cultural standards. Like other forms of popular entertainment, the hip swiveling and the footwork of the twist put on full display "vulgarity, sensuality," and "downright filth." "Now, America today is just as strong as it needs to be," he nonetheless assured the crowd. "America is the strongest nation in the world, and she will never be defeated or damaged seriously by anyone from the outside. Only Americans, only Americans can ever hurt us." He closed by exhorting his listeners to look to the great political leaders of America's storied past. "So, my prayer is merely this: That all of us will be inspired by the examples of those men long gone." Lincoln and Washington, not Presley or Checker, should be moral guides.[32]

The *New York Times* took stock of the former president's jeremiad by convening a panel of experts. Was the country really in a moral tail-spin, as indicated by the latest dance craze, abstract expressionism, and other signs of the times? No, answered most. The American historian Allan Nevins was particularly dubious. "Americans have been especially open to castigation," he mused, "because they had a golden opportunity to create a bright new society in an unpolluted continent." In the long arc of American history, declension narratives often helped make sense of change.[33]

But the wisdom of professors and pundits was no match for wider, popular feelings or the words of the president and former general. Americans in this era worried about the pernicious influence that communism, secularism, and pop culture were having on society. Adding to their worries, the Gallup organization found that the percentage of those who thought that religion "is increasing its influence on American life" was down from 69 percent in 1957 to 45 percent in 1962, the year Eisenhower delivered his speech excoriating the twist.[34] Whether real or imagined, some Americans perceived that things were getting worse. Popular culture, and rock 'n' roll music in particular, with its more expressive and shocking forms, was a large part of the problem. Beginning in the 1950s, numerous evangelicals, Catholics, and other American Christians worried about the pernicious influence of rock 'n' roll music, dance crazes, and other fads that surrounded the genre. The crusades of these years against rock 'n' roll—tied as they were to views about race, gender, sexuality, and decadence—reveal much about the fears and anxieties of American believers. From the mid-1950s forward, church leaders, lay people, and denominations grappled with the problems of assertive youth and the challenges of modern times.

By the late 1960s, however, such persistent and powerful fears of moral decline, ironically, inspired a new willingness to blend popular music, and even rock, with an evangelical message. The Jesus people movement that first emerged out of nondenominational churches in California,

Georgia, New Jersey, and across the country inspired young believers with a countercultural-style faith. This was a new kind of relevant hippie Christianity. Its young longhaired and beard-wearing adherents eagerly played rock music during their worship services, adopted the tastes and fashions of the Age of Aquarius, and called for a revolution in the practice of evangelism and church worship.

There was some precedent for this within the fold. The British founder of the Salvation Army, William Booth, had declared roughly a century before, "The music of the Army is not, as a rule, original. We seize upon the strains that have already caught the ear of the masses, we load them with our one great theme—salvation—and so we make the very enemy help us fill the air with our Saviour's fame."[35] Salvationists drew from spirituals, Victorian ballads, drinking songs, and patriotic anthems.[36] Hence, it was not completely out of step with tradition when America's most well known evangelical, Billy Graham, lent his support to the pop Jesus cause in the early 1970s. He adopted the language of the counterculture when speaking to teenagers and college students. He also supported the mixture of rock and pop music and evangelicalism. Performers, pastors, and church leaders eventually found a way to sanctify the loud, electrified, and beat-driven music. To make the transformation complete, the lyrics of what would be called Jesus rock implored listeners to repent, celebrated the joys of being a believer, warned of the apocalypse, or counseled fans to live a life of purity and devotion.[37]

Still, it was a surprising, seemingly unimaginable transformation. Graham, like many other Christians, had lashed out at rock 'n' roll in previous years. This shocking new genre was a clear sign of degeneracy and modern sin, they vented. At Graham's 1960 crusade at Griffith Stadium in Washington, DC, he enjoined teenagers to live clean lives. Desperate for direction and security, many youngsters had made heroes out of Elvis Presley and the television rock 'n' roll host and promoter Dick Clark. Elvis, preached Graham, was a clear and potent indication of the moral decline and sin that so pervaded society.[38] His earlier judgment was similar to that made by many other Americans, who had long opposed music of "low" or "profane" origin. Victorians scorned bawdy barroom songs and vulgar Irish tunes. In the early twentieth century, jazz and Dixieland were new targets of moral outrage. Certainly such disdain and indignation did not just come from religious circles, however influential churches and clergymen were when policing the boundaries of taste and entertainment. Representatives of the black middle class and social elite had made strong nonreligious arguments about popular music. Revved-up dance songs, in this rendering, were unseemly and uncivilized.[39] That was the tack taken by the music editor of W. E. B. Du Bois's journal *The Crisis.* "Let us hope that it is true that the makers of entertaining music have learned a lesson," observed Maud Cuney-Hare in 1936. Such entertainers should "come to realize that no seeker after Beauty can find inspiration in the common combination of unlovely tones and suggestive lyrics. Music should sound, not screech; Music should cry, not howl; Music should weep, not bawl; Music should implore, not whine."[40]

For conservative Christians, too, pop music often channeled bad taste and was beneath their exacting standards. Among America's many Christians, evangelicals raised the loudest complaint. Others might find the songs of Elvis, the Beatles, Led Zeppelin, or Madonna degraded and artless. But for evangelicals, fundamentalists, and other conservatives it was much more than that. The music was sinful, deranged, and demonic. Conservative Protestant and Catholic magazines sounded the alarm with headlines like "Musical Smut," "What Is the Disease in Modern Popular Music?," "Rock and Roll: The Devil's Heartbeat," and "Are the Beatles Minstrels of the Antichrist?"[41] For the author of the last, the question quite simply answered itself.

Such definitive hostility makes it all the more unusual that by the late 1960s and early 1970s, millions of conservative Christians decided that rock music could serve the church and the cause of evangelism. Christian rock bands—equipped with electric guitars, drums, tambourines, and synthesizers—became an important feature of pentecostal and charismatic churches. (The latter tradition, originating in the 1950s and 1960s, brought the theology and practice of pentecostalism—speaking in tongues and divine healing especially—into mainline, established churches.) Soon the music and styles of rock also made their way into Southern Baptist, Nazarene, Presbyterian, and other denominations. The change was evident to anyone who listened to the new sound of worship bands or witnessed sermons by longhaired pastors and youth ministers who donned bell-bottom jeans, wore faded denim jackets, and used the idioms of the counterculture.

How did believers go from shouting down the devil's music to fashioning what would come to be known as Christian rock? The answer can be found in the enormous cultural, political, and generational changes that shook postwar churches in America. Never in living memory had the divide between young and old been so vast. The perilous generation gap would plague conservative Christians while also inspiring them to adapt the form of rock music for a higher, holy purpose. But too great a focus on later developments obscures an important aspect of this convergence. Rock 'n' roll music and pentecostalism had been closely related from the earliest days of the genre.[42]

Ironically, the religion of the spirit helped inspire rock—the soundtrack of youth rebellion—which stalwarts spent so much time and energy responding to and sermonizing against. Tensions between the sacred and the profane loomed large. Pentecostal music, preaching styles, and performance inspired rock 'n' roll's early pioneers. Adventurous performers in the Eisenhower years—who hailed from Mississippi, Arkansas, Georgia, and Louisiana—borrowed directly from their regional religious traditions to craft a new form of pop music. In subsequent years, Christian hippies and unconventional youth pastors, coffee shop owners, and pentecostal ministers adopted and enhanced music and performance styles from more secular forms of pop culture and reached massive new audiences. Pentecostalism proved critical at every stage. As a relatively new religious movement, it was not inhibited by tradition and formality as mainline white and black churches were. Adherents were more likely to innovate around the use of media and the formation of musical styles. The unrestricted format of the sanctified, tongues-speaking faith had a lasting impact on rock 'n' roll.

In fact, the culture of southern pentecostalism influenced early rock in startlingly powerful ways and helped give birth to the new genre. Such dynamic performers and chart toppers as Elvis Presley, Johnny Cash, Little Richard, B. B. King, Sister Rosetta Tharpe, Jerry Lee Lewis, and James Brown all were nurtured by close associations with pentecostal and holiness churches in the South. It is no coincidence that rock music and pentecostalism were at first strongest in Dixie. The sensuality and driving rhythm of rock 'n' roll owed much to outsider pentecostal church worship. One of America's most important cultural exports, rock 'n' roll, had first emerged among religious groups functioning on the geographic and social fringe of society.

The potent religious connection was played out in the tumultuous lives of some of rock 'n' roll's most famous stars. Johnny Cash, Jerry Lee Lewis, and Little Richard struggled with the heavy weight of the devil's music and what they thought to be its sinful excesses.[43] In 1957, a peak year for the new music, Little Richard claimed to have seen the light and thus walked away from his successful career. He prepared to become a revival preacher. "I wanted people to forget Little Richard as a Rock 'n' Roller," he said. "I was soon to be qualified as an evangelist like Billy Graham."[44]

Twenty years later, in the winter of 1977, a reporter interviewed Jerry Lee Lewis, who was making his way around the nation in his shag-carpeted tour bus (and dressing room on wheels). It was just months before Elvis would finally succumb to the numerous pills he had been popping since his days in the army. Jerry Lee had been unhealthily obsessed with Elvis and had brooded over the King of Rock 'n' Roll's fame and wealth that had somehow eluded him. His arrest outside Graceland the year before was just the most visible aspect of an unhealthy fixation. Now the rock 'n' roll celebrity, in a nostalgic, somber mood, was muttering, "I wish I were strong enough to quit right now and go back to preaching." His cousin Jimmy Lee Swaggart had long ago taken up the call and had devoted his life to ministry in the Assemblies of God church. "I can't give up rock 'n' roll," Jerry Lee lamented. "It drives me crazy man!" He was not able to shake the nagging guilt. He held out hope, however. Maybe he could still set things right, abandon the devil's music, and renew his pentecostal calling.[45]

Since pentecostalism's emergence in the early twentieth century, its devotees had emphasized healing, prophecy, and millennialism while fostering revved-up music and experimenting with unorthodox worship forms. At the churches that Jerry Lee and Jimmy Lee attended as children, worshippers regularly spoke in tongues. These ecstatic utterances had marked pentecostalism off from other groups since the early years of the century. The faithful's beliefs in healing, miracles, and prophecy were unlike the beliefs of other Christians as was their willingness to cross the color line despite the reigning segregation in other

Protestant churches. In the postwar era some music in pentecostal services, outside observers noted, sounded surprisingly like rock 'n' roll. In their houses of worship, black and white pentecostals strummed guitars and played rollicking tunes on the piano or the fiddle. These were not like the sedate services of most mainline churches but rather drew on the music most familiar to their adherents. The critic and Jerry Lee Lewis biographer Nick Tosches even ventures, with a dash of hyperbole, that "if you took the words away, there were more than a few Pentecostal hymns that would not sound foreign coming from the nickel machine in the wildest juke joint."[46] Elvis, Little Richard, and Johnny Cash, like many other early rockers, looked back with fondness on the pentecostal services they attended in their youth.

Religious leaders inside and outside the pentecostal tradition, however, did not see these rockers as kindred spirits. Some believers even worried that the cacophony, shaking, and singing of a rock 'n' roll show looked too much like an old-fashioned pentecostal revival.[47] Conservative religious leaders reacted adversely to the big-beat music because they thought that performers borrowed too heavily from the worship styles and music of their churches. Stars like Elvis, Ray Charles, and Jerry Lee Lewis faced the occasional charge of sacrilege. But even more problematic for rock 'n' roll's many white religious despisers, especially in the South, was the mixing of musical styles and the intermingling of black and white performers on stage and teens on the dance floor. For those critics, the music produced ungodly and unnatural behavior.

Often lurking behind the rock 'n' roll panic were deep fears of racial contamination and religious impurity. "To us, rock and roll is bad enough with Elvis Presley," wrote the polemicists and arch segregationists Lambert and Patricia Schuyler in 1957. In the year that Elvis's hit songs "Teddy Bear" and "Jailhouse Rock" were shooting up the charts, the Schuylers were warning of the dangers integrated music posed to American purity. In the previous decade Lambert had called attention to the supposed Japanese menace to American society. Now he and his wife turned their attention to a new, equally disturbing development. They were mortified to see that "one Negro orchestra or singing group follows after the other on the [movie] screen, all rocking and rolling." The Schuylers said, "[We] simply can't stand it. But teenagers can." That was the rub. White, wholesome teenagers were learning to "love it and never does the thought cross their minds that this incessant emphasis upon the Negro with his repulsive love songs and his vulgar rhythms is but the psychological preliminary to close body contact between the races."[48]

Those most resistant to the civil rights movement joined in the debate. To its horror the White Citizens' Council reported in 1958 that a church in Manchester, England, set sacred music to a "rock-n-roll beat." In the same piece the segregationist group alarmed readers with news of a televised British update on the passion play. Jesus, in this scenario, was played by a juvenile delinquent, "complete with long sideburns, a black leather jacket, tight-fitting blue jeans, and motor-cycle boots." To the editor in Jackson, Mississippi, it smacked of "Religion a la NAACP."[49]

Few, though, could match the racist fire-eating of Alabama's Asa Carter, who eagerly portrayed black and white rock 'n' rollers as equally licentious, vicious, and pagan. The Klansman and White Citizens' Council leader, who stirred up so much discord and violence in Birmingham, had been waging his campaign since the new music was first played on national airwaves. In 1956, Carter demonized rock 'n' roll as "sensuous negro music" that was destroying the "entire moral structure of man, of Christianity, of spirituality in Holy marriage . . . of all the white man has built through his devotion to God."[50]

White Baptists, pentecostals, Methodists, and Presbyterians were usually not as explicit or racist as Carter or the outraged Schuylers. Still, across America in the 1950s and 1960s, churchmen and parents had similar worries. White Christians might not have been so brazen and vocal in their denunciations of the savage rhythms of the electrified music, but they fought it and its influence nonetheless. Many whites feared that the new wild, mixed-race music—along with the intermingling of black and white bodies on the dance floor—would overturn their evangelical Zion.

A Cassandra-like advice columnist for the white pentecostal Assemblies of God echoed this racialized view of calypso and rock. A youngster wrote to him with a dilemma. She had received a radio for Christmas but did not know if it was appropriate for her to tune in to rock 'n' roll stations. God did not seem to be giving her a clear answer about it. Whereas God was silent, the columnist wrote back with strong advice. Rock 'n' roll music was designed to incite passions and unbridled emotions, he said. "The first time I heard the beat of rock and roll," he wrote, "was listening to juju drums in the jungles of Africa." He then concluded, "I cannot enjoy that type of music." It reminded him too much of the worship routines of sensual pagans.[51]

After the 1954 *Brown v. Board of Education* decision that declared school segregation unconstitutional, and as Martin Luther King Jr. emerged as a national leader of the black freedom struggle, white ministers and laypeople, especially in the South, feared that rock-inspired amalgamation would destroy the country. In the South, sermons, editorials, and pamphlets ominously warned of racial disorder. Early fears of rock 'n' roll race mixing and concern about "jungle music" rattled ministers and laypeople.[52] Evangelical missionaries warned that rock 'n' roll dancing, stage antics, and wild music were much like the savagery and heathenism they witnessed in the global South. Missionaries and church officials made direct connections between the work of the church "in darkest Africa" and their outreach to teens at the soda shop or local rec center. Preachers and laypeople pointed the finger at Elvis, Fats Domino, Bill Haley, and other early rockers who were crossing the color line and leading the big-beat rebellion. At the same time, believers felt menaced by juvenile delinquency and the unbridled sexuality on display at rock shows and in the lyrics of popular acts. For Methodists, pentecostals, Baptists, and more it was quite simply godless and anarchic.

In the years between 1958 and 1964, evangelicals and fundamentalists were less threatened by rock 'n' roll because of significant shifts among the first-generation rock 'n' rollers who had so inspired rage, racial fears, and reaction. A victory for conservative Christians began in 1957 as Little Richard, who was touring Australia with Gene Vincent and Eddie Cochran, announced that he would ditch rock 'n' roll and enter the ministry. Then Elvis Presley was drafted by the U.S. Army and spent the next two years being a model soldier in Germany. His recording, film, and performance career came to an abrupt halt. Also in 1958, Elvis's former Sun Records label mate Jerry Lee Lewis saw his career eaten away by scandal after Lewis married his thirteen-year-old cousin. In 1959, Buddy Holly died in a tragic plane crash, alongside tour mates Ritchie Valens and Jiles P. Richardson, otherwise known as the Big Bopper. That same year Chuck Berry—a major star, musical pioneer, and touring giant—faced federal prosecution for violating the Mann Act by transporting an underage Apache girl across state lines. He would spend twenty months in a federal prison.[53] The rock 'n' roll legends of the 1950s fell from the *Billboard* charts as they dropped out of the public eye.

Meanwhile, the new music trends of the late 1950s and early 1960s seldom registered in the minds of conservative believers. Isolated from cultural trends, evangelicals responded only to the most ubiquitous forms of pop culture. Baby-faced crooners with velvet throats, girl groups, and surf bands did not appear as threatening as pelvic-grinding rockers. By the early 1960s, worries of a miscegenationist, antireligious rock revolution had largely subsided. Yet Southern Baptists, Catholics, pentecostals, Presbyterians, Lutherans, and Methodists soon spied new threats on the music horizon.

Ministers and laypeople were unprepared for the frenzy that the Beatles would inspire shortly after the English foursome appeared on American television in February 1964. Carl F. H. Henry, editor of the premier evangelical magazine *Christianity Today,* tried to read the signs of the times. Believers had "taken comfort in the fact that rock and roll seemed to be dying here." However, he noted with dejection, "the ecstatic reception accorded the Beatles bears a rather appalling witness to the emptiness of youthful heads and hearts." He made light of the situation to some extent. America had exported its fair share of rock 'n' roll to Britain. Maybe, Henry grumbled, "there is in the latest exchange a certain poetic justice."[54] Other concerned Christian leaders scoffed when mainstream journalists called the group a harmless fad. What they saw were the Fab Four's tight clothes, long hair, and silly affectations leading youngsters down the road to perdition. In the wake of Beatlemania, Billy Graham earnestly cautioned, "Ancient historians tell us that one of the symptoms of declining civilization is a desexualization of the human race, with men becoming more effeminate and women becoming more masculine."[55] That gender reversal appeared to him to be happening now.

Opposition culminated in 1966 in response to John Lennon's controversial comment that the Beatles had become more popular than Jesus. Christianity would fade away, he confidently told a reporter. Rock 'n' roll, by contrast, was here to stay. In an increasingly secular England

Lennon's remarks caused little concern. American evangelical and Catholic outrage, by contrast, burned hot. A leading religious reporter rated the story the top news item of 1966.[56] Boycotts, concert protests, and large-scale bonfires of their records sponsored by radio stations and churches dogged the band as they toured across the country. Even before the controversy, the Beatles had become a target for conservative Christians who feared that the young men who listened to them were becoming effeminate and rebellious. Girls, too, appeared to lose their senses when they heard the wailing of the Fab Four. The group disrupted the lives of respectful churchgoers. Even worse, though, it appeared that the band and the fanfare surrounding them had become a kind of religion for some impressionable teenagers.[57]

Fundamentalist, evangelical, and pentecostal parents had waged battles against pop culture crazes before. Fads had come and gone. Ragtime music. Bobbed hair. Panty raids. Elvis. But the Beatle menace—along with the threat posed by other British-invasion rock groups like the Rolling Stones—seemed far more destructive. Churchmen had no intention of losing ground to what some were calling an innocent trifle. Thus, commentators took on the Beatles-as-religion issue squarely. Hence, the fundamentalist magazine *King's Business* printed "Ten Commandments for Teen-Agers" in a 1964 issue. The tenth admonished, "Thou shalt not bow the knee to 'Elvis' (Presley) or 'Frankie' (Sinatra) or 'The Beatles.' God alone is worthy of thy worship."[58] That might have been written with tongue in cheek. Still, there was sincerity behind it.

Denominational editors, broadcasters, and pastors hoped their readers and listeners would understand the seriousness of the challenge in their midst. "It may be all right to be patient with harmless clothing fads or Beatle haircuts," observed a concerned pentecostal woman, yet such styles could signal more worrisome trends to come. Key moral principles were at stake when it came to teenage rebellion. Laypeople and clergy should take a firm stand, she remarked.[59]

Did this new obsession with the Beatles mean that youngsters were paying less attention to the sacred truths of old-time religion? One Southern Baptist Sunday school teacher at a large church in North Carolina worried about this very shift in values. In early 1965, he asked his students if they could name the twelve apostles. The average for the boys was two. Then he took his questioning into the pop culture realm, asking if any knew the names of the Beatles' songs. One of his pupils rattled off twenty titles without hesitation.[60]

There was much to fear. For evangelicals and other conservative Christians the counterculture and the social revolutions of the 1960s appeared to be destroying the moral fabric of their country and Christian faith. The sheer size of the baby boom generation, whose members had large disposable incomes, made the problem of youth rebellion and apostasy all the more critical. The free speech movement, opposition to the Vietnam War, looser morality, civil rights protests, college students' flirtations with Eastern religion and leftist politics, and widespread drug use only compounded evangelicals' sense of a frightful downward moral spiral.[61] Conservative Christians struggled mightily with youthful unrest. Rock music, the accompaniment to these radical shifts, provided the blaring soundtrack of destruction in evangelicals' apocalyptic scenario.

And yet many evangelicals as well as Catholics made peace with the *form* of rock music in the late 1960s. Conservative Christianity proved remarkably elastic. Believers had long used nearly any means necessary to steady the faltering or rescue the unconverted. Billy Sunday, the most well known fundamentalist preacher of the century, allegedly declared, "I'd stand on my head in a mud puddle if I thought it would help me win souls to Christ."[62] Evangelical ministers would not stand upside down in a puddle of mud, but many would grow their hair long—as did Billy Graham—and open wide their church doors to hippies and countercultural youngsters. By the late 1960s, folk masses and traditional songs geared to a young audience had become commonplace from California to Georgia. Celebrity revivalist Billy Graham, like a growing number of the faithful, decided that pop songs could be baptized for godly purposes, if that's what youth wanted. This coincided with a generational shift in which baby boomers and their parents—many of them pentecostals, holiness people, or charismatics—played a new role in crafting a vibrant, more culturally flexible faith. The new openness to the counterculture inspired millions and lured them into churches.

Experiments with countercultural and bohemian faith proliferated. Even mainline Protestants took part. In the late 1960s and early 1970s, the Berkeley Free Church in California reached out to wayward young people, hippies, and runaways. The church offered health care, housing, free food, and a variety of other services. It won the support of Presbyterian and Episcopal churches. One witness to a July 1967 colorful evening event, self-described as a "be-in," later wrote about the unusual religious festivities. The Free Church–sponsored gathering drew over "a thousand hippies from nearby Telegraph Avenue." They filled up a Presbyterian church parking lot. The observer noted that "booths had been set up for the sale of incense, beads, and trinkets admired by hippies, and four rock bands provided music. Halfway through the six-hour-long be-in, in which the hippies decorated themselves with beads and crosses, burned incense and danced, the religious ceremonies started." They took part in a large procession, replete with a ten-foot papier-mâché Virgin Mary. Hippies pulled the makeshift statue along on a cart. Episcopal and Roman Catholic priests joined in, along with a Presbyterian minister. The be-in culminated with a ritual foot washing.[63]

Evangelicals or pentecostals in the Midwest and South might have found all this just a little too baffling, if not outright pagan and disturbing. Harvard University professor Harvey Cox tried to make sense of these scenes of religious excess. A public intellectual and a keen observer of religious trends, Cox figured that there was not so great a difference between America's historical religious movements and the newfound spiritualism and communalism of the counterculture. In his view the hippie phenomenon

> does have religious overtones and . . . its growth in America today has a message for both the church and the society. Hippieness represents a secular version of the historic American quest for a faith that warms the heart, a religion one can experience deeply and feel intensely. The love-ins are our 20th century equivalent of the 19th century Methodist camp meetings—with the same kind of fervor and the same thirst for a God who speaks through emotion and not through the anagrams of doctrine. Of course, the Gospel that is preached differs somewhat in content, but then, content was never that important for the revivalist—it was the spirit that counted.[64]

Cox was one of the first to notice and analyze these transformations. Many others followed his lead. In 1972, a *U.S. News and World Report* journalist speculated that "hippies began reading the Bible in large numbers. Suddenly the Bible is better than drugs. Suddenly it was hip to be holy. It was hip to get high on Jesus."[65] So-called Jesus freaks cast a suspicious eye on old-fangled institutional churches, just as hippies had been skeptical of the government, universities, and traditional institutions in general. These Jesus people formed house churches, with acoustic guitars, bongos, and hirsute chorus leaders to guide them in their worship music. Jesus for them was a way of life. He was personal. They were turned on to him. The born-again, pentecostal Johnny Cash became a guiding light for the movement, as did other celebrities who claimed Christian rebirth in the late 1960s and early 1970s, like the English rock sensation Cliff Richard and the American folk-rock singer Barry McGuire.

In many ways the Jesus people remained staunchly conservative, despite their clothes, long hair, countercultural slang, and freeform music.[66] Their songs ushered in a new obsession with the end of the world and helped make Hal Lindsey's apocalyptic guidebook *The Late Great Planet Earth* (1970) the best-selling nonfiction title of the decade. A wave of new Jesus rock and Christian pop groups and solo artists—including Phil Keaggy, Larry Norman, 2nd Chapter of Acts, Chuck Girard, Love Song, and Andraé Crouch—sang of God's love, redemption, the coming of the end of the world, and the perils of youth. This vogue in religious music soon found its way onto FM radio and then Broadway, with hit musicals like *Joseph and the Amazing Technicolor Dreamcoat* (1970), *Jesus Christ Superstar* (1971), and *Godspell* (1971).

The Christian turn in pop music was still strong a decade later. The musicologist and blues musician Robert Palmer took note of popular Christian rock in 1981. Roughly a decade after the music first received widespread attention, Palmer observed that "when rock-and-roll enjoyed its initial surge of popularity in the mid-50s, many fundamentalist Christians recoiled in horror." The lyrics, the beat, and sexuality of it all made it seem like "the Devil's music." Now, declared Palmer in the *New York Times,* rock and fundamentalism "have become more and more closely entwined since the 50's." He pointed to the many popular performers who identified with some variety of Christianity, including Bob Dylan, Al Green, Johnny Cash, B. J. Thomas, Donna Summer, Van Morrison, and Arlo Guthrie. Dylan's *Slow Train Coming* (1979) was the best of the "born again" albums, he judged. Palmer even figured that many Christian artists "write and record music that is more or less indistinguishable from conventional rock and pop."[67] Indeed, the Christian music industry became a big business and a handful of artists even achieved enviable chart success. For some critics of the era, the conservatism and the perceived conformity of Christian pop music never sat well. Rock music was meant to liberate and break with convention, so said doubters. It could never be the theme music of born-again Christianity.

Regardless of their conservative credentials, Jesus hippies, along with Christian rock stars, came under heavy suspicion from other quarters as well. The highly publicized record burnings of the early 1980s were one of the most visible signs of fundamentalist discontent. The rock music that inspired them offended fundamentalist Christians, who were now on the defensive against not just secular rock but Christian rock too. Such critics—who adhered to strict lifestyle standards and held conservative views on gender and sexuality—could not be persuaded by the music's popularity. The controversy over music and style within the conservative Christian world revealed deep, long-standing fissures. Evangelicals were far more elastic when it came to popular culture. Unlike fundamentalists, evangelicals had been more willing to engage with society and had tended to have less of a polemical and dogmatic edge. Accordingly, Carl F. H. Henry rebuked his fundamentalist brethren in 1947 for their inattention to "the evils of racial hatred, the wrongs of current labor-management relations, the inadequate bases of international dealings." For many evangelicals, fundamentalists were out of touch, irrelevant, and overly combative. In turn, fundamentalists thought evangelicals were weak on doctrine, compromised, and too worldly. Evangelicals could more easily borrow from pop culture if and when it suited their needs. But fundamentalists stood their ground, upholding a stubborn culture of separatism from the secular world.[68]

The genre, linked as it was to pentecostalism and the counterculture, raised hackles particularly on the far right. Fundamentalist newspapers like *Sword of the Lord, Christian Crusade, Christian Beacon,* and *Moody Monthly* brimmed with denunciations of the movement and its new sound. The popular Jesus-themed musicals *Jesus Christ Superstar* and *Godspell* also earned their ire. The traveling ministers Sketch Erickson, Bob Larson, Frank Garlock, and dozens of others spoke in churches from coast to coast, authored diatribes about Christian rock, produced sermons on record and tape, and worked tirelessly to halt the advance of rock and pop gospel. Within fundamentalist circles arguments called into question the clothes, hairstyles, and pentecostal heresies of Christian rock.

Fears of race mixing and savage music diminished among fundamentalists in the 1970s, but bulwarks like Bob Jones University in South Carolina still cautioned against the unnatural and dangerous barbarity, as well as the racial anarchy, the music carried with it. For fundamentalists, the gender and social rebellion that post-Beatles groups represented remained threatening. But more importantly, the innovations of both the Jesus people and associated pentecostalism were as biblically unsound to critics as they were threatening.[69] Controversies continued to rage within communities of faith.

Regardless of the fundamentalist holdouts, Christian rock would become a dominant force in pop music by the 1980s and 1990s. Over the decades, evangelicals had become less culturally insular, adopting the fashions and the loud, drum-heavy music of the counterculture. They did so as the movement aligned itself, as never before, with the Republican Party. By the Reagan and George H. W. Bush years, Christian pop music and rock ranked among the most profitable entertainment industries in America. Crossover artists like the glam metal group Stryper, the soft rock star Amy Grant, or alternative acts Switchfoot and Jars of Clay logged successes on radio and in record stores. Simultaneously, famous bands and artists like the postpunk U2, the progressive heavy metal King's X, and the white soul singer-songwriter Van Morrison enriched their songs with Christian imagery and themes. These defied easy categorization.

Contemporary Christian music was raking in almost a billion dollars annually by the late 1990s. Christian bookstores, which by then dotted the suburban landscape of America, sold records by heavy metal acts, rap groups, new wave bands, indie artists, and a range of others. Evangelical rock festivals attracted hundreds of thousands of believers in Illinois, California, Pennsylvania, Tennessee, and Georgia.

Rock 'n' roll's exciting, unconventional mix of country, gospel, and rhythm and blues was first broadcast on the nation's radio stations in the mid-1950s. What had seemed like an undeniable abomination would, after the 1960s countercultural revolution, appear less and less problematic. American Christians eventually made an uneasy peace with the pop music that they had once battled so relentlessly. With each passing decade, it had come to seem less and less threatening to the faithful. Pop genres would become key to American Christian identity and church growth, helping make evangelicalism the largest American religious tradition by 2008.[70] As organs and pianos dominated religious music in earlier eras, guitars, drums, keyboards, and bongos were now typical in evangelical churches. Stripped-down praise choruses became the order of the day. Much of what animates evangelical churches in the twenty-first century comes directly from the unlikely fusion of pentecostal religion, conservative politics, and rock and pop music.

• 1 •

Pentecostalism and Rock 'n' Roll in the 1950s

I just sing like they do back home.
—Elvis Presley, 1956

Elvis wore a red jacket, black shirt and pants, a silver belt glittering with rhinestones, and a yellow tie. It was October 1957 and the star was about to take the stage at the Pan-Pacific Auditorium in Los Angeles. Thousands of fans waited, screaming. Amid the chaos and noise, Elvis made time for a reporter from a teen magazine called *Dig.* His loud outfit and gravity-defying coif contrasted with his humble, polite responses. The reporter wondered how "the reputed King of Rock 'n' Roll" felt about Frank Sinatra's comments that rock fans were just a bunch of "cretinous goons" and that rock 'n' roll was "the martial music of every side-burned delinquent on the face of the earth"? "He has a right to his opinion," Elvis replied, "but I can't see him knocking it for no good reason. I wouldn't knock Frank Sinatra. I like him very much." Then, asked why he gyrated on stage, Elvis said that he didn't really think about his movements. "I just sing like they do back home," he commented. "When I was younger, I always liked spiritual quartets and they sing like that."[1] Elvis, like so many other first-generation rock 'n' rollers, looked back with fondness on his pentecostal upbringing and the gospel quartets that inspired him.

Regardless of such personal associations, in the popular imagination a large gap still separated rock and Christianity. The widespread preaching against rock, which first began in earnest when the music broke onto the national scene in the mid-1950s, sowed the seeds of the idea that the big beat had nothing to do with Christianity in general or evangelicalism and pentecostalism in particular. Although some have paid attention to the impact of gospel music on rock 'n' roll, the more specific religious and cultural roots of the music remain mostly unexplored.[2]

The culture of southern pentecostalism helped give birth to the new genre of rock 'n' roll. That religious stream was one of many that fed into the larger river of rock 'n' roll, but it was an important tributary. Burning controversies, inside and outside churches, surrounded the new musical hybrid. Through it all pentecostalism continued to shape first-generation performers like Elvis Presley, Johnny Cash, Little Richard, and Jerry Lee Lewis. Even before the new music made big news and created a stir, church leaders and laypeople argued about the relationship of popular music to church music. When performers like Ray Charles or Jerry Lee Lewis borrowed from sacred tunes for their recordings and performances, it only confirmed the worst suspicions of black and white believers. The supposed boundaries that existed between religion and nonreligion, sacred and profane were not as formidable as conservative Christians imagined or hoped.[3] In the American South, a region that consistently ranked as the most conventionally religious section of the country, musical influences crossed back and forth over the thresholds of church doors.[4]

In 1960, Flannery O'Connor, the South's most famous Catholic writer and a keen observer of southern zeal, remarked, "I think it is safe to say that while the South is hardly Christ-centered, it is most certainly Christ-haunted."[5] Indeed, since the early nineteenth century black and white evangelical Christianity had dominated below the Mason-Dixon Line. In the mid-1960s, the Southern Baptist scholar and critic Samuel Hill Jr., summed up southern religion, which he considered "a medley of revivalistic and fundamentalistic strains. On its revivalist side, it conceives of Christian faith in definitively inward terms. Faith is a reality to be experienced at the deepest level of one's inner life." For Hill, then, some of southern religion's most representative traits included "the seriousness with which it takes its business; the subjective orientation of its life; its attitude toward change; its high self-estimate; and the peculiar relation which exists between the church and its culture."[6] Evangelicals in the South and elsewhere tended to emphasize the born-again experience, the workings of God in daily life, the wiles of the devil and the perils of sin, the importance of church attendance, the reality of hell, biblical literalism, and strict moral codes.[7] In the first decades of the twentieth century, all the main pentecostal churches in America were headquartered in the South. But even then Baptists and Methodists claimed the largest share of believers. Historically, Catholics, Jews, and nonevangelical Christians had a very small presence. In 1950, two of the country's largest Protestant denominations, the white Southern Baptist Convention and the black National Baptist Convention, boasted over seven million and four million members, respectively.[8] The majority of their adherents resided in the former Confederacy. The South was, and still is, the most homogeneous religious region in the country.[9]

In the middle decades of the twentieth century, pentecostalism was a relatively new offshoot of evangelicalism. It grew out of the holiness movement of the late nineteenth century. Holiness people, many of them former Methodists, looked to key passages of scripture and the writings of John Wesley and proclaimed that believers could be *sanctified,* or set apart, living holy lives, unburdened by sin. Holiness shared some of its optimism with other Victorian movements of spiritual abundance or limitless divine potential, including Christian Science, Seventh-day Adventists, and mind cure. Some of what the psychologist and scholar of religion William James said of mind cure in 1902 also applies to perfectionism and holiness. "The fundamental pillar on which it rests," James observed of mind cure, "is nothing more than the general basis of all religious experience, the fact that man has a dual nature, and is connected with two spheres of thought, a shallower and a profounder sphere, in either of which he may learn to live more habitually. The shallower and lower sphere is that of the fleshly sensations, instincts, and desires, of egotism, doubt, and the lower personal interests."[10] Further, higher spiritual experiences and insights awaited holiness folk who devoted themselves completely to God.

Holiness people stressed heart purity and a strict life of obedience to God. Preachers often targeted lax mainliners for allowing card playing, theater attendance, or even dancing. Such secular amusements, deceptively harmless, led straight to hell, they warned. Critics thought the exuberant, overzealous holiness folk went too far. Mark Twain aimed his satire sights on the most famous southern holiness preacher of the Gilded Age. The Georgia revivalist Sam Jones, wrote Twain in an 1891 short story, unpublished in his lifetime, was an unbearable ignoramus. The story followed the preacher's trip to heaven aboard a celestial train. Jones hollered "hosannahs like a demon" and was scolded by Saint Peter. The evangelist made a complete nuisance of himself in paradise, "preaching and exhorting and carrying on all the time" until "even the papal Borgias were revolted."[11]

Jones and other preachers took it all in stride. The people continued to show up at their revivals and to embrace holiness and Christian perfectionism. Following the mass meetings of Jones and the spread of holiness, pentecostalism first took root in the American West and the American South in the first years of the twentieth century. A protracted interracial revival in Los Angeles, which erupted in April 1906, drew thousands to a former barn and tombstone shop. William J. Seymour, a traveling black preacher from Louisiana, led the devotees. Men and women, young and old, black and white, sang, shouted, spoke in unknown tongues and believed that they were witnessing a new age of the spirit unlike anything since the Holy Ghost descended on the apostles in the second chapter of the New Testament book of Acts. Women ministers played a conspicuous role in both holiness and pentecostalism. The color line, adherents liked to proclaim, was washed away in the blood in these last days before Jesus's Second Coming.

Stalwarts testified to other signs and wonders. At the Azusa Street revival, the key founding event of American pentecostalism, men and women, touched by the spirit, claimed to be able to take up and play instruments that they had no familiarity with. Observers in the press and pilgrims who ventured across the country to experience this "outpouring of the spirit" marveled at the scene. Blacks and whites sang, clapped, and shouted "Hallelujah!" together.[12]

Interracial services and prominent woman preachers largely went the way of the horse and buggy. By the 1920s and 1930s, most pentecostals had divided into all-white or all-black fellowships, and fewer and fewer women received ordination. Other peculiarities lasted throughout the century. Energetic worship styles and revved-up music marked pentecostal churches from one generation to the next. From the earliest days, believers liked to compare their spirit-filled churches with the lifeless drudgery of mainline congregations. As one early convert put it, "Compared with [the pentecostal revival], any meeting of Baptists is as the silence of death."[13]

Black storefront churches and rundown glory barns, the sites of pentecostal meetings, did not tend to attract members of the Rotary Club or the Chamber of Commerce. Adherents clung to their outsider status with pride. The establishment of Jesus's or Paul's day had accepted neither, they pointed out. So-called respectable churches turned away from true Christianity and had a "Bible full of holes," not a "Holy Bible." But animosity went both ways. "Holy roller," "tonguer," "religious fanatic," and "bible thumper" were typical epithets hurled at the pentecostals by Baptists and Methodists. Even within evangelical circles pentecostalism was still suspect in the 1950s and 1960s. In 1963, a discontented Louisiana Methodist wrote to *Christianity Today*, concerning what he thought were proud, boastful pentecostals. "I have found Pentecostalists choosing to dissociate themselves from the major orthodox denominations," he sneered, "because they claim to offer the Holy Ghost (pronounced HO-lyghost) as a bonus to people already 'saved.' " Was this some kind of "Christian aristocracy"? he asked rhetorically.[14]

One folklore and religion scholar notes that "Pentecostals are creating distinctive models for members to follow that will differentiate them from others, [and] they are aware that many outsiders consider their behavior extreme. . . . [But by] creating standards that seem extreme to the outsider," she writes, "Pentecostals create boundaries between themselves and others. They recognize that in so doing they often create negative images that are difficult to combat. The balance between 'different' and 'freakish' is not an easy one to maintain."[15]

In many ways, however, as pentecostal and holiness churches grew, becoming less "freakish," even outpacing the mainline, they moved haltingly from the fringe to the American religious mainstream. In June 1958, *Life* magazine ran a cover story on what its editors called a "third force in Christendom." That third force—made up of pentecostals, Adventists, holiness groups, and a host of what were derogatorily called fringe sects—seemed likely to outpace Catholicism and Protestantism. One observer in the *Life* feature cautioned that not all third force Christians were rowdy, barnstorming, chandelier swingers. Still, the reporter ventured, "Swingy hymns and passionate preaching stir up the congregation's emotions, and worshipers respond with hand clapping, arm-waving, loud singing, dancing in the aisles, shouted 'amens.' "[16] This was not like the calm, measured services of most mainline churches. The innovative, dynamic aspects of the self-proclaimed "old-time faith" offered more effective communication to members than dry sermons from a minister.[17]

Relatively new to the American religious scene, pentecostalism drew the disapproval of mostly outside critics, whether mainline Protestants, journalists, or academics. In the view of typical skeptics, the movement catered to overly emotional, simple-minded types. Charismatic, sordid ministers, in the Elmer Gantry mode, were seen to prey on weak-willed and uneducated poor people.[18] The Congregational Church sponsored a detailed report on "the Pentecostal Sects" in 1939. "The Pentecostal churches," concluded an observer in one of the denomination's magazines, "undoubtedly belong to the group of the eccentric and even of the regressive." The critic found it hard to fathom pentecostals believing that something that "darts into their mind without their seeming to have anything to do with [it]" was of supernatural origin.[19] By these lights, the Holy Ghost religion of blacks and whites was at best a kind of escapism. Some observers found more positive features in the sanctified faith, however. In the 1960s, an Ohio anthropologist interviewed members of black urban storefront churches. Congregants made up a "warm, understanding, enthusiastic band of baptized believers." Their lively worship services, thought this eyewitness, allowed for a freedom of expression missing in other areas of life. One subject interviewed responded directly to doubters: "A lot of folks talk about getting too emotional," he confided. "I wouldn't give two cents for a religion that wouldn't make me move. My God is a living God." Energetic services, and spirited music, in this telling, proved the truth and godliness of the movement.[20]

Hard-driving, powerful music and worship in holiness and pentecostal services could be mesmerizing. Two mid-twentieth-century novelists drew on this theme directly. Critically acclaimed African American author James Baldwin well expressed the excitement, emotion, and ecstasy of pentecostal services in his semiautobiographical *Go Tell It on the Mountain* (1952). Setting the story in 1930s Harlem, Baldwin narrated the life of young protagonist John. The congregants of his family's pentecostal church

> sang with all the strength that was in them, and clapped their hands for joy. There had never been a time when John had not sat watching the saints rejoice with terror in his heart, and wonder. Their singing caused him to believe in the pres-

> ence of the Lord; indeed, it was no longer a question of belief, because they made that presence real. . . . While John watched, the Power struck someone, a man or woman; they cried out, a long, wordless crying, and, arms outstretched like wings, they began the shout.[21]

The lesser-known white novelist Jack Conroy presented similar scenes of religious pandemonium in his semiautobiographical Depression-era, proletarian novel *A World to Win* (1935). The humorist Conroy's story of two vagabond, bohemian brothers in Missouri included a subplot of a "Holy Roller Church" with its "sagging frame building." Drawing on his early familiarity with holiness-pentecostal faith and preaching in Missouri, Conroy described the white church's interior, with its pot-bellied stove and walls bedecked with colorful charts plotting out all the details of the end of the world. The saints, or the elect of the church, might be hit with the power of the Holy Ghost and fall to the floor in a heap. The pastor of the "Holy Rollers," a man named Epperson, wrote Conroy, was a divine healer with a bad track record, who "could be heard bellowing pleas or threats at the unsaved, or, 'the gift of tongues,' having fallen upon him, mouthing unintelligible gibberish." Congregants "expressed their exuberance by dancing violently for hours at a time." Epperson might fall to the floor in a trance, wrote Conroy. At such times "he muttered to himself: 'Yes Lord! I understand, Jesus! It shall be done! Praise Thy holy name! Whooooooeee! *ashanagi makeesha mahio heeshana hyshen a lia genoa!* Whoooooeeee!' " In Conroy's fictional Missouri town, locals thought the saints' behavior as scandalous as it was amusing.[22]

In between the publication of these two provocative novels that featured the power and passions of pentecostal religion, a concise sociological study of black pentecostal churches in Chicago took stock of transplanted southern churches. The researchers accounted for various worship styles and rituals across the spectrum of black religious experience. The sociologists who fanned out across the city classed their forty subject churches into four broad categories: "(1) the crowd that dances, (2) the group which indulges in demonstrative assent, (3) the congregation which prefers sermon-centered services, and (4) the church with formal liturgy." According to the researchers those in the first group—which consisted of pentecostal and spiritualist churches—were put off by the formality of traditional black churches. These recent arrivals from the rural South turned to more expressive and ecstatic houses of worship for spiritual sustenance.[23]

The study certainly reveals the class and cultural biases of social scientists in this era. (Many of those views were shared as well by African American Baptists and Methodists.) In this telling pentecostals are primitive, isolated, ignorant, and crude. Nonetheless, the project also recorded the activities in these store-front tabernacles with a careful eye and a documentarian's attention to detail. The laborers and domestic servants that made up such churches worshipped with a kind of vigor and abandon unimaginable in staid, established congregations. The principle investigator, Vattel Elbert Daniel of Wiley College in Texas, summarized the worship, sermon topics, and music of nine "Ecstatic Cults." Their instruments included piano, "percussion, such as drums, tamborines [*sic*], triangles and sometimes a wind instrument, usually a trumpet." The conduct of the services was "highly theatrical and it is recognized by rapid and rhythmic movement; at times, in some of the cults, the ecstasy becomes so great that pandemonium reigns." Participants testified to healings, praised their risen Lord, or warned of the imminent Second Coming of Jesus. Taking in what seemed like chaos, Daniel scrutinized the bodily exercises of laypeople and their preachers:

> In most cases, the frenzy includes yelling, tapping, stamping, shouting, and, in some instances, running and jumping, including the type which resembles the movements of a jumping jack. Loud praying while standing with hands uplifted, and speaking in tongues while in a similar position constitute the climax of the ecstatic behavior, although this was not so prevalent as were the rhythmic hand-clapping and foot-patting.[24]

For Daniel this all contrasted quite astonishingly with the services in African American churches that he described as upper middle class. Scenes in fourteen so-called deliberative churches—Episcopal, Presbyterian, and Congregational—seemed positively quiet by comparison. Daniel summed up the order of the service: "Formality without a great amount of liturgy; activity of the pastor shared by ministerial and lay assistants." Daniel marked off the newly arrived pentecostals from their religious competitors in the Windy City. Believers in these churches, commonly lumped together as "holy rollers," set themselves apart by

> speaking in tongues, in which the believers repeat rapidly and loudly unintelligible symbols; . . . healing ritual, in which the sick are anointed with oil and surrounded by a praying, singing, and dancing group; saint-making ritual, in which believers are supposed to receive the Holy Ghost, after white-robed saints kneel with them and pray loudly, accompanied by rapidly repeated rhythmical assent, while the pianist plays a revival hymn.[25]

In 1942, the same year that the Chicago study was published, to the west in California, James Bright Wilson, a Ph.D. student in sociology at the University of Southern California, made notes while attending the pentecostal churches of white agricultural workers. Some services looked almost formal, he wrote, whereas others seemed like a "wild frenzy from beginning to end." The devout set themselves apart from other common laborers. They distanced themselves from what they considered "worldly" concerns. The enthusiasts that Wilson observed won few friends among labor organizers when they refused to join unions. Their fast-paced music and loud singing also provoked the scorn of outsiders. Wilson noted that the chief concern of the service seemed to be to awaken the congregants:

> This is done through prayer, testimony, songs, sermon, shouting, clapping the hands, and vigorous physical activity on the part of the leader or leaders. Occasionally, banjos or other instruments are used. The songs are especially emotional in nature. Their appeal is never made to the intellect. It is rhythmic, loud, and joyful. It is catchy, and never difficult. It is decided in its emotional coloring and so serves to arouse the particular emotions of awe, hope, repentance, and the like. Choruses are often repeated eight or ten times while bodies sway back and forth, and feet

> beat out the music upon the floor. Lusty "Amen's" and vigorous "Hallelujah's" resound all over the room.[26]

Each of these accounts of high-energy worship and holiness belief was similar to what regionalist painter Thomas Hart Benton saw in white churches on a trip that he made through the mountain South in the early 1930s. With a far more sarcastic, even Menckenesque tone, Benton spoke of believers' "Dionysiac madness," which he nonetheless found deeply moving. His account of mountain holiness emphasized the exotic, grotesque, and thinly veiled eroticism of devotees, a common theme in journalistic and popular portrayals. At roughly the same time, the lawyer and poet William Alexander Percy pilloried the riotous religion of Mississippi's poor whites, who "attend revivals and fight and fornicate in the bushes afterwards."[27]

In Benton's account, stalwarts were primitives and zealous hardliners. As he made his way through West Virginia he encountered a banjo-picking preacher, recently hounded out of Baptist country by a shower of stones. The headstrong itinerant had written "Holiness" on his instrument. Benton observed such figures playing in up-tempo services, carried by rhythmic music and shouts of "Amen. Blessed be His name." He made numerous sketches, one of which became the study for his masterful painting *Lord, Heal the Child* (1934), depicting a female preacher ministering over a young disabled girl in a ramshackle church.[28] Pentecostal and holiness people embraced the new; they played stringed instruments and danced about. The music, to the famous painter's ears, sounded like dancehall music.[29] Much of the initial energy of pentecostalism burst forth in the hills and hollers of the South that Benton traveled. It also took root in growing cities and towns along the Mississippi River and followed migrants on the Great Migration. Even the lively church of James Baldwin's fictional Harlem, the Temple of the Fire Baptized, was populated by recent arrivals from Dixie.

First-generation rock music was also largely a southern phenomenon. Even as Elvis became an international star, write historians Bill C. Malone and David Stricklin, "neither he nor the other young southern singers who followed in his wake could ever escape, even had they desired, the marks of their southern bred culture." Furthermore, "singers such as Carl Perkins, Roy Orbison, Jerry Lee Lewis, Charlie Rich, and

Conway Twitty carried the dialects and inflections of the Deep South in their speech and singing styles."[30] The same could be said of black singers. Many of both races first sang in public in pentecostal or evangelical churches. Such links are not altogether coincidental. Yet hot music in the service of the Lord, believers assured themselves, was very unlike the riotous new rhythm and blues or rock 'n' roll music. But they were more similar than the devout were willing to concede.

The leap from unbridled sanctified music to rock was not a great one. Unlike their condescending critics, pentecostals were not burdened with the trappings of tradition or the weight of convention. That may explain why something as new and scandalous as snake handling would originate in white pentecostal churches in the upcountry South. The saints had long used the latest technologies to distribute tracts and newspapers. They sang new, up-tempo hymns and worshiped in ways that made other Protestants shudder with disgust. Yet their passion and intensity would take them forward to pioneer radio and television ministries to the masses.[31]

Free of a variety of constraints, pentecostals held uninhabited, unconventional revivals. Black and white pentecostal music tore down the walls of genres as well. Arizona Dranes, Eddie Head, and other black sanctified performers in the early twentieth century borrowed instruments and melodies from the secular scene. Arkansas native Sister Rosetta Tharpe, called the Godmother of Rock and Roll, achieved critical acclaim in the late 1930s for her skillful guitar-accompanied gospel. All over the South foot-stomping, boogie-woogie pianists, jazz trumpeters, and jug bands led worship in the African American Church of God in Christ. That denomination spread into the urban North with black migration. Beginning in the 1940s and 1950s, black pentecostal quartets began to exert a greater influence on mainstream black gospel music. This new style was louder, more rhythmic, and more affective than what had dominated the scene before.[32] The jazzy shout music that shook church windows paralleled the development of rhythm and blues.

Similar musical innovations took place in white pentecostal churches. Washboard players, flatpicking guitarists, and fiddlers stirred hearts in white congregations. The impact of these musical trailblazers reached well beyond the walls of tumbledown churches. Many of the first-generation rockers who grew up in pentecostal denominations credited

The influential trailblazer Sister Rosetta Tharpe with the Lucky Millinder Orchestra singing "Lonesome Road," 1941. Mick Csáky, *The Godmother of Rock & Roll: Sister Rosetta Tharpe.* A film by Mick Csáky (Directors Cut Films, 2014), an Antelope South Limited production. Screenshot by the author from Vimeo, Directors Cut Films (https://vimeo.com/101093967).

sanctified music with giving them new, exciting ideas. It was how they first experienced live performances. They said that the unrestrained style of tongues-speaking churches made an indelible impression.[33]

One of those was Johnny Cash, who attended a branch of the Church of God (Cleveland), a pentecostal denomination headquartered in the upcountry of Tennessee. In his hometown of Dyess, Arkansas, Cash came to Jesus when he was twelve during the congregation's singing of the altar call classic "Just as I Am."[34] (That tune would later be a kind of theme song for Billy Graham's highly publicized revivals.) Local initiates held animated meetings in an old schoolhouse. Years later, the Man in Black remembered scenes of religious ecstasy. "[The] writhing on the floor, the moaning, the trembling, and the jerks" along with hellfire sermons and frenzied religious excitement struck him to the core. "My knuckles would be white as I held onto the seat in front of me."[35] Worshipers hollered in unknown tongues. Cash thought that the uninhibited music, improvisation, and variety of instruments played were liberating and powerful. The future country star Tammy Wynette, from nearby Mississippi, frequented a Church of God congregation as a youngster. She also went to a Baptist church that was stuffy by comparison. With the pentecostals Wynette pounded out hymns and spirituals on the piano. Unlike the starchy Baptist minister, Wynette recalled, the Church of God preacher "would let you bring in guitars and play rockin' gospel more like black gospel music."[36]

The southern-born rocker Little Richard and blues titan B. B. King, who both attended black pentecostal churches, recalled similar scenes.[37] Nonpentecostals, too, looked back with nostalgia on the church music of their youth. Chuck Berry, whose father was a deacon in the Antioch Baptist Church, was first exposed to rousing gospel music in a house of worship. As a youngster, he sang in the choir.[38] Berry's family, with its Baptist roots, was in the black middle class. Others came from the lower end of the economic spectrum.

Little Richard Penniman, the son of a part-time moonshiner, cultivated a loud, vibrant stage persona when he first toured through the South in the early 1950s. He was raised in a devout Seventh-day Adventist home. "Of all the churches" in Macon, Georgia, he said, "I used to like going to the Pentecostal Church because of the music." And why not—his favorite musician was the pentecostal guitarist Sister Rosetta Tharpe. So the young Penniman could not believe his luck when he had the chance to sing with the famous performer at the Macon City Auditorium on October 27, 1947. It marked his first secular public performance. Tharpe, with her plump frame and unique picking style, played a large solid-body Gibson electric guitar. Little Richard and the fans at the show were spellbound. "I was just a kid," he recalled over sixty years later. "I'd get lost in the music. I was singing on my own when Sister Rosetta heard me. She asked me to come up on stage with her to sing 'Five Loaves and Two Fishes.' When I heard the audience go wild when we were finished, I knew what I wanted to do."[39] But he also felt called to the ministry. From the time he was a boy, he remembered, "I wanted to be a preacher. I wanted to be like Brother Joe May, the singing evangelist," who was called the Thunderbolt of the Midwest. He styled his hair into a curly pile, much like "the singing evangelist" did. Richard heard impressive sermons at one pentecostal church, at which he and his friends would do the holy dance and "imitate them talking in tongues, though we didn't know what we were saying."[40]

Jerry Lee Lewis, roughly the same age as Little Richard, was born into a dirt-poor family in Ferriday, Louisiana. He attended a Church of God congregation, as Cash did, as well as an Assemblies of God church with his family. From his earliest years he absorbed the traditional hymns and spirituals along with the culture of pentecostalism. Jerry Lee's aunt, Ada, underwent what pentecostals called a baptism of the spirit at a camp meeting in Snake Ridge, Louisiana. Her grandson—and Jerry Lee's cousin—Jimmy Lee Swaggart recalled her experience, common in pentecostal settings. To anyone who would listen she said, "You've got to get it. You've got to have it. You really don't know the Lord like you should until you receive it." She exclaimed, "The presence of God became so real." In an instant, "it seemed as if I had been struck by a bolt of lightning. Lying flat on my back, I raised my hands to praise the Lord. No English came out. Only unknown tongues."[41] The family followed her example and became committed believers. At the Assemblies of God church in Ferriday, Jerry Lee sang alongside Jimmy Lee, who would go on to fame as a TV preacher and a singing evangelist. With a local minister Jerry Lee toured briefly around the South, playing the piano and speaking. He abandoned that for a shot at fame with a Sun Records recording session in November 1956. Not long after that he became an international celebrity. Jerry Lee and Jimmy Lee parted company. Said Swaggart years later, "Why do I need forty suits, I'm clothed in a robe of righteousness! Why do I need Cadillacs and Lincolns when I can ride with the King of Kings? Jerry Lee can go to Sun Records in Memphis, I'm on my way to heaven with a God who supplies all my need according to His riches in glory by Christ Jesus."[42]

Undoubtedly, the most famous performer to emerge from a tongues-speaking church was Elvis Presley, Sun Records' celebrated star. Born into poverty in Tupelo, Mississippi, Elvis and his parents moved to Memphis in 1948. His mother, a committed believer, searched for a local church. The growing Memphis First Assembly of God initially met in a tent. With membership swelling, the congregation moved to a storefront. Then it finally settled in its own building, a sign of the firm establishment of pentecostalism in the South. The church sponsored a radio ministry and then a TV program in the 1950s. Not long after the Presleys arrived in town, a First Assembly bus drove through the family's ragged neighborhood. They boarded it and became regulars of Pastor James Hamill's congregation. The teenage Elvis was shy, awkward, and quiet. The country boy's trousers were hitched too high and his hair was long, remembered Hamill, but he was a courteous, respectful teen. Elvis

The Jerry Lee Lewis Trio performing the hit song "Great Balls of Fire," 1957. Jerry Lee Lewis "Great Balls of Fire" *(Disc Jockey) Jamboree* (Warner Bros. Pictures, Inc., 1957), Vanguard Productions, Inc. Screenshot by the author from YouTube, The Tumtrah (http://www.youtube.com/watch?v=JzvBx8sniVA).

did not drink or smoke, which Hamill found commendable. Elvis attended Sunday school. He also snuck out of his church from time to time to attend a black church nearby. The music and the preaching at Reverend W. Herbert Brewster's East Trigg Avenue Baptist Church was like nothing Elvis and his young friends had experienced. Brewster penned such gospel classics as "God Is Able" and "Move on up a Little Higher." The latter was gospel icon Mahalia Jackson's first hit. In Jim Crow Memphis, Elvis's attendance at a black church might have been considered inappropriate, or worse. So he and his fellow absconders would sneak back to the First Assembly before services ended there.[43]

He would become an enormous fan of black gospel music as well as rhythm and blues. The star spoke animatedly about his musical tastes and favorite records. There were certainly plenty of doubters, black and white, who accused Elvis of musical theft across the color line. White performers made millions playing and recording rhythm and blues tracks, whereas their black counterparts never achieved the same level of fame and financial security. How could a performer like Elvis, asked numerous critics, gain fame and fortune, while "colored" artists were either ignored or pushed aside?[44] Black gospel singer Mahalia Jackson was even more explicit, calling out Elvis for his "deliberate theft from religious music" and misusing "the best qualities in music which had been sacred to Negro people for years."[45] She and other critics ignored that rock music, as played by Elvis and contemporaries, drew on a variety of styles and genres, including honky-tonk country, rhythm and blues, swing, as well as white and black gospel in the sanctified tradition.

Perhaps more than anything else, Elvis's first and most enduring influence was white southern gospel music. At Memphis First Assembly, the impressionable teen witnessed the gospel stylings of the Blackwood Brothers and the Stamps Quartet. Those two groups pioneered white southern gospel. Members from each attended First Assembly. Speaking about the Stamps Quartet in 1972, Elvis, his sleepy eyes obscured by massive sunglasses, said, "We grew up with it. From the time I was . . . like two years old . . . because my folks took me there. When I got old enough, I started to sing in church." Asked if that's how he got into singing, Elvis remarked that it was one of the ways. "The gospel is . . . what we grew up with, more than anything else."[46]

Elvis was exposed to the best in pentecostal music. In 1956, after he became world famous, Presley spoke to an Associated Press reporter about the impact of church music:

> We used to go to these religious singins all the time. There were these singers, perfectly fine singers, but nobody responded to 'em. Then there were these other singers—the leader wuz a preacher—and they cut up all over the place, jumpin' on the piano, movin' every which way. The audience liked 'em. I guess I learned from them singers.[47]

Energetic pentecostalism gave the young Elvis new ideas. He marveled at the fiery rhetoric and acrobatics of traveling preachers at Memphis's First Assembly of God.

Elvis's style—his long hair combed back into a pompadour, loud outfits, and showmanship—owed much to pentecostal-flavored gospel groups. J. D. Sumner, of the Stamps Quartet who sang backup for Elvis, recalled that in the early 1950s southern gospel singers donned flashy

A scene from Elvis Presley's performance of "Don't Be Cruel," with backing by the gospel quartet the Jordanaires. *Ed Sullivan Show*, CBS-TV Studio 50 (Ed Sullivan Theater), New York (CBS, January 6, 1957), Sullivan Productions, Inc. Screenshot by the author from YouTube, *The Ed Sullivan Show* (http://www.youtube.com/watch?v=COFHGFZxtnY).

clothes and, before it came into vogue, wore their hair long, combed back in a swoop. That this influenced an impressionable young Elvis is not at all surprising. His childhood dream had been to be part of a tight, harmonizing gospel quartet.[48] According to one music historian, "Elvis admitted to copying the singing style of Jake Hess," leader of the Statesmen Quartet from 1948 to 1963. "The source for so much of Elvis Presley's music and personal style," he notes, "came from the southern gospel world. The attitudes, tastes, and style in his dress and performances were then passed on to a whole generation of teenagers who had never heard of southern gospel or, if they had, probably despised it."[49] A Presley family friend from Memphis echoed that view, remarking, "Undoubtedly Elvis' free form and almost involuntary style of dancing [that] the world would discover was strongly shaped by his experiences at church."[50]

Elvis spoke little about the possible pentecostal sources of his outrageous outfits, vocal style, or stage moves. In 1956 when asked about the influence of his "holy roller" faith, Elvis snapped back, saying he would never use a derogatory term like that. "I belong to an Assembly of God church, which is a holiness church," the young star told Paul Wilder of *TV Guide*. In the long interview held on August 6, 1956, at Lakeland, Florida's Polk Theatre, Elvis continued, "I was raised up in a little Assembly of God church. And some, uh, character called them 'holy rollers.' Uh, and that's where that got started. I always attended a church where people sang. Stood up and sang in the choir and worshipped God, you know. I have never used the expression 'holy roller.' " Clearly on the defensive, he then denied that his music had much connection to his religious roots.[51]

A bit more direct about the matter was South Carolina music legend James Brown. In his autobiography the Godfather of Soul reflected on how important the bravura of one pentecostal preacher was for him. As a young man—living with his aunt, who operated a brothel in Augusta, Georgia—Brown frequented the United House of Prayer for All People. Bishop Daddy Grace, an immigrant from Cape Verde and a controversial black pentecostal prophet, founded the denomination in 1919. Grace, recalled Brown, would "get to preaching and the people would get in a ring and they'd go round and round and go right behind one another, just shouting. Sometimes they'd fall out right there in the sawdust, shaking and jerking and having convulsions." The posts in the church even had to be padded so that enthusiasts, taken up in the spirit, would not inadvertently hurt themselves.[52]

In typical fashion a reporter for the *Augusta Chronicle* offered up a colorful, exotic portrait of a 1938 meeting of the House of Prayer that Brown frequented. The church "rocked and swayed to the rhythm, shouts and dances of hundreds of worshipers yesterday," the journalist wrote. The night meeting began an hour before Grace, who intermittently visited the Augusta outpost, made his way to the front. "The tambourine band, the Queen's band, the string band, the Bishop Grace staff band, the rhythm band and assorted chanting, singing and clapping" all put the congregation in a heightened state. The correspondent then noted that one older woman convulsed and dropped to the sawdust floor, where she remained for the rest of the service. Others twitched, shouted, and danced with joy. Once Daddy Grace joined the assembly, shouts of "yeah man" and "Hail Daddy" burst from the audience.[53] In 1940, Columbia, South Carolina, officials closed a House of

Prayer church for creating a disturbance in the neighborhood. Grace himself was anything but sedate. His flowing robes, shoulder-length hair, and thin mustache captured the attention of his rapt followers. Often arraying himself in luxurious suits with gold piping, donning a cape, or sporting hand-painted ties, Grace won much notoriety and even more negative newspaper coverage for his religious practices and extravagant claims. Equal parts showman and patriarch, he conducted mass baptisms of hundreds of parishioners at outdoor services by using a fire hose.[54]

When Grace died in 1960, *Ebony* magazine eulogized him as a holy father to the 375,000 members of his United House of Prayer for All People. Although, noted the obituary, to others he remained a "Cadillac-riding materialist" or "a brown-skinned P. T. Barnum who cracked the whip in a circus of gaudy costumes, wildly gyrating acrobats and brass bands that played as if God were a cosmic hipster."[55] Even the young James Brown doubted Grace's legitimacy. But the powerful preacher still seemed "like a god on earth" to him. The same held true for others. Rhythm and blues and soul legend Solomon Burke, Grace's godson, served for some time as a minister in the United House of Prayer. The impressionable young Brown took in the blasting trombones and the passionate worship, and he admired the show that the caped Daddy Grace put on for churchgoers. "Those folks were sanctified," he said, looking back years later. "They had the beat. . . . Sanctified people got more fire."[56]

Although Brown and Presley had a high opinion of pentecostals—their music, their "fire"—such sentiments were not mutual. From the early days of his stardom, Elvis's childhood pastor, James Hamill, knew that the singer could no longer attend church, pursued by fans and the hungry media as he was. But the trouble with Elvis, thought Hamill, went much deeper than his spotty church attendance. Writing to the Assemblies of God's general superintendent in 1956, Hamill confided that Elvis "seems to be caught in a 'web,' spun by Satan and those around him who have suddenly brought him to fame and fortune." The celebrity rocker should be prayed for earnestly, he recommended.[57]

For the devout there was much to pray about. From 1955 to 1958, headlines announced a new wave of juvenile delinquency and social degeneracy that was linked to the big beat. In 1955, *Life* magazine reported on a "frenzied teen-age music craze" that was kicking "up a big fuss." Soon the rock 'n' roll scare swept across the South. Police in Atlanta halted dances at the City Auditorium.[58] Fearing that rock 'n' roll incited violence and promoted sexual promiscuity, the San Antonio, Texas, Parks Department banned big-beat records from jukeboxes located at city swimming pools, special sites of segregationists' anxieties.[59]

Journalists and opinion makers rushed to explain the phenomenon. Newspaper editors trotted out experts to weigh in on the origins of the music and the dangers of the craze. In 1957, a psychiatrist and an educational psychologist compared the mayhem to religious fits and trances that had occurred in the Middle Ages. Others claimed it was nothing more than the latest youth fad.[60] Violent, loud music naturally generated violent behavior, additional authorities informed a worried public.[61] A churchgoing mother made these connections and fretted about the influence Elvis might be having over her daughters. After *Life* ran a photo essay on the star in late summer 1956, she wrote a letter to the magazine's editor. Elvis was a novelty, she admitted, and youngsters probably flocked to him because he was a dazzling performer. But she hoped that all the "years the church and I have spent on training my teen-age daughters" would not be "obliterated by watching a performance or two by Elvis."[62]

Lurking behind many such criticisms was a deeper fear of rock 'n' roll's sexually explicit nature and the feline masculinity that stars like Little Richard, Jerry Lee Lewis, or Presley exuded. For decades, critics had claimed that pentecostals had pushed the boundaries of decency, mixing sex and salvation. Now rock 'n' roll came under much greater, but similar, scrutiny. Even the term "rock 'n' roll," like "jazz" before it, was a euphemism for sex. Fans, many of them teenage girls, said critics, were exposed to a host of vile profanities. With these criticisms lingering in the air, Elvis tore into the song "Long Tall Sally"—written by Little Richard, Robert "Bumps" Blackwell, and Enotris Johnson—while over twenty-six thousand teens roared at the Dallas, Texas, Cotton Bowl Stadium on October 11, 1956. A reporter in the crowd took in the sights and sounds. Elvis's "gyrating pelvic motions," he observed, "are best described as a cross between an Apache war dance and a burlesque queen's old-fashioned bumps and grind."[63] Earlier in the same year a writer at *Time* thought much the same. Elvis's "movements suggest, in a word, sex." Likewise, "his hips swing sensuously from side to side and his entire body takes on a frantic quiver, as if he had swallowed a jackhammer."[64] Fittingly, a scholar notes of the pop icon, "in an anxious Cold War culture that demanded the demarcation of gender difference—gray-flanneled businessmen versus the Marilyns and Moms of American womanhood—Elvis clearly violated mainstream sexual roles."[65]

Fears of a gender dystopia plagued the minds of pastors and educators. A Catholic teacher in 1957 was positive that rock 'n' roll music and styles were disrupting the rules of nature. Girls and boys in classes now wanted to look like their strange teen idols. In a normal society, the teacher observed, boys should become more manly and girls should become more womanly. To the horror of many, the educator reported, "boys of today are getting girlish; putting their hair up into 'pretty' waves and curls, wearing long hair, showing over-preoccupation with their looks and clothing." Some had even lost interest in manly pursuits, like hiking, building, and camping. "Girls on the other hand," who had come under the influence of the music and its upside down values, "tend to become more boyish." They now sported "slacks, sloppy jackets, men's shirts hanging out, hacked off hair styles," smoked cigarettes, and talked about all manner of tough and vulgar things. "God help us," the educator concluded with hands in the air.[66]

Deep in America's Bible belt, rock music lit a raging fire of controversy. The rebellious, loud anthems of black and white teenagers threatened the good order of the white Christian South and stirred the leadership and laity in black churches as well. As rock 'n' roll music hit big in 1955 and 1956, southern ministers and laypeople lined up to condemn the new genre. If rock *did* owe something to pentecostalism, said detractors, it was only a perverted, blasphemous copy. Churchmen had long guarded their Zion from encroaching threats—whether those were in the form of religious rebels, political radicals, or deviants of any stripe. It was not only white conservatives, though, who registered such dangers. The African Methodist Episcopal Zion Church, with a geographic concentration in the Carolinas and Alabama, took aim at Elvis Presley. Vulnerable youth were being led on a "march of destruction," complained church officials.[67]

Additional church leaders in the 1940s and 1950s worried that popular music, syncopated beats, and boogie-woogie piano were tainting white as well as black gospel music. They thought churches should fortify themselves against the encroachments of worldly entertainment. For instance, at their annual meeting in the summer of 1956, New Jersey Seventh-day Adventists denounced all those songsmiths who "are capitalizing on the current religious revival in the form of platter-chatter and gospel boogie." Little Richard's denomination had nothing but condemnation for the star's hits and his influence. Church officials finally warned, "It is impossible to harmonize holiness and hep-cats, sanctification and swing."[68]

Already in 1938, one harsh critic of jazz, who attended a Benny Goodman concert in Cleveland, Ohio, had made the links between the new music and the pentecostal faith explicit. Was swing music "really as bad as I thought it was"? he asked. It was. His mind raced back to the camp meetings his parents forced him to attend in his youth, wherein a "much publicized evangelist who knew how to play on the heart strings" would cast his spell over the gathering. Goodman's show, the dancing, and the whole scene reminded him of "the halls where Holy Rollers held their meetings in the camps of colored people of the southland." Concertgoers, like ecstatic worshippers, "gave free rein to their emotions when someone tapped the right nerve."[69] In the following decade another anxious commentator in a gospel music magazine cautioned against songs like the Homeland Harmony Quartet's 1948 rendition of "Everybody Gonna Have a Wonderful Time Up There (Gospel Boogie)," which had been popularized by Sister Rosetta Tharpe. "Why should men who are supposed to love the Lord make for their most popular phonograph records and 'song-hits' the type of song that is too cheap in the light of God's holy purpose to deserve mention?" asked the critic with outright disgust. The popular new style of gospel music appeared to such naysayers to be dangerously close to the debased secular music of the age.[70]

In the mid-1950s, questions concerning the direction of influence gave way to intense debate. The dispute about the links between rock 'n' roll or rhythm and blues and church music enlivened the pages of African American newspapers across the country. In 1955, the rhythm and blues singer LaVern Baker made the scandalous claim that gospel singers, like Philadelphia's Clara Ward, fired their music with a rock 'n' roll beat. Baker had recently risen to stardom with her 1955 Atlantic Records hit "Tweedle Dee." Ward, who with the Ward Singers toured alongside Minister C. L. Franklin and played before crowds of up to twenty-five thousand, angrily shot back. "We've been singing gospel music long before the public ever heard of rock and roll," she told a reporter. She was not opposed to rock music and actually enjoyed listening to it. But, in fact, claimed Ward, it was rock and pop performers who lifted from the gospel tradition, not the other way around. She asked, "Where else did they copy their styles but from church groups?"[71]

Were popular performers using gospel melodies and styles for debased purposes? It certainly seemed so to churchgoers in the mid-1950s. The rock 'n' roll revolution was counterfeiting the gospel sound. Records and concert ticket sales owed something to the religious element, opponents implied. An influential white Baptist preacher and broadcaster summed up the fears of many in 1956. "The 'spirituals' are the heartcry of a people for freedom and for God," he sternly observed. "Sadly, almost blasphemously," the minister lamented, "they have been taken over by the entertainment world in our day, their purpose misdirected, the melodies adapted to the cheapest of swing."[72]

Quite a few of the faithful, then, watched with horror as Ray Charles borrowed heavily from church music for his unabashedly worldly hits. Between 1953 and 1955, Charles experimented with spirituals, drawing sacred songs into the secular realm. In his hands, "You Better Leave That Liar Alone" became "You Better Leave That Woman Alone." A version of the latter appeared on his 1958 album *Yes, Indeed!!* (Atlantic) along with a song called "Lonely Avenue," which Charles claimed was based on a popular spiritual Jess Whitaker sang with the Pilgrim Travelers. The most powerful and effective of these retooled spiritual numbers was the 1954 smash hit "I've Got a Woman," co-written with Renald Richard. The song drew closely from "It Must Be Jesus" by the Southern Tones. The coda repetition in Charles's song, "she's alright," used the standard gospel form. "I've Got a Woman" climbed to number two on *Billboard*'s rhythm and blues chart in 1955 and was one of the most played jukebox hits of the year, beating out rivals like the Penguins' "Earth Angel" or the Drifters' "What'cha Gonna Do?" "I've Got a Woman" also helped usher in the new genre of soul music. The basic formula for so many of

Charles's early hits harkened back to the gospel quartets from the South that inspired him. One of his favorites, the Dixie Hummingbirds, emerged from the black holiness tradition.[73]

Decades later, Charles's genius would be celebrated at the highest levels of society. In December 1986, President Reagan hailed the famed musician, who had just received a prestigious Kennedy Center honor. Speaking at a White House reception, the commander in chief proclaimed, "Today Ray Charles is known the world over for his infusion of gospel fervor into rhythm and blues and rock and roll and for the quality—the sheer lilting, rolling musical quality of his singing."[74] At the time that the talented pianist and songwriter was putting "gospel fervor into rhythm and blues and rock and roll," however, the religious reaction to Charles's innovations was immediate and fierce. Even the Chicago blues legend Big Bill Broonzy thought Charles had taken things too far. Broonzy, who briefly worked as a pastor in Pine Bluff, Arkansas, said that although Charles had "got the blues, he's cryin' sanctified. He's mixing the blues with the spirituals."[75] Letters arrived in Charles's mailbox, accusing him of "bastardizing God's work," and a prominent preacher in New York City denounced the performer from his pulpit. Charles brushed it all off, later saying, "I really didn't give a shit about that kind of criticism."[76]

With some trepidation, others followed Charles's phenomenal success. Crossover stars, from gospel to pop—like Sam Cooke, Johnnie Taylor, Dionne Warwick, and Lou Rawls—produced chart-topping songs. In the 1960s, Aretha Franklin perfected a pattern that had been well established, says critic Hollie West. Much like what Charles had done before, Franklin had "once said Jesus, [whereas] she now cries baby. She hums and moans with the transfixed ecstasy of a church sister who's experiencing the Holy Ghost."[77]

Without a doubt, the line separating godly and worldly music had long been a thin one. Sometimes there was no line at all. The life and work of Thomas Dorsey, the father of the gospel blues, illustrates as much. In the middle of the Great Migration, he began his career in Chicago as the accompanist of blues sensation Ma Rainey, calling himself Georgia Tom. Alongside writing partner Tampa Red he composed classic double entendre blues numbers in the late 1920s and early 1930s, with bawdy titles like "It's Tight like That," "Pat That Bread," "It's All Worn Out," and "Somebody's Been Using That Thing." His duet "Show Me

What You Got," recorded with Kansas City Kitty in 1930, included racy lyrics about an old profession: "Come in momma, you lookin' mighty swell. Now, you say you got somethin' to sell. So let me see what you got." At the same time, Dorsey, tugged in the direction of the church, was composing sacred songs for the National Baptist Convention and scoring his first big gospel hits like "If You See My Savior."[78] He eventually turned all his efforts to sacred music.

One black minister who bore the heavy influence of Dorsey mixed together blues, gospel, and even rock 'n' roll with surprising ease. Ironically, his sung sermons targeted the very music he performed. "Rock & roll has just about brought about the disintegration of our civilization," thundered Elder Charles D. Beck in 1956 in a legendary sermon recorded in Memphis, Tennessee. As he shouted down rock 'n' roll records and the bad influence of performers, his backing guitarist plucked rocking blues licks on an electric guitar and the pianist played bluesy trills. Beck peppered his delivery with long, gravel-throated shouts of "Oh Lord!" and "Yeah!" while "Amen!" came back from the congregation. Referring to impending judgment, he howled, "This whole world is gonna rock and roll!" The closeness of Beck's raucous, gospel blues style to contemporary rhythm and blues as well as rock 'n' roll was simply unmistakable.[79]

Only a handful of white and black ministers actually came to the defense of blues or rock 'n' roll music, although none would have defended deliberately salacious songs like those credited to Georgia Tom. In early 1957, the black pastor of Jersey City's Deliverance Temple challenged all those naysayers who linked Elvis Presley with sexual depravity and immorality. In a forceful sermon, Milton Perry noted that Elvis, unlike Ray Charles, did not rework gospel songs into secular ones. Moreover, Elvis, said Perry, was raised in a strict Assemblies of God home, "a home of Orthodox 'sanctified Pentecostal' parents who taught a boy to love and fear God." This could also account, the minister speculated, "for Presley's abstention from tobacco and alcoholic beverages." Perry was particularly impressed, after a visit to Memphis, with what he heard about how the young rock star conducted himself. By all accounts Elvis was humble, polite, and progressive on the race issue. Stories of Elvis's participating in a charity event for orphaned and needy black children impressed the reverend greatly. So too did positive anecdotes of Elvis's interaction with Memphis's black community.[80]

Like Perry, black and white teens were eager to counter the negative reaction to the music. They proudly defended their gold-lamé-jacketed heroes. "We want to thank you for that picture spread you had about our 'dream baby'—Elvis," gushed a teenage girl in a letter to the editor of *Life* magazine in 1956. "It was the 'badest [*sic*],' that means the 'greatest.' " She continued, "The 'cats' here in Philly are wild about Elvis. He's the 'king,' the supreme ruler."[81] Other teenagers enthusiastically offered their opinions to newspapers, magazines, and radio reporters. Elvis "hits me right between the eyes," a teenage fan told a *Washington Post* reporter in 1956. "Every time I hear his records," the youngster confessed, "I get weak in the knees. Oooooh."[82] Such devotees claimed the music had been unfairly panned by parents and pastors who failed to understood its appeal or appreciate how it spoke directly to youngsters. When ministers or tastemakers took a dim view of the music, some teenagers were ready with barbs and insults. After *Chicago Tribune* journalist William Leonard penned a scorching critique of the big beat, one young reader resorted to caustic sarcasm.[83] "Did your parents lock you up so you couldn't dance or sing the way you wanted to?" snapped Jo Ann Burke. She asked, "Why not let us have rock and roll?"[84] Another hissed that rock 'n' roll was here to stay, but critics like Leonard would fade into obscurity.[85] Other approaches tried a more subtle, conciliatory tone. Mothers, pleaded a young woman in the *Boston Globe,* "please try to understand Elvis." Surely the new music and dance fads were no worse than the Charleston, she reasoned. Rock 'n' roll also "has a lot more sides to it," she argued, "including ballads and peppy songs."[86]

More often than not, pentecostals all over the South thought they understood Elvis and his rabid fans all too well after he hit the big time in 1956. He might claim to be a member of an Assemblies of God church, they huffed, but he certainly did not behave like one of the saints. "I am sure you agree," a congregant from Richmond wrote to the Assemblies' general superintendent, "that this boy certainly should not be allowed to be [a] member of any 'Bible believing' church." A Macon, Georgia, Sunday school teacher told the superintendent that she was "stunned over this thing they call 'Rock & Roll Music.' "[87] All the light and heat generated by concerned laypeople and pulpit pounders obscured the religious roots of the new music.

Some pentecostals did sense that the scenes at rock concerts looked a little too much like a Holy Ghost revival. The pentecostal youth pastor, and later author of the influential book *The Cross and the Switchblade,* David Wilkerson saw the connection between rock 'n' roll and sanctified music all too clearly.[88] In 1959, he railed against rock, a godless cult. For each Youth for Christ rally, "Satan is now staging a rock and roll rally!" Wilkerson blasted. "Satan has used rock and roll to imitate the work of God at Pentecost!" As the world was approaching its final hour, "Satan has come down to baptize with an *unholy ghost* and *unholy fire*!" In his estimation rock concerts looked shockingly like perverted pentecostal services: "the shaking, the prostration, the tongues" at rock shows "are imitated by this unholy baptism—as far even to speaking in vile tongues!"[89] Wilkerson continued with these themes in a small pamphlet he published to warn teens and their parents that rock 'n' roll "is the pulse and tempo of hell! It is not music—it is not a dance—it is not energetic exercise—ROCK AND ROLL IS A RELIGION! IT IS A CULT! IT IS A SUPERNATURAL MANIFESTATION FROM HELL." The new genre, hardly a harmless fad, was an "invention of Satan to ensnare and enslave the millions of 20th century teenagers." The up-and-coming youth leader pointed out that on the day of Pentecost the followers of Jesus received power to preach from Christ. Elvis, by contrast, "RECEIVED POWER from below." His startling rise to national and international fame could only be explained, Wilkerson figured, as the payoff from his bargain with Lucifer.[90] Another pentecostal, Tennessee's self-anointed "King of the World" Homer A. Tomlinson, agreed: Presley was only a "guitarist and singer from one of our churches in Mississippi," and Elvis's wiggling was "just a vulgar adaptation of our dancing and rejoicing in the Spirit of God in our Church of God services."[91]

Elvis, who could be quite sensitive about aspersions cast on him, commented now and then about what he saw as a kind of persecution. To a reporter in Louisiana he remarked, "If there wasn't somebody on my side, I'd be lost." He went on to say, "There's people, regardless of who you are or what you do, there's gonna be people that don't like ya." Adding to what appeared to be a martyr complex, Elvis then commented, "There were people that didn't like Jesus Christ. They killed him. And Jesus Christ was a perfect man."[92]

Youth for Christ magazine, an outlet for celebrity evangelist Billy Graham and mainstream evangelicalism, featured numerous articles on rock music in the late 1950s. All were negative, and most took direct aim at the King of Rock 'n' Roll, the most visible target. None of the big beat's detractors in its pages described the wild music, as did Wilkerson, as a kind of inverted pentecostalism. Yet some detected that the music took something that could have been beautiful, true, and godly and twisted it into something gnarled, hideous, and even satanic. One teenage girl who wrote a short piece for *Youth for Christ* magazine in the fall of 1956 picked up on that common theme. "Elvis Presley has taken the graceful harmony of God's music and transformed it to that which is contrary to God's purpose." She concluded with a lament: "How much better it would be if Elvis Presley were singing and making melody in his heart to the Lord." In line with the name of the magazine, another young woman surmised that Elvis needed Christ in his life. "Because of his church background," she reasoned, "I feel that if we Christians would really pray, we would see the Lord work with Elvis. . . . I detest all he stands for, but I would love to see him won to Christ."[93]

Responding to such rebukes, one high-profile rocker traded pop music stardom for a pentecostal ministry. Jimmie Rodgers Snow, the son of country legend Hank Snow, counted Elvis and Buddy Holly as friends. He toured the United States with both as well as alongside Bill Haley and His Comets. While still very young, Snow landed a record contract with RCA, producing minor hits like the innocent "The Rules of Love" (1958).[94] In the late 1950s, Snow felt torn between his pentecostal church, which he began attending with a girlfriend, and the unbridled life of a rock 'n' roll celebrity. In late 1957, Snow confessed to Elvis that he was thinking of becoming a preacher. Presley was glad to hear it, although he surely did not realize that Snow would become a thundering evangelist against rock.[95]

Even before officially entering the ministry, Snow took to the pulpit to testify of his conversion experience and to convince fellow pentecostals, teens, and their parents, that rock 'n' roll music led to all kinds of vice and was destroying the country. In a short 1961 essay he penned for his denomination's youth magazine, he recalled his close friendship with Elvis and the things he figured he was best at before being saved from the fires of hell: "lying, stealing, and telling dirty jokes." He felt

The cover of C. M. Ward's *From Rock 'n' Roll to a Passion for Souls: With Questions & Answers on Youth's Problems Today* (Springfield, MO: Assemblies of God, 1960). Depicted are Jimmie Rodgers Snow and his wife, Carol. Reproduction courtesy of the Flower Pentecostal Heritage Center, Springfield, Missouri.

pursued by God. Eventually he "cut all ties with show business and started preaching full time for the Lord." God then gave him special power and boldness to preach, claimed Snow. He wrote this testimony for teens, he said, "to show you the depths the devil can pull you down to. He hates you and wants to destroy you." But salvation was at hand for anyone.[96]

Similar to Snow, the rockabilly legend Billy Adams also turned his life around. He had achieved minor fame as a solo artist with the twangy "Rock, Pretty Mama," a song inspired by Elvis and Jerry Lee. His late 1950s group Rock-a-Teens' novelty track "You Gotta Have a Ducktail" (1958)—featuring a baritone talking voice, heavy guitar strumming, and slap-back reverb—achieved a modicum of success, too. *Billboard* and

Cashbox magazines gave the group's work strong reviews. Adams felt called to the ministry in 1965, long after his band broke up. Years later, he liked to tell his audiences that he played only gospel after that moment. He toured the country, preaching and singing in the Pentecostal Holiness Church and in other denominations. One of his special targets from the pulpit was rock 'n' roll. Decades after his road to Damascus experience, he enthralled a crowd of two hundred pentecostals in Saluda, South Carolina, with a ninety-minute sermon demonizing rock. He knew well the evils of the music, he proclaimed, having performed it once himself. Teens rebelled automatically after listening to it. "It affects the pituitary gland," the evangelist said, "and breaks down moral inhibitions. Rock music promotes drugs, illicit sex and satanism."[97]

With so much scrutiny and negative attention from religious and secular quarters, it is no wonder that a few early rockers felt scorched by guilt. Raised on turn-or-burn theology, as Jimmie Rodgers Snow had been, they harbored grave doubts about the music they played and the lives they led. Jerry Lee Lewis famously wrestled throughout his career with a deep sense of conviction. The Killer's baroque hedonism—womanizing, drugs, and alcohol and accompanying violent behavior—only added to his gargantuan sense of remorse. While the tape rolled during an October 1957 Sun Records session for "Great Balls of Fire," Lewis preached on the evils of the devil's music. Lewis, who had been expelled from a pentecostal Bible school in 1950, turned to producer Sam Phillips:

> **JERRY LEE LEWIS:** H-E-L-L . . . that's right. It [the Bible] says "MAKE MERRY with the JOY OF GOD, only." But when it comes to worldly music, rock and roll, anythin' like that, you're in the world, and you haven't come from out of the world, and you're still a sinner. And you're a sinner. You're a sinner unless you be saved and born again, and be made as a little child, and walk before God, and be holy. And brother, I mean you got to be so pure, and no sin shall enter there. No SIN! Cause it says "no sin." It don't say just a little bit. It says, "no sin shall enter there." Brother, not one little bit. You got to walk and TALK with God to go to heaven. . . .

SAM PHILLIPS: Now look, Jerry . . .
LEWIS: Mr. Phillips, I don't care . . . it ain't what you believe. It's what's written in the BIBLE. . . .
PHILLIPS: Nah, gosh, it's not what you believe, it's how do you interpret the Bible.[98]

Jerry Lee was not interested in the subtleties of Phillips's hermeneutical argument. The Bible said what it said, Jerry Lee answered in typical pentecostal or fundamentalist fashion. The hard lessons of the Good Book could not be watered down or explained away. The brute fact of rock 'n' roll's sinfulness chased him like a demon.[99] As late as the 1970s, Lewis still contemplated giving up showbiz for a full-time ministry. Other first-generation rock 'n' rollers, like Lewis, continued to sing religious music and, in some cases, devoted increasing attention to the Lord's work.

Little Richard took up the call. A blazing comet on stage, Richard had one of the most tumultuous lives in the business. He flaunted his homosexuality, even though he was tormented by what he believed to be its innate sinfulness. The first draft of his 1955 hit song "Tutti Frutti," an homage to anal sex, included the lines "Awop-Bop-a-Loo-Mop-a-Good Goddam" and "Tutti-Frutti good booty—if it don't fit don't force it. You can grease it, make it easy." The record was sure to flop with lyrics so obscene. So, in production at a New Orleans studio, he and the song's co-creators cleaned it up. The final version—replete with Richard's gospel-tinged, high "whoo," which he confessed to borrowing from the gospel legend Marion Williams—rose to the number-two slot on *Billboard*'s rhythm and blues chart.[100] But success came at a heavy cost. Richard faced the scorn of critics, both secular and religious. A representative of WAMM radio in Flint, Michigan, pulled one of Little Richard's songs off the air. "I banned Little Richard's 'Lucille' because I feel the lyrics advocate immoral practices," he said bluntly. He was sure that his listeners thought it was the right decision.[101] As Little Richard's career took flight, the star performer was tormented relentlessly with inner doubts.

In 1957, after being confronted by a door-to-door preacher, Richard decided to give up the rock stage for the pulpit while on tour in Australia. Richard spoke about his change of heart on the October 11, 1957, broadcast of the live Ampol Radio Show in Sydney. He had just completed a dazzling performance of his brand-new hit song "Lucille." The song was about a drag queen, although most radio programmers and record shop clerks were none the wiser. The song that WAMM had banned sat on the rhythm and blues chart for twenty-one weeks and was also number one on the "Most Played R&B in Juke Boxes" list.[102] Richard, however, had other things on his mind besides his successful songs and his meteoric rise to stardom. The Soviets had just launched their beach-ball-sized Sputnik satellite on October 4. Richard spoke to the Australian radio show host, Jack Davey, about the ominous signs of the times and his decision to leave the world of rhythm and blues behind him. "I understand you're leaving here pretty soon, because you're anxious to get back to America," Davey said to the performer from Macon.

LITTLE RICHARD: Yes, uh. I'm anxious to get back to America, but I'm coming out of show business.

JACK DAVEY: Out of show business?

RICHARD: That's right.

DAVEY: You're going back for that reason?

RICHARD: That's right. I'm going to be an evangelist.

DAVEY: That's, that's, your, your heart is set on that apparently.

RICHARD: Yes. Uh, um, the reason, I would like to say this, I'm glad that you asked me. [*laughs nervously*] But, the reason I, I want to come out of show business, you see all these different kinda lights going up in the sky.

DAVEY: You mean the, the satellites. [*audience laughter*]

RICHARD: Thaaaat's right. That's it. That's a sign that the Lord is coming soon and I wanna dedicate my life to God.

DAVEY: I see, Little Richard. Well that's, that's a very good thought. . . .

RICHARD: . . . I know that if I don't get it right, I know that the, that the plans that the Lord is going to put on the world they gonna worry me, so I might as well be worried one way or the other. So I'm going back and I'm gonna study so I can help the other people that are doing wrong where they can be saved too.

DAVEY: Yes, I, I daresay I really agree with you. Music is pretty close to that sort of thing actually. I suppose you throw so much into your music that it, it gives you a feeling of goodness. You think it brings good in people?

RICHARD: Yes, I think that the music do a lotta good to the people, in one way. But I can't serve the Lord while I'm doing this, because he say you either love one and hate the other, you either hold one or turn-a loose the other. So I got to get completely from this to dedicate my life directly to God.

DAVEY: Well, that's very nice, and I think so sincere.[103]

It was an enormously costly decision. Little Richard walked away from half a million dollars in cancelled shows and faced a string of lawsuits.[104] To convince his doubtful saxophonist of his sincerity, Richard threw four diamond rings, valued at $8,000, into Sydney's Hunter River. Said Richard to a reporter, "If you want to live with the Lord, you can't rock 'n' roll too. God doesn't like it." He added that he was preparing for the end of the world.[105] Richard then trained for the ministry at a small Seventh-day Adventist school in Alabama.

His turnaround, however, proved short lived. He still enjoyed hanging out with young men more than with his wife, and he could not shake the rock music bug. In 1962, he signaled his rock comeback with shows in England alongside Sam Cooke and Gene Vincent. He later toured with a relatively unknown band from the port city of Liverpool called the Beatles. Would he perform gospel songs? asked some who were befuddled by his zigzagging career path. Promoters eagerly informed fans that "Little Richard has been booked purely as a rock and roll artist."[106] Richard continued to record gospel music, though. And in the late 1970s, he again quit rock music and denounced homosexuality. Then, in no uncertain terms, he declared, "I believe this kind of music is demonic. . . . I believe God wants people to turn from Rock 'n' Roll to the Rock of Ages."[107]

Like Little Richard, Johnny Cash spent much of the 1960s struggling mightily with what he considered the power of sin. Unable to control his alcohol and amphetamine use, he reached a low point in the late 1960s. Cash underwent a second, very public, conversion experience in

Little Richard performing "Long Tall Sally" in the 1956 film *Don't Knock the Rock* (Columbia Pictures, 1956), Clover Productions, Inc. Screenshot by the author from *Don't Knock the Rock/Rock Around the Clock* (Sony Pictures Home Entertainment, 2013), DVD.

1971 at the pentecostal Evangel Temple in Nashville, pastored by Jimmie Rodgers Snow. Thereafter Cash made frequent appearances at Billy Graham rallies and was the headline act at one of the first major Christian rock festivals in the country, Explo '72, in Dallas, Texas. Over the decades Cash continued to perform gospel music and released a string of gospel records, among them *Hymns by Johnny Cash* (1959), *The Holy Land* (1969), *The Gospel Road* (1973), *A Believer Sings the Truth* (1979), *I Believe* (1985), and *Goin' by the Book* (1990).[108]

Elvis, too, recorded a variety of gospel albums and continued to sing hymns as part of his regular repertoire, especially from the time of his comeback in 1968 until his death in 1977. He loved to sermonize, even while wearing an amphetamine crown. The King's Memphis mafia called him the "evangelist." One of his favorite hymns was the bombastic "How Great Thou Art," a nineteenth-century evangelical standard.[109] Throughout his career Elvis performed live and made recordings with the Jordanaires and the Imperials, both gospel quartets. For Elvis's final *Ed Sullivan Show* appearance on January 6, 1957, the Jordanaires backed him on a version of the classic Thomas Dorsey song "Peace in the Valley." He was especially fond of singing gospel songs as a way to calm down after a high-stress performance. With backing by the Jordanaires, Elvis's "Crying in the Chapel" made it to number three on the American charts in 1965. The song also sat at number one on the British charts for two weeks that summer, briefly beating out the Beatles, who had been dominating the charts on both sides of the Atlantic, a development that Elvis found particularly galling. In this same period Elvis had become the highest-paid star in Hollywood.[110]

All the while, Elvis was a religious seeker. Under the tutelage of his hairdresser–cum-guru Larry Geller, Elvis began to devour spiritualist and new age texts in 1964. A special favorite was Timothy Leary's *The Psychedelic Experience: A Manual Based on the* Tibetan Book of the Dead (1964), which he coaxed members of his Memphis mafia to read as well. He also pored over the pages of Joseph Benner's 1914 god-within book, *The Impersonal Life,* along with the writings of the Indian holy man Paramahanse Yogananda, the philosopher and writer Jiddu Krishnamurti, and the occultist and spirit medium Madame Blavatsky.[111] Over the Christmas holiday of 1964–1965, he experimented with LSD. (He spaced out while watching the sci-fi classic film *Time Machine* on television and eating pizza.) Still, Elvis—certainly not as conflicted as Jimmie Snow, Jerry Lee, Little Richard, or Johnny Cash—continued to call himself a Christian, although he was stung by rebukes from pulpits. He did not think that his dabbling in mysticism or numerology somehow meant that he was anything but a follower of Jesus.[112]

America's most famous preacher, Billy Graham, certainly doubted Elvis's faith. In the 1950s and through much of the 1960s, Graham disparaged the rock 'n' roll craze. At the height of Presley's fame in 1957, Graham lamented that "the American people are now plagued with a peculiar phenomenon of a young man whose songs emphasize the sensual, having the highest record sales and television audiences in the country." America's preacher asked how this could possibly be. It was the mystery of iniquity, he declared, "ever working in the world for evil."[113]

Despite Graham's certainty of the hellish origins of rock, the new genre bore the deep imprint of religion. The influence of pentecostalism on the first southern rockers to achieve national and international fame reveals the specific nature of that imprint. In an ironic twist, at the same time that Graham and other critics condemned the music as the demonic soundtrack of immorality and juvenile delinquency, some commentators were linking the famous preacher with the Memphis rock 'n' roller.

Billy Graham conducting his Glasgow crusade, March to April 1955. *Billy Graham's Glasgow Crusade*, Kelvin Hall, Glasgow, Scotland (Pathé News, 1955). Screenshot by the author from YouTube, British Pathé (http://www.youtube.com/watch?v=ftLWfmFdMrc).

They were both "popular heroes," claimed a critic in a May 20, 1957, issue of the *Hartford Courant*. At the time, Graham was conducting his famous sixteen-week Madison Square Garden Crusade, which over two million would attend. Presley's "All Shook Up" topped the charts in the United States, Canada, and England; his Technicolor blockbuster for Paramount, *Loving You,* had recently finished shooting. However different the entertainer and the revivalist might seem, wrote the critic, "both are crowd pleasers. Both are handsome. Both spring from south of the Mason-Dixon line." And more importantly for the riled editorialist, both emerged from the "unsophisticated" realm of fundamentalism. Neither appealed to the intellect. With a parting shot the critic observed that their fame spoke ill of America. The minister of the Protestant Episcopal Church of St. John, in Greenwich Village, agreed. The Reverend Charles Howard Graf, speaking to a church that was three-fourths empty, compared Graham's crusades to a circus. The celebrity evangelist's crowd appeal, said the minister, was like that of rock 'n' roll's

Elvis Presley. If only laypeople were informed and intelligent, he mused, "there never would have been a Billy Graham, or even a Billy Sunday." (Graf failed to realize that the mass appeal and innovativeness of evangelicalism was at the root of the movement's success.) One of America's most celebrated novelists, John Steinbeck, added his voice to that of other skeptics. In an op-ed drenched with sarcasm, he upheld the supposed "great men" of our time: "Billy Graham and Elvis Presley."[114]

The linking of America's premier evangelist and the King of Rock 'n' Roll was not entirely outrageous. The religious innovations of evangelicalism in general, and pentecostalism in particular, surely helped launch the vibrant new genre. By the mid-1950s, both black and white pentecostals had long been using the newest technologies to deliver their message to the widest possible audience. Believers also played passionate music, used stuttered vocalization and syncopated singing, and practiced holy dancing like no other religious conservatives would. Gospel groups—including Elvis's favorites, the white Stamps Quartet and the black Golden Gate Quartet—sang and performed in ways that excited crowds and inspired early rock 'n' rollers.[115]

Accordingly, the Arkansas native and music and art legend Tav Falco observes that "Gospel and rock 'n' roll were cut from the same cloth, even though one is considered to be the devil's music, and the other sanctified music. It was played by the same people, and appealed to the same audience."[116] The two styles were woven together closely in the 1950s. Looking back a little more than a decade after Little Richard, Elvis Presley, Jerry Lee Lewis, and Johnny Cash first shot up the charts with their high-energy songs and stage antics, a critic at the African American *Chicago Defender* reflected on the influence sanctified music exerted on rock and rhythm and blues. It was ironic, thought Earl Calloway, that the church had become a "virtual training ground for the entertainment world." He was sure that all the "energy, the music, style, the clapping of the hands, stomping of the feet, whoopin' and hollerin' are all a part of the sounds" these performers encountered in the sanctified holiness tradition.[117]

In a region like the South—where religious institutions and religious culture were so pervasive—popular, or so-called nonreligious, music, certainly bore the stamp of religion. The religious, especially pentecostal, influence on rock shows also that categories of religion and nonreligion, or sacred and profane, sometimes do not reflect a more nuanced reality.[118] The exuberant religion of the spirit certainly influenced life in the South, and the nation as a whole, well beyond the walls of churches.

It was in the 1950s South as well that rebukes of rock 'n' roll as "jungle music," "savage," and modern-day "voodoo" rhythms would stir up the religious imagination of white southern evangelicals. As the genre grew and thrived, performers would face new charges of defiling the racial purity of the white Christian South.

• 2 •

Race, Religion, and Rock 'n' Roll

On main street and in African jungles,
the beat of this wild rhythm is the same.
—Jessie Funston Clubb, 1957

It was Sunday afternoon, May 20, 1956, in Birmingham, Alabama. Bill Haley and His Comets were set to headline a rock 'n' roll and rhythm and blues show at the city's municipal auditorium. They would be joined on this leg of the tour by African American sensations like LaVern Baker, the Platters, Bo Diddley, Clyde McPhatter, and from Britain, Freddy Randall and His Band. The previous May, Bill Haley and His Comets had topped the *Billboard* chart with "Rock Around the Clock," and the song remained in that position for eight weeks. In January 1956 their "See You Later Alligator" had climbed to number six.[1]

But the Chester, Pennsylvania, group's success came at a high price. Visible representatives of the new rock and roll craze, they faced the ire of the Deep South's arch segregationists, especially the White Citizens' Council and the Ku Klux Klan, who were intent on maintaining racial purity, sometimes using threats, intimidation, and violence to achieve their goals. The council, founded in 1954, became a grassroots white bulwark against integration and bitterly challenged black social advancement. One month before Haley's Birmingham show, three white men associated with the North Alabama Citizens' Council had attacked Nat King Cole while the velvet-throated crooner performed on stage. In the city that would come to be called Bombingham in the tumultuous years ahead, rock-inspired interracialism lit a fuse.[2] Denominational editors and leaders, along with other secular observers of the rock 'n' roll revolutions, linked the black-and-white music to the exotic worlds of Africa, the Caribbean, and pagan religions. One month before his Birmingham show, Haley took the stage as part of a star-studded, mixed-race bill in Toronto. "Like natives at a voodoo ritual," noted a reporter with what was proving to be a common theme, "the crowd writhed and reeled until their pent-up emotions burst the dam of reason and they clambered onto the stage and into the aisles to dance."[3]

As Haley and his entourage made their way south to Birmingham, their truck tipped over in Mississippi. It was a bad omen. The Birmingham concerts would be divided—one for a white audience in the afternoon and one for a black audience at night. Civil rights activists were chipping away at Jim Crow laws in Montgomery, Alabama, in 1955 and 1956. But Birmingham's city ordinances remained secure, requiring segregated bus seating. Lunch counters and housing were organized by the color line as well.[4] That Haley's shows would conform to Jim Crow measures could not dispel hardcore opposition. White English trumpeter Freddy Randall was met with shouts of "jungle music!" Upon their arrival in Birmingham, Haley, Randall, and the other performers discovered fifty to sixty North Alabama Citizens' Council picketers. "Negro music," said council members, was degrading white youth and poisoning the South. They marched with placards that read "Why Negro Music," "Down with bebop," "Christians will not attend this show," "Bebop is communism," and "Ask your preacher about jungle music!" A much smaller group of teenage counterprotesters held up their own signs, which proclaimed "Why don't you drop dead, because rock 'n' roll is here to stay!" and "Three cheers for Bill Haley."[5] The show of support and the 2,500 concertgoers did little to rally Haley. Exhausted and rattled, he wrote in his tour diary, "They picketed the auditorium and we played to about half the people we had last time here. Made front page news all over the country." In his view, the Citizens' Council picketers were "fanatics." Maybe the city should even "stop shows coming here until the race situation is straightened out," lamented Haley.[6] Two days later, one of Haley's two integrated shows in Greenville, South Carolina, was cancelled after a bomb was discovered at the venue.[7]

Racial fears and anxieties about wayward youth gripped white America's conservative Protestants whenever they switched on their radios or television sets, only to hear the blaring of rock 'n' roll's uncouth shouters. As the American studies scholar Jack Hamilton aptly puts it, "A fundamental panic surrounding rock and roll's emergence was that its racially indeterminate character would threaten the racial order."[8] Accordingly, segregationist leader Asa Carter, who the *Montgomery Advertiser* dubbed the "loathsome fuhrer," and White Citizens' Councils throughout the South pressured owners of teenage hangouts to ban "Negro music" from their premises. The eccentric, maniacal Carter was even to the right of many a segregationist, but numerous others shared some of his views about the big beat. Jukeboxes in particular were to stock no rock and roll records. Carter said bluntly of rock that it was "the basic, heavy-beat music of Negroes. It appeals to the base in man, brings out animalism and vulgarity."[9] Councils blanketed their communities with flyers warning of the un-Christian, hideous perils that rock 'n' roll posed to white purity. The moral wholesomeness of the region was at stake, they claimed. The White Citizens' Council of Greater New Orleans printed up a dire warning for distribution throughout that storied, racially mixed city, where African Americans made up 37.2 percent of the population.[10] "NOTICE! STOP," read the alarmist handbill. "Help Save The Youth of America DON'T BUY NEGRO RECORDS." With urgency, the flyer continued, "The screaming, idiotic words, and savage music of these records are undermining the morals of our white youth in America. Call the advertisers of the radio stations that play this type of music and complain to them!" It concluded by pointing out the real victims of this music: "Don't Let Your Children Buy, or Listen to These Negro Records."[11]

This era of race-baiting and blatant white supremacy was also a time of great religious and social stability, especially for the middle class. Seldom in American history had church attendance been so high and public religious expression so ubiquitous as in the postwar years and the 1950s in particular. The Southern Baptist Convention and other white evangelical bodies celebrated their denominational successes with a flurry of church building. Religious organizations took in an astonishing twenty million new members in the 1940s. In the next decade, membership rose by another twenty-eight million. By 1960, religious affiliation in the United States hovered around 65 percent. This heightened religiosity also found expression in popular culture. Openly religious songs like "Vaya con Dios" (1953), "I Believe" (1953), and "The Man Upstairs" (1954) achieved chart success and high sales. On a larger stage, America's Cold War ideological battle with "godless communism" unified citizens against a common foe. The revivals of cold warrior preacher Billy Graham, the pronouncements of President Eisenhower, and the best-selling, self-help, soft evangelicalism of Norman Vincent Peale were just some signs of the spirit of the age.[12]

Skeptics called the civil religion of the Eisenhower era shallow, conformist, and self-congratulatory. By the end of the decade, Lutheran minister and religious historian Martin Marty acknowledged that the country was "reaching a point of near-saturation so far as religious interest goes." He thought, however, that

> the religion involved is largely so inoffensive that the pendulum of reaction is not likely to swing far. In other words, the current revival, while extensive, in many of its aspects lacks depth. There has been less investment; there need be less withdrawal. For this is that utterly new thing: A revival that goes not against the grain of the nation but with it; a revival that draws its strength from its safe residence in the mores of the nation.[13]

Two years after Marty's warning of the perils of superficial religiosity, Gibson Winter equally castigated complacent and conformist Christianity in *The Suburban Captivity of the Churches* (1961).[14]

Resting just beneath the surface of denominational confidence, successful religious crusades (however shallow), church membership campaigns, and church building were strong fears and social anxieties. Accordingly, rock 'n' roll music inspired numerous jeremiads in the 1950s. The music, for its many detractors, embodied almost everything that was wrong with the country. But for teenage fans it was the antidote to the disease of bland conformity. In the wake of Elvis Presley's stunning record sales and live TV performances, and as Chuck Berry, Little Richard, Fats Domino, and Bill Haley packed out auditoriums of white and black youths, denunciations of rock and roll as uncouth, vulgar, and reprehensible became commonplace. Race weighed heavy on the minds of rock 'n' roll's countless critics. One month after the Birmingham picketing, in a relatively restrained take on the new riotous music, a journalist in Florida called rock 'n' roll "a combination of many forms of music, from the most primitive jungle beats to the sensuous rhythms of the Negro blues to the monotonous cacophony of hillbilly

Teenage girls make their marks on a poster for Elvis's 1956 film *Love Me Tender*. Photo by Phil Stanziola, New York World-Telegram and the Sun Newspaper Photograph Collection, Library of Congress Prints and Photographs Division, Washington, D.C. (LC-USZ62-114912).

happiness numbers." Commenting on the 1956 hit song "Hot Rod Henry," popularized by the white teen phenom Lola Dee, another observer found that "the strong down-beat is strictly from the jungle, but in this unorthodox age the jungle casts its spell the same as anything exotic—anything but home is supposed to be marvelous." Whatever shape the Frankenstein genre took, it looked stronger and more popular with each passing week.[15]

Race was typically central to secular and religious press coverage of the music. An editor in the African American *Pittsburgh Courier* newspaper figured that the anti-rock-'n'-roll hysteria gripping the nation, and especially the South, had a distinct racist tinge. The insistent pronouncements of the White Citizens' Council were clear enough. In the view of the *Courier* journalist, all the outrage amounted to an "attack against Negroes, of course, because they invented rock 'n' roll . . . and because it so captivated the younger generation of whites."[16] Elvis himself acknowledged as much when he said in 1956 that "colored folks been singing it and playing it just like I'm doing' now, man, for more years than I know. They played it like that in the shanties and in their juke joints and nobody paid it no mind 'til I goose[d] it up. I got it from them."[17] Sam Phillips—the boastful, larger-than-life owner of Sun Records who first launched the star's career—made similar comments about the interracial genius of the music. Phillips first thought Elvis was rough around the edges, he recalled a few years after their first studio sessions together in Memphis in 1954. Elvis, he said, "was just a raw kid with no training, but he had an interesting sound. He was a white boy, but he was singing like a Negro."[18]

Others were anything but excited or proud of rock and roll's supposed black or interracial roots. Within black communities, and especially in churches, clergymen and churchgoers fretted that they would be associated with the wild new rhythmic songs and the dances the music inspired. In Bedford, Massachusetts, an AME Zion minister preached to his congregation that traditional black spirituals were being "mixed up with some crazy rock 'n' roll song, their purposes have been misdirected—their melodies adapted to the cheapest of swing." Now performers were infusing such classic spirituals as "Swing Low Sweet Chariot" with racy rhythms. These sinful tunes had "sacrilegiously become the media of entertainment in theaters and nightclubs amid drunkenness and moral dishevelment."[19] Rising civil rights leader Martin Luther King Jr. cast aspersions on the new music as well. So too did A. Philip Randolph's Brotherhood of Sleeping Car Porters, which considered black popular music degrading to women. Within black communities there were even some attempts to censor or ban records that were judged offensive or troublesome.[20]

Typical white denunciations focused much attention on race and called into question rock 'n' roll's supposed low African origins. Critics had, in fact, used the tag "jungle music" long before the advent of the big beat, largely to warn off listeners from degenerate tunes performed by black, white, or integrated groups.[21] In 1938, one white observer was drawing direct connections between black sanctified services and wild music. A Milwaukee reporter sat in on the religious services of Father Divine, the southern-born, quasi-pentecostal promoter of interracialism and his own cult of personality. Congregants at Divine's church on the

Hudson River, said the witness, sang the same droning tune, "clapped their hands and stomped their feet to the jungle music of a Negro band."[22] Divine's rival Depression-era black pentecostal prophet, Daddy Grace, whose church a young James Brown attended in Augusta, gained as much notoriety for his church's novel, so-called primitive music and unorthodox practices. Upon Grace's death in 1960, a reader of the *Baltimore Afro-American* penned an outraged response to the iconic leader's church and his religious spectacles: "Their disgraceful baptizing with fire hoses, their rock 'n' roll jungle music and their speaking in so-called unknown tongues added nothing to our struggle for first-class citizenship."[23]

Even in the halls of power ideas about race, ethnicity, rhythmic music, and immorality took center stage. In a 1932 session of the House of Representatives Committee on Immigration and Naturalization, a parade of experts weighed in on the menacing influence of unwanted, "foreign" entertainers. Tawdry race music came under the scrutiny of one witness who denounced "sex dramas, strip shows, gangster heroics, mushy love, jungle music" in equal measure. These, he said, "all leave a mark, a mark deep and telling, and the result of some years of such is beginning to be felt in society in general and in the youth of the nation, in particular."[24] It is little wonder that white Southern Baptists feared that jazz music, as one North Carolina believer put it, "is so immoral that it cannot be described in the columns of a religious paper." Parents, he urged, should never allow their daughters to go to dances where "the strains of this jungle music" were played.[25] The horrors of black and white dancers holding each other closely on the ballroom floor haunted the minds of such outraged evangelicals. But what struck some as debased and wretched was a selling point to others in the boom-and-bust era. In the 1920s and 1930s, for instance, marketers used primitivism to pitch jazz. The storied Cotton Club promoted the "Jungle Music" of Duke Ellington and outfitted dancers with stylized "native" dresses.[26]

When rock 'n' roll music gained widespread attention in the mid-1950s, its interracial dimensions seemed to pose a new, even more substantial threat to youth. Jazz looked almost quaint by comparison. The exposure of fans to integrated music was never far from the conversation. Officials in cities across Alabama, Louisiana, Virginia, and Arkansas passed laws that banned interracial dances and concerts.[27] Fights between blacks and whites broke out at the Memorial Auditorium in Chattanooga, Tennessee, during the Drifters concert there in early 1956. The manager of the venue felt certain about the real problem. The "mixing of the races at these dances," he reasoned, "should be stopped before an unnecessary tragedy occurs."[28] Numerous conservative white religious critics took such warnings to heart.[29]

Over and over again between 1955 and 1959, commentators hoped to reveal the savage, twisted roots of this music. They did so with massive resistance to the 1954 *Brown v. Board of Education* Supreme Court decision as a backdrop. Ten years after that landmark decision, Martin Luther King Jr. would reflect on the economic and social pressures of the era in *Why We Can't Wait.* "Negroes are still at the bottom of the economic ladder," he lamented. "They live within two concentric circles of segregation. One imprisons them on the basis of color, while the other confines them within a separate culture of poverty."[30] But even in the 1950s, there were signs of change for the better. Basic transformations in postwar America made it more and more difficult for African Americans to settle for marginalization or Jim Crow justice. A younger generation that was better educated, the expectations of returning veterans from World War II and Korea, the growing black middle class, and a new engagement with the market economy and with politics made blacks in the 1950s press for greater opportunities and the rights they deserved.[31] Simultaneously, African American performers had a larger presence in film and on television. Black solo artists and vocal groups were also gaining new white fans and rising in popularity. In the early years of the decade, the black electric blues bands of Chicago claimed few white fans. But after 1955, greater and greater national attention focused on black artists and the music that had formerly been almost invisible to whites. Only 7.5 percent of the musicians on the top forty charts were black in 1955. Two years later, that had doubled.[32]

Bohemians and white teenage hipsters drew on black and African themes in significant ways in the postwar years. A younger generation of Americans and Europeans turned to the imagined exoticisms of Afro-America, in part out of disillusionment with war, conformity, and the banality of a staid mass culture. As one scholar observes, "Paris and Harlem were the main centres of this cult of 'negrophilia.'"[33] Observing these trends, Norman Mailer penned his influential, controversial 1957 essay "The White Negro" for *Dissent.* "So no wonder that in certain cities of America," Mailer wrote,

> in New York of course, and New Orleans, in Chicago and San Francisco and Los Angeles, in such American cities as Paris and Mexico, D.F., this particular part of a generation was attracted to what the Negro had to offer. In such places as Greenwich Village, a ménage-à-trois was completed—the bohemian and the juvenile delinquent came face-to-face with the Negro, and the hipster was a fact in American life.[34]

In Dixie such cultural influence and black striving would be challenged vehemently. That young black performers exerted any kind of influence over white teenagers threw segregationists into a rage. From the U.S. Senate floor, Mississippi's segregationist senator James Eastland held fast to the divinely ordained, immutable racial status quo. He defied the federal government's efforts to alter the arrangement. Turning to the region's history, Eastland argued in late May 1954, "The Southern institution of racial segregation or racial separation was the correct, self-evident truth which arose from the chaos and confusion of the Reconstruction period. Separation promotes racial harmony." Segregation, he went on, "is the law of nature, it is the law of God, that every race has both the right and the duty to perpetuate itself."[35] Two years after Eastland's stern pronouncement, nineteen U.S. senators and seventy-seven representatives signed on to the "Southern Manifesto," a document that encouraged resistance to federally mandated integration. "Without regard to the consent of the governed," the resisters warned, "outside agitators are threatening immediate and revolutionary changes in our public school systems. If done, this is certain to destroy the system of public education in some of the states."[36]

For critics of desegregation, rock 'n' roll's ungodly race mixing posed grave threats similar to those posed by integrated public school classrooms. Thus, denominational attention to the big beat's roots and its possible impact on teens took on a new urgency in the years immediately after the *Brown* decision. The Sunday School Board of the Southern Baptist Convention took up the question of the music's origins. Was it a harmless fad or something far more sinister? they asked. The Kentucky Baptist newspaper the *Western Recorder* weighed in as well. "The Rock and Roll craze is not actually a thing in itself," a writer reasoned, "it is the symptom of a disease in human nature—sin. . . . Christ is the answer to the total problem of sin! When He comes into the life the 'disease' goes out."[37] Integrated dances and performances from 1955 forward made these fears about the *disease* that preyed on youth even more real.[38]

Disc jockey and youth-market entrepreneur Alan Freed did more than perhaps anyone to promote this novel, much-reviled, integrated, and teen-geared music. He was tireless in his efforts to spread what some were calling the gospel of rock 'n' roll. Nicknamed Moondog, the brash promoter won over devoted young fans who flocked to concerts that he hosted and eagerly awaited his radio broadcasts. On January 14 and 15, 1955, Freed's "Rock 'n' Roll Jubilee Ball" set the tone for numerous future shows. The New York City boxing arena that served as the venue held six thousand attendees. The crowd was roughly half black and half white.[39] The police did their best to rid the show of fainting youngsters and assorted hooligans. Freed's extravaganza showcased an all-black cast of performers, including Buddy Johnson, Joe Turner, Fats Domino, the Clovers, Clyde McPhatter and the Drifters, the Harptones, Red Prysock, and the Moonglows. More famous even than most of the performers was the charismatic, energetic Freed himself. Early on, the popular DJ had been clear about the churches, White Citizens' Council, and civic officials who demonized the music. Writing in *Down Beat* magazine in 1955, Freed said, "To me, this campaign against Rock and Roll smells of discrimination of the worst kind against the great and accomplished Negro songwriters, musicians and singers who are responsible for this outstanding contribution to American music."[40]

In that same year, *Variety* noted Freed's influence and the Pied Piper role he had assumed. "The big beat in the pop music biz these days is rhythm & blues," wrote Herm Schoenfeld. The "top name in the r&b field is Alan Freed, the 'rock 'n' roll' disc jockey who recently moved from Cleveland to WINS [radio station] in New York." As with Elvis and many other key figures who were crossing the musical color line, Freed, the teenage culture broker, was turning white youth on to black music. Schoenfeld observed as much, noting, "Once limited to the

Negro market, the r&b influence has now crossed all color lines into the general pop market." Freed had "stepped into the role of a rhythm and blues evangelist."[41] The famous DJ, yelling into the mic at mixed-race shows, would beat on a phone book like a revivalist on the circuit. The African American bandleader Lucky Millinder thought that Freed had all "the fire and excitement of a Reverend Billy Graham."[42]

For worried white evangelicals, Freed's was a false gospel, and for some, unnatural race mixing in low-lit dance halls made it even more pernicious. They would not have been shocked when scandal began to plague Freed. He was once again in the national spotlight in May 1958 after his Big Beat show in Boston, headlined by Jerry Lee Lewis, ended in a fit of teenage violence. Following that, Boston's mayor John Hynes suspended licenses for rock and roll concerts, and a Boston grand jury issued an indictment against Freed as part of an antianarchy law. *Time* magazine called what happened in Boston a "Rock 'n' Riot." Catholics in the city especially thought the disturbance distasteful and indicative of the rock menace. But Freed, confident as ever, was defiant. "Those kids in Boston were the greatest—swell, wonderful kids," he pleaded. "But the police were terrible." Such authorities, like religious leaders, were just using the incident to lash out at the music, Freed continued to claim.[43]

For the faithful, there seemed to be a war going on for the souls of their teens. The Baptist General Convention of Texas even produced a short pamphlet for youngsters to warn them against the wiles of Freed and others like him. "Most of the blame for the cheap taste in music of our young people," it spelled out, "goes to those conscientiousless [*sic*] disk-jockeys who intersperse their spiels for toothpaste with the course and vulgar drivel of pop platter."[44] Questions about the impact of DJs hung heavy in the air. Would good churchgoing parents lose their children to the new, integrated dance music? Or would their youngsters remain safely within the confines of the church and Sunday school? Could the sanctified entertainments that pastors and laypeople approved hold teenagers' attention? The struggle for the teen soul reached into Canada. "During my junior year in college in the Maritimes in the mid-50s," recalled Pat MacAdam over forty years later, "Billy Graham exploded on the scene like a meteor. His book, *Peace with God,* was a mega-bestseller. On cold, crisp winter evenings we could pull in radio stations from New York and Boston—1,300 kilometres away." While MacAdam stayed glued to his set, he "could also pick up Alan Freed's new kind of music (rock 'n' roll), Bill Haley and the Comets and a galaxy of other musicians who would become household names."[45] For this reminiscing baby boomer, though, Graham won the day. Alan Freed, hounded by a payola scandal and losing out to changing teenage tastes, faded away.[46]

In the South, others fretted that perhaps the church could not compete with new music idols, Pied Piper DJs, and the pleasures of the flesh that rock 'n' roll offered so easily. In the fall of 1960, a North Carolina Baptist editor was asking if there was a "Spiritual Recession" taking place. Maybe it was the ecclesiastical analog of the Eisenhower Recession of 1958. Low turnout at a five-day Charlotte, North Carolina, preaching and missions conference did not bode well, said the editor. The event gathered some of the "finest preachers" and even several sports celebrities. But only three thousand showed up for it. Across town, a rock 'n' roll show, to the editor's consternation, drew an astounding five thousand teens. "Attendance at the rock 'n' roll show contrasted with the attendance at the Preaching Mission," he concluded. It made one thing abundantly clear to the Baptist editor: "People do what they want to do." Maybe the church was losing out to the "world," he suggested.[47]

Blame fell not only on the DJs that promoted the music but also on the juke joints, teen hangouts, and concert halls that dotted communities around the country. Ministers and church members eagerly pointed out the grave problems posed by concerts and poorly supervised youth. Preachers needed only to pick up their morning papers to collect material for their Sunday sermons attacking rock 'n' roll.[48] A Dallas rock 'n' roll show at the city's Sportatorium on July 14, 1957, led to a particularly intense national uproar. The city was a stronghold of the Ku Klux Klan and had earlier gained notoriety for public lynchings. Dallas would remain the largest segregated southern city until 1961, when its school board finally set in motion a desegregation plan. And yet, in the late 1950s, the Sportatorium was sponsoring interracial rock 'n' roll concerts.[49] Elvis played the arena early in his career. Texas native Buddy Holly and "Blue Suede Shoes" legend Carl Perkins mounted its stage as well. Just a few months before the July 1957 show, the storied venue hosted Jerry Lee Lewis, Chuck Berry, Johnny Cash, and Fats Domino. The latter played to mixed-race audiences of twelve thousand in two separate shows in February. The crush of fans outside the concert hall was so tremendous that twenty-five fainted. Fats Domino saw repeated outbreaks of mayhem and violence at his performances in these years.[50]

At first the July 1957 concert, once again featuring New Orleans native Fats Domino, seemed to be going off without incident, although crowd security guards ejected some of the fans for dancing at the mixed-race event. The arena did not have a dance permit. After the Sportatorium concert concluded, thousands of youths poured out into the streets, their ears still ringing. Fights broke out as the crowd milled about. The staccato pops of gunfire could be heard overhead. In all, police arrested and jailed twenty. Amid the melee, four young white men were stabbed, two of whom were summer students at North Texas State College. That school, forty miles northwest of Dallas, had admitted Irma E. L. Sephas, its first African American student several months before. The college's newspaper claimed that a twenty-year-old black man was one of the perpetrators. Police also reported that a sixteen-year-old assailant, wounded in the ruckus, was overheard at a café near the arena saying he had just "cut some white men at the rock 'n' roll show."[51]

Shortly after the bloody incident, the *Dallas Morning News* was asking its readers, "Was this music in any way responsible for what happened later? Can rock 'n' roll exert wicked influence on the behavior of people who listen to it?" Many white Texans certainly thought so. A student at North Texas State reflected on the chaos and drew dire conclusions. "In both Monday's fracus [*sic*] and a previous incident in March," observed the student, "Negro entertainers played rock 'n roll music before mixed audiences."[52] The interracial violence after Fats Domino's Dallas show was even logged as evidence of racial strife in U.S. Senate hearings on constitutional rights.[53] The committee also made note of a similar incident that happened five months later in Spartanburg, South Carolina. Committee members recorded that the Spartanburg "City Council passed an ordinance in November requiring municipal approval for outdoor public meetings. The action came after fights broke out between whites and Negroes during a street 'rock and roll' party sponsored by a local radio station."[54]

Religious leaders in Dallas quickly drew connections between race-mixing, rock 'n' roll music, and violent disturbances. The pastor of First Baptist Church of West Dallas, Carey Daniel, delivered a jeremiad to his congregation on the new music fad. He titled his July 1957 sermon

An illustration for a Southern Baptist anti-rock-'n'-roll article. Jessie Funston Clubb, "What about Rock 'n' Roll?" *HomeLife*, April 1957, 42. Reproduction courtesy of the Southern Baptist Historical Library and Archives, Nashville, Tennessee.

simply "That Rock 'n' Roll Fight and What We Should Learn from It." The unruly fans surrounding the Sportatorium were part of a much larger problem. "Those people were worked up to a hysterical pitch by that sexy music," Daniel told a local reporter. He went on to venture that "Negroes" excelled at rock 'n' roll music because it was "straight out of the African jungle." Worse still, in the pastor's opinion, "the stupid American white public is going crazy over it."[55]

Across town, Dallas's most influential minister, W. A. Criswell, served in the pulpit of the largest church in the Southern Baptist Convention. The downtown First Baptist Church boasted eleven thousand members in 1956.[56] Like his fellow preacher at West Dallas, Criswell, who would later serve as the denomination's president, was a diehard segregationist. He warned attendees of a 1956 South Carolina evangelism conference of the dangers of integration:

> If you want this group, or that group, or that group, or that group, brother, it's a free country. If I want my group, let me have it. Let me have it. Don't force me by law, by statute, by Supreme Court decision, by any way that they can think of, don't force me to cross over in those intimate things where I don't want to go. Let me build my life. Let me have my church. Let me have my school. Let me have my friends. Let me have my home. Let me have my family. And what you give to me, give to every man in America and keep it like our glorious forefathers made it—a land of the free and the home of the brave.[57]

Criswell was joined by other men of the cloth on the subject. Lawrence Neff, an Atlanta Methodist, wrote a pamphlet in 1958 confidently titled "Jesus: Master-Segregationist." "Let the fact be calmly and deliberately stated and stressed," argued Neff, "Jesus was the most consistent and inflexible segregationist the world has ever known. . . . His gospel is equally valid for every nation, tribe and tongue. But it could flow only through specific human channels."[58]

Criswell's and Neff's views aligned closely with those of the so-called reading-and-writing Klan, the White Citizens' Council. By 1957, that group boasted an estimated membership of between 250,000 and 300,000. Their greatest recruitment was logged in Alabama, Louisiana, Mississippi, South Carolina, and Virginia. By some estimates, race relations were growing worse after 1954, and the council was a sign of severe social strain. A twenty-two-year-old reporter traveled through the region to take stock of local Citizens' Councils and the religious responses to racism. David Halberstam had just graduated from Harvard University and was working for the Nashville *Tennessean.* "Before the advent of the Councils a man who spoke up against Jim Crow merely ran the risk of being known as radical," reported the young journalist. Now, "he faces an organized network of groups consciously working to remove dissenters—his job and his family's happiness may be at stake."[59] Indeed, members of the growing white supremacist group pressed southerners to conform to its social and even religious agenda.

Early in 1957, the organization's chief newspaper published a "Manual for Southerners" that tutored grade school children that "God put each race by itself." Accordingly, it reasoned that God "wanted the colored people to live alone. That is why He put them off by themselves."[60] Such racial certainties shocked some in the region. Another Baptist pastor in Dallas took issue with the Citizens' Council and Criswell's staunch, God-ordained segregation. Reverend T. H. Wicks, of the Griggs Chapel Baptist Church for Negroes, challenged Criswell. "Looking at the question from the gospel of the New Testament church," stated the African American minister, "there is no race distinction." What were the theological implications of racism? he wondered. "If we are to be separated here, are we to be separated in heaven?"[61] Many white southern evangelicals, who had long maintained Jim Crow cemeteries, seemed to believe just that.[62]

Along with his preaching on the moral certainties of segregation, Criswell occasionally spoke to his large congregation and radio audience about the snares of liberal trends, popular culture, and secular music. In early 1957, he devoted one of his sermons, broadcast over the radio, to the falsehoods of evolutionary theory. He found occasion to take a swipe at rock 'n' roll and its primitivism as well. "Well, there are a lot of poisons that look exactly like sugar and like salt, but that does not make them all alike," he said with a southern twang, his voice rising to a crescendo. Scientists were trying to confuse believers and convince them that men came from apes. To make the matter plain he used an illustration:

> I can go down there to the record shop and I can buy two records, and they look exactly alike, and to all appearance they are alike. And I can put one of them on the record player and it plays a beautiful aria by Caruso entitled "Martha," and I put the other record on and it plays "You Ain't Nothing but a Hound Dog," by Elvis Presley. Isn't that right? Isn't that right? Yet the evolutionist comes along and says they are exactly alike. . . . Why there is no such thing in this earth as those things being exactly alike just because they look alike.[63]

A year later, the popular Dallas pastor used the example of regressive, debauched music to show how ungodly the world had become. The country was a modern "Babel." He shouted, modulating his voice between high and low pitches, "There is something wrong with America when the radios . . . of Dallas . . . by the hours, and the hours, and the hours, and hours play nothing but the sorriest, sorriest, most inexcusable type of rock 'n roll." The music was an "abomination"! If anything, returning to his anti-Darwinism, it all proved devolution.[64] Behind much of this and similar rhetoric was the implication of degraded, mongrelized music.

Other Baptists in the area shared Criswell's views about popular culture and divinely sanctioned segregation. Among those was E. K. Oldham, a vocal pastor from Grand Prairie, just to the west of Dallas. The Citizens' Council upheld both Criswell and Oldham as examples of true, untainted Christianity. God, said Oldham in a 1956 sermon, wanted "every Bible believer to make protest against desegregation." In his mind the integrationists' ultimate goal was interracial marriage, a typical racial apocalypse for ardent segregationists. Contrary to what so many liberal Protestants believed, Oldham emphasized that "all men are not brothers."[65]

At the dawn of the modern civil rights movement, white evangelicals were asking just who was their brother. In the Bible Belt, worries about interracialism, rhythmic music, and uncontrollable teenagers were woven together. In the late 1950s, evangelicalism claimed an enormous portion of the American public in the South and beyond it. The National Association of Evangelicals, founded in 1942 as a counter to the liberal National Council of Churches, soon represented millions, drawing together some of the largest denominations in the country. By the early 1960s, the expanding National Association of Evangelicals totaled roughly twenty-six million constituent members.[66] Billy Graham, the most visible representative of the movement, at first bowed to the pressures of Jim Crow and segregated his meetings in Dixie, but he was soon holding integrated revivals in the early 1950s. During these same years Graham considered racism an individual sin, not a social or collective sin in need of structural reform, and he seldom addressed the systemic nature of race prejudice. When believers got right with God, Graham assured interviewers, they would see the light and repent of their bigotry. A critic in Graham's magazine *Eternity* was less sanguine. "Let's face it," he wrote, most white "evangelicals, whether they are from the North, South, East, or West, are supporters of the *status quo,* and consequently tend to be segregationists."[67]

In the postwar period, Graham's denomination, the Southern Baptist Convention, with roughly 10.2 million members and thirty-three thousand churches, cautiously broached the topic of segregation, often referred to as the "race problem."[68] In the late 1940s and 1950s, the denomination's Christian Life Commission instructed members on the cruel discrimination and prejudice that African Americans regularly faced. In 1954, the Southern Baptist Convention held its annual convention in St. Louis. Thus removed from sections of the country most adamantly opposed to integration, convention delegates nonetheless wrangled over whether to support the *Brown* decision. Gallup polling revealed that 72 percent of easterners supported school desegregation and 77 percent of westerners did. Only 20 percent of southerners polled said they supported it.[69] Even official Southern Baptist Convention endorsement of school integration mattered little to the average man and woman in the pew. As one observer noted roughly fifteen years later, "The near-unanimous approval of the commission's resolution at the 1954 convention was not an accurate measure of Southern Baptist feeling about desegregation."[70] Some congregations even forced the resignations of pastors who appeared to favor integration. Churches in the Deep South, bristling at the thought of what the *Brown* decision would do to their schools, also threatened to withhold financial support from the Southern Baptist Convention.[71] Three years after *Brown,* the Alabama Baptist State Convention firmly committed itself to segregation. Progress for the races, said representatives, "could best be achieved for all concerned by not integrating our schools." Integration, in this view, would only make race relations worse.[72] In many ways, white evangelicals in the postwar years did not see racism as a widespread societal problem but, as Graham did, as a matter of the heart. If anything, it was a personal sin to be a racist. In the mid-1960s, the Southern Baptist minister and academic Samuel Hill observed that white Christian responsibility amounted to converting and befriending blacks. Hill remarked that conservative and moderate whites did not "consider altering the social traditions and arrangements which govern his (and everyone else's) life to so significant a degree."[73]

Supporters of some measure of desegregation, especially those in the South, were painfully aware that the word "integration" had come to mean something far more threatening to their parishioners and to the larger public. Moderates and progressives were at pains to lay out in detail what integration did *not* mean. Just as a single rock 'n' roll concert in a community might obliterate the color line, school desegregation posed a similar danger. Just two months after Senator Lyndon Johnson helped push a tepid Civil Rights Act through Congress in 1957, a gathering of white clergy in Atlanta tried to clear up the matter surrounding integration. "The use of the word 'integration' in connection with our schools and other areas of life has been unfortunate . . . since to many that term has become synonymous with amalgamation."[74]

The conservative Southern Presbyterians represented one part of the backlash to integration and the modern civil rights movement. In the late 1950s and early 1960s, numerous ministers and laypeople had had enough of "tolerance," racial and otherwise. One minister wrote to the denomination's publication, edited by Billy Graham's father-in-law, to offer his adamant opinion. "Our interest in civil rights these days," he challenged from Prattville, Alabama, "makes it almost impossible to see clearly the demerits as well as the merits of every effort to 'overcome racial, social and religious prejudice.' " Not every group or individual was deserving of support, he proclaimed. The minister then concluded, "Not every prejudice is bad."[75]

When instances of extreme prejudice or outright white supremacy did arise, the Southern Presbyterians and the Southern Baptists could stand in opposition to them. For instance, in the summer of 1957 the Southern Baptist Convention demanded that a group of white supremacist laymen drop the word "Baptist" from that group's name. The segregationist organization vowed to fight ideas that were "foreign to our beliefs as Christian white men."[76] Otherwise, the Southern Baptists' record on race relations on the local level, as with that of the Southern Presbyterians and the Assemblies of God, proved ill suited to the times, nonexistent, or starkly segregationist.[77] Religious historian Andrew Manis remarks that "the more local the responses, the more likely southern Baptists were to reject the civil rights movement."[78]

In 1957, as the final impact of *Brown* still remained uncertain, the Southern Baptist Convention's Chicago annual convention called on the nation to heal "racial tensions" and protect the rights and ensure the safety of blacks while cautiously avoiding specifics. The editor of the *Baptist Record*, based in Jackson, Mississippi, reassured readers that any direct action on the "race problem" would be left up to individual churches. "The truth of the matter is," he observed, "that the Southern Baptist Convention in Chicago said nothing of consequence and did nothing newsworthy concerning the race issue. . . . The question of segregation or integration of public schools was not discussed." Perhaps more importantly, he reassured readers, "there was no consideration whatsoever of integration in the churches."[79]

Clear ideas about race, civilization, and barbarism emerged from such religious conversations and debates about public school integration and missions in the southern hemisphere. Simultaneously, church leaders and laity continued to speculate about where this wild, disorderly teenage music originated. Their answers often took them to the southern hemisphere of their imaginations. On furlough back in the United States, white evangelical missionaries who ministered in Africa, the Caribbean, and South America would regale congregations with tales of witchcraft, polygamy, and the strange customs of their adopted homes. On these campaigns to raise funds and increase interest in world evangelism, white missionaries would bring with them weapons, tools, totems, and other artifacts to show puzzled parishioners.[80] In characteristic fashion, a holiness missionary described the exotic "dark continent" to fellow believers in the 1950s. "Africa—the very word has a fascinating ring about it," said H. K. Bedwell. "It conjures up visions of great forests and roaring lions, slave-caravans and cannibals, great missionary explorers and bloodthirsty chiefs." The continent was "full of mystery and unnamable horrors."[81]

At the same time in missionary circles, even among select evangelicals, the old exotic and primitive tropes were being replaced with a fuller picture of African countries, cultures, and foreign religions. For instance, Southern Baptist missionaries and members of the denomination's mission boards tended to be more progressive about race than state officials and laypeople.[82] After racial turmoil and violence broke out in her home state of Mississippi, one Southern Baptist missionary wrote back to fellow believers with concern. From Nigeria she reported, "You send us out here to preach that Christ died for all men. Then you make a travesty of our message by refusing to associate with some of them because of the color of their skin."[83] As anthropology and ethnography increasingly influenced evangelical and liberal Protestant missiology, stock ideas about civilization versus barbarism appeared less frequently than they had earlier in the twentieth century. In fact, anthropology so influenced mainliners that proselytizing and missionary activity seemed less and less relevant with each passing year. During the Cold War era, evangelical leaders, as the historian Molly Worthen notes, "more than ever before began to realize the costs of prejudice on the mission field." But evangelicals' lofty ideal of converting the "noble savage" in far-off countries, says Worthen, "did not always temper their reactions to African-American children bound for their own neighborhood's newly integrated school."[84]

In many other cases, though, the experiences of white missionaries appeared to confirm the worst fears panicked believers harbored about rock 'n' roll. White missionaries from the pentecostal Assemblies of God sent dispatches back to the denomination's headquarters in Springfield, Missouri. They were thrilled to be doing work in the Caribbean in the summer of 1962, although the stubborn persistence of African religious practices that they witnessed in Haiti gave them pause. In their view, "Transplanting these people from Africa to Haiti has done little to change their customs." At one point the missionaries' preaching was overpowered by the distant banging of drums. Appalled, they could not believe what they were witnessing. "Voodoo dancers, to the accompaniment of jungle drums, are doing a twisting dance in the door of the church." The white missionaries thought that the "demonism" on display rivaled anything on offer in Africa.[85] Believers expanded on this well-established theme. In the summer of 1962, a group of pentecostal youth evangelists, who had taken Coney Island as their mission field, witnessed similarly wild scenes that brought them to tears. The amusement park where they preached was little more than a "wicked playground." Across from their outpost was a rock 'n' roll dance hall named the Devil's Pit—for them, it was a den of sinners. According to one account, the venue gathered together "homosexuals, Lesbians, teen gangs, drug addicts and professional swindlers." The "most shocking sight of all," observed one of the ministers, "was the young piano player," perhaps under the influence of Jerry Lee Lewis. The animated performer "was beating out his chords in a demon-possessed manner with his head and hair twisting and flopping like a savage under the influence of voodoo."[86]

One of the most well-known Christian crusaders against rock music in the late 1950s was not a southerner or a pentecostal. He did, though, use many of the same racial tropes that his southern and pentecostal brethren had employed. Canadian-born William Ward Beecher Ayer made direct connections between voodoo in the Caribbean and sexually explicit dancing that accompanied concerts around the country. Ayer bore the name of his famous grandfather, Henry Ward Beecher. His illustrious, occasionally controversial forefather had been an abolitionist, social reformer, and minister of the influential Plymouth Church in Brooklyn. Like his famous grandfather and great-grandfather Lyman, Ayer, too, seemed destined for the pulpit. In 1916, he attended a life-changing Billy Sunday revival. After that, Ayer enrolled in the fundamentalist Moody Bible Institute. During his successful ministerial career, he hosted the popular radio show *God's Truth Marches On.* Pastor of the famed "skyscraper church," Calvary Baptist in New York City, he became a full-time evangelist in 1950.[87] In the fall of 1956, Ayer took to the pages of *Youth for Christ* magazine to caution parents, teenagers, and their pastors against the "Jungle Madness in America." The sixty-four-year-old Ayer proclaimed, "Every low idea that can be raked out of the dives of New Orleans, the wild, unbridled sensuousness of semi-civilized Caribbean rhythms, and even in the dark and dank jungles of seething Africa, are being set to incendiary music to thrill the squealing mob and set them to moaning, groaning, twisting and twirling in empty-headed ecstasy." Ayer told of his recent trip to Haiti, which convinced him that the connections between rock and sex-crazed voodooism were hardly imaginary. "The jungle is transported to America's dance halls," he concluded. "Demons seemed to have leaped the seas from tribal West Africa to the Caribbean Isles" and then to America's shores. It was an invasion of the worst kind, the fundamentalist radio minister preached.[88]

In the late 1950s, the Youth for Christ organization continued to relay stories and news items about rock 'n' roll. Leaders of the organization clearly sensed that even teens in evangelical churches were not immune to the bewildering charms of the music. In 1958, the Youth for Christ Club's president, like Ayer, had a chance to travel from the chilly climes of Flint, Michigan, to tropical Haiti on a short mission trip. The young man described, in vivid detail, the foreignness of his surroundings and, as he put it, the natives' "heathen religion, the worship of the devil and all his demons." Upon hearing the pounding of drums late at night and seeing what he described as a "voodoo dance," the president reflected on the sights and sounds before him. He realized it was just the sort of music that he had witnessed at high school dances. His mind raced back home to the Wolverine State and to the calypso fad. He still had hope. If God could change the hearts of the benighted people of Haiti, he could do the same for teenagers in America.[89]

The racial scare and references to Africa and the Caribbean were certainly not limited to the South or to Protestants in general or evangelicals in particular. Catholic church leaders raised their own concerns about the big beat in the mid-1950s. Their response was in keeping with earlier pronouncements from the princes of the church. For instance, in 1938 the Dubuque, Iowa, archbishop, Francis J. L. Beckman, addressed a gathering of the National Council of Catholic Women in Biloxi, Mississippi, on the subject of vulgar music. For Beckman, swing music represented a particularly troubling peril for youth. Swing and jazz were "denigrated and demoralizing," said the archbishop. "We permit, if not freely endorse, by our criminal indifference," he scolded those present, "jam sessions, jitterbug and cannibalistic rhythmic orgies to occupy a place in our social scheme of things, wooing our youth along the primrose path to hell." Modernist trends in art, including surrealism, came under his intense scrutiny as well.[90] A little more than thirty years later, the racial theme returned in relation to rock 'n' roll. The priest John P. Carroll spoke to a group of teachers in Boston on the matter in late summer 1956. Not all DJs were corrupters of youth, he assured his listeners. But those who played rock 'n' roll music contributed to the moral destruction of the nation's young people. "Rock 'n roll music inflames and excites youths like the jungle tom-toms readying warriors for battle," he told them. Explicit lyrics and suggestive dancing, said the priest, accompanied this debased music.[91] To the west in Chicago the sixty-nine-year-old Cardinal Samuel Stritch sensed something similarly ominous. "When our schools and centers stoop to such things as 'rock and roll' tribal rhythms," he intoned, "they are failing seriously in their duty." The thinly veiled critique of savagery-read-as-black-music was prominent.[92]

Southern Baptist, pentecostal, and even Catholic allusions to voodoo, shamanism, and jungle drumming were ubiquitous. Underneath the rhetoric lay anxious questions. Were churches and families losing their teen boys and girls to bewitching rock 'n' roll icons? Was the new leisure and consumerist economy destroying piety? The veneration of recording stars and the wasting of money on concerts and records left parents and youth pastors scratching their heads in worried incomprehension.[93]

The growing rift between parents and their children was a new hard fact of life. That divide owed something to economic realities. The economic miracle of the postwar years set in motion cultural and social trends that were unmatched in American history. In the postwar era the gross national product rose from $353.3 billion in 1950 to a staggering $487.7 billion in 1960. The automobile industry, defense spending, housing, and an ever-expanding market of consumer goods drove much of this. Families could afford one or even two cars, and many more than in previous decades could now buy their own homes. As the historian James Patterson fittingly put it, "By the late 1950s millions of Americans were enjoying the bounties of affluence and the consumer culture, the likes of which they had scarcely imagined before. In the process they were developing larger expectations about life and beginning to challenge things that had seemed set in stone only a few years earlier."[94] The esteemed Harvard economist John Kenneth Galbraith summarized the achievements of the age in *The Affluent Society* in 1958.[95] There were other clear limits to such affluence that Galbraith only hinted at. African Americans, poorer whites, and other ethnic groups remained the have-nots of society.

The rise of a robust white middle class—and to a lesser extent a black middle class—had an ancillary effect. Youngsters eagerly took part in the consumer market and had expendable incomes as never before. In early 1956, *Scholastic* magazine's Institute of Student Opinion revealed that America contained around thirteen million teenagers. They had a combined income of $7 billion per year. Surprisingly, that was 26 percent higher than it had been in 1953. The typical teen now made about $10.55 a week. They spent their money at movie theaters, dancehalls, and diners and bought up the latest hit singles.[96]

Young people clearly did not share their parents' tastes in goods and entertainment. In 1959, researchers at Ohio State University conducted a survey of radio listeners. Those ages fourteen to eighteen preferred rock 'n' roll music over seventeen other categories of music by a margin of 82 percent. By contrast, for those ages nineteen to seventy rock 'n' roll was disliked more than any other type of music. According to the survey, housewives ages twenty-six to fifty-five proved to be a target radio audience. Among their top four favorite types of music they placed "familiar hymns, spirituals."[97]

Churchmen might have little or no control over teen tastes, but they nonetheless exhorted young men and women to obey the biblical commandment to "honour thy father and thy mother: that thy days may be long upon the land which the Lord thy God giveth thee" (Exodus 20:12). Youth needed to listen to the sage advice of teachers and their elders as well. Such voices occasionally guided teenagers on relations between the races. Too-close contact with those of other races was unnatural, so went the logic. According to a Gallup poll, that view was overwhelmingly the norm when it came to interracial marriage. In 1958, a national Gallop poll showed that when asked if they approved of "marriages between white and colored people" only 4 percent of those surveyed said yes.[98] When a number of girls wrote in to the Southern Baptist Convention's youth magazine to ask about interracial dating, they received a direct, clear reply. The advice columnist responded that couples with common backgrounds had a better chance of a successful, happy marriage. "Just to be 'in love' is not enough," she instructed, concluding, in a strange twist, "A House divided against itself cannot stand."[99]

Such statements looked cautious, even timid, when compared with the heated rhetoric in other quarters. The White Citizens' Council stoked fears of integration and amalgamation as few other groups did. The white supremacist group regularly highlighted theological opposition to "mixing," as it typically put it, and focused heavy attention on the problems of interracial dancing, dating, and social interaction. In late summer 1959, the group's chief newspaper reported with alarm on an incident in Cincinnati involving the African American doo-wop and rock 'n' roll quartet the Platters, "part of the dark-skinned menace to America's teenagers." The group had achieved international fame with its number-one 1955 hit song "The Great Pretender." Four years later, the editor indignantly recounted, "Police arrested the rock-and-roll group, along with three white girls and a Negro girl, in a raid on a downtown hotel room where the Negroes were staying." The writer hoped the scene, with the girls reported to have been in various stages of undress, might lead to the quartet's members facing federal charges for taking the young women across state lines and thus violating the Mann Act against human trafficking.[100]

White perceptions of integration and dangerous savagery took on new meaning in the mid-1950s. And it was not only extreme segregationists from the Deep South who spoke of civilization versus savagery; the racialization of rock 'n' roll was widespread in American Christianity. Such language, though, was mostly among white evangelicals, fundamentalists, and to a lesser extent, Catholics. Liberal mainliners largely ignored rock 'n' roll and other youth trends. In the eyes of liberal establishment ministers these fads ranged from harmless to mildly tasteless. The *Christian Century*, flagship magazine of liberal Protestantism, was indignant about the money Elvis earned and the fame he garnered. His career said something about "the depth of decadence into which our scale of values has sunk."[101] But that proved a tame assessment alongside the racist screeds and denunciations that emanated from conservative Protestant pulpits or rolled off their presses. Fundamentalists scorned the liberal ecumenical body the National Council of Churches, a typical target of right-wing religious groups, for its cultural permissiveness. When the National Council of Churches sponsored a jazz program on CBS in 1956, a representative of a conservative group in Virginia cried foul. "Everyone knows that 'jazz' music originated among the Negroes in the deep South," he fumed. Fewer knew that its roots lay in "the ancient tribal music of Africa" or that it was used "in Africa in ancient times for sexual orgies."[102]

In the same year that the conservative critic penned his article decrying jazz, Elvis's hit songs rocketed up the charts and made millions. Also in 1956 the perceived savagery of jungle primitives dominated headlines across the country. In early January, Auca natives in Ecuador murdered five young white American evangelical missionaries. The atrocity became one of the most widely publicized news items of twentieth-century American Protestantism. The religious and secular press highlighted the Stone Age ferocity of the natives and upheld the martyred figures as middle-class representatives of Christian decency. Feature stories in *Life* magazine, *Time*, *Reader's Digest*, and a host of major national newspapers vividly recounted the murders by the bloodthirsty Indians, misidentified as headhunters, and told of their brutality in explicit detail.[103] As American evangelicals and Catholics read about the wild new "jungle music" blasting from jukeboxes and radio sets and the moral turpitude that accompanied it, tales of Amazonian horrors would not have been far from their minds. An advertisement for the subsequent book that described the missionaries' fate called it "the saga of five young missionary martyrs . . . ambushed and slain with savage lances."[104]

The predominately white Church of the Nazarene, with its concentration of membership in the Midwest and the West, used the story of martyrdom to teach valuable lessons to its teenagers. Youngsters might not have to face cannibals, yet they could still be shining examples of uprightness and decency in the face of a degenerate culture. One of the missionaries, James Elliot, served as a particularly strong role model for young Christians who were eager to resist the temptations of popular culture. Elliot, observed a Nazarene author in a youth magazine, "is one of the finest of a recent group of martyrs." His exemplary life was cut short "by the chonta-wood lances thrown by savage, Stone Age Auca Indians of Ecuador, South America." In this lesson Elliot stood apart. To illustrate his teenage evangelical bravery, the Nazarene author looked back on Elliot's life. Pressured to attend a dance at his Portland, Oregon, high school, Elliot had allegedly responded, "I'm a Christian and the Bible says that I'm in the world but not of it. That's why I'm not going to the dance."[105]

Like the Nazarenes, the Youth for Christ organization told teens of the grisly attack and the saintly courage of the young missionaries. Such tales recounted not just the cruelty of the natives but also their alleged sacrileges. "All men whose bodies were found had been killed by lances," went the report, "with further damage by machete blows. One of the lances had the pages of a Spanish New Testament wrapped around it."[106] Just months later, a teen from Ontario, Canada, wrote to *Youth for Christ* magazine about her contempt for Elvis. Her piece seemed to draw together the latest news from mission fields and what was happening in pop culture. She reserved pity for Elvis's fans. Many of them walked the halls of her high school under Presley's spell. "Watching gals 'moon' over a picture of his swinging body," she wrote, "reminds me of their lost condition." Immediately she thought of a similar "picture with the heathen dances of darkest Africa." The mission fields of her school and the southern hemisphere seemed to blur together.[107]

Like the Canadian teenager, other white evangelicals in the United States used primitive and exotic imagery to convey the African-roots message. Articles, pamphlets, and tracts denouncing rock 'n' roll bore illustrations of tribesmen, scantily clad and performing wild dances. The American Tract Society in New Jersey, for instance, produced a booklet titled "Jungle to Jukebox" to advise teens on the effects of the music. On the cover danced a cartoon version of a witchdoctor, wearing a devilish mask and holding a human skull on a stick. "Where did it come from?" asked the author of the short tract. "This type of music originated with tribesmen in backward areas," claimed the writer, using authorities to back him up. "Accompanied by such music they performed tribal dances which were ritual prayers to the Gods."[108]

Evangelicals drew on this primitive or savage imagery to describe salvation from sin. A white pentecostal publication in early 1961 published an article on what it called the "Juvenile Jungle." The title appeared in a cut-out, disjointed modern font next to an image of an African American teen who was a converted drug addict. The author led off the article with a description of the jungle: "dark, dangerous and infested with beasts." He reckoned that "no other words so vividly described large sections of metropolitan New York–New Jersey." Teen evangelism and outreach, in this scenario, was conducted in a juvenile jungle, filled with gangs, blaring music, drugs, and crime.[109]

Church leaders and national media linked rock 'n' roll music not only to the southern hemisphere and race mixing, but also to what was thought to be a rising wave of teenage crime and senseless violence. The delinquency scare astonished pastors, police officers, teachers, and parents around the country.[110] The feral teenage boy—wearing blue jeans, sporting a greasy pompadour with a ducktail, and smoking a cigarette—became a stock villain in film and pop culture, joining aliens and communists on the silver screen. Experts took center stage to make sense of the alleged jump in crime, truancy, and teen violence. In 1954, the psychologist Frederic Wertham wrote *Seduction of the Innocent*, which blamed comic books for leading youngsters astray. Benjamin Fine published *1,000,000 Delinquents* in 1955 while he served as the education

The cover illustration for an anti-rock-'n'-roll pamphlet. Vic Erickson, "Jungle to Jukebox" (Oradell, NJ: American Tract Society, circa 1958). Reproduction courtesy of the Southern Baptist Historical Library and Archives, Nashville, Tennessee.

editor of the *New York Times.* Robert Altman's 1957 dramatic film *The Delinquents,* set in his hometown of Kansas City, now joined a roster of teens-gone-wrong films, including *The Wild One* (1953), *Rebel without a Cause* (1955), and *Blackboard Jungle* (1955). At showings of the latter in England riots broke out as Bill Haley and His Comets' "Rock Around the Clock" played during the rolling of the credits. In early September 1957, *Life* magazine jumped into the fray with a lead story and a series of reports on "Crime in the U.S." The cover featured a stylized watercolor of loitering New York gang members. Clad in leather and satin zip-up jackets, they wear their hair greased back and have long sideburns. "The nation in the fall of 1957 appears to be threatened by a catastrophic wave of crime," reported Robert Wallace.[111]

The head of the Federal Bureau of Investigation, J. Edgar Hoover, who had made fighting juvenile delinquency nearly as much of a hobbyhorse as he had made battling the red menace, regularly appeared in the pages of evangelical and fundamentalist publications. In 1957, he recommended firm discipline in churches, homes, and communities. "The Biblical charge," he advised, "to 'Train up a child in the way he should go; and when he is old, he will not depart from it' is as sound today as it was many generations ago."[112] Billy Graham used Hoover's crime statistics as an opportunity to evangelize. "Many people are trying to analyze the delinquency problem," Graham remarked, "but in most cases they are dealing only with symptoms." It was not really the result of suggestive music, smutty films, comic books, or bad parents. The cause, simply, was sin and depravity.[113]

For fearful Americans, rhythmic, big-beat music had become the soundtrack of juvenile delinquency. In 1955, the Houston, Texas, Juvenile Delinquency and Crime Commission petitioned local radio stations to ban a list of objectionable rhythm and blues and rock 'n' roll songs. Almost all of the twenty-six records were by black artists. The full list included Ray Charles's "I've Got a Woman" and Elvis Presley's "Good Rockin' Tonight."[114]

Those on the lookout for links between the music and black crime pointed to the actions of celebrated performers. In early 1960, the escapades of a sixteen-year-old African American boy in New York City circulated widely. Police nabbed David Campanella, the son of a former Brooklyn Dodgers catcher, along with three "other Negro boys on a street corner." This was not the first of the teen's arrests. Before this he had broken into a drugstore and had also been arrested for involvement in a street fight. One front-page article on his misfortunes noted, "Recently he has made two rock 'n' roll recordings." The piece mentioned that David Campanella and the Dell Chords had appeared on TV and had scored a couple of minor rock and doo-wop hits for Kane Records. But his notoriety as a "hoodlum" overshadowed his music career and, in the eyes of white readers, confirmed the connections between rock 'n' roll music and black hooliganism.[115]

Did the music really contribute to juvenile delinquency? asked the famous revivalist and evangelical radio broadcaster Jack Wyrtzen. It most certainly did, he proclaimed emphatically. Citing examples of social unrest—riots that took place at dances and at the showing of rock 'n' roll films—he presented a bleak picture, colored with apocalyptic tones. "Evil seducers are waxing worse and worse," he stated. For Wyrtzen, the many connections between juvenile crime, rock 'n' roll music, and race were clear enough. "This 'rock and roll' business," he preached, was marked by "wild, savage dancing to jungle drums and blaring disharmonies that have caused riots and bloodshed."[116] Such racially charged language was often missing in more official accounts of delinquency. But even in the corridors of power, government officials were connecting the dots between crime and rock 'n' roll. A member of the Senate Subcommittee on Delinquency addressed the issue head-on. "Elvis Presley is a symbol, of course, but a dangerous one," he noted. "His strip-tease antics threaten to 'rock-n-roll' the juvenile world into open revolt against society." Time was of the essence. "The gangster of tomorrow," he went on, "is the Elvis Presley type of today."[117] In such judgments teachers, community leaders, and especially parents needed to take decisive action.

In the view of one prominent Alabama Southern Baptist, parents shared much of the blame for the antisocial and unbalanced behavior of their children. "The tragedy of neglecting to teach a child to direct and control his emotions and to give the emotions definite outlets results in such outlandish fads as 'rock 'n roll' music and dances." Young people who were emotionally balanced would not take part in the "orgies" of popular music.[118] Evangelist and fellow Baptist Billy Graham thought that in the absence of strong parental or social guidance American teens were becoming "soft and flabby." According to Graham's logic, teens were weak and susceptible to dangerous trends and sinister influences. Unlike their robust European counterparts, American young people, said Graham in 1957, had grown wealthy and complacent. "They spend their time before television," he preached to thousands of teens at New York City's Madison Square Garden. They wasted away "listening to rock and roll, or going to the joints." Looking out over the sea of young faces, he counseled, "Give yourself to Christ, right now, without reservation."[119]

Teenagers, though, seemed increasingly unreachable. Parents were baffled by the lingo used by their sons and daughters. Teen values and ideals appeared upside down. In one effort to bridge the gap, in late spring 1957 the *Chicago Daily News* and the Kiwanis Club made an unusual attempt to harness rock 'n' roll to a greater good. The two groups sponsored a youth rally at the Chicago Stadium, where, according to *Life* magazine, teens were led in prayer "and took a mass pledge to 'keep out of trouble.'" To sweeten the deal, the rally also featured artists like the rockabilly shouter Gene Vincent. To the reporter at *Life*, it looked to be a success.[120]

Efforts like this seemed to represent a compromise, thought conservative white evangelicals. But even conservative Protestants were trying to reach teens of the rock 'n' roll generation in new ways. For instance, Youth for Christ and Gospel Films produced dramatic movie features that treated controversial topics like juvenile delinquency, race prejudice, and rock 'n' roll. Churches and schools then showed these movies at youth rallies and teen retreats. One such film, the 1959 *Teenage Rock,* promised audiences it would be "provocative!" "action-packed!" and "dynamic!"[121] In reality, however, movies like this showcased poor acting and were anodyne imitations of major motion pictures. Still, they did achieve some success. Similarly, from its base in Wheaton, Illinois, Youth for Christ offered up white Christian musical alternatives to all the pop artists that the organization found so repugnant. It praised the guitar- and accordion-playing brothers the Palermos; Billy Graham's song evangelist, the Canadian-born George Beverly Shea; and the recently converted crooner Tony Fontane, who traded singing his secular hit single, "Cold, Cold, Heart" for the decidedly evangelical "Give Your Heart to Jesus."[122]

For all such efforts to reach youngsters, church officials would not relent when it came to dancing. White and black evangelical prohibitions against dancing had long been in place, and white churchmen, especially in the South, were increasingly embarrassed that something as low and debauched as rock 'n' roll dances could be allowed to infiltrate their communities. To drive this point home, a North Carolina Baptist editor reported that "American rock 'n' roll dances have been banned in several Indonesian cities because of opposition by cultural and religious groups which consider them 'degrading and immoral.'" It all seemed beyond comprehension. "Congratulations to the Indonesians," the editor wrote, his pen heavy with sarcasm. "Perhaps they should send some missionaries to America to teach our people how to practice Christian virtues and live more decent lives." Dancing, in the view of one Texas Baptist in 1955, was a "sexual exercise." Modern dancing, he speculated, had its roots in Paris brothels. The Church of the Nazarene's "General Rules" forbade dancing, along with a litany of similar vices that ranged from attending movies and gambling to drinking and swearing.[123]

Southern Baptists had much to worry over when it came to the potential troubles that dancing could bring. The proximity of blacks and whites was just one problem. On very rare occasions believers caved in to the will of teenagers or college students. Administrators at the Baptist Wake Forest College in North Carolina, after considerable pressure from students, decided in 1957 to allow dancing on campus. Officials were not prepared for the backlash of alums, preachers, and other fellow Southern Baptists. A *Life* magazine photo essay of rowdy coeds flailing about at the school stirred up conservative forces in the denomination. The ban on dancing was put back in place in October 1957; however, maintaining the prohibition proved far more difficult than school administrators had imagined. The controversy led to the largest-attended Baptist State Convention in history and a shake-up of the school's administration. Students responded with a frenzied protest. In a large gathering on campus they burned an effigy of the state convention president, set off firecrackers, and blasted trumpets in the cool night air. They also cranked up the volume on their record players and spun the Everly Brothers' "Wake Up, Little Susie" and Jerry Lee Lewis's controversial "Whole Lotta Shakin' Goin' On." In a sign of the growing generational divide, one female student told a reporter what she really thought about the grandees of the church: "We ought to go and dance with those old men and see if they get shook." The state's denominational editor reported on the scandal with a palpable sense of disgust and moral outrage. "In what appeared to be a prearranged revolt, the student body walked out of chapel" and staged "a 'Rock 'n Roll' exhibition." In his view the affair was about as dignified as a panty raid. It was little more than "an orgy of fancy footwork by some of the young people," huffed the editor.[124] Dances, whether interracial or not, by his lights, were dangerous and morally inappropriate.

Champions of white purity could point to instances of dreaded race mixing. Rock was "the most miscegenated popular music ever to have existed," proclaimed the journalist Sasha Frere-Jones in the pages of the *New Yorker* decades later.[125] It was not just rock 'n' roll and dreaded juvenile delinquency that seemed to stalk the nation's youth. The raucous music drew together a range of Cold War–era fears. Lewd stars claimed the hearts and minds of their impressionable young fans. Asa Carter was convinced that the music was a hell-hatched NAACP plot to bring young whites down to the level of blacks. Denunciations of rock 'n' roll as a communist plot also circulated in the early years of the genre and in the 1960s as well.[126]

Pentecostalism, too, had once been decried as an antisocial, dangerous interracial movement. Early ministers and believers faced local hostilities for holding mixed-race revivals and playing music that sounded unruly and improper. Now, similar denunciations dogged rock 'n' roll's celebrity performers.[127] There was a certain logic to these accusations of pop-inspired miscegenation. Youngsters, both black and white, bought the records of Elvis, Chuck Berry, Jerry Lee Lewis, Little Richard, and a host of other stars. In 1957, Buddy Holly and the Crickets took to the road as part of an otherwise all-black review. Whites and blacks showed up at the same performances.[128] There was, of course, no way to segregate the airwaves. In Memphis, for instance, the first African American–oriented radio station in the country, WDIA, gained an enthusiastic white listenership. Its devotees could hear black gospel, blues, along with the antics of their favorite DJs. "Rock and roll does help to combat racial discrimination," Bill Haley remarked, voicing an opinion shared by numerous white and black artists. Haley recounted that he "performed to mixed groups all over the country and have watched the kids sit side by side just enjoying the music while being entertained by white and negro performers sharing the same stage."[129]

Fans, too, eagerly shared their vision of the healing power of the music. Writing in the *New York Amsterdam News,* a black teenager editorialized about the subject in 1958. Whites "do not demand special billboards or dressing rooms. In the audience, fair-skinned boys do not complain about sitting next to girls with Negroid features." Youngsters like him were especially awakened to the integrationist impulse.[130] Several years later, the civil rights leader Andrew Young reflected on the matter: "I say all of the time that rock and roll did more for integration than the church and if I was going to choose who I was going to let into the Kingdom . . . I might have to choose Elvis." Whereas so many white church leaders, Sunday school teachers, and pentecostal youth ministers saw Presley as rebellious and deeply sinful, Young viewed him as a significant catalyst for positive racial change.[131]

Few within black churches would have shared Young's upbeat view of Presley. Rock 'n' roll, for most black church officials, pastors, and laypeople, was disruptive and immoral. Teens in their churches, thought concerned parents, had no business listening to it. In Elvis's hometown of Memphis, W. Herbert Brewster, a pillar of the African American National Baptist Convention, preached against rowdy, lewd music that seemed to be infiltrating the churches. Supposed gospel quartets, he warned, were really just "racketeers who prey on churches."[132] Likewise, when a teenager asked Martin Luther King Jr. about rock 'n' roll and the Christian calling, King made clear his opposition to the music. "The real question," King told the youngster in his *Ebony* advice column, "is whether one can be consistent in playing gospel music and rock and roll music simultaneous." It was unthinkable in his estimation: "The two are totally incompatible."[133]

African Americans who defended black respectability against the obscene threats of low culture seemed to have less to worry about in the coming years as the first wave of rock 'n' roll music crashed in on itself. The negative and even racialized white reaction to the big beat also diminished somewhat as the late 1950s gave way to the early 1960s. In the years between 1959 and 1964, evangelicals and fundamentalists were paying less and less attention to so-called jungle music. In some ways white conservatives could tell themselves that they had beaten back the forces of moral degeneracy.

By the last years of the decade, white and black critics of rock 'n' roll were hoping the chaotic, morally degenerate teen music would soon be in the dustbin of history. In the last year of the decade, a Southern Baptist Sunday school teacher was speculating on the demise of the vilified genre. At its height, she wrote, the music had inspired ungodly hero worship, rioting, and emotional anarchy. Now the fad seemed to have run its course.[134] In 1960, *Youth for Christ* magazine gathered seven of its teenage readers to mull over the question "Is Rock 'n Roll on the Way Out?" Their responses were mixed. Some thought it still had staying power, vile though it was. Others were sure it was dead or dying. Elvis was no longer a presence, commented two of them. In the view of one boy from Arlington, Virginia, there were "several signs that show that rock 'n' roll is losing its popularity." Ballads were in. Rock 'n' roll was out. Evangelical parents, pastors, and teachers who read such lines might have breathed a sigh of relief.[135]

At the same time, key first generation rock 'n' rollers had died (Buddy Holly, Ritchie Valens, the Big Bopper, and Eddie Cochran), fallen victim to scandal (Jerry Lee Lewis and Chuck Berry), or stopped playing and recording altogether (Elvis Presley and Little Richard).[136] The album charts subsequently changed in the late 1950s and early 1960s, reflecting a cleaner, softer style of rock 'n' roll promoted by the television program *American Bandstand* and large music labels. *Billboard* magazine put a positive spin on the shift in taste and a decline in sales. "This is not to say that rock and roll isn't fading, or actually evolving into pop music," it reported, "but the fade is one of the slowest yet recorded."[137]

By the early 1960s, worries of a miscegenationist, antireligious rock 'n' roll revolution were slowly subsiding. That might have been the result of the changing complexion of the genre as the Eisenhower years gave way to the 1960s. The public, the press, and even teenage fans tended to consider rock 'n' roll a black-roots phenomenon.[138] As the most critical stars of the early years faded from the national scene, new solo artists and bands took their place. Fresh-faced, white teen idols—such as Frankie Avalon, Fabian, Pat Boone, and Ricky Nelson—offered a safe, parent-friendly brand of pop music. A sobbing girl from Kansas rhapsodized about Nelson to *Life* magazine in late 1958, "It's like he was Elvis and my brother at the same time."[139] Rolling Stones guitarist Keith Richards sums up the change in early 1960s American pop music in his autobiography: "White American music when I arrived was the Beach Boys and Bobby Vee."[140] Surf and hot rod bands (writing "love songs to the carburetor," as one savvy observer put it) were either benign or completely invisible to believers.[141] Prepackaged white male performers stood in contrast to popular black musicians associated with Motown, soul, and later, funk.

Still, if first-generation rock 'n' roll's royalty had been dethroned, their influence was far from gone. In fact, in the early 1960s a new band from the English port city of Liverpool, which would go on to achieve unimaginable fame, had been enormously influenced by Chuck Berry, Little Richard, Buddy Holly, Jerry Lee Lewis, and most importantly,

Elvis. The Beatles bore the heavy influence of black American artists, country groups, and white rockabilly. The four of them, like countless other teens in their country, were influenced by gospel music indirectly. Elvis Presley loomed especially large. "I worshiped him," said the Beatles' John Lennon of the King of Rock 'n' Roll.[142] In fact, without such strong American musical influences the Beatles could not have existed. Their skill at channeling icons from across the Atlantic was uncanny. So said one of the Beatles' close German friends of the band's early sixties Hamburg period. "For me it was like hearing every great rock-'n'-roll tune there had ever been," Klaus Voormann rhapsodized. "They were like chameleons," he continued, "John would be Gene Vincent, then he'd be Chuck Berry. Paul would do Elvis, then he'd do Fats Domino, then he'd do Carl Perkins."[143] Lennon met one of his many idols, Jerry Lee Lewis, in 1973 when the legend played a show at the Roxy in Los Angeles. The former Beatle got on his hands and knees to kiss the Killer's boots. Embarrassed by this worshipful display, Jerry Lee put out his hand and said, "That's all right, son, that's all right."[144] The Beatles would go on to achieve a kind of lasting fame, influence, and critical praise Jerry Lee Lewis never could garner.

Evangelicals cared little for the Beatles' presumed artistry. There was nothing redeemable about the group. In that band from northern England, and many others in the 1960s, Southern Baptists, pentecostals, and Presbyterians saw a new alien menace to their churches and homes. Millions of American baby boomers brought up on the Beatles' records, memorized the lyrics to songs and followed the styles, fashions, and trends set by the beat group from Liverpool. Following Beatlemania, evangelical pastors and parents worried about the gender confusion the band introduced, from long hair on boys to the wild enthusiasm of the band's girl fans. The Beatles' views on religion also came under deep suspicion. Subsequent youth revolutions in the mid to late 1960s that were tied to politics, opposition to the Vietnam War, campus protests, and feminism would also stir up Zion.

• 3 •

The Beatles, Christianity, and the Conservative Backlash

It's as if they've founded a new religion.
—Derek Taylor, 1964

During the hot, stormy summer of 1966, a tempest of controversy raged in the United States over remarks that John Lennon of the Beatles made about his band and its popularity. It all began with journalist Maureen Cleave's candid interview with Lennon for the London *Evening Standard* in March 1966. The reporter was a close friend. The pop celebrity let Cleave into his inner sanctum. At his mansion in Weybridge, Lennon gave Cleave a tour of his collected oddities. A young man with money to burn, the Beatle had acquired a suit of armor, luxury cars, five television sets, a massive Bible he bought in Chester, an enormous altar crucifix, and a gorilla suit. The lonely, somewhat isolated twenty-five-year-old, who lived in the stockbroker belt southwest of London, appeared to be bored and a little bit listless.[1]

Always a voracious reader, Lennon spent some of his downtime devouring books on religion. One of those, a popular revisionist treatment of Jesus, squared with Lennon's ideas about the phoniness and irrelevance of Christianity. Hugh J. Schonfield's *The Passover Plot* (1965), a shocking best seller, was first only available in Britain.[2] It created a stir there, but in the far more religiously observant United States, it was positively scandalous. Schonfield, a biblical scholar from England, described himself as a nonpracticing Jew. He had mastered Latin, Hebrew, Aramaic, and Greek. He could read a variety of other languages, too. *The Passover Plot* would sell over two million copies, was reprinted more than twenty times, and was even adapted for the big screen in 1976.[3] A few years after the book hit the shelves, Schonfield told a reporter what he made of the contemporary church. "The whole position of the papacy and the Vatican," he ventured, "the very nature of all church authority, is being questioned today." Hitting on one of his common themes, he continued, "The things that the church prizes are not the things that Jesus Christ stood for."[4] Thus, *The Passover Plot* had a conspiratorial tone, likely making the book all the more appealing to a skeptical Lennon and other post-Christian British readers. Schonfield's Jesus is the mastermind behind a planned crucifixion hoax, meant to fulfill Old Testament prophecies. Jesus's revolutionary plot, which was also meant to free the Jews from Rome's grip, was foiled when Jesus died after being pierced with a spear while on the cross. Jesus, in Schonfield's telling, did not intend to create a church movement. His disciples, as such, were naïve bunglers, or worse.[5]

Lennon, equipped with Schonfield's argument and relaxed by the tone of the interview, told Maureen Cleave what he really thought about Christianity. Rock music was here to stay. Christianity would fade, said Lennon. "We're more popular than Jesus now," Lennon remarked, in an almost offhand way. "I don't know which will go first—rock 'n' roll or Christianity. Jesus was all right but his disciples were thick and ordinary. It's them twisting it that ruins it for me."[6] Lennon's comments made little to no impression in England, where church attendance and traditional belief were on the decline. At first, Americans did not take much notice of his statement either. That all changed when his provocative remarks reappeared in the pages of an New York-based teen magazine called *Datebook.*[7] In an accompanying interview in the same issue of *Datebook,* Paul McCartney had also commented on race relations. He lashed out at the persistence of Jim Crow laws in the United States. But McCartney's comments, a kind of social heresy in some quarters of the South, did not receive the same attention or criticism.[8]

As John and the three others boarded their Pan Am flight from London to Chicago on August 11, 1966, to kick off their American tour, five hundred fans milled about, dizzy with excitement. One of those, aware of the growing controversy, shouted out, "John, please don't go. They'll kill you." That warning was not all that far from the realm of possibility. As they set out, Lennon did not think he would receive death threats—as he, in fact, would. "We've never left for America with this sort of feeling before," he admitted in a moment of candor. Then he added, "Frankly, I'm worried."[9]

Brian Epstein, the group's manager, cut short a European vacation and flew to America to do damage control. Cleave, too, stepped into the breach: Americans had misunderstood John's words and unfairly targeted the group. Such efforts did little to stem the tide of negative opinion.[10] By the time the Beatles landed in Chicago to start what would be their last tour, articles on the scandalous statement had already been making front-page news in the United States and were the subject of TV and radio commentary. Radio stations across the South quit playing the group's albums. WRNB in New Bern, North Carolina, was one of those that pledged to stop spinning the band's records. "Any one making a sacrilegious remark like that," a WRNB rep declared, "has no place on our station."[11] Altogether, at least thirty-five stations, but likely more, climbed aboard what was being called the Beatles "ban wagon." WAKY in Louisville, Kentucky, aired silence, meant for prayer time, in place of Beatles music.[12] KOB in Albuquerque conducted a phone poll to gauge listener opinion. Six hundred called in; 65 percent favored the ban. Not to be outdone, a Longview, Texas, station received eleven hundred calls as a result of its poll. A staggering 97 percent of those, deep in the Bible Belt, supported the ban. Another Texas station proclaimed it was banning the Beatles "eternally." A South Dakota station offered listeners the unique chance to come out to witness shotgun fire blasting the English group's records, which were to be launched into the sky like clay pigeons.[13] Three state senators in Pennsylvania even introduced a resolution in the capitol, urging the legislature to "express its shock at the irresponsible statement of Beatle John Lennon" that "the Beatles are more popular than Jesus." The proposed resolution also encouraged jukebox operators to get rid of the group's songs and asked that radio and television stations stop playing their harmful music.[14]

Compared to these, some other reactions were positively frightening. The South Carolina grand dragon of the KKK, for instance, burned a cross with a Beatles record affixed to it. A Klavern in Mississippi sponsored a Beatles wig burning and accused the group of "atheistic" leanings. In Memphis one Klansman described Lennon's comment as "nothing but blasphemy." "And we're gonna try to stop it," he stated menacingly, even if it meant the use of "terror." Imperial wizard Robert Shelton served up what he likely thought would be the ultimate insult. The former Tuscaloosa tire salesman told a British reporter, "It's hard for me to tell through the mop-heads . . . whether they're even white or black."[15]

Churchmen and denominations responded as well, although without the threats of actual violence. Baptist ministers, Catholic priests, and concerned Christians across the United States, and especially in the American South, raised a collective complaint. Sensing the cultural moment, preachers and deejays lit up night skies in Dixie with Beatles paraphernalia bonfires and Beatles effigy burnings. In Longview, Texas, seven thousand showed up for one such conflagration. At a similar event in Birmingham, Alabama, a protestor stood with a large sign: "Deposit Beatle Trash Here." The popular DJs at Birmingham's WAQY Doug Layton and Tommy Charles, who launched the effort, watched with glee as the ban went national.[16]

For some, the whole affair seemed to draw a line between the saved and the lost. The scandal rippled down to individual congregations. The African American pastor Thurman H. Babbs of the New Haven Baptist Church in Cleveland threatened to expel anyone in his church who had the temerity to attend the Beatles' 1966 Cleveland show. (Two years before, Cleveland's mayor, Ralph Locher, had actually banned the group from playing in his city after fans rushed the stage in a frenzied crush. Now that had been lifted.) Babbs promised to cast out of his congregation those who agreed with Lennon's comments. "It's high time Christians spoke out on this atheistic remark," said the twenty-eight-year-old preacher. Some might accuse the minister of being a dictator, but he did not mind that. He prepared a special fire and brimstone sermon to coincide with the group's tour, in which he compared the four to "heathen idols." In the pulpit, Babbs thumbed through his Bible to a particularly foreboding passage in the Old Testament. He read out, "As soon as all the peoples heard the sound of the horn, pipe, lyre, trigon, harp, bagpipe, and every kind of music, all the peoples, nations, and languages fell down and worshiped the golden image that King Nebuchadnezzar had set up" (Daniel 3:7).[17] Such hardliners were clearly riled, but the report of Lennon's comments echoed well beyond conservative circles. It is little wonder that a leading reporter rated the story the top religious news item of 1966.[18] It made ministers and laypeople ask themselves, How could this member of what seemed like a novelty act have anything to say about the place of Jesus in the lives of young people?

Even before the 1966 flap, believers were mulling over the group's popularity and questioning the band's influence over youth. Such worries would only grow with each passing year, as the tame beat music of the British invasion gave way to loud, experimental psychedelic rock, laced with overt references to drugs, sex, Eastern mysticism, political protest, and cultural liberation. In 1964, when the Beatles first made headlines in the United States, evangelicals and fundamentalists still remained largely isolated from or hostile to most of what passed as popular culture. They spoke up to denounce Elvis and rock 'n' roll with a fury to match the wild new music, although in the 1950s they remained unaware of most other pop music groups and personalities. A decade later, these conservative Christians, who would form a powerful political force in the coming years, reacted fiercely against the 1960s counterculture, of which the Beatles were the most obvious, high-profile representatives. Related leftist political and radical cultural movements of the latter half of the decade looked shockingly anarchic and anti-Christian to evangelicals. In December 1968, Billy Graham told reporters at a press conference that campus demonstrators were determined to destroy the "American system." Six months later, Graham judged that worldwide "moral deterioration" was a clear sign of the approaching apocalypse. Campus protests and violent antiwar rallies seemed to spell doom for civilization in the eyes of believers.[19] An evangelical critic in *Eternity* magazine declared that rock music reflected the twisted values of youth culture and leftist politics. The lyrics of folk-rock star Bob Dylan, he reported, promoted freewheeling liberation. "The individual does what he feels as long as he does not interfere with others," claimed the writer. "Morality is determined not by social standards but by the individual—largely guided by his intuitive feelings."[20] In the same Philadelphia magazine another troubled voice reflected on campus unrest in June 1967, the same month the Beatles released their groundbreaking album *Sgt Pepper's Lonely Hearts Club Band.* Evangelical parents, educators, and pastors thought that the political and cultural experimentation from Berkeley to Boston was dangerous and gravely troubling. Protesters called into question America's foreign and domestic policies, the legal system, the modern family, the institutional church, and much more. "Loudspeakers cracked obscenity across the University of California's Berkeley campus last year," the author reported. A downward trend was evident to anyone with eyes to see and ears to hear. "Crusaders for free speech and filthy speech have given way, in recent months, to the advocates of free love." In what sounded like one of Ronald Reagan's diatribes, the *Eternity* correspondent continued, "Six off-campus student sex orgies" took place in the Bay Area, a modern-day Sodom in the view of such stalwarts.[21] The Beatles, who encouraged young people to throw off the chains of tradition, bore special blame, said detractors.

Two years before Lennon's alarming 1966 Jesus remark, believers were finding much to dislike in the Fab Four. Even though it would take an epic sacrilege for the faithful to rise up with a unified voice, long before Lennon weighed in on Jesus and his disciples, evangelicals and fundamentalists were discussing and debating the Beatles and their impact. Preachers and parishioners wrote op-eds and articles, and delivered sermons and radio talks. Beatlemania was an unmistakable, massive pop cultural phenomenon. Troubled conservatives were again finding fault in the emotional chaos rock and roll seemed to stir among teenage girls in particular. But the staying power of the Beatles, the extreme devotion of fans, and the ways that youngsters, especially girls, emulated their new idols made it seem even more threatening than so-called Presleyism. (Elvis, at least, had never targeted Christianity.) Boy Beatles fans came under a watchful eye, too. These turned-on teenagers grew their hair out, blasted Beatles songs from their radios, and were caught up in the whirl much as their sisters and female classmates were. Conservative believers in the United States sensed real trouble here. The band from Liverpool was preying on naïve youth. In responding to the group from across the Atlantic, the devout questioned the styles, trends, tastes, and attitudes of youngsters. Evangelicals, who were paying much greater attention to the family and children in these years, saw in the English band a declension in morals and a turning away from long-standing cultural and spiritual norms.

In the 1960s, many conservative adherents continued to define themselves by their social prohibitions. Those in the largely white Nazarene or Assemblies of God churches opposed moviegoing, short skirts, worldly music, drinking alcohol, smoking, and in some more-strict circles, even the reading of newspapers or novels on Sunday.[22] By contrast, all members of the Beatles chain-smoked, and in the early years the foursome listed rum and Coke as one of their favorite drinks. In part, the massive Beatles phenomenon, and the cultural changes and

The Beatles arrive in the capital, February 11, 1964, before their Washington Coliseum concert. Photo by Marion S. Trikosko, *US News & World Report* Magazine Photograph Collection, Library of Congress Prints and Photographs Division, Washington, DC (LC-DIG-ppmsca-41593).

attitudes the group ushered in, forced evangelicals to confront pop culture and youth culture in ways they seldom had before. Other prohibited amusements now seemed tame when compared with this new imported brand of rock, which marked a new beginning for Christian crusading against the music. What had become of society? evangelicals and Catholics asked, while watching the four Scousers break television-viewing records on the *Ed Sullivan Show* on February 9, 1964. Why did teenagers shriek and flail about at Beatles performances? What was at the root of Beatlemania?[23]

The conservative Christian response to Beatlemania, from 1964 through the 1966 bigger-than-Jesus controversy, sheds light on how the faithful came to engage pop culture and reveals something about the culture wars that ensued. The America that conservatives grew up in seemed to be transforming beyond all recognition. Some felt powerless to stop the march of change. The Christian pop psychologist and child-care expert James Dobson, who graduated from Pasadena Nazarene College in 1958, would later reflect on an idyllic, pre-1960s America. "Virginity was still in style for males *and* females," he recalled of the halcyon days of his youth. With a rosy view of the past, he looked back:

> I attended high school in the "Happy Days" of the 1950s, and I never saw or heard of anyone taking an illegal drug. . . . Occasionally a girl came up pregnant, but she was packed off in a hurry and I never knew where she went. Homosexuals were very weird and unusual people. I heard there were a few around but I didn't know them personally. Most of my friends respected their parents, went to church on Sunday, studied hard enough to get by and lived a fairly clean life. There were exceptions, of course, but this was the norm.[24]

This black-and-white picture, the product of selective memory and political boundary work, was hardly in line with more complicated realities. But such evangelicals liked to look back on an Edenic age, unspoiled by social strife or rebellious youth. Through the 1960s, evangelicals like Dobson sensed with alarm the erosion of paternal authority and the displacement of Christian and patriotic ideals. The world they had grown up in seemed to be swiftly changing, especially when misremembered, and they did not recognize it as their own.[25]

The process was well under way in the early 1960s. Numerous conservative believers registered shock at the prospect of the Catholic John F. Kennedy becoming president. Billy Graham and Christian self-help author Norman Vincent Peale, along with other prominent voices, mulled over how to make their discomfort known. In that election year, denominations containing roughly eleven million members issued official statements against electing a Catholic to lead the free world. Evangelical fears of government overreach would rise in the years of the Kennedy and Johnson administrations.[26] New controversies related to the secular government's power involved the nation's youth and intensified anxiety levels.

Little bothered the faithful as much as the decisions made by the highest court in the land. The Supreme Court's *Engel v. Vitale* (1962) decision banned official school prayer and *School District of Abington v. Schempp* (1963) forbade the reading of scripture in public schools. Even those on the left worried about the backlash such decisions would provoke. Bastion of liberalism the *New Republic* thought that *Engel v. Vitale* had "provided the occasion for the most savage controversy concerning the Court since the 1954 desegregation decision." As with the *Brown* decision the banning of prayer seemed likely to "strengthen the bitterness felt in the South, and among conservatives in both parties across the country, against the Supreme Court itself."[27] That was an accurate prediction. Cardinal Richard Cushing, Norman Vincent Peale, and Billy Graham considered the decision as unwise as it was ominous, and they publicly condemned it. "If the Supreme Court keeps up the present trend," Graham cautioned in June 1963 while conducting a crusade in Stuttgart, Germany, "they will vote God out of our national life." To drive his point home, he pointed out, "This is what naziism and communism did."[28] Outrage rippled across America. Religious groups and the John Birch Society funded billboards that read "Save Our Republic! Impeach Earl Warren."[29] In 1963, the evangelical *Christianity Today* reflected a national mood of discontent. "The Supreme Court decision" against school devotions, said the editor, "seems to have given atheism in the United States a new lease on life."[30] The American public largely disapproved of the decision to bar the reading of scripture in public schools. The Gallup polling agency found that 70 percent of Americans did not support the decision in 1963.[31] Conservative Christians, though, were some of the most ardent critics of the liberal establishment and the Warren Court.

The general moral tone of the country appeared to be in trouble. National headlines and television reports about American crime and depravity fit well with religious believers' apocalyptic outlook.[32] A fundamentalist pastor in Oregon felt he was "Lot" in the "Sodom" that America was becoming. "Certainly our society has not reached that state?" he asked rhetorically in *Christianity Today.* "No," he answered, "but our literature well nigh has!" Smutty novels and magazines corrupted youth, he and many others proclaimed. Hence, believers needed to be vigilant. Numerous fundamentalists hoped Barry Goldwater, running for the presidency in 1964, could set the nation on the right course, before it was too late. "My sympathy is very much with young people these days," lamented a conservative Presbyterian pastor in 1965. "They're getting filth thrown at them from every conceivable source," he concluded.[33] Long-standing laws that had censored suggestive literature and films were being weakened or eliminated.[34] Nihilism and immorality had even spread into the world of high art, complained one evangelical in the middle of the decade. The Pop Art craze, grumbled a woman in *Eternity* magazine, revealed the stark impersonality of a godless society. "The non-Christian quality of society has spread increasingly throughout the western world," she observed frankly. Nietzsche's prophecy about the "death of God," she felt sure, was becoming a new, disturbing reality.[35]

By 1966, related trends in modern theology upset evangelicals, too. Some of these developments even appeared to bear out John Lennon's scandalous remarks. The cover story for the April 8, 1966, issue of *Time* magazine asked "Is God Dead?" The text was set in a bold red font with an ominous black background. The piece drew from three hundred interviews with church leaders and prominent theologians conducted by a team of thirty-two *Time* reporters. It hit newsstands before the Easter season and generated a twenty-year record for the magazine's sales. "Is God dead? The three words represent a summons to reflect on the meaning of existence," wrote one contributor with solemnity. The reporter continued,

> No longer is the question the taunting jest of skeptics for whom unbelief is the test of wisdom and for whom Nietzsche is the prophet who gave the right answer a century ago. Even within Christianity, now confidently renewing itself in spirit as well as form, a small band of radical theologians has seriously argued that the churches must accept the fact of God's death, and get along without him. How does the issue differ from the age-old assertion that God does not and never did exist? Nietzsche's thesis was that striving, self-centered man had killed God, and that settled that. The current death-of-God group believes that God is indeed absolutely dead, but proposes to carry on and write a theology without theos, without God. . . .
>
> If nothing else, the Christian atheists are waking the churches to the brutal reality that the basic premise of faith—the existence of a personal God, who created the world and sustains it with his love—is now subject to profound attack.[36]

Evangelicals, their faith built on a personal God of love and judgment, found the story quite unsettling. Modern life, the cover story implied, could be lived and comprehended without pointing to the divine. *Time*'s reporters introduced Middle America to "Christian atheists" and "religionless Christianity." The purported demise of the triune God provoked evangelicals, who viewed the piece as a sign of the immoral, godless age in which they lived.[37]

Fittingly, *Time*'s "Is God Dead?" feature drew the magazine's highest volume of letters to the editor, some 3,500 in all, many from outraged conservatives. Said one critic, a retired colonel from Laguna Hills, California, "TIME'S story is biased, pro-atheist and proCommunist, shocking and entirely unAmerican." A student at the conservative Missouri Synod Lutheran Seminary in St. Louis said simply, "God is dead to those who wish him so; he lives for those who hope in him." Far more caustic was a critic from Mount Vernon, New York, who castigated *Time:* "Your ugly cover is a blasphemous outrage and, appearing as it does during Passover and Easter week, an affront to every believing Jew and Christian."[38] Christian America, so thought the devout, looked to be unraveling. Billy Graham stepped into the fray, writing a rebuttal chapter titled "God Is Not 'Dead'" for a 1966 book on the topic.[39]

From the far right, other preachers and public personalities dove into the controversy, too. The fundamentalist and anticommunist Christian Crusade in Tulsa, Oklahoma, rushed to print fifty thousand copies of a book that intended to refute the radical theologian Thomas J. J. Altizer and the so-called Christian atheists. Billy James Hargis, the organization's leader, was at the peak of his powers in the early and mid-1960s. Tipping the scales at 270 pounds, the preacher was called a "bawl-and-jump" evangelist by fellow Sooners. His morally urgent tone, tireless anticommunist efforts, and hyper patriotism made him seem like a character from Stanley Kubrick's classic 1964 satire film *Dr. Strangelove.* Hargis's Christian Crusade organization might well have been the best-funded far-right organization in the country. The tax-exempt, nonprofit group drew in roughly $1 million in contributions in 1963.[40] His radio broadcasts ran on over a hundred stations, and he branched out into television as well. In 1966, Hargis was pleading with his constituents across the South and Midwest, "We need your immediate help! The 'God is Dead' Movement is both an insult and a plague to New Testament Christianity." Fellow countrymen had to be made aware of this latest "satanic movement."[41] Along with fighting what Hargis considered radicals and communists in the mainline churches, he also targeted the civil rights movement and later turned his attention to rock music and the counterculture. Amid the uproar over civil rights and leftist theology, student protests began on the West Coast, and the generational divide appeared to be widening. Hargis was prepared to fight it all.

This was an upsetting turn of events, because during the previous decade evangelicals had ridden high on a wave of religious fervor. Billy Graham's crusades still drew massive audiences. In 1962, seven hundred thousand turned out for his Chicago series of revivals. Church building and attendance had been at a new high during the Eisenhower years, and threats to good order appeared to diminish.[42] Rock 'n' roll seemed to lose much of its edge and fury in the late 1950s and early 1960s. But the respite that the faithful had after Elvis went into the military in 1958 and the first stars of rock dimmed would not last. In 1964, with the mass appeal of the Beatles, new dangers to Christian decency appeared. In that first year of Beatlemania, the press coverage, astonishing concert ticket and album sales, and intense fan enthusiasm dominated headlines of America's leading newspapers and magazines.[43]

Thousands of fans awaited the Beatles on February 7, 1964, as the foursome touched down at the newly christened John F. Kennedy International Airport in Queens, New York City. CBS first aired a short story about the group on *CBS Morning News with Mike Wallace* on November 22, 1963. The piece was slated to air again on *CBS Evening News with Walter Cronkite* that same day, but was preempted by the assassination of the president.[44] In a strange way, the group helped America's youngsters out of the anxiety and gloom of national mourning. In the weeks of December and January, U.S. radio airplay picked up for the still obscure Liverpool band. Then, their first wildly successful tour featured television appearances in Miami and New York City as well as concerts at Carnegie Hall and the Washington Coliseum, where the band played through the deafening screams of thousands of roaring fans. Covering the group's visit for the New York *Herald Tribune,* the new-journalist-in-the-making Tom Wolfe witnessed unusual scenes of teenage abandon. The excited fans wore "goony smiles" on their faces. Wolfe reported that "one group of girls asked everybody who came out, 'Did you see the Beatles? Did you touch them?' " A police officer strolled by and one of the girls shouted, "He touched a Beatle! I saw him!" The girls around leapt onto the officer in a frenzy of excitement.[45]

On the other end of the journalistic spectrum was the CBS television anchorman Walter Cronkite, who would win the nickname "the Most Trusted Man in America." Little did he know that his daughters, too, would be caught up in the clamor. When the four lads arrived in Manhattan in February, Cronkite and CBS News featured them prominently. He managed to get his two daughters, Nancy (age fifteen) and Kathy (age thirteen), into the band's *Ed Sullivan Show* rehearsals. A reporter on hand observed the "lucky teen-aged girls" who "whined and squirmed and covered their mouths with their hands, perhaps to avoid speaking in tongues."[46] Kathy told a reporter from *Life* magazine, "Their accents are so heavenly and their hair is so adorable. Our father doesn't really like our reaction very much, but we can't help it."[47] The veteran journalist thought his daughters' behavior was bizarre. He was not a fan of the band's music either.

Neither were a host of others, including a critic at *Newsweek.* The four looked nightmarish, with their "tight, dandified, Edwardian-Beatnik suits and great pudding bowls of hair." Their music was no better, pronounced as "a near disaster" by the skeptical reporter: "guitars slamming out a merciless beat that does away with secondary rhythms, harmony, and melody." The lyrics, too, came in for a drubbing: "Punctuated by nutty shouts of 'yeah yeah yeah!, [the lyrics] are a catastrophe, a preposterous farrago of Valentine-card romantic sentiments." Never had such "ritualistic crazes" gripped the country. The *Milwaukee Sentinel* offered a standard establishment opinion with a sigh: "Fortress America has been breached. The Beatles, unkempt, untalented, lunatic noisemakers, are inside our gates."[48]

Let the cultured despisers rage on, American teens seemed to say, as girls and boys responded with enthusiasm bordering on worshipfulness wherever the Beatles played on their short first tour. Thus victorious, they flew back to England on February 22. Two months later, the band held the top five positions on the American *Billboard* Hot 100 singles chart, with (1) "Can't Buy Me Love," (2) "Twist and Shout," (3) "She Loves You," (4) "I Want to Hold Your Hand," and (5) "Please Please Me." So enormous was the teen buyer's hunger for all things Beatles re-

The Beatles' Ringo Starr adjusts the revolving stand for his drums, Washington Coliseum, February 11, 1964. Photo by Marion S. Trikosko, *US News & World Report* Magazine Photograph Collection, Library of Congress Prints and Photographs Division, Washington, DC (LC-DIG-ppmsca-41598).

lated that even recorded interviews with the group, released as LPs, achieved chart success.[49]

The four young stars from northern England touched down on American soil again in August 1964. This time it was for a well-publicized, one-month, thirty-concert tour. They received a minimum of $50,000 for each gig. Charles O. Finley, owner of the major league baseball team the Kansas City Athletics, was desperate to get the band to play in Kansas City, Missouri. The band was meant to have the day off, but Finley offered their manager, Brian Epstein, a record-setting $150,000. The band performed a thirty-one-minute set to twenty thousand roaring fans in Kansas City's Municipal Stadium on September 17, 1964. The tour netted $1,000,000 just in ticket sales.[50] Beatles merchandise—wigs, handbags, lunch boxes, trading cards, jigsaw puzzles, bubble bath, magazines, harmonicas, bedspreads, games, jewelry, sweatshirts, and dolls—tallied up millions more. Fans prized cheap paraphernalia like sacred relics. They made pilgrimages to concerts, some traveling hundreds of miles.

The tour began in San Francisco's Cow Palace, which had recently hosted the Republican National Convention, scene of candidate Barry

Goldwater's ascendancy. On August 30, the group also played the Atlantic City Convention Center, which just a few days before had been the site of the Democratic Convention that nominated Lyndon Johnson. The Johnson White House had even asked the Beatles to be photographed with the president as the commander in chief placed a wreath at the tomb of Kennedy. Manager Brian Epstein politely declined, saying only that the group did not accept formal invitations like this. The final concert of the tour took place in New York City, scene of their first stateside triumph. Each city greeted the group with the pomp and circumstance befitting a visiting dignitary or the pope. The Beatles' arrival made front-page news in cities across the nation.[51]

The quasi-religious dimensions of fans' devotion struck observers of all stripes. In *Variety* magazine a humorist sent up a religious version of the Beatles' first performance on the tour. In mock King James Bible prose, he wrote that Beatles "idolization had begun and their fame had spread by numerous scriptures, images, artifacts and objects purporting to contain the sound of their voices." "At last it was time for the immortals," he joked. The resulting show led to sixteen "maidens" becoming "ill with hysteria at the rites . . . one was strapped and raving, moaning and shaking her head and screaming 'George' as she was taken to a place for the healing of minds."[52] In the national Jesuit weekly magazine *America,* a writer observed, with a similar dose of humor, the chaos generated by the Beatles' September 1964 Cleveland concert, which had provoked the city's mayor. Teenage fans staked out the group's hotel in the days preceding the show. Acolytes were looking for exits, secret entrances, and fire escapes where they might be able to hide. The Catholic critic noted that a "virtual state of martial law was about to go into effect." It all drove him to sing the classic hymn "Hide Thou Me," he said.[53]

Other eyewitnesses thought the behavior and mania on display was anything but funny. Dr. Bernard Saibel, a child guidance expert, sat through one of the concerts at the Seattle Coliseum on August 21. He reported on his upsetting experience on the front page of the *Boston Globe.* The concert was "unbelievable and frightening," he said. "The hysteria and loss of control," he cautioned, "go far beyond the impact of the music." Youngsters in attendance "became frantic, hostile, uncontrolled, screaming, unrecognizable beings." It was hardly advisable to give up teens to this kind of environment. In his estimation, normal, polite "girls behaved as if possessed by some demonic urge, defying in emotional ecstasy the restraints which authorities try to place on them." His verdict: it was "unholy bedlam."[54] Youngsters were quick to cry foul. "Maybe parents are jealous because their children are giving the Beatles so much affection," snapped a teen from Cohasset, Massachusetts, in the pages of the *Boston Globe.* She concluded, "I'll bet that's the reason that parents can't stand to see their kids give love to strangers." She said, "They aren't really strangers to us."[55] But evangelicals and fundamentalists agreed wholeheartedly with Saibel. They, too, could hardly believe what was happening at these concerts.

Three weeks after the horrors Saibel endured, the band played to twenty-three thousand screaming, flailing teens at the Gator Bowl in Jacksonville, Florida, on September 11, 1964. It was one of twenty-four cities they would visit on the tour. The next was Boston.[56] Tickets for that show had gone on sale on May 25. Prices ranged from $3.50 to $5.50 for the best seats. It was a sellout in two days, making box-office history. Scalpers were quickly offering up tickets for $20 and $30 a pair.[57] In the hours before the Beatles' arrival in Boston, thousands of anxious, twitchy teenagers waited expectantly outside the Madison Hotel to get a glimpse of the celebrity rock 'n' rollers.[58] The intense devotion of local fans made front-page news in the *Boston Globe.* One enthusiast wrote to an area hotel, imploring, "If the Beatles stay at your fine hotel . . . please save me something that Paul, George, or Ringo touched. It would mean so much to me."[59] Scores of teens camped out at North Station, next to the group's hotel. A fifteen-year-old teen from Boston kept vigil, remarking that she and her friends "just want to see them—a finger, an eyebrow, any part of them."[60]

At the Boston Garden on September 12, one hundred local policemen and one hundred military policemen were on patrol. The combined force, hailing from Bedford, Lincoln, Concord, and Lexington, came to the city to protect John, Paul, George, and Ringo. Handlers hustled the four from the airport in hired limousines. They used a private ramp and freight elevator at the venue to avoid their zealous devotees. Inside the Garden 13,909 fans endured the heat of a packed, un-air-conditioned arena for what observers described as one of their most exhilarating concerts. The venue had once hosted Winston Churchill and John F. Kennedy. For the Beatlemaniacs present in September 1964, though, nothing could compare with this.[61]

The concert lasted two hours, but the Beatles played for only thirty minutes. "Yeah, yeah, yeah" could hardly be heard over the sheer noise of the fans. "Little girls were paralyzed by excitement," reported one journalist at the performance. "They stood trembling, hands shaking and sweat coursing down their faces." Some fans, observed the journalist, "collapsed from fatigue. Other children wept." Six girls, having fainted, had to be carried away to first-aid stations by police officers. Twenty minutes after the show ended, one sixteen-year-old girl from Reading was found in a venue restroom, lying in a pool of water, debilitated by "hysteria."[62] Leaving the chaos behind, the Beatles were off for their next show in Baltimore.

Not all New England teens were swept into the commotion. Young religious conservatives largely kept clear of such unholy displays. Just days after the Beatles' show another mass meeting in Boston made front-page news. "If the Beatles had walked into Boston Garden Monday night," wrote a *Globe* reporter, "they might have been greeted by cold stares, and heads bowed in prayer for their salvation." The 13,500 teens that gathered in the Boston arena came to hear America's most famous preacher, the sensational Billy Graham. He was launching his ten-day Greater Boston Crusade. Longtime partner George Beverly Shea, with his deep resonant vocal style, led the crowd in hymn singing. A 1,600-voice choir, its members ranging from young to old, also joined the revival team. They sang the standard, somber revival classic "Just as I Am." The audience applauded enthusiastically when Graham stepped to the podium and announced triumphantly, "Today, the Beatles have left for home."[63] The British foursome might have caused mass delirium, or "unholy bedlam," among Boston teens in previous days, but the youngsters gathered to hear the Reverend Billy walked forward to the altar to give their hearts to Jesus and heed the call to moral purity. The seriousness of these youths, in Graham's view, stood in marked contrast to the obscene devotion of Beatles converts. A veteran usher at the Garden marveled at the audience's polite serenity. A reporter asked how the revival crowd compared with the audience that came to

Young fans scream and clap with delight at the Beatles' Washington Coliseum performance, February 11, 1964. Photo by Marion S. Trikosko, *U.S. News & World Report* Magazine Photograph Collection, Library of Congress Prints and Photographs Division, Washington, D.C. (LC-DIG-ppmsca-41599).

hear the Liverpool rock quartet. The usher thought for a moment, then said, "It's incredible! The Beatles' crowd was indescribable! This crowd just pours in, but tonight it's going to be a breeze."[64]

In the first stages of the Beatles' global popularity in 1964, Graham weighed in on the group that had produced so much pandemonium. "I'm afraid I'm on a different wave length than the Beatles," said Graham to a curious reporter. He even broke one of his long-standing rules, not watching television on the Sabbath, to catch the band's record-breaking performance on the *Ed Sullivan Show.* He wanted, he claimed, to get a better understanding of today's youth. The music was washed out by what he thought sounded like the pointless screaming of three thousand teenagers. Perhaps, he speculated, the church could use some of the excitement and emotion these young performers generated. "Watch the kids' reaction to the Beatles," he told an audience in Omaha, "and you'll know that man is an emotional creature." What accounted for the group's rise to worldwide fame? journalists asked. "I think the Beatles are a product of our time," Graham confidently answered. "They represent the restlessness and the longing of young people today for something off-beat, something different." But it was certainly not all harmless. He branded Beatlemania as a dangerous kind of escapism. The group revealed something about the strains of the era and the "confusion about us."[65]

There is more to Graham's brief comments on the Beatles than one might first think. More than two years before the upheaval caused by John Lennon's 1966 Jesus remarks, evangelical Christians, and especially fundamentalists, were casting a suspicious eye and waving a censorious finger at the four mop tops from Liverpool. In later years—as the Beatles and the counterculture championed recreational drugs and sexual freedom and embraced Eastern meditation—American believers had even more reasons to be troubled. At best the Beatles filled youngsters' minds with frivolous nonsense.

Maybe they were a fad, Graham speculated in 1964. Elvis, too, had once been enormously popular. The evangelist introduced some humor into the national conversation about crazes and the fleeting nature of fame. Teenagers were always chasing about after the latest thing, although parents did not typically know what that was and usually did not understand the lingo their sons and daughters adopted. "Now, don't ask me what they mean," Graham told a crowd at his 1965 Houston revival. From teens, he discerned that the "Beatles are the 'rock 'n' rollers.' The Rolling Stones are the 'rhythm and blues'; Ray Charles is 'pure soul,' and Elvis is 'an old man still trying.' " Audiences chuckled and were comforted to know that, as Graham put it, such tastes, along with "the vocabulary changes about every six months."[66]

Humor could not completely dispel the darker fears of evangelicals and their fundamentalist brethren. At worst the Beatles and the Rolling Stones were leading youth down the wide road to hell. Some in the mainline Protestant world and nearly all evangelicals hoped that the days of this teenage hagiography would be numbered. They may have thought back to the wise words of America's most famous ethicist and theologian, Reinhold Niebuhr. Hero worship was fleeting, observed Niebuhr decades before. In his view heroes could "not survive the coldly critical temper of modern thought, when it is functioning normally, nor can they be worshiped by a generation which has every facility for detecting their foibles and analyzing their limitations."[67]

Guesswork about the Beatles' beguiling popularity and the spell their music cast over teen girls dominated national attention for much of

1964 and 1965. The mainstream media treated the band as a lovable, silly, or ridiculous act. A few outliers, like the conservative commentator and gadfly William F. Buckley, panned the group in harsh terms. "The Beatles are not merely awful," he scoffed. "I would consider it sacrilegious to say anything less than that they are godawful. They are so unbelievably horrible, so appallingly unmusical, so dogmatically insensitive to the magic of the art, that they qualify as crowned heads of anti-music."[68] A year later, the American TV host David Susskind was as blunt and hyperbolic, venturing that the Beatles were "the most repulsive group of men I've ever seen."[69]

There were many reasons to be a Beatlephobe. Mainstream media critics and taste monitors attacked the band for its gimmicky qualities and a lack of style, depth, and artistry. At the same time, conservative religious folk saw something far more baleful. Sure, they might seem fun, wrote Betty Jane West in a Southern Baptist women's magazine. One year after the group first landed in New York City, she observed that the Beatles seemed like playful clowns. But when girls lost control at their concerts it was "really no different from the girl who insists on using alcohol to boost her fun." It amounted to a different kind of addiction and a dangerous conformity. In the end all the time spent on this supposed fad, like wasting away on strong drink, hurt teenagers.[70] In the mid-1960s, a Church of the Nazarene teen penned a poem about the Beatles' malicious influence. She called it, simply enough, "I Hate the Beatles." She wondered, "How many of you reading this / Could say *that* to your crowd."[71]

Even worse than problems of self-control and teenage conformity, the Beatles appeared to be taking the place of religion in the lives of many young people. Such rebukes appeared over and over again in evangelical and fundamentalist magazines as preachers warned of the British invasion from their pulpits. As months went by and as the Beatles gave way to other, rowdier, and hairier English groups—the Rolling Stones, the Animals, the Kinks, the Who, and the Yardbirds, for instance—the threat appeared to grow in intensity. By then, the Beatles looked tame in comparison. As Tom Wolfe aptly put it in 1965, "The Beatles want to hold your hand, but the Stones want to burn your town."[72] Regardless, all such pop cultural celebrities had achieved a quasi-sainted status in the eyes of youth. It looked as if teens had turned their hearts from Jesus to John, Paul, George, Ringo, and an array of other new unkempt stars from across the Atlantic.

Conservative Christians worried about the harmful effects of the Beatles' profane music and seemingly anti-Christian message. Their signature sound came from the gutter, sneered a pentecostal music teacher. Unlike decent Christian musicians, the Beatles made millions by playing the low, savage music that had been popular in America in previous years. Such critics could not speak to specific influences, but they would not have been surprised to know that the Beatles, like the Rolling Stones and countless other art school blues rockers from England, covered the music of black performers such as Chuck Berry, Little Richard, Larry Williams, and Berry Gordy Jr. For this pentecostal detractor it was damning enough to say that the Beatles borrowed from "primitive rhythmic instincts of aboriginal peoples." Their songs were "stripped of much of the restraint" of culture.[73] By these lights the Beatles were profane and wanton.

As early as 1964, fundamentalists had picked up on similar themes as they tried to figure out Beatlemania. The far-right, fundamentalist newspaper *Sword of the Lord* of Murfreesboro, Tennessee, offered its verdict. The newspaper that had printed attacks on the civil rights movement, Presidents Kennedy and Johnson, wayward ecumenical liberal Protestants, and Billy Graham now turned its attention to the pop group from northern England.[74] Its editor looked no further than the Beatles' own press officer, Derek Taylor, for confirmation of the group's vulgar, anti-Christian outlook. The editor quoted Taylor, who in 1964 proclaimed,

> It's incredible, absolutely incredible. Here are these four boys from Liverpool. They're rude, they're crude, they're profane, and they've taken over the world. It's as if they've founded a new religion. They're completely anti-christ. . . . The only thing left for the Beatles is to go on a healing tour.[75]

Sword of the Lord then followed up the Taylor excerpt with a solemn peroration: "That ought to settle the Beatle question once and for all for anyone and everyone who even claims to be a Christian."[76] Far more moderate was Carl F. H. Henry, the editor of the flagship evangelical magazine *Christianity Today*. He observed that young people would cling to their idols, and "the Beatles were hardly the worst of all human possibilities." The Bible, of course, admonished believers to "keep yourselves from idols." But, said Henry, taking a cue from the apostle Paul, idols were really empty objects. They were nothing and would soon pass.[77]

Unfortunately for Carl Henry, Billy Graham, and others in the evangelical fold, the extremely popular, revered band could no more be ignored than it could be wished away. Something like a cult even developed around the group. The excitement that accompanied their shows was unparalleled. Parents looked back almost longingly to the harmless antics of starstruck fans of Rudolph Valentino, Frank Sinatra, or Elvis Presley. Now Beatles concertgoers described the mayhem and rank smell that accompanied performances. Youngsters in the front rows, delirious with elation, occasionally wet their seats or fainted.[78] Many rushed to the stage in a crowded mass. Fans treasured the close contact with the sainted Beatles. Like the young fan in Boston who wrote to a hotel owner, they wanted relics and totems. A piece of a bedsheet. A guitar string. A lock of hair. Lennon and the others were painfully aware of their new, unwelcome holy status. Not long after the group's breakup in 1970, the former front man, with his trademark glasses giving him an owlish look, told *Rolling Stone* magazine about the strange aura that surrounded them. "Wherever we went on tour," Lennon complained,

> there's always a few seats laid aside for cripples and people in wheelchairs. Because we were famous, we were supposed to have people—sort of epileptics and whatever they are—in our dressing room all the time. . . . They would just say hello and go away, they're pushing them at you like you're Christ or something, or as if there's some aura about you, which will rub off on them. . . . It got *horrifying*.[79]

The group's press agent, Derek Taylor, recalled much the same. The hysteria and quasi-religious fanfare of the 1964 tour struck him to the core. The Beatles' tour "routes were lined solid," he said, "cripples threw away their sticks, sick people rushed up to the car as if a touch from one of the boys would make them well again." When airplanes carrying the Beatles touched down at airports around the world it was as if the Messiah had come back, Taylor exclaimed in bewilderment.[80]

Meanwhile, parents, religious and secular, registered new concerns about the craze. Writing to *Playboy* magazine, of all places, in March 1965, a San Francisco father worried that his daughter was taking Beatles worship to new, ridiculous heights. "It may seem sort of silly, but things have reached the stage where" even this reader of the titillating bachelor magazine was "getting worried." He related how his "daughter and a number of the other kids in the neighborhood have formed a real cult over the Beatles." The enthralled teens had "built an altar in one girl's bedroom and they burn candles and recite Beatle prayers they have written." They even went so far as to compose "a Beatle Bible which starts out, 'in the beginning the Beatles created rock and roll.'"[81] Such accounts would have struck the jet-set magazine's relatively affluent, male readership as humorous, if not absurd. Its target audience preferred jazz to rock 'n' roll, drank more martinis than rum and Cokes, and thought the Beatles were a novelty act.[82]

Far removed from the world of *Playboy,* matters were much more serious in the sin-and-salvation environs of conservative Christians. Why had so many youngsters fallen for Beatlism? asked a well-known fundamentalist revival preacher. Such stalwarts turned to scripture for answers. It was simple, he figured. "The devil has control of this world right now." Moreover, "the Devil knows that if teenagers and adults hear the 'glorious gospel of Christ' that they will be saved and begin to live for Christ."[83] Accordingly, Lucifer had blinded youths and turned their attention to the Beatles. Similarly, a fundamentalist pastor from Panama City, Florida, asked his congregants, "What can we learn from the Beatles in the light of the Bible?" In his sermon the Baptist minister repeatedly pointed out that the Beatles were from "the slums of Liverpool," and he spoke of the demonic, evil powers at work in their music. Turning to scripture he quoted 1 Timothy 4:1: "Now the Spirit speaketh expressly, that in the latter times some shall depart from the faith, giving heed to seducing spirits, and doctrines of devils." The Beatles were the apocalyptic minions of Satan, he thundered to his audience.[84] Such experience was shared by a member of the holiness and fundamentalist denomination the Christian and Missionary Alliance. This churchman penned a letter to his denomination's digest to warn others. For all those who doubted the reality of demon possession, he offered his daughter as a clear example. "I watched my Christian daughter dance, frenzied, to Beatle music and rock 'n' roll records for five months," he declared. It stopped only when "the Lord condemned her in a still voice."[85]

Such pulpit-pounding ministers and concerned parents had plenty of anecdotes to work with. Young female fans especially spoke about the Beatles in personal, intimate terms, their language of devotion sounding nearly like that of evangelicals speaking about Jesus. A fan might claim to know all about her favorite member. If she could only meet Paul in person, life would be complete. A sixteen-year-old girl from Milwaukee said she wrote her own fan fiction about the group. "Let's face it," she sighed, "I worship the Beatles." Some hoped to prove their love by buying up every record or knickknack available. Others, half jokingly, said they would kill themselves if they could not secure a much-sought-after concert ticket. The obsession of fans was variously dubbed Beatleitis and Beatleadoration.[86] For fundamentalists, only the workings of sinister forces could help them make sense of the strange behavior of their teens and the weird, inappropriate clothing and hairstyles now being adopted by so many youngsters.

Typically, Baptists, pentecostals, and conservative Presbyterians fretted that the Beatles' feminine hairstyle, tight clothes, and emotional performances produced gender and social anarchy. Others were also thinking these fads marked a major shift in attitude. But for a handful of secular intellectuals, these were positive, revolutionary developments. So said feminist Betty Friedan. The leading voice of second-wave feminism told a Canadian Broadcasting Corporation interviewer in the mid-1960s that young men were drastically changing their outlook. Boys who wore their hair long were "saying no to the *masculine mystique,*" Friedan reasoned. "They are saying no to that brutal, sadistic, tight-lipped, crew-cut, Prussian, big-muscle, Ernest Hemingway" manliness. Such young men, according to the best-selling author, now felt liberated to say "I can be tender and I can be sensitive and I can be compassionate and I can admit sometimes that I'm afraid."[87]

The editor at one interdenominational magazine hoped to dissuade teen boys from breaking with tradition, as Friedan spelled it out, and emulating their ballyhooed idols. Warned the evangelical critic, "The things that 'bug' girls about boys' styles are long hair, skinny pants and fads that tend toward the effeminate. No matter how popular the Beatles become, American girls still like boys to look like boys!"[88] When

Tulsa-based Christian Crusade leader Billy James Hargis ventured to England in September 1964 he was shocked to find what he termed "the beatnik crowd represented by the Beatles." Youngsters on the streets, in his estimation, had swapped natural traits. Teenage boys even curled their hair, he reported with outrage to his constituents. Should they be called "he," "she," or "it"? he wondered.[89] Worries about hair and dress proliferated outside the church as well. The North Carolina attorney general even allowed the banning of Beatles haircuts in public schools. The style was not, he said plainly, "normal."[90] Not "normal," in this sense, could serve as a code word for being effeminate or homosexual. The famous cartoonist Bill Mauldin's fifteen-year-old son David told *Time* magazine that his dad did not approve of his new, long bowl cut. "My father thinks it makes me look like a faggot," he said candidly.[91]

Indeed, the Beatles had adopted the androgynous clothes as well as the bohemian hairstyles of young German artists and intellectuals. In the band's Hamburg, Germany, days they took on the attitudes and poses of German "exis," so named because of their embrace of existentialism, and clad themselves in the gender-neutral leather outfits of young hipsters. The group had long performed and recorded the songs that African American girl groups—the Marvelettes, the Cookies, the Donays, and the Shirelles—had made popular. The foursome played the hits of gender-bending rockers like Little Richard, who sang frankly about sex.[92] The Beatles' tight, collarless, silver-gray Edwardian suits, Scouse accents, and their ankle-high Cuban boots all struck mainstream observers as bizarre.

But it was the long, bushy hair that seemed the oddest feature of all. Keen observers noted the strangeness of the group. The British-based Granada Television commissioned the American documentarians Albert and David Maysles to cover the group's first visit to the United States with a fly-on-the-wall film. "This was a historical moment," recalled Albert decades later. "These guys, the Beatles, they were almost, like, from another planet."[93] That was especially true in the age of pompadours, flattops, and buzz cuts. Judging from the 1963 edition of Amy Vanderbilt's ever-popular *Complete Book of Etiquette*, long, shaggy hair on men appeared to be as gauche as it was rebellious. "The well-groomed man," the guide counseled, "never allows his hair to get so shaggy his new haircut is all too apparent. His hair is trimmed as often as necessary to keep it from colliding with his collar or his ears."[94] Young boys had long hair. Grown men or teens who adopted the style were out of place, eccentric, or worse.

Commentators around the country in 1964 and 1965 wondered about the impact of the Beatles-style haircut. Teens might be sporting or admiring it because it was new or unusual, but teachers, pastors, and numerous commentators in the media, like North Carolina's attorney general, found it unattractive and problematic. Anne Francis, the star of the TV detective drama *Honey West,* summed up much of the disapproval. "I don't understand it," she mused in 1965. In her view it was "unhealthy for girls to admire men who are female-looking."[95] But the appearance of long hair on young men revealed something deeper for religious conservatives. When Billy Graham was asked about the meaning of recent attitudes concerning gender and attire, he wondered aloud if long hair on boys and men spelled the end of civilization.[96] In spring 1966 a United Press International reporter noted the very trend that Graham feared. "Some boys are going in for shoulder-length hair, lip pomades, false eyelashes, and sweet-smelling perfumes," the journalist observed. On the other end, "Girls are affecting male haircuts, workmen's boots, [and] have belt[s], and apparel bought from the army-navy store."[97]

The relative androgyny of the new Beatles style slowly caught on and became fashionable. High school and college yearbook portraits documented the trend with each passing year. It came to be identified with youth and with a kind of cultural liberation. The Beatles-influenced, made-for-TV band the Monkees, with their zany irreverence, embodied that spirit. Those subtleties and the cultural meaning of hair style—its novelty and independence—was largely lost on religious critics. As young men grew their hair longer, critics and supporters battled over the meaning of it all.[98] Popular evangelicals like Billy Graham called it a bad sign of the times. Another prominent minister and friend of presidents, the Quaker Elton Trueblood, agreed. Speaking to students at the Baptist Wake Forest College in 1964, Trueblood denounced "those four stupid boys from Liverpool who can't even sing." But perhaps worse for the former chaplain of Stanford University, the Beatles had "tried to make themselves look like girls."[99] Over the next four years, more and more young men appeared to be trying to "make themselves look like girls," and young women were putting on dungarees and cropping their hair. By 1967, Graham's and Trueblood's feared gender mix-up was well under way.

It seemed to be getting worse as the Beatles' popularity continued to grow along with the length of their hair. Some dealt with the problem by joking about it from the pulpit, as did a Baptist minister in Saint Paul, Minnesota. In Pastor Ernest Ruark's estimation the four musicians looked like "victims of a barber's nervous breakdown" or "refugees from the Australian bush country."[100] Where sarcasm and shame would not work, church guardians resorted to discipline. One Southern Baptist church in North Carolina took the drastic step of expelling several youngsters from its congregation. "They were kicked out for having long hair like the Beatles," observed a parishioner.

> It's the first time we've had anybody booted out of our church in 48 years. (That's not including preachers.) We've had drunkards, women-chasers, man-chasers, thieves and just about everything else in our little church, this is the first case that was serious enough to take drastic action.[101]

The church's deacons self-assuredly proclaimed that "any male who wore his hair long was just plain bad."[102]

The Beatles hair fad went beyond bad taste for the faithful. It denoted rebellion and ungodliness. In the view of an editor at a Georgia pentecostal paper, the long, floppy Beatles haircut surely marked a breakdown in parental authority.[103] Bill Goetz of the conservative holiness group Christian and Missionary Alliance agreed. While fans of the Beatles plastered the walls of their rooms with glossy posters of the shaggy-haired group and devotees deluged the four with letters, telegrams, and mementos, Goetz raged, "If you are a Christian teen" and a "Beatle bug" then "THERE'S SOMETHING RADICALLY WRONG!" He believed that the Beatles urged young people on to rebellion against parents and made youths lose all sense of dignity. "Now," he sternly pronounced, "I scarcely need to point out that no Christian teen will go along with those two ideas."[104] Fundamentalists associated with the Bible Institute of Los Angeles asked believers to seek guidance in the word of God. In May 1965, one worried evangelist affiliated with the conservative school pointed to Exodus 23:2: "Thou shalt not follow a multitude to do evil." The preacher concluded that the four young rock 'n' rollers from England "have caused more frustration and evil excitement among the teenagers (and many adults) than could have been imagined."[105]

Surprisingly, fundamentalist critics like these, with Bible in hand, and academics agreed on some of the basics. *U.S. News and World Report* turned to one such academic, the Harvard professor and eminent sociologist David Riesman, for his expert opinion. The author of the 1950 best-selling *The Lonely Crowd* considered the Beatles to be tamer, and much less a threat to parental authority, than was Elvis.[106] Presley rose to fame with his "swagger and his aggressiveness and his defiance." The four Liverpudlians, heavily influenced by the King of Rock 'n' Roll, were nonetheless a sign of teenage restiveness. "It's a form of protest against the adult world," said Riesman in an interview. Their fans were "hoping to believe in something, or respond to something new that they have found for themselves." Riesman, unlike conservative religious voices, felt that this pop cultural import from Britain was a relatively innocent trend. It was "not at all dangerous."[107]

Beatles devotion and the moral chaos the group inspired were especially grave concerns for devout southerners. A few of the more zealous anti-Beatles crusaders in the Tar Heel state went beyond mere words. Roughly one year before Lennon made national news with his incendiary remarks about the Beatles' fame, some pentecostals targeted the band directly. The group led young people astray, thought Jim and Tammy Faye Bakker. The two revivalists, who would much later rise to national prominence and infamy, preached against rock 'n' roll music in their youth campaigns. On a tour through North Carolina, the Michigan-based evangelists warned congregants of the hazards of rock. Jim delivered what had become a standard autobiographical sermon, "From Rock and Roll to Rock of Ages." In his youth, Bakker had been a fan of the big beat and Elvis in particular. While still in high school in Muskegon, Michigan, he had even managed the nationally known female Elvis impersonator Marlene Way. Bakker felt torn between two worlds in these years before he met Tammy Faye. "Should I be good or should I be a hood?" he asked himself. In the end he decided that rock 'n' roll, Elvis, and all that these stood for, were wrong. In 1965, the Bakkers ended their large teen evangelism campaign with a "Beatle

Burning." They encouraged local youth to toss "objectionable books and magazines" and rock 'n' roll records into the flames.[108]

Records and paraphernalia could be consigned to the bonfire, but baleful, immoral ideas were harder for stalwarts to eradicate. The greatest threat was that the Beatles made children rebellious, unruly, or sacrilegious. Pop and folk music, said some religious conservatives in the early and mid-1960s, could even serve as tools of communist subversion. However fantastic such theories might seem, they had a ready audience in some sections of the country.

Though the red scare had waned in the United States since the 1950s, conservative evangelicals were still united in their belief that communism posed a major threat to America, both at home and abroad. Quite a few believers were just beginning to be energized in reaction to the liberal rights revolution that they felt was at odds with everything that they stood for. Leading pastors reacted to the midcentury liberal consensus and liberalism in mainline Protestant churches with a militant brand of anticommunism. Adherents were eager to provide, as one publication phrased it, "the Christian answer to communism." Billy Graham staked much of his early career on battling the red menace. So too did the Los Angeles Methodist and fundamentalist Fighting Bob Shuler and the New Jersey fundamentalist radio preacher Carl McIntire. Graham, by comparison, would mute some of his militancy in the coming decades. Campaigns involved monitoring school curricula, pointing out the supposed communist infiltration of Protestant churches, calling for the censorship of leftist books and speakers, and keeping a watchful eye on national and international politics.[109] Uneasy evangelicals rightly sensed that the larger culture was moving left at a speed they could hardly comprehend. Looking back on the turbulent 1960s from the vantage of 1980, the Yale University historian of American religion Sydney Ahlstrom mulled over the radical developments in religion and ethics. "Never before in the country's history," he concluded, "have so many Americans expressed revolutionary intentions and actively participated in efforts to alter the shape of American civilization in almost every imaginable aspect—from diet to diplomacy from art to the economic disorder."[110]

In the early 1960s, evangelicals and fundamentalists fretted that their youngsters were falling under the influence of liberal or even atheistic curricula and teachers. What would happen to their teenage sons and daughters in the classrooms of secular America? asked troubled ministers and laypeople. So contentious were the fights against communist influence and the efforts to ferret out reds in the United States, that even those within the conservative fold came under scrutiny. Robert Welch, the head of the far-right John Birch Society, had accused even President Dwight Eisenhower of communist sympathies.[111] In much the same vein, the segregationist and fundamentalist Bob Jones painted Billy Graham with the red brush in 1958. "When Billy Graham insists that he will not hold meetings anywhere unless the races are desegregated," said the founder of Bob Jones University, "he is playing into the hands of the Communists even though it may not be his intention to do so."[112] That smear was especially ironic, because Graham had made anticommunism a key part of many of his campaigns from the late 1940s through the 1960s. Graham's hatred of communism burned hot. The famous evangelist's later hawkish support of the Vietnam War was just one manifestation of that outlook.[113] The accusations, counteraccusations, and slanders revealed the persistent anxieties evangelicals had about their government, foreign affairs, and presumed leftist and amoral influences on young people. For Graham and millions of other evangelicals, communism and its explicit atheism threatened to undermine American values and to do away with Christianity. Likewise, revolutionary rock music jeopardized the future.[114] Youth appeared to be particularly vulnerable.

They had good reason to worry. A 1963 nationwide survey of college students on twelve campuses revealed that liberalism was in the ascendancy. The survey asked undergraduates about their religious beliefs and political ideals. The poll showed that students were reacting against the religious values of their upbringing. Startling to evangelical adults, the survey found that only a minority of those questioned "affirm the existence of a God capable of exercising an effect on their lives." Undergraduates supported pro-union laws and were less ardently anticommunist than their parents had been. One journalist concluded that Billy Graham's brand of evangelism had not taken hold.[115]

Some conservative activists, convinced that pop culture and public education were against them, took action. In Tulsa, Billy James Hargis was so worried that he and his organization decided to intervene in more direct ways. "Most of our Christian Crusade rallies are attended by middle-aged couples and older folks," he admitted with some embarrassment. "We need to reach out to youth," he said. "We are all aware of the liberal poison being spread in our high schools, especially in the metropolitan areas, by the National Education Association." Maybe worse yet, colleges and universities across the country failed to invite the anticommunist military and religious leaders that Hargis and his followers put forward. Instead, they invited left-leaning folk singers like Peter, Paul, and Mary, Bob Dylan, and Joan Baez or speakers such as Gus Hall, Herbert Aptheker, Elizabeth Flynn, and other crimson archvillains. Christian Crusade responded by launching a summer training institute in Colorado for college students and by placing its broadcasts on more college and university stations.[116]

College campuses would remain a kind of battleground for Hargis and like-minded fundamentalists. Folk music, and later, folk-rock, they thought, was particularly to blame for anarchy and communist ideas. "Satan is concentrating full-time on America's youth," warned Hargis in early 1967. The Oklahoma political evangelist singled out popular university performers like the once-blacklisted folk performer Pete Seeger. The hawkish Hargis was livid. "Two of the most popular folk songs on college campuses today across the land are 'Draft Dodger Rag' and 'I Ain't Marching Anymore,' written by another pro-Red, Phil Ochs," stated Hargis. The folkie *Sing Out!* magazine was a popular university publication. It all rang of treason, or something even worse, to him.[117]

The most ardent, well-known anti-Beatles campaigner in these years was the youth minister and far-right anticommunist activist David A. Noebel. An associate evangelist and youth coordinator for Hargis's Christian Crusade, Noebel took aim at the Beatles as no one else in America would. Before heading to Tulsa and taking on the Fab Four, he had served as pastor of the Fundamental Bible Church in Madison, Wisconsin. The young right-wing pastor from Oshkosh had attended Milwaukee Bible College and then went on to the evangelical Hope College. He subsequently studied philosophy as a graduate student at the University of Wisconsin. Along with his pastoral duties, he spent time in the college town, squaring off against campus leftists, denouncing the American Civil Liberties Union, dashing off op-eds to the local newspaper, and pointing out fellow travelers across the political and religious spectrum. In 1962, at the tender age of twenty-six, Noebel even ran for Congress, facing off against an Eisenhower Republican for the GOP nomination. He lost the bid by an overwhelming margin.[118]

In 1964, with the encouragement of Hargis, Noebel was linking the Beatles' antics to communist subversion. By the fall of that year, Noebel was traveling on the anticommunist speaking circuit, delivering his message about the red Beatles. An October 1964 talk at the Veterans Memorial Building in Eugene, Oregon, was billed as "Communist Hypnotism and the Beatles." The lecture promised to reveal that "much present-day recorded music . . . is in reality nothing but an effort to control the thoughts and behavior of American children and youth."[119] Noebel's central thesis was that the Beatles were softening up America's impressionable young people for Soviet indoctrination. He added to this warning the now-standard line about the African origins of the music. Rock music, even the kind that the Beatles played, came directly from the dark, ferocious jungles of the southern hemisphere. These roots might have been hidden from teenagers, but that made the music all the more suspect, Noebel cautioned. Communism, too, when coupled with rock music, was surreptitiously influencing teenagers. This was Noebel's line of reasoning in his 1965 Christian Crusade book on the topic. "The communists, through their scientists, educators and entertainers," claimed Noebel in grave prose, "have contrived an elaborate, calculating and scientific technique directed at rendering a generation of American youth useless through nerve-jamming, mental deterioration and retardation."[120] If action was not taken, brainwashed, mentally challenged youth would soon be hoisting the Soviet flag over America.

Noebel's ideas were not entirely out of the blue, however bizarre and conspiratorial they seemed. He was, in fact, drawing on Cold War theories about thought control, which had been a particularly useful explanatory device since the Korean War. This theme of mind control even drove the plot of Hollywood films like *Prisoner of War* (1954), starring Ronald Reagan; *The Hypnotic Eye* (1960); and *The Manchurian Candidate* (1962). In the early 1950s, government officials commissioned leading psychologists to help explain the confessions of American POWs. These studies focused on the Soviet conditioning of animals and subsequent thought control of humans.[121] Psychiatrist and public intellectual Robert Jay Lifton's 1961 *Thought Reform and the Psychology of*

Totalism: A Study of "Brainwashing" in China continued this thread of reasoning. But when compared with such nuanced research, Noebel's efforts were slapdash, amateurish, pretentious, and a perfect expression of far-right paranoia. The plan, in which the Beatles would play a critical part, said Noebel, "involves conditioned reflexes, hypnotism, and certain kinds of music. The results, destined to destroy our nation, are precise and exacting." Drawing on a dizzying parade of experts and communist figures, Noebel concluded that in the twenty-nine minutes of a Beatles concert, young fans had lost all inhibition and sense of right. In this state, Noebel declared, teens "can be told to do anything—and they will." Youngsters needed to pack their Beatles records off to the city dump, before it was too late.[122]

Noebel's fevered speculations were not too far removed from those floated by the Young Americans for Freedom or the John Birch Society. "Fluoridation, mental-health programs, and the United Nations are," cracked a critic in *Newsweek,* "as every Right-thinking fundamentalist well knows, insidious Communist plots to soften up America for Bolshevik takeover."[123] The writer went on to skewer the twenty-eight-year-old Noebel, who was offering his usual lecture on the Beatles at a Baptist church in Claremont, California. When the time was just right, Noebel told his crowd, the communists would put the Beatles on television to hypnotize hollow-headed teens. One reader wrote in to *Newsweek* from Lenoir, North Carolina, to set the record straight. Noebel's "witless theory," he claimed, "could scarcely come from the lurid and frenzied dreams of an opium smoker, much less a supposedly sane and sober 'patriot.'" The skeptic concluded that "far-rightism" might be a stronger hallucinogen than LSD.[124] Hargis and Noebel considered such denunciations to be a kind of confirmation of the righteousness of their cause. The more they felt persecuted, the more they believed they were in the right. Hargis wrote to supporters in the mid-1960s about the mistreatment he and his band of anticommunist crusaders faced regularly. "If all our friends only knew the satanic pressures that are exerted against us daily . . . trying to stop this activity . . . trying to discourage and frighten the workers," he claimed, then supporters would be far more generous with their donations.[125]

Noebel, who occasionally met with hisses, boos, and restless commotion by the teens who showed up to his lectures on a lark, would

Rev. David Noebel
Billy James Hargis' Executive Assistant, Dean, Christian Crusade Anti-Communist University . . . and one of the most outstanding and dramatic conservative spokesmen in America today.

CHRISTIAN CRUSADE RALLY
PRESENTS

DAVID NOEBEL'S

"COMMUNISM,
HYPNOTISM,
AND THE BEATLES"

ADMISSION
FREE

KANSAS

Friday, April 23, 7:30 p.m.
ARKANSAS CITY
Kansas Gas & Electric
Hospitality Room

Sunday, April 25, 2:00 p.m.
WICHITA
Twentieth Century Club Aud.

Monday, April 26, 7:30 p.m.
HUTCHINSON
Baker Hotel -Kansas Room

Tuesday, April 27, 7:30 p.m.
NEWTON
Ripley Hotel - Ballroom

Wednesday, April 28, 7:30 p.m.
ABILENE
Sterl Hall - Eisenhower Park

Thursday, April 29, 7:30 p.m.
TOPEKA
Hotel Pick-Kansas - Roof Garden

Friday, April 30, 7:30 p.m.
LAWRENCE
Eldridge Hotel - Ballroom

MISSOURI

Sunday, May 2, 2:00 p.m.
KANSAS CITY
First Bible Presbyterian Church

Monday, May 3, 7:30 p.m.
SPRINGFIELD
Kentwood Arms Hotel
Crystal Room

Tuesday, May 4, 7:30 p.m.
JOPLIN
Mickey Mantle Holiday Inn
Oriental Room

A Christian Crusade poster for David Noebel's anti-Beatles speaking tour through the Midwest, 1965. Reproduction courtesy of the Wilcox Collection of Contemporary Political Movements, Kenneth Spencer Research Library, University of Kansas Libraries.

not be silenced by scoffers. They were likely fellow travelers and pinkos anyhow, he reasoned. For the next several years, he churned out other articles and books and traveled across the Midwest and border South, delivering lectures on the destructive powers and hidden agendas of the four Liverpudlians and taking on red folk musicians.[126] He spoke to concerned parents, teachers, and pastors who filed into hotel ballrooms, community centers, and city auditoriums in Lawrence, Kansas; Des Moines, Iowa; Minneapolis, Minnesota; and Joplin, Missouri, to hear his elaborate theories about Merseybeat, the Liverpool subgenre that the Beatles led.[127] Hargis sent out advance notices about Noebel's anti-rock-'n'-roll tour to his constituents and churches across the region. "We are in a war, a war to save our young people," proclaimed Hargis. Teens, glued as they were to their transistor radios or hovering over their record players, were being brainwashed and parents needed to know how to act.[128] Noebel received a good hearing from evangelicals and fundamentalists. His theories may have been a little hard to believe, but his general message of caution was convincing. His articles, books, and speaking engagements from 1964 to 1969 likely made believers more resistant to the Beatles and what they represented.

It is not surprising, then, that after Lennon's 1966 Jesus remark pastors' and laypeople's suspicions turned into full-blown condemnation. Numerous record bans, sermons, and public burnings illustrated just how seriously evangelicals were now taking popular culture and its appeal to youth. A Baptist pastor from Georgetown, Massachusetts, took a counterintuitive look at the controversy. "I think that there is no question that the Beatles are more popular than Christ," he mused. But what did the Beatles actually offer to their putative followers? the minister wondered. They "cannot do for man what Jesus Christ can do." He went on, "They cannot forgive sins; they cannot give Divine direction to man so that he can do the will of God."[129] Doe-eyed teenagers might worship John, Paul, George, and Ringo, but these entertainers were no deities.

The promoter of positive thinking and renowned clergyman Norman Vincent Peale offered his thoughts on Lennon's comments about Jesus, saying they were an "adolescent remark of one of the Beatles." Peale's uplifting evangelical message had won a wide readership as well as an enormous radio and television audience in the 1950s and 1960s. A close associate of Graham, Peale, like the famous revivalist, had a common touch and spoke earnestly and directly to middle America. The best-selling self-help author had made a national name for himself with sunny, optimistic sayings, like "Believe in yourself and release your inner powers. . . . You can develop creative faith in yourself, faith that is justified." Anyone who took these steps, he wrote in his multimillion-selling *The Power of Positive Thinking* (1952), "will feel like a new person, for in fact you will be a new person."[130] His homey, day-to-day, upbeat wisdom appealed to multitudes. Peale's audience listened as well to his conservative advice on politics and culture. His response to Lennon had an uncharacteristic note of bitterness in it. Lennon's British cynicism and caustic wit clearly bothered Peale. Jesus had never intended to be "popular," said Peale in fall 1966. "The brash remark of the cocky girl-haired young man" missed the whole point of who Christ was and is. He elaborated, like the Baptist pastor from Georgetown, comparing Jesus and the Beatles,

> We have seen Jesus at work in the lives of people who go into the ghettos, into the dark and miserable places of the world lovingly ministering in His name. And by motivation from Jesus they have dedicated themselves to remove the causes of poverty and crime and human misery. I have never heard of the Beatles getting involved in any such activities. And one wonders what they do with all their dough. Does any of it go to help the unfortunate in the slums of their own city?[131]

Regardless, concluded Peale, Jesus had had many critics before. He ended on an assuring note and reinforced the gender biases of his readers. Some of these former skeptics, unlike the Beatles, were "real tough man-sized opponents who make these long-haired musicians appear infantile."[132]

Angry critics wanted the "infantile" Lennon and the group to elaborate, apologize, or leave the country. The press, religious leaders, and even former fans badgered the Beatles for a retraction. Johnny Midnight, a DJ at KTEE in Idaho Falls, Idaho, expressed the feelings of many others. "Until John Lennon retracts his anti-Christ statement," he roared, "KTEE will play no more Beatles records."[133] Such reactions ran all the way to the top of the religious organization chain. The Vatican's newspaper, *L'Osservatore Romano,* lent its voice to other detractors in America, Spain, South Africa, and Mexico. Certain "subjects must not be dealt with profanely," it counseled, "even in the world of beatniks."[134]

Hounded by negative attention, the Beatles' manager Brian Epstein and the group knew that something clearly had to be done. Lennon eventually did apologize for his remarks about Christianity and Jesus. On August 12, 1966, Lennon tried to make amends during a special press event held at the Astor Towers in Chicago. It had the feeling of a courtroom proceeding. A reporter piped up, asking, "Mr. Lennon, do you feel you are being crucified?" Lennon, perhaps now more aware than ever that his answers could pose serious problems for himself and the band, said with a laugh while chewing gum nervously, "No, I wouldn't say that at all." Paul McCartney sarcastically observed that the band would now probably get blamed for the "fall of Christianity." Lennon's eyes looked tired as he sat next to his three, less talkative, somewhat subdued bandmates. Eager to move beyond the whole affair, he admitted, "I just said what I said and it was wrong, or was taken wrong, and now it's all this." Clearly uncomfortable, Lennon admitted, "I can't express myself very well, that's my trouble. I was just saying, in my illiterate way of speaking, what I gleaned from [Hugh J.] Schonfield's book." Lennon said he was just pointing out a fact. If he had said the band was more popular than television, he pleaded, no one would have batted an eye. Besides all this, he claimed, the Beatles were probably more popular than Jesus in England, not America. "Even church people are trying to be with it," he said, reaching for a further example, "with sort of pop groups and things."[135]

Perhaps nothing Lennon said in Chicago and elsewhere would have been enough for those committed to the boycott. The Nacogdoches, Texas, radio station KEEE received over five hundred phone calls after Lennon's apology. The majority of these callers, perhaps to the consternation of DJs, wanted the ban to continue. In Birmingham, WAQY's station manager, who had started it all, was satisfied with the apology. He called off the airplay ban and decided not to destroy a collection of Beatles records.[136]

In the coming months and years, Lennon viewed the whole horrible episode in a slightly different light. Exactly two months after the Beatles performed their last show at Candlestick Park in San Francisco, Lennon was on the set for a movie he was starring in. It was being filmed in the arid, moonlike environment of Spain. Between takes for *How I Won the War* (1967), the Beatle, now wearing his trademark National Health round-frame glasses, made some time for reporters and friends. Fred Robbins made his way over from America for a quick interview to

"Would you believe Confucius?"

A Bob Bastian cartoon commenting on the scandal swirling around the Beatles after John Lennon's "more popular than Jesus" remark. The cartoon appeared in the *San Francisco Chronicle* on August 8, 1966. Courtesy of the *San Francisco Chronicle*/ Polaris Images.

be broadcast by the radio show *Assignment: Hollywood.* They joked about Lennon's short haircut, which he was sporting for his theatrical role, and the chaos of the last concerts, with their bomb scares, boycotts, lower ticket sales, and pressure from the Christian right and the KKK. Lennon was surprisingly low key. Some answers came out as near whispers. "Well, now it's just like a bad dream, you know?" he confided. "It's just way in the back of my mind somewhere, and it just comes back when you read things, just odd things that crop up now and then—'Cardinal So-and-so says it's OK,' or things like that." The star laughed at the incongruity of his remark. "But it's really WAY in the back of my mind," he trailed off. But it could not be denied, he said, that it "was very frightening."[137]

The public apology helped quell the matter, at least somewhat. In private Lennon poked fun at the protesters, who were, in his typically sarcastic words, "middle-aged deejays burning a pile of LP covers for an audience of 12-year-olds."[138] But the damage done to the group was real. The fiasco, the pressure, the threats were indeed "very frightening." All the band members felt the sting of negative publicity. Epstein was especially worried about putting "his boys" in harm's way. Eight years after that last tour, Lennon recalled their Memphis show at the Mid-South Coliseum, picketed as it was by members of the Klan. During the concert, said Lennon,

> somebody let off a firecracker while we were on stage. There had been threats to shoot us, the Klan were burning Beatle records outside and a lot of the crew-cut kids were joining in with them. Somebody let off a firecracker and every one of us—I think it's on film—look[ed] at each other, because each thought it was the other that had been shot. It was that bad.[139]

For fellow Beatle George Harrison, it was all too much. The terror and fierce opposition to the Beatles, along with the death threats Lennon received, helped Harrison decide that touring had to come to an end.[140]

The militant language religious conservatives used to denounce the band, the well-publicized Beatles bans, and the uproar that spread over radio stations swept over the Bible Belt, but did not reach into all quarters of American Christianity. Mainline, liberal Protestants and some Catholics tended to stay out of the fray or brushed off the controversy and the band's supposed pernicious influence.[141] A writer in the liberal Catholic weekly *America* thought all the handwringing to be a little bit ridiculous. Elderly Cassandras expected the Beatles "to carry-on in a style more brazen than Presley's and more saccharine than Sinatra's." But the Beatles did no such thing. "How disconcerting," said the Catholic journalist, "to discover four tea-drinking young adults (one already a father), with nothing more noxious about their demeanor than a weird tonsorial get-up."[142] The editor of the liberal magazine *Christian Century* poked fun at crusaders like David Noebel, weighed down as Noebel was with conspiracy theories about communism and rock mesmerism. The *Christian Century*'s staff figured that "Beatlism isn't so bad." It was a marked improvement over Presleyism, anyway. "We're not even bothered by the fact that the Beatles say that they are 'anti-Christian,'" said the editor. Of course, this was before Lennon delivered his opinion on Jesus and his disciples. But in early 1965, at least, the *Christian Century* considered John Lennon's comments about Christian hypocrisy to be sensible, "if naive."[143]

Some in the Lutheran Church of America and the United Methodist Church followed a similar course. A reporter from *The Lutheran* national magazine went on a kind of fact-finding mission of the Beatles. After interviewing parents and their teens and going to see the group's film *A Hard Day's Night*, Rachel Conrad Wahlberg came away with some clear insights. In the theater, caught up in the excitement, she said she "nearly chimed in [her]self, all the while thinking how silly, how utterly ridiculous."[144] She came away with a better sense of the purpose of the Beatles in the lives of young girls. Her restrained take on Beatlemania contrasted sharply with denunciations on the right. She nodded to Freud and child psychology in general. "These young girls aren't ready for love," concluded Wahlberg.

> They are still in the period of idolizing Daddy. He is their image of man. The Beatles are a transition, a pleasant escape from school and homework and music lessons, a form of hero-worship for adolescents. Many of these girls still have stuffed animals on their beds.[145]

Where others saw idolatry, she saw benign "hero-worship" and teenagers who were, slowly, fitfully, becoming adults.[146] The Methodist student magazine *Motive*, a haven for social activists and up-and-coming critics, took seriously the Beatles' influence, appeal, and key place in pop music history. An earnest grad student in its pages reflected on the artistic achievements of the 1965 album *Rubber Soul* and the song "Norwegian Wood" in particular. "It is not that we can or should understand" the Beatles, he wrote with some solemnity, "but that we can and should appreciate them."[147]

Unlike evangelicals, some mainline Protestants responded to the bigger-than-Jesus scandal with a little well-intentioned soul searching. Writing for *Presbyterian* magazine, William Stringfellow even ventured that the "Beatles' premise is correct" in some measure. True, he wrote, the "churches in Great Britain and, increasingly, the churches in North

America endure significant public disfavor, I venture, because they are so much preoccupied with themselves and so little attentive to the common needs of human beings in modern society."[148] So said Lennon himself in his attempt to clarify what he had said. As mainliners tried to understand and appreciate the Beatles phenomenon or even sympathize with Beatlemaniacs, pentecostals, Nazarenes, Southern Baptists, and others remained on the defensive. The latter would reap new rewards in the growing culture wars of the late 1960s and 1970s. Their membership numbers swelled and they appealed to Americans who felt the cultural excesses of the 1960s needed to be countered.

When the fires of the bigger-than-Jesus controversy finally began to die out in September and October of 1966, one Southern Baptist offered a parting shot. Will ten thousand books be written about the Beatles in years to come? he asked rhetorically. The Beatles might have drawn crowds of twenty thousand, he commented—perhaps unintentionally deflating their turnouts—"but a North Carolina preacher named Billy Graham has drawn over 100,000 at a time."[149] Norman Vincent Peale chimed in on the matter as well, saying, "One cannot help wondering if the boys will be remembered at all one hundred years from now." Jesus's name, however, would be.[150]

That confident fist-shaking could not dispel deeper insecurities, however. Were conservative Christians losing out? Billy Graham did not think so, but even he thought it a shame that the Beatles missed their opportunity to influence American youth for the better. It was sad that John Lennon, so young and hailing from a Christian nation, as Graham put it, would make a comment like that. In fact, the Beatles "could lead the way and set the moral tone for the youth of the world," he lamented. "But unfortunately, they do not seem disposed to make the right kind of capital of their great success and popularity."[151] Fellow Southern Baptist W. A. Criswell, who counted Graham as a member of his First Baptist Church in Dallas, was even bleaker about the Lennon incident. From his pulpit the revered Criswell, with typical bombast, chalked up Lennon's observations to a "colossal, indescribable, unbelievable, indifference, secular indifference to the things of God, and of Christ, and of the faith." A decade before, Criswell had denounced Elvis with a similar fury, but the extent of the Beatles' influence and their anti-Christian attitude marked a new low. Criswell's flare for the apocalyptic shined through. "This is the spirit of the new day and the new age," he told his congregants and his radio and TV audience. "And these are the idols," he announced, "of millions and millions of teenagers in America and in the whole world."[152]

Criswell seemed to be acknowledging the cold logic of Lennon's remarks. In truth, the rock star's comment, however flippant, was certainly in line with the prevailing wisdom of critics, opinion makers, and academics. Throughout the 1960s, numerous observers were sure that organized religion, even in America, was on the decline. The uproar that surrounded the *Time* magazine God-is-dead story was only one manifestation of that consensus. Secularism was the order of the day. Those who denied it, said sociologists and philosophers, were deluding themselves. Secularization theory served as the master model of the era. In 1959 the Columbia University sociologist and public intellectual C. Wright Mills summed up what he thought was an undeniable religious disenchantment. "Once the world was filled with the sacred—in thought, practice, and institutional form," Mills declared. "After the Reformation and the Renaissance, the forces of modernization swept across the globe and secularization, a corollary historical process, loosened the dominance of the sacred. In due course, the sacred shall disappear altogether except, possibly, in the private realm."[153]

Few described the process more clearly and in greater detail than did Peter L. Berger. The Austrian-born sociologist summed up his ideas about the decline of religion for a *New York Times* reporter in early 1968. Protestant churches had reached a stage of "self-liquidation," claimed the New School professor. Social pressure to give up religion would continue to be powerful. "I think people will become so bored with what religious groups have to offer that they will look elsewhere," he predicted.[154] Churchmen, too, could not help but sense the winds of change. Even the Vatican's official newspaper, after accepting John Lennon's apology, admitted that the Beatle was likely on to something. "It cannot be denied," said a church official, "that there is some foundation to the latest observations of John Lennon about atheism or the distraction of many people."[155]

The Beatles' soft revolution of values and tastes, their later dabbling in Eastern mysticism and celebration of hallucinogenic drugs, and their promotion of a kind of be-true-to-yourself religion illustrated the excesses and dangers of the decade. The LSD guru and bête noire of evangelicals and conservatives of every stripe Timothy Leary hailed the Beatles—with paisley, purple prose—as "a new young race of laughing freemen. Evolutionary agents sent by God, endowed with a mysterious power to create a new human species." In 1967, he went on to describe their Pied Piper status. "The Beatles have taken my place" as drug gurus, he ventured. In his estimation their latest effort, *Sgt Pepper's Lonely Hearts Club Band,* was "a complete celebration of LSD!"[156] Fittingly, since 1964 tens of thousands of screaming American fans sensed that the Beatles *had* changed things for good. On that point several women authors noted the difference the British foursome made. Even if the group did not spark a traditional political or social movement, they wrote, "Beatlemania was the first mass outburst of the sixties to feature women—in this case girls, who would not reach full adulthood until the seventies" when they would form "a genuinely political movement for women's liberation."[157]

Less than a month after the Beatles first touched down in New York City, the conservative Missouri Synod Lutheran denomination was already reflecting on the generational meaning of the band. A church spokesman said that it would be easy for believers to dismiss Beatlemania. They could class it with goldfish swallowing, the twist, or the Hula-Hoop fad. But that would be missing the point. Accordingly, this concerned Lutheran leader called on church people to understand the phenomenon in a different light. The music seemed to be designed especially for children and teenagers. Adults did not understand it, and that made it all the more appealing. Of his fellow Lutherans he asked, "When and where and how are local churches giving their 12-to 16-year-old members such markedly special attention that they feel: 'This is for us'?" Lutherans needed to show young people that they mattered and that their tastes in music and worship mattered.[158] Some Protestants on the left were asking similar questions about their sons and daughters. A prominent Baptist minister in Washington, DC, thought the Beatles and their music could serve as a wake-up call for the church. The liberal Clarence W. Cranford, who had served as president of the American Baptist Convention in the years of rock 'n' roll's rise, believed that the Beatles could illustrate a larger generational problem. The church was failing to meet the needs of youth, he preached from his pulpit in the summer of 1964. Beatlemania represented "the cry of youth for a greater recognition of their problems." Perhaps it was true that the church had, as the minister put it, "failed to speak out on great moral issues."[159] Such views were shared by a scholar of religion and history at Yale University who witnessed the social fracturing of the nation firsthand. The era was marked by growing "tendencies to alienation." A gloom set in, he said, and "neither the moral attitude nor the traditional theology of the major denominations had much appeal." For many, "the religious establishment was apprehended as both conventional and authoritarian."[160] Conservative Christians, now engaging in a little soul searching themselves, were asking: Was the religious establishment in trouble? Did a younger generation reject the ancient faith of their parents for the latest pop culture fads?[161]

The answer to those questions mattered dearly during the turbulent 1960s. The stakes were high for conservative Christians. By 1966 and 1967, it almost seemed to many observers inside and outside the church that, in fact, the Beatles were now more popular than Jesus. The devout feared the threat the Beatles posed to their churches, their youth, and society as a whole. Yet despite the confident predictions of secularization theorists or the many evangelical sermons about widespread apostasy, born-again Christianity was growing. At the same time, mainline, moderate American Protestantism was shrinking. Conservative groups that denounced Lennon and the Beatles with the most ferocity were poised to reap some of the biggest rewards in the coming decades. And their growth owed much to the strident tone and cultural stand the most conservative stalwarts were now taking.[162]

• 4 •

The Advent of Jesus Rock

Why should the devil have all the good music?
—Larry Norman, 1972

At the Woodstock Music and Art Fair in August 1969, four hundred thousand youths gathered to listen to some of the biggest-name rock bands of the era. For youngsters who thronged to the Catskill Mountains farm in New York, it was a pilgrimage like no other. Performers, some having to play through the steady summer rain, included Janis Joplin; the Who; Creedence Clearwater Revival; the Grateful Dead; Jimi Hendrix; Joan Baez; Canned Heat; Crosby, Stills, Nash, and Young; and Ravi Shankar. Rumors circulated that even the Beatles would join the star-studded roster. Their absence did little to diminish the once-in-a-lifetime gathering. The massive outdoor event helped define a generation. With typical hippie embellishment it was dubbed "An Aquarian Exposition: 3 Days of Peace & Music."

The *Guardian*'s New York–based correspondent Alistair Cooke was on the scene. The veteran journalist saw "hippies, rockers, pot people, and soul people" who "converged over the weekend on 600 acres rented out to them for $50,000 by a dairy farmer who believes 'we older people have to do more than we have done if the generation gap is to be closed.'" Cooke reported that there had been real fear that the festival would be "a rural version of the Chicago Democratic Convention riots" that took place almost exactly one year before.[1] It was anything but. Reporters at *Life* magazine were dazzled by the success of the festival. The whole affair was less a series of concerts "than a total experience," gushed a journalist with heady prose to match the flower-print optimism of the youth movement. It was "a phenomenon, a happening, a high adventure, a near disaster and, in a small way, a struggle for survival." A multipage photo essay commemorated it all, from scenes of skinny-dippers to the colorful hundreds of thousands spread out across a hillside. The wide eyes of stoned teenagers stared out at *Life*'s middlebrow readers.[2] All the fanfare proclaimed that this was *the* iconic event of 1960s youth culture.

Several years later, another large-scale rock event took place 1,500 miles to the southwest. Unlike Woodstock, this festival would not draw pot smokers and LSD droppers. There would be no displays of puckish nudism. Also unlike the cultural milestone of Woodstock, this latter festival would seldom be remembered or commemorated in the coming years and decades. Still, the Jesus Music Festival of Dallas's Explo '72 bore the unmistakable imprint of the counterculture. Dallas's streets were clogged with Jesus hippies, longhaired teens wearing bell-bottom jeans, bearded pentecostal youth pastors outfitted with sandals and tattered denim jackets, and a smattering of buttoned-down parents. Mothers and fathers looked generations apart from their sons and daughters. In early June, a range of rock and folk acts, along with high-profile preachers, took to a three-level, thirty-five-foot stage. The designer of the Pop Art psychedelic set had also created backdrops for the Grammy Awards.[3] The visual cues on display revealed how evangelical Christianity was now borrowing heavily from the aesthetics of the underground and the counterculture, replacing the message of liberation and personal freedom with the good news of the gospel and pentecostal power. Save for Johnny Cash and Kris Kristofferson, few of the performers who mounted the multicolored, cartoonish stage—Larry Norman, Love Song, Great Commission Company, Katie Hanley from *Godspell*, and Barry McGuire—had the cachet of Woodstock's celebrity lineup.[4]

Still, the 1972 fest—Godstock, as it came to be known—drew roughly two hundred thousand fans and marked a turning point for evangelicalism. The believers on hand were loud, committed, and engaging with pop culture in vibrant new ways. They hoped to spread the message of Jesus to the whole country by 1976. They pledged to do the same for the entire world by 1980. The new Jesus rock, influenced as it was by pentecostal beliefs and practice and indebted to folk rock, country, and hard rock, led believers to think about politics by way of theology. Bands and solo performers—influenced heavily by the charismatic movement and pentecostalism—sang of spiritual gifts, the embrace of Jesus as the only way to achieve happiness and avoid

A candid shot of Larry Norman at the Explo '72 festival, Cotton Bowl, Dallas, Texas, June 1972. Photo by and courtesy of Garry Slabaugh.

damnation, prophecy, the place of Israel in world history, the fast-approaching end of the world, and God's creation of the world in six literal days. Musicians described a personal Jesus who was an intimate friend, a moral guide, and the ultimate judge. Performers called for a revitalization of the church and admonished believers for failing to care for the poor, the sick, and the elderly. The music would later take on secular humanism, the pro-life movement, gays and lesbians, and religious pluralism. Already in 1972, an Associated Press reporter observed that Jesus people in California were registering Republican. "The conservative Republican viewpoint is closest to the laws of God," a twenty-five-year-old believer said bluntly.[5] In these early years, for the most part, Jesus hippies kept their distance from partisan politics. By the late 1970s and early 1980s that began to change, as Christian rock reflected the growing political conservatism of its artists and its audience while also mirroring the rightward turn of evangelical denominations. Simultaneously, new styles and musical experimentation would reshape church music and evangelical listening habits for decades to come.[6] Even some of the most revered leaders of conservative Protestantism would come to endorse Christian rock.

At the helm of Explo '72 stood Billy Graham, now fifty-three years old, his hair grown out a little longer in keeping with the times. (Ever aware of the latest trends, the famous evangelist had been reaching out to Christian hippies since 1971.) Clutching his Bible, he scanned the mass of youngsters and admonished them to grow in their faith. Three years before, *Life* magazine had highlighted Woodstock. Now its focus turned to the surprising story of so-called Jesus freaks, Billy Graham, and Godstock. Those gathered were largely evangelicals who were theologically conservative, but they did not look it. Reported *Life*, "Young people listened to hours of rock religious music and heard encouragement from [Billy] Graham, Dallas Cowboy quarterback Roger Staubach and Florida governor Reubin Askew." Pleased with the event, and glad to be recapturing the youth of America, Graham proclaimed, "We've sort of made an end run around the church." *Life*'s full-color cover story called Graham, "a hero to many of Explo's young evangelicals." He "spoke six times during the week."[7] America's preacher had made his peace with rock music and the counterculture, that is, in their sanctified incarnations. By the early 1970s, there were scores upon scores of Christian rock and folk outfits. Hard and psychedelic garage rock bands formed on the West Coast. Folk troubadours toured churches, coffeehouses, and teen hangouts in the Midwest. Beatlesque, guitar-driven bands performed for thousands at Jesus music festivals around the country. Men and women played country rock and acoustic music styled after Joni Mitchell, Gene Clark, Carole King, Graham Parsons, or Bob Dylan.[8]

It was a surprising turn of events. In the 1950s and through much of the 1960s, Graham, like many other evangelicals, had lashed out at rock 'n' roll. This degenerate genre was a clear sign of modern apostasy and disobedient youth. Screaming, crazed Beatlemaniacs seemed to prove as much. In the words of others, especially in the white South, rock 'n' roll was debased "jungle music." Such opposition had clear racist overtones. But mostly, for the conservative faithful, the music spawned disobedience and outright sin. In 1956, Billy Graham said he wished he could sit down and talk to the King of Rock 'n' Roll. He would, he remarked, try to convince Elvis to be a wholesome influence on the nation's youth. On stage at a 1958 youth rally held in San Francisco's Cow Palace, Graham told the youngsters in the audience about a young girl who "switched from Elvis to Jesus." Christ, rather than the side-burned, snarling singer, could become their personal hero. At other times Graham and his contemporaries were far more direct about rock music, linking it to wickedness and juvenile crime.[9]

By the standards of the late 1950s and 1960s, Graham's remarks were tame. Sermons, radio programs, and articles in denominational magazines routinely condemned rock 'n' roll. It is true that the American establishment opposed rock music as well. But what was sinful or debauched to conservative Christians was merely silly, absurd, or tasteless to mainstream critics. Journalists from the establishment press graded rock 'n' roll as crude and vulgar. It had slithered out of the swamps of Mississippi. But the music, for many such critics, was harmless and novel, if idiotic.[10]

By the mid-1960s, as rock proved to have longevity and as the music dealt with more serious themes, major newspapers and magazines began to favorably review the album-oriented releases of the Beatles, the Rolling Stones, Bob Dylan, the Mamas and the Papas, the Kinks, and the Lovin' Spoonful. By 1966, a Louis Harris poll revealed that 21 percent of adults in America listened to rock 'n' roll. That was small when compared with the 87 percent of teens who listened to the music.[11] As the genre matured, adult interest grew. It was still largely anathema in conservative religious circles. Evangelicals feared any softening of musical standards. It represented a kind of bargain with the devil. One Southern Baptist minister illustrated his late 1950s sermon with references to the evil fruits of rock 'n' roll. The preacher highlighted the violence and mayhem that accompanied concerts. He drew on psychiatrists and others to explain the allure and power of the music. It was surely "the work of the devil among those who do not yield to Christ."[12]

Strangely enough, though, less than twenty years after the start of the rock 'n' roll revolution, and as conservative Christians came to endorse pop music and youth culture, even America's pastor had changed his mind. By the time Elvis had finally succumbed to his insatiable appetite for prescription drugs, Graham had largely accepted the southern entertainer and rock 'n' roll pioneer into the fold. "I never met him," said Graham shortly after Elvis's death in August 1977. "But I believe I will see him in heaven," Graham remarked, "because Elvis Presley was very deeply religious, especially in the last two or three years."[13]

If opposition to wild, devil-inspired rock music and all it represented was once so pervasive among conservative Christians, it is a wonder that something as unusual as Jesus rock emerged at all. The generational dynamics of the 1960s played a key role in the rise and acceptance of the new genre. By the middle of the decade, an older generation of evangelicals had begun to fear that they had lost touch with teens. Youngsters, even those within the church, were dissatisfied with the staid, bland denominational music handed down to them. Beyond that, millions of men and women who were under thirty were taking part in what some were calling "the great refusal." They rejected, at least for the time being, the values, aspirations, and ideals of their elders. Beat music, soul, surf rock, and then psychedelic music were cultural expressions of this "great refusal." So too were other new or changing art forms, as well as a more avid leftist brand of politics.

Much commentary and debate in the 1960s centered on the yawning divide between young and old. The critically acclaimed 1967 films *The Graduate,* starring Dustin Hoffman, and *Bonnie and Clyde,* featuring Warren Beatty and Faye Dunaway, projected the tensions between young and old onto the silver screen. Social activists and antiwar radical Jerry Rubin's oft-repeated words "Don't trust anyone over thirty" became a kind of slogan for restless, dissatisfied youth. One of those not to be trusted was Columbia University president Grayson Kirk, who helped define the term "generation gap" in 1968 and became a walking symbol of the maligned establishment. Kirk was convinced that youth had rejected the authority of their elders. The teens and twenty-somethings, slouched and shuffling onto his campus, he said, were nihilists with a violent streak. When Columbia's campus shut down as a result of student protests and the occupation of buildings in spring 1968, it seemed to only confirm Kirk's horrible suspicions.[14]

The Students for a Democratic Society, scourge of President Kirk and college administrators around the United States, laid out an agenda in 1962 that spelled trouble. The New Left group's *Port Huron Statement* displayed its optimism about the potential of youth and its scathing pessimism about a corrupt establishment. "Men have unrealized potential for self-cultivation, self-direction, self-understanding, and creativity," it challenged. "It is this potential that we regard as crucial and to which we appeal, not to the human potentiality for violence, unreason, and submission to authority."[15] With each passing year, the SDS gained in influence and, for conservatives, notoriety. At protests that the group and like-minded organizations sponsored from Berkeley to Columbia, students sang out the lines of the Beatles' unlikely 1966 hit song and title track to their animated feature *Yellow Submarine*. There was a more anxious, menacing side to such protest activity as well. A Columbia University student and a leader in the university's SDS chapter, Mark Rudd, penned a caustic letter to Kirk. In it he addressed the generation gap. "I see it as a real conflict between those who run things now—you, Grayson Kirk—and those who feel oppressed by and disgusted with the society you rule," Rudd lashed out. He ended his philippic on a provocative note, signing off with the words of a black radical activist and author: "LeRoi Jones, whom I'm sure you don't like a whole lot: 'Up against the wall, motherfucker, this is a stick-up.' "[16]

A year later, Grace Slick, of the San Francisco–based psychedelic rock band Jefferson Airplane, included a version of that inflammatory line in the band's 1969 song "We Can Be Together." She sang it out, unedited, when the group performed live on the *The Dick Cavett Show*.[17] The profane posturing of rock stars was just one of the many ways they set themselves apart from the thirty-and-up crowd. "For the youth of the 1960s," says folk musician and critic Elijah Wald, "the 'generation gap' between our elders and us was an article of faith, and rock music was its most potent symbol."[18] Accordingly, the folk troubadour Bob Dylan warned elders of the youthquake to come in his influential 1964 song "The Times They Are A-changin'." Writing in the *Nation*, Theodore Roszak used Dylan to trace the transformation of the era's soundscape. The Minnesota-born singer-songwriter, said Roszak in 1968,

> commands respect among all segments of the dissenting youth culture. Dylan's early songs are traditional folk protests, laying forth obvious issues of social justice: anti-boss, anti-war, anti-exploitation. Then, quite suddenly, rather as if Dylan had come to the conclusion that the conventional Woody Guthrie ballad didn't reach deep enough, the songs turn surrealistic and psychedelic.[19]

Other groups followed Dylan's lead and began experimenting with aggressive protest songs that challenged the powers that be and raised the generational flag. The English mod rock band the Who stuttered out their lyrics of defiance in their 1965 hit "My Generation," which climbed to number two on the UK singles chart. Their stage routine, which they first brought to the United States in March 1967, had developed into a self-destructive act, with band members smashing, throwing, punching, and kicking their instruments before awestruck crowds. They were a tornado of fury, frantic drum fills, and whirring guitar feedback. The Who were soon one of the most talked about, popular bands in the United States. They performed "My Generation" on *The Smothers Brothers Comedy Hour* on September 15, 1967. In the crashing finale, smoke rose behind the amplifiers while songwriter Pete Townshend hurled his guitar into the air, whacked it onto the stage, and then rammed it into a speaker. The color televised performance ended with a pyrotechnic explosion that ripped apart Keith Moon's drum set and permanently damaged Townshend's hearing.[20] It was a performance designed to shock and thrill. "Rock is subversive," said a critic in *Life* magazine in 1968, "not because it seems to authorize sex, dope and cheap thrills, but because it encourages its audience to make their own judgments about societal taboos."[21] Worried evangelical parents would have agreed in horror. For them the distorted music had become the theme music for cultural liberation, drug experimentation, and campus riots.

The divide between young and old, child and parent, had already taken center stage in the years before the Who's explosive performances lit up television screens and before the major campus uprisings of 1968 and 1969. The generation gap entered the lexicon and joined other anxiety-producing "gaps" of the age. In the late 1950s, Democrats had charged that a growing missile gap would damage America's military might. Critics of President Johnson spoke of a credibility gap, especially in relation to the commander in chief's clandestine policies on Vietnam. The country had an abundance of disconnections. *Life* magazine joked that at least "there will never be a gap gap."[22] Richard Nixon speechwriter and columnist William Safire pointed out the kind of suspicion inherent in all the gap rhetoric: "shortage, lack, insufficiency, a falling short, or a gulf between."[23] Editorials about the "gulf between" young and old not only filled the pages of *Life*, *Reader's Digest*, and *Newsweek* magazines but also inspired handwringing essays in dozens of Christian magazines and denominational journals. It was also, especially from the late 1960s forward, regular sermon fodder.[24]

The sheer size of the segment of the population that was under thirty made it impossible to ignore. In 1964, the year that marked the end of the baby boom, 40 percent of the population of the United States was under the age of nineteen.[25] In that same year students were crowding onto college campuses in ever-greater numbers. Before World War II only roughly 14 percent of America's college-age students went on to higher education. With the GI Bill (1944) and the coming of postwar prosperity, a university education was in reach of even those in the lower economic brackets. By 1961, 38 percent of college-age students were enrolled. Then, by 1970, that had jumped to 50 percent.[26]

Who were these new college students and teens? asked preachers from their pulpits and Sunday school teachers in their basement classrooms. Youth appeared to have lost respect for most of what evangelical pastors, parents, and teachers held so dear. Teens and college-age sons and daughters subjected military service and patriotic love of country to scornful critique. By these lights the church and the political establishment were corrupt and out of touch. The ballads, hymns, and swing music of the World War II generation sounded nothing like the popular beat, rhythm and blues, soul, and garage rock that teens in the swinging sixties preferred.[27]

Writing in the *New Republic,* Henry Fairlie fretted, "We are in danger of becoming obsessed by the young: in our lives, in our thinking, in our politics."[28] Such warnings did little to halt the national fascination with youth and with teens in particular. Echoing some of the romantic countercultural superlatives of the day, Theodore Roszak served up a "heroic generalization" about contemporary youth in the pages of the *Nation.* What those under thirty were "up to" in 1968, he proclaimed, was "nothing less than a reorganization of the prevailing state of personal and social consciousness."[29] By the time he made that hyperbolic observation the national focus on youth had become almost obsessive. Reading the tea leaves of the "now generation" occupied television commentators, editorial teams, campus administrators, and denominational officials. *Time* magazine named those who were "Twenty-Five and Under" its "Man of the Year" in early 1967. In line with the generational stereotyping of the day, *Time* proclaimed that this was certainly not the "silent generation," whose members came of age in the 1940s and 1950s. "Today the young are anything but silent," it reported in its cover story.

> Americans under 25, who will soon outnumber their elders, exhibit many features, make many statements, suggest many pictures, often conflicting—they are well-educated, affluent, rebellious, responsible, pragmatic, idealistic, brave, "alienated," and hopeful. Who they are and what they stand for are the subjects under study. . . . To a generation that seems to be saying, "Pay attention to us," we might well reply that indeed we do. In the past three years, TIME has run more than 150 stories on one aspect or another of youth, including covers on U.S. teenagers, on London's youthful takeover of staid English culture, on young Americans' feelings about the draft. The essay section also examined the problem of "Not Losing One's Cool about the Young."[30]

That, of course, was easier said than done. Many evangelicals, like conservative Americans in general, seemed to be losing their cool when they discussed baby boomers' values, politics, and musical tastes.

The well-known journalist and political operative Clayton Fritchey summed up the views of many in 1967, reasoning that the "alienation between those who fought the last war and those who have come of age since then is almost certainly the most severe in the history of America."[31] It was nearly impossible to avoid the debate about youth. Church leaders stepped into the debate, armed with their own opinions. "Teenagers are bugging America," observed one fundamentalist in the middle of the decade. For proof, he said, "go no farther than the magazine rack of the nearest drugstore. Take a look at the most popular publications. Those that are appealing directly to teens are usually discussing them." The large size of the baby boom generation, he suggested, was one reason teens were on the minds of so many.[32] That was also the view of experts on the topic. In 1966, an academic observer suggested that the generation gap was as wide as it was because of the sheer number of those under twenty-five. These youngsters had also not weathered the hardships that their parents and grandparents endured.[33]

Young people, said evangelicals picking up on this theme, were inexperienced. They were easy prey. And now teens were much more exposed to bad influences through television, the movies, rock music, and questionable literature. Worst of all, concluded some observers in the church, Christian teenagers represented a very small minority of the overall population. That holy remnant could have only a limited impact. A leader of the Church of the Nazarene in Kansas City figured he knew why this minority of the young faithful was being ignored by the larger culture. In 1969, W. T. Purkiser observed that "the bizarre and the off-beat always get more attention than the 'ordinary.'" He denounced those "dozen long-haired, unwashed yippies shouting obscenities [who] can provoke a riot and the story is flashed around the world." These made the front-page news and won the attention of TV anchormen. When thousands of clean-cut Nazarene young men gathered for a missionary rally—with their crew cuts, penny loafers, and holiness hymnals in hand—the local press would bury the story on the last pages.[34]

This was the same kind of logic that President Nixon broadcast to the entire country in his famous Silent Majority speech on November 3, 1969. With a homey sentimentality that had now become the president's trademark since his famous Checkers speech, Nixon looked into the camera and said gravely, "I know it may not be fashionable to speak of patriotism or national destiny these days. But I feel it is appropriate to do so on this occasion."[35] Numerous evangelical parents identified with Nixon's America. Embattled and bruised, they *were* that silent majority. But now loud youths, singing profane rock songs and marching with signs, seemed to be taking their country in another direction.[36] The historian Daniel Williams notes, "Evangelicals were ecstatic about Nixon because he positioned himself as a moral leader defending religious values against secular attack." In 1968, says Williams, Nixon's "image as a moral traditionalist was crucial in winning the evangelical vote" and helped him appeal to Catholics as well.[37] They wanted a president who could stand up for what was good and true.

They wanted their children to be similarly prepared for righteous service. Evangelical teens might have been few and not able to get the kind of attention their disrespectful, longhaired classmates garnered, said the education secretary for the Church of the Nazarene, but they could still have a large influence on their peers. Willis Snowbarger asked what it was that teens and college-age youths in his church wanted. In an act of ventriloquism, he stated in 1967, "Like their unchurched peers, they face fearsome challenges of revolutionary times and feel deeply and intensely some of the timeless questions of mankind." They wondered who they were, how they fit in, and what the meaning of life was, Snowbarger surmised. They wanted to be genuine, never phony. Taking a jab at the prevailing "new morality" on college campuses, he thought that Nazarene teens wanted to know if there were "changeless values or is everything relative to time and situation." Those students who were not poisoned by the New Left or professors at secular schools would discover the right answers.[38] Another in the Nazarene denomination counseled youngsters to embrace the landmarks of the faith, the General Rules. A version of these had been in place since the founding of the church in 1908 at Pilot Point, Texas. These included prohibitions against dancing, drinking, smoking, wearing revealing clothing, and viewing movies. "But don't sell them short," pleaded Leslie Parrott from Portland, Oregon. "And don't rule them out as irrelevant because of *your* generation gap."[39] That was a tough sell. Nazarene youths, like those in the Campus Crusade for Christ, would make halting attempts to evangelize their campuses at a time when universities and colleges were overcrowded with new students, many of them questioning the faith of their parents and the ethics of the political establishment.

Rare was an outright dismissal of the much-discussed generation gap. Southern Baptist minister W. A. Criswell, now serving as president of his denomination, weighed in. The supposed generation gap was a ubiquitous topic of conversation, he admitted from his Dallas pulpit in 1969. But, in fact, he retorted, "there has always been a generation gap."[40] Anticommunist fundamentalist crusader Billy James Hargis was another doubter. From his Tulsa headquarters he reckoned that there was nothing all that novel or unusual about the generational divide. "Historically, young people feel that they know more than their parents and can solve problems a lot differently and more successfully," the controversial leader said with confidence. "This is nothing new, and, actually it is not a bad feeling." But concerning the campus radicalism, the new rock music, and violence of the era, Hargis was adamant. Hippies and yippies, in his telling, were only the dupes of communist conspirators and radical professors.[41] Evangelical ideals of purity and forbearance looked to be endangered, especially on the nation's private and state campuses. Like Hargis, Norman Vincent Peale had mocked the boyish, unkempt Beatles in 1966. Now Peale jumped into the debates about campus politics and the new morality. He rebuked the professors and "the treason of some of our intellectuals—writers, thinkers, philosophers—who have done their best to make sex immorality seem natural and normal, and self-control in sex puritanical, old fashioned, or downright queer."[42]

Some of those vilified professors, however, hoped to bridge the generation gap. Unlike Hargis or Criswell they did not dismiss the generational dilemma out of hand. A psychology professor at Stanford University offered some remedies. Parents could try to engage their children in conversations that interested youngsters, suggested John D. Black. Mom and Dad should also ask more questions and listen better. He suggested they listen to their sons' and daughters' LPs. "Your auditory system can adapt," he assured parents. "The music of each generation is an integral part of its culture and a clue to its concerns."[43] Parents might have preferred the traditional pop of Rosemary Clooney to the growling blues of Janis Joplin. Yet, said Black, they might never really understand their sons and daughters if they refused to bridge the musical gap.

It was little wonder, then, that youngsters did not seem to be enjoying church worship, which like music, was stamped with the tastes of an older generation. A writer in a Baptist student magazine thought that church worship—ritualistic, wooden, and formal—seemed "to be a remnant of another age and another generation."[44] Some, like Professor Black at Stanford, were asking their fellow believers to take a moment to consider just how different the world of a teenager was from the world of an adult. In 1968, a Methodist educator was asking just that. He used the local teenage hangout, called the Cellar, to illustrate his point. It was housed in an old converted factory building. Teens flocked to it, where they danced to loud, heavy music. The lighting and decorations were bizarre. He summed up his impressions: "They dress differently, think differently, have a style different from any previous generation. Altogether they are around 19 million strong." His church needed to adjust its curriculum and its approach to better minister to youth. There had not been a major overhaul of his church's educational materials since 1952. The new curriculum, put together with a painful awareness of the need for relevance, asked youngsters to consider milestones in life and to debate the major social issues of the day. Perhaps that would work, hoped Methodist educators.[45]

Similar reevaluations took place around the United States. Amid the social and cultural ferment of the age, faculty and administrators at Catholic universities and colleges rethought what had seemed to be the time-honored truths of higher education. The introduction of coeducation, the relocation of campuses, and the adoption of relevant curriculum all helped reshape Catholic identity, following the changes of the Second Vatican Council. On campuses across the country in the late 1960s and early 1970s, student groups and allied professors pressed for a more inclusive curriculum that spoke to the concerns of minority groups and the disenfranchised and called for new ways of teaching. Universities haltingly responded with the creation of black studies, Chicano / a studies, and women's studies. Some of the changes would prove short lived. One historian describes the cynical maneuvering of higher education officials in these years. "American university authorities," writes Gerard J. DeGroot, "proved remarkably adept at containing, manipulating and re-directing the tide of change, so much so that, when the shouting ceased and the sit-ins ended, status returned resolutely to quo."[46] Regardless, though, the shift in teaching as well as the new programs and curriculum represented a broader accommodation to the demands of youth and the ceaseless quest for relevancy. Church youth leaders, pastors, and denominational officials awakened to new needs within their organizations.[47]

Still, quite a few conservatives refused to budge. "Relevance" sounded to them like just another word for "compromise." Numerous evangelicals dealt with the problems of youth through scolding rebukes, biting ridicule, or telling morality tales about rock-addled teens gone astray. The president of the evangelical Fuller Theological Seminary in Pasadena, California, figured that the usual way of reaching the lost just would not work. Generalizing heavily, he reasoned that all appeals to the Bible or a higher law would be shouted down as authoritarian. The "typical high school or university student," he remarked, "has neither a philosophical nor a theological world-view by which truth is gauged." Teens cared nothing for historical context. The typical student shrugs "at the law of contradiction, he sneers at the traditions of the elders. His own private opinion is his sole authority."[48]

Evangelicals like Fuller's president could turn to experts. For example, Marshall McLuhan described how different the "now generation" was in his *Understanding Media.* With breathless prose, McLuhan observed,

> The young people who have experienced a decade of TV have naturally imbibed an urge toward involvement in depth that makes all the remote visualized goals of usual culture seem not only unreal but irrelevant, and not only irrelevant but anemic. It is the total involvement in all-inclusive *nowness* that occurs in young lives via TV's mosaic image.[49]

Put simply, the old ways of reaching young people would no longer work. Drawing on McLuhan's summary of youth, a writer in one evangelical magazine figured "the medium is the message, and the medium of rock music is an all encompassing sound." The resultant "gratification of the senses" strictly appealed to youth. The church's response to the community of rock 'n' roll, observed this critic, amounted to a "refusal to confront the world in which youth are living." It then followed that teens were right to think that the church had little or nothing to offer them.[50]

Some in the conservative Christian camp thought all this talk seemed too pessimistic and deterministic. Doubters scoffed at the cult of nowness. "Can the Church Reach the Teens of '65?" asked a headline in the conservative *Moody Monthly* magazine. For an answer the editor turned to the director of Youth for Christ International, Bill Eakin. That organization had long been a model of youth engagement. Its rallies featured peppy music and premiered evangelical films about rock 'n' roll, juvenile crime, and the pitfalls of youthful indiscretion. Teenagers were not entirely lost to the church, Eakin reasoned, although there were significant challenges facing conservative believers. Had the church lost touch with youngsters? he was asked. "Not completely," Eakin responded, "but certainly in part. . . . But unless we get moving and rapidly, we're going to keep on losing our kids."[51] The church had become far too associated with its moral prohibitions and stringent rules. (Nazarene officials who took pride in their General Rules could not change that hard fact.) The Bible, too, seemed irrelevant to teens.

For others, the old tried and true ways of Christian ministry, church music, and solid Bible education needed no altering. Chasing after nowness and relevance or the latest musical fad would not do. But even the most rock-ribbed, right-wing Protestant had reason for concern. A conservative Methodist organization in North Hollywood worried about the growing divide between young and old. In 1970, the group frantically asked, "Who is to blame for our generation gap—for youth's war on the ideas and ideals of their parents' generation? Where did so many of today's youth learn to despise their parents, their religion, their country, their flag, and the Western culture?" In their firm warnings, they blamed liberal leaders and weak-willed Sunday school teachers. Answering the cry for social and political liberation, they offered the firm, conservative truths of the Bible.[52]

Questions lingered. Could the Good Book provide answers to problems that seemed so new, so unique to this younger generation? Teenagers had always misbehaved. There had always been barriers between young and old. But youths had certainly not used recreational drugs as they now were doing in ever-greater numbers. A 1969 Gallup poll revealed that 22 percent of college students had tried marijuana. It was the drug of choice for rock musicians, who celebrated its use in songs like Bob Dylan's "Rainy Day Women #12 & 35" (1966), the Yellow Balloon's "Panama Red" (1967), the Beatles' "With a Little Help from My Friends" (1967), Fraternity of Man's "Don't Bogart Me" (1969), or Commander Cody and His Lost Planet Airmen's "Seeds and Stems (Again)" (1971). Gallup first began its college drug survey in 1967. The new poll was just one sign of the relatively recent rise of recreational drug use. In that first year only 5 percent of students said that they had tried pot. In 1971, Gallup polling agents fanned out to fifty-seven campuses across the country and interviewed 1,063 students. By then, 51 percent said they had smoked grass. A study of 2,141 students at the University of Maryland calculated that pot use was on the rise in the late 1960s, climbing from 15 percent in 1967 to 35 percent in 1969. Most staggering of all were the studies done on particular locales, like San Francisco, where a third of women and a half of men surveyed in 1968 said they had tried marijuana. Particularly shocking to religious conservatives was another growing drug statistic. Gallup reported in its 1969 survey that

10 percent of students had taken barbiturates and 4 percent had dropped LSD.[53]

In early 1966, the *Christian Science Monitor* spotlighted the rise in drug abuse. Seekers of kicks still represented only a minority of the population. "But the spread of the problem," observed a reporter, "has caused concern in two areas: Casual addictions slipped into by youth. Addictions secretly developing in the home among bored housewives and overwrought businessmen." More typical were stories that focused on youth. Marijuana and amphetamines, the preferred mood elevators for rock stars and their millions of fans, had a new appeal for teens in the mid-1960s.[54] So too did LSD.

As early as 1966, *Time* reported that LSD use had spread across college and university campuses. As many as ten thousand University of California students had used it by March 1966. For its psychedelic apostles, like former Harvard professor Timothy Leary or the British band the Moody Blues, LSD was a balm that could heal a broken nation. In the fall of 1966, one evangelical writer commented on the frightening aspect of LSD use that was "sweeping college and university campuses." The drug was reported to make young men and women feel that they had divine powers. Satan was using this mind-altering substance, and the wild music that accompanied its ingestion, to destroy a generation, he worried.[55] Another reported that Leary's followers used the drug as a sacrament in their folk-rock masses.[56]

Controversy about the drug and its use by rock stars awakened evangelicals and other conservatives to new risks in the late 1960s. In June 1967, Paul McCartney gave a *Life* magazine reporter his opinion about the recent vogue for mind-altering chemicals. Soon to turn twenty-five, McCartney had been the last of the Beatles to drop acid, preferring alcohol, amphetamines, and marijuana instead. He was now sporting a droopy Victorian mustache and was often kitted out with the latest in quasi-historical, urban dandy apparel: capes, gaudy ties, vintage hats, a burgundy velvet jacket. He had also become the latest spokesman for LSD. The influential singer and London scenester told a journalist, "After I took it, it opened my eyes." The bachelor Beatle viewed LSD as a kind of "universal cure-all," the reporter said. "We only use one tenth of our brain," Paul gushed, combining the latest in science with the mystical panaceas of the paisley underground. "Just think what all we could accomplish if we could tap that hidden part! It would mean a whole new world. If politicians would take LSD, there wouldn't be any more war, poverty or famine."[57] Several months later, a *Time* magazine writer declared that the Fab Four's pronouncements were taking on the weight of prophecy for their young, impressionable fans.[58] Perhaps with this in mind, reporters prodded McCartney with further questions about his use and promotion of the hallucinogen. McCartney told newsmen in London that LSD made him a more adjusted and tolerant person while also bringing him closer to God. Pressed about it, he backpedaled some, saying that he did not advocate its use. One year after John Lennon's scandalous comment about the group being more popular than Jesus, Paul was now in the glare of the limelight. Members of Parliament and British medical professionals denounced him.[59]

Stateside, ministers, politicians, and laypeople had even more ammunition to use against the "prophetic" Beatles. But Paul was not alone in his outlook. Others in the emerging counterculture blurred the boundaries between the sacred and the revolutionary. At a 1967 happening on the streets of Berkeley, one marcher held aloft a sign that read "Jesus was a hippy."[60] This was not the Jesus of the Southern Baptist Convention. It was not the Jesus that Billy Graham described in his crusades. Graham was now offering his opinions about the LSD rage among pop stars and youth. He targeted what he considered to be the spiritual confusion of misguided hippies. With McCartney's psychedelic evangelism comments making headlines, Graham counseled, "The Bible says, 'Be not drunk with wine wherein is excess, but be filled with the Spirit.'" It was beyond doubt, he warned, "that LSD and its advocates are about as far away from First Century Christianity as one can get." For anyone confusing Jesus with modern-day hippies, Graham hoped his remarks would settle the matter.[61]

Even before McCartney's psychedelic epiphany, evangelicals had been striking out against acid and the rock musicians and gurus who championed it and other hallucinogens. Graham's brother-in-law and fellow evangelist Leighton Ford similarly took aim at LSD and the pseudo-religious culture that surrounded it. The handsome evangelist—described by some as a "latter-day Jimmy Stewart"—was leading a youth crusade in Seattle in May 1967. At the rally Ford looked out over the mass of 3,500 young people seated in the Seattle Center Arena. "A new religion has been calling to the 'turned on' generation," he told them. "This is the gospel according to LSD and the apostle of this cult is Timothy Leary." Borrowing from the very words of that vilified ex–Harvard professor, Ford admonished his listeners that only through a commitment to Christ could youngsters "turn [their] life on all the way."[62]

Believers cheered on the efforts of politicians and pastors in their fight against the nihilistic culture of new bohemians and rock stars that they thought prevailed on university campuses. Governor Ronald Reagan, who like Nixon became a revered politician in conservative religious circles, had to stay away from University of California campuses. His presence could lead to a riot. In 1966, Reagan delivered a jeremiad at San Francisco's Cow Palace on the moral dangers of the rock counterculture. He held in his hand a report from the district attorney of Alameda County. In urgent tones he read from it the lurid details of a multimedia psychedelic rock show. The Berkeley University event had attracted more than three thousand impressionable youngsters, "including a number of less than college age juveniles," Reagan related.

> And all during the dance, movies were shown on two screens at the opposite ends of the gymnasium. These movies were the only lights in the gym proper. They consisted of color sequences that gave the appearance of different colored liquid spreading across the screen, followed by shots of men and women on occasion, shots where the men and women's nude torsos on occasion [appeared]. And persons twisted and gyrated in provocative and sensual fashion.[63]

Richard Nixon was later to the culture wars battlefront, but took to the field much as Reagan had. Nixon proclaimed, "It is not too strong a statement to declare that this is the way civilizations begin to die." He warned, "The process is altogether too familiar to those who would survey the wreckage of history: assault and counterassault, one extreme leading to the opposite extreme, the voices of reason and calm discredited."[64] Nixon's prophecy resonated with evangelicals. In the mid and late 1960s, they were becoming painfully aware of the rise in drug use in high schools and on college campuses from coast to coast.

When Nixon confidant Billy Graham surveyed the so-called new morality of the 1960s and the culture of permissiveness that it bred on college campuses, he was sure about the negative impact it all would have. Rock music accompanied the hedonism of youthful abandon. Was it any wonder that college campuses had become so wicked and so lost? he asked rhetorically in 1965. "Even churchmen are encouraging them in immorality," he said with astonishment. Graham denounced the liberal, tolerant culture that had invaded even large denominations. To counter that pernicious influence of relativists, Graham offered granite-solid advice from scripture: "The Bible says . . . The Bible teaches . . . The Bible also tells us . . ."[65]

Others were not so convinced of the power of staunch biblicism. Something had to give. Youth leaders needed to reach out to teens and twenty-somethings, even meeting them on their own terms if they had to. Denominational leaders cast about for political and cultural solutions. A former professor from Pennsylvania State University established the Christian World Liberation Front, which aimed to evangelize countercultural college students and wayward young people.[66] Others in mainline denominations "turned on" to youth culture and rock music in ways that proved shocking to more skeptical pastors and parishioners. The stodgy Episcopal Church, quipped a religion commentator during the so-called 1967 Summer of Love, "always the symbol of The Establishment, good manners and white gloves," housed priests who were now "in the forefront of what might be called the new, swinging, blue-jeans religion." One representative minister turned up at a fund-raiser in a bow tie and madras shorts. Another showed up at hippie hangouts to discuss marijuana and LSD with longhaired teens and twenty-somethings. Paul Moore, the suffragan bishop of Washington, DC, even allowed the playing of rock music in the National Cathedral's Bethlehem Chapel.[67]

Few would help believers better understand the secular culture around them than one particularly eccentric and influential native of Philadelphia. In the 1960s and 1970s, Francis Schaeffer—an aging, longhaired, and lederhosen-wearing American prophet—attracted a growing following of baby boomers and those evangelicals and fundamentalists who were dissatisfied with the cultural isolationism of their traditions. With his wife, Edith, he had founded L'Abri in the Swiss Alps in 1955.

The lecture and study programs held at this center and retreat offered religious seekers, disaffected evangelicals, and hippie drifters the solace and religious answers they had been looking for. Schaeffer, who *Newsweek* would later call a fundamentalist guru, spoke directly to those under thirty about the philosophy of existentialism, trends in modern abstract art, and the music of the Rolling Stones and the Beatles.[68] That was a major departure from the standard approach to evangelical ministry. Writing in *Christianity Today* in 1966, a youth worker remarked, "Christian colleges have generally kept their students roped away from the dangers—real or imaginary—of the outside world."[69] Schaeffer, by contrast, freed young believers to think critically about pop culture and to critique what he considered to be the morally bankrupt worldview of the modern West. The decline of moral absolutes, he regularly thundered, was leaving a civilization in ruins.

Decades after Schaeffer's death, the English Christian social critic Os Guinness reflected on his legacy and influence. He recalled how a friend had brought him along to hear "a strange little man in Swiss knickers" speak about the critical issues of the day. "He had a massive impact on the lives of individuals, including me," said Guinness, "but his wider significance was as . . . a door opener. When almost no Evangelicals were thinking about culture and connecting unconnected dots, Schaeffer not only did it himself but blazed a trail for countless others to follow." Guinness then made the pilgrimage to L'Abri after finishing his undergraduate degree in 1967.[70] Some of those dots Schaeffer was connecting for his rapt young listeners included the lyrics of Led Zeppelin songs, the experimental music of John Cage, the modernist theology of Paul Tillich, and the splatter paintings of Jackson Pollock. Many evangelicals and fundamentalists, long cut off from the fresh air of cultural engagement, found such explorations to be exhilarating.[71]

Even those who were not as adventurous as Schaeffer and his followers were finding it harder and harder to avoid pop culture and pop music. That was the case even though the decision to use pop songs to carry an evangelical message was not easy to make. Would such music defile the message? asked troubled believers. Would it amount to an unforgivable compromise? others wondered. "We evangelicals," proclaimed a speaker at a 1969 Wheaton College convocation, "are a conservative lot—conservative because we have something worth conserving." He said to the crowd at Billy Graham's alma mater,

> We don't change our methods and materials very easily because we do not want to tamper with the gospel itself and sometimes we are not sure just where the unchangeable gospel leaves off and the methodology of proclaiming it begins. In spite of our conservative attitudes we are affected more than we sometimes realize by the rest of the Christian world as well as the non-Christian world about us.[72]

Such challenges of the era and the need to reach youth sparked numerous innovations in ministry.

In 1966, a Methodist minister from Elgin, Illinois, wrote in *Christianity Today* that he had long tried to ignore the "caterwauling and frenetic beat, beat, beat" of rock music. He came to believe that his disdain and disinterest was a mistake. "We dare not chew our fingernails and lament about popular music as an affront to the soul and the senses," he now thought.[73] Lincoln B. Justice, a Methodist pastor in Nebraska, went a step further in 1967 and 1968. Knowing the kind of influence popular musicians exerted on young people, he played songs by Simon & Garfunkel; Peter, Paul, and Mary; Pete Seeger; Bob Dylan; and others to illustrate his sermons. An eighty-year-old great-grandmother in his congregation, somewhat perplexed, told him, "I never listened much to that kind of music before, but you know, I kind of like it." The pop cultural pastor admitted that he would not have done something like this just two years before. But now, like so many others in evangelical and mainline churches, he "had a growing dissatisfaction with the effectiveness of the conventional sermon." The temper of the times seemed to demand something more. Some adventurous souls were plainly calling it *relevance.* The generational gap seemed to make it necessary for clergymen and their denominations to find new modes of outreach: rap sessions on politics and war, work with the poor in urban centers, rock record listening groups, or debates about pop culture and faith. In Nebraska, Justice asked himself, "With all the modern techniques of communication that are available, why do we seem to think that a 'sermon' must be a monologue to a silent audience?" The standard approach looked as hopelessly out of date as the hand-crank Victrola or the icebox.[74]

A University of Southern California professor of choral and church music, along with numerous like-minded Protestants, hailed the updating of creaky and old-fashioned sacred music. Californians would largely lead the charge for new, experimental music in congregations. "Much of the musical, liturgical and multimedia experimentation that has been going on is healthy," he reasoned. "The traditional overconservatism of the church in the arts is at last being challenged and in not a few cases the church has been involved in some artistic pioneering."[75] Another religious music educator and composer was certain, from the vantage of 1967, that the church was "in the midst of a transitional period that marks the end of one great creative epoch and the beginning of an era of uncertainty, unknown experimentation, a transition that may well take at least a century."[76] Just how to deal with such shifts in musical taste and new aesthetic sensibilities dominated the attention of Catholics, evangelicals, and mainline Protestants for at least the next decade.

The design of Christian magazines slowly began to change, reflecting the era's obsession with youth and novelty. Many of these visual innovations laid the groundwork for Explo '72's vibrant stage artwork and packaging. By the time of the large Dallas festival, numerous conservative denominations and parachurch groups had been toying with the fads of Aquarian design. A growing number of Catholics and mainline Protestants began to wrap their message in youth culture packaging. By the late 1960s, even conservative evangelical magazines and newspapers like *Christian Life* and *Eternity* had adopted the bulging or wavy psychedelic typography and the mod Pop Art swirls then in vogue. Methodist and Baptist student publications used the buzzing, garish color palette of rock music posters and gatefold LP covers. Some fundamentalists made this aesthetic concession as well. Hippie, art nouveau–inspired design; knock-off Yellow Submarine graphics; and dazzling Day-Glo colors proliferated in an effort to bridge the generation gap.[77] Not all older readers thought the changes in design were appropriate or fitting. After the Missouri Synod's *Lutheran Witness* featured a modern-style, heavy-brush-stroke painting of the holy family on its cover in

December 1966, one reader upbraided the "deplorable and vulgar" depiction. Another felt the image was "grotesque and offensive." "It was almost as if the artist was ashamed of the human face," wrote a disgruntled woman from Port Townsend, Washington. One more thought the "baby Jesus looks like a circus clown!"[78]

In the years ahead, conservative Christians became more and more comfortable with changes in design and visual culture, inspired largely by the pervasiveness of the world of entertainment and fashion as well as rock and pop music. Hence, the cover of Billy Graham's 1971 book *The Jesus Generation* clearly took America's pastor into new fields of youth ministry. Its cover features bright yellow and orange colors and a silhouette of Jesus, his pierced hands at his side turned upward. The title, in a bold, blocky font, bends around the silhouette as a halo would. Puffy cartoon clouds billow behind him. In the middle is an arm outstretched with an index finger pointing heavenward. Below the blazing, haloed image of Christ are the upturned faces of young men and women, rendered in the new rotoscope style popularized by Bill Sewell in the Beatles' *Yellow Submarine* film of 1968.[79]

By the early 1970s, Graham had taken another page out of the Beatles' playbook. The evangelist let his curly, thick blond hair grow out longer, as his sideburns lengthened about an inch. Some of the old guard in the evangelical world thought that he had given in too much. Why did he have to conform to the hollow trends of the era? critics hissed. Writing in to Graham's syndicated newspaper advice column, one individual expressed doubts about the new style. "I saw you on TV recently and was amazed and disappointed to see that you have conceded to the 'long hairs,'" stated the disgruntled writer. That look was tolerable when adopted by young people, claimed the critic, but on the middle-aged Graham it looked like a gimmick, or something worse. Beyond this, asked the reader, how would Graham interpret the New Testament passage in 1 Corinthians: "If a man has long hair it is a shame unto him"? Graham fired back that his hair had always been a little longer than his contemporaries; besides, Saint Paul did not mean what the reader thought he meant in the biblical passage. Moreover, Graham replied, Jewish men in the days of Jesus wore their hair longer. So did America's revered founding fathers, with their "hair down to their shoulders."[80]

Even the look and words of scripture changed to reflect the latest trends. The American Bible Society rolled out its new Bible translation, *Good News for Modern Man,* in 1966. It looked nothing like the standard Good Book. Gone were the typical leather cover, gold title, and somber tone of the King James Version. It seemed like a modern paperback, complete with specially made illustrations. It cost only a quarter. Its up-to-date language was combined with a modern font. It won key endorsements from Billy Graham, the Southern Baptist Convention, and the United Presbyterian Church in the USA. The cover of *Good News for Modern Man,* illustrated with the mastheads of international newspapers, promised "the New Testament . . . in Today's English." Scripture, the American Bible Society seemed to be saying, was as current and relevant as a news flash. Over the next twenty-five years it would sell seventy-five million copies. Other with-it translations followed, including *The Way* (1971), geared for readers in their late teens and early twenties. Up-to-date Bibles, new goods, and designs were meant to project relevance as well as an earthy authenticity.[81]

Others, similarly inspired, crafted new, heartfelt, youth-oriented church music. By 1967, even the usually staid *Christianity Today* had to admit that rock 'n' roll was here to stay. One of its contributors noted that it was the music that Jackie Kennedy danced to. *Time* featured rock on its cover, and the Beatles made millions. Rock-inspired music could open "a new avenue of witness for the evangelical church," the *Christianity Today* author noted. "Great care should be taken in making use of this," cautioned the writer, but creating Christian music that was commercially viable and intellectually provocative was possible. Finally, he reasoned that "the Gospel must be communicated," even on the top forty charts.[82] Such developments inspired the editor of another prominent evangelical magazine to rhapsodize about the potential of a new sound. "The youth interest in contemporary music is apparently sparking spiritual revival," he enthused. "And this comes at a time when the older generation is despairing, when churches are losing hope, when denominations are panicking." He was happy to see that "young people with long hair and beards, who have been ostracized sometimes from their churches, are picking up their guitars, writing their own tunes, and witnessing to their peers." He thrilled at the thought that young Christian artists were "capturing the rock sound for the service and glory of God, whatever its earlier associations."[83] The new eagerness to incorporate pop music would have been largely unimaginable just five years before.

For younger church leaders and music directors, folk music—with its sincerity and communal spirit—looked like a good vehicle for the gospel. Jesuits at Saint Louis University and folk-loving Catholics on the West Coast led the way. They pioneered new folk masses in the 1960s, after Vatican II's significant reforms.[84] Ray Repp, a seminarian in the Golden State, released his 1965 album *Mass for Young Americans.* Within just a few short years one-third of American Catholic churches reported using folk masses.[85] Thus, by the early to mid-1960s publications like the *Catholic Voice* and even mainstream newspapers such as the *San Francisco Chronicle* and the *Oakland Herald Tribune* reported on a flurry of folk guitar services in Catholic churches.[86] Evangelicals, too, embraced the genre. Evangelical folk music concerts took place across the country from the mid-1960s forward. One Christian folk group performed before eight thousand Oregon State University students as a warm-up act for Robert F. Kennedy's speech. The group also played to twenty thousand during an evangelistic crusade in Calgary, Canada, and gave an outdoor concert to three thousand students in front of Berkeley University's Sproul Hall.[87]

By the end of the decade, greater numbers within evangelical churches had decided that rock music, too, could be incorporated into youth events and could be used for sermon material, as the young Methodist minister in Nebraska had done. One Catholic laywoman reflected on why such openness had once been impossible. It had something to do with "all the notions about the world and worldliness," she figured. Although, she said in a roundabout fashion, "right now I'd be more confident saying that I don't think God is always that far from the enjoyment of rock."[88] Others had earlier drawn the same conclusions about jazz.

Jazz worship and concerts had been tried out in some Catholic and Protestant churches as early as the late 1950s, to the great consternation of critics. In 1959, the editor of the *Alabama Baptist* drew attention to jazz music in the church. A Presbyterian church in Little Rock debated whether to incorporate the music into its services, in an attempt, said the Baptist editor, to reach the "beat generation." It was foolishness, he concluded. Churchmen were merely looking for "something to take the place of a genuine spiritual experience with Christ."[89] Writing about the new jazz masses for the *San Francisco Chronicle* in 1966, the journalist Lester Kinsolving said the movement was "regarded by some church members as a sincere attempt to attain contemporary relevance in worship," but others viewed it as "a bizarre and deliberately contrived stunt, designed for the sole purpose of attracting crowds."[90] Debates about the appropriateness of the music roiled Baptist, Methodist, Catholic, and Nazarene congregations. Typically, detractors feared that their churches had gone too far in crafting a contemporary, hip gospel.[91]

Jazz might impress sophisticated urbanites or the discriminating nonchurchgoer, but rock 'n' roll was far more appealing to teens. Some of the earliest experiments with sacred pop took place in the United Kingdom. The Church of England, suffering a loss in membership and social influence in the 1960s, hoped to revitalize congregations with lively beat music. Beatles-style groups formed across the country. New bands like the Envoys and the Brian Gilbert Group combined pop melodies with a traditional gospel message. One of the most successful, and unusual, combos was the Salvation Army's the Joystrings, fronted by Joy Webb. The band, which performed in churches and on street corners, wore their traditional Salvation Army uniforms. The Joystrings even appeared on the BBC and in newsreels, and they scored a record deal with EMI. They also won some chart success, drawing on beat groups and Peter, Paul, and Mary for inspiration.[92]

It may be that the first self-professed Christian rock band, in the evangelical mold, was an American group called the Crusaders. There had been other, fleeting experiments with beat, folk, and rock taking place in the United States and United Kingdom before the Crusaders began performing. The Joystrings were one such example. But the Crusaders were much more deliberate in carving out their music as something new and exciting. On the cover of their 1966 album, *Make a Joyful Noise with Drums and Guitars,* was a photograph of the five young men, shot from a low angle, wearing turtlenecks and staring intently into the camera. A burst of the setting sun shines behind them. On the back of their LP the band was described as "five sincere young men—all of them in their teens—who have chosen the Big Beat as the means of expressing their religious faith." All the young members came from Christian homes. They staked out the territory with a clear sense of pride. They were, in their own estimation, pioneers who fit in a long tradition of freighting popular music with the gospel. "Now, for the first time," they declared, "God is praised in song through the most contemporary musical expression: The Beat." Their sound was on the amateurish side, but evoked the vocal harmonies and electric guitar work of the Association, the Byrds, the Yardbirds, and the Mamas and the Papas.[93]

At about this time, some mainline congregations sponsored rock shows, hoping to draw in youth who were otherwise unreachable. A rock combo called the Strangers performed at the All Saints Episcopal Church in Palo Alto, California, in 1967. Scandalizing conservatives, the band featured drums, organ, tambourine, harmonica, and two shouting vocalists. The group's manager, Chaplain David Baar, described their music as "Hard or Nashville Rock."[94]

A couple of years before and roughly three thousand miles away in St. Petersburg, Florida, the twenty-six-year-old youth pastor Fred Bischoff struck on the idea of having rock music pull in the crowds to his teen services. Newspapers in California and Florida reported on these "Holy Rock 'n' Rollers!" and their "Christian hootenanny." Bischoff's weekly radio program *Truth for Youth* was aired on eighty-five stations and was reaching more than a million high school students from New York to Miami. Bischoff, who looked a little like an insurance salesman, kept his hair short and sported a business suit, horn-rimmed glasses, and well-polished shoes. A newspaper report described him as a fundamentalist. But he tooled around Florida's Gulf Coast in a hot rod that combined the engine of an Oldsmobile and the body of a 1932 Ford. He peppered his radio broadcasts with the occasional "man," "keen," and "cool." "Hell," he told his young listeners, was "Downsville." Unlike others in that movement he heartily borrowed from pop culture. His youth services incorporated a guitar band and folk singers. Teens, said Bischoff, wanted to go to a service that they would not be ashamed of. He was happy that his youth center did not look like a church, and when he climbed onto the stage in his short-sleeve plaid shirt, he did not look like a typical minister.[95]

In the mid and late 1960s, Bischoff was part of a growing trend. Youngsters at a similar gathering at New Mexico State University eagerly reported on their experiences, revealing the generational divide that so many fretted about. "The pulpit-pounding evangelist," said one young enthusiast, "was good for a certain generation, but that is past and perhaps our generation needs something else." He and his friends formed a folk outfit called the Icthusians at the university's Christian student center.[96] College campuses fostered harder-rock Christian groups as well, who honed a decidedly psych-rock sound. The interracial Christian rock group Mind Garage, from Morgantown, West Virginia, released a self-titled debut on RCA Victor in 1969. But even before that, the band's 1968 performance "Electric Liturgy" marked perhaps the first Christian hard rock fusion. All band members were university students. The campus Episcopal priest cheered them along. They took to the road, playing in Washington, DC, and New York City in 1968. "Radically socially conscious clergymen are a marvel to me," reported a *Village Voice* correspondent in July 1968. Church, however, "that unimaginative ecclesiastical bag," still held no allure. "But last Sunday I went to church, and I swear, if church were really like that, I'd go back. It was a gas." At St. Mark's Church-in-the-Bowery the writer witnessed one of Mind Garage's rock masses. The psychedelic Christian rock outfit played "a very mysterioso 'People Get Ready,'" along with "'Love Is the Answer' and 'Let's Get Together." Congregants in the balcony swayed and danced in place to the rhythms of "theo-rock." Mind Garage reminded the writer of the trippy hard rock of Long Island's Vanilla Fudge. The group even played a Vanilla Fudge–inspired version of "Stop! In the Name of Love," a major hit for Motown's the Supremes.[97]

It's not entirely surprising that one of the largest denominations in America, the Southern Baptist Convention, was soon trying to reach teenagers with similar chart-topping rock, rhythm and blues, and Motown singles. Roughly a decade before the denomination hardened along political and theological lines, youth workers explored new routes of evangelism. The church's Radio and Television Commission launched the teen talk and music show *Powerline* out of Fort Worth, Texas, in 1969. On the half-hour radio program, DJs interspersed top forty hits with comments about the problems of modern society and the hope of the gospel. On a typical program in 1969, they spun the following for their overwhelmingly white listeners: "Crimson and Clover" by Tommy James and the Shondells, "Soulful Strut" by Young-Holt Unlimited,

"Everyday People" by Sly and the Family Stone, and "I Heard It through the Grapevine" by Marvin Gaye. Jesus was a soul man, the DJs told their audience. Let him into your heart.[98] Letters from listeners, many seeking day-to-day advice, flooded *Powerline*'s office. By 1971, six hundred radio stations around the United States were broadcasting the program.[99]

In the same year that the Southern Baptist Convention launched *Powerline*, a DJ and former assistant director of music for the influential WINS radio station in New York City also took to the airwaves with a Christian hippie message. Scott Ross made a name for himself as one of the new cultural brokers of the technicolor, swinging sixties. He was a co-emcee for the Beatles' famous Shea Stadium concert in 1965 and socialized with Bob Dylan and the Rolling Stones. Married to the Ronettes' singer Nedra Talley, he was a rock music insider. But his WINS career was cut short by a drug bust. After his conversion experience, Ross began to explore the intersection of pop styles and Christianity. In some ways, it was a return to his roots. His father was a pentecostal minister, and his mother was a devout believer. In 1967, Scott and Nedra started working for the charismatic minister Pat Robertson's Christian Broadcasting Network (CBN) in Portsmouth, Virginia. Here the young couple also joined Jim and Tammy Faye Bakker, although the Bakker's older style of pentecostalism stood in stark contrast to the more experimental and countercultural Christianity of Scott and Nedra. By 1973, *The Scott Ross Show* was airing on a hundred radio stations around the country. Ross grappled with the philosophies of rock stars, offered an antidrug message, and spun the latest hits. In a short time, the program was airing on two hundred stations. Ross later branched out into television with CBN.[100]

When it came to an openness to new types of music and more lively services, few could match the pentecostals. Black and white pentecostals, perhaps more than any other Protestants in America, had long experimented with new styles of music and instrumentation. Their worship services, led by the spirit as they liked to say, were open and subjective in ways that other mainline liturgical services were not. The white Assemblies of God and the black Church of God in Christ made early forays into radio ministry, too. The African American celebrity holiness minister Lightfoot Solomon Michaux even made the transition from radio to TV broadcasts in the pioneer days of the late 1940s.

Visitors to Church of God (Cleveland) services or Pentecostal Holiness Church revivals could not but help notice the vivacity of the singing, preaching, and congregational participation. At a 1953 convention of the Assemblies of God in Milwaukee, a reporter on hand listened to the shouts of "Hallelujah" and the fervent prayers of the attendees. They sang full-throated songs of praise. They cried out and spoke in tongues. Some women in the crowd turned their heads upward, yelling out their prayers while clutching their babies in their arms. These believers did not have any intention of settling down or making their music tamer for the sophisticated crowd. One leader from California strode to the podium in the Milwaukee auditorium. During his forceful prayer he rumbled loudly, thanking God that his church "dared to call [them]selves Pentecostal," and promised that the denomination would not turn into "another fat, ecclesiastical body."[101] Adherents were happy to be outside the norm. In his history of his own Assemblies of God denomination, Carl Brumback painted a scene of a typical twentieth-century revival. Looking back from 1961, he described days gone by. Brumback reminisced about "one little boy" who directed a stranger to the pentecostal church in the community and informed him, "When you get about a mile away from the church, you'll hear 'em singin'!" Brumback reckoned that "this very singing which was so repulsive to a few was a drawing card to multitudes. It was bright, lively singing with a lilt that corresponded to the experience of the singers. It was a testimony in music. Subjective? Yes, but so are many of the Psalms."[102]

All this engagement with lively new music and pop in pentecostal and mainstream denominations set the tone for later developments. Christian rock as a distinct, sustained genre, though, really had its roots on the hippie fringe of California and among holiness and neo-pentecostal converts. In 1967, a group of young believers, street Christians in the parlance of the day, set up a storefront mission in San Francisco's Haight-Ashbury district. The mission that Ted and Liz Wise established would come to be called the Living Room.[103] Ted, who had struggled with LSD addiction, and Liz reached out to the burnouts, runaways, and hippies that flooded into the city. The Living Room served as the heart of an evangelical bohemian community and drew together countercultural believers and musicians. A reporter for an evangelical magazine described the twenty-nine-year-old Ted Wise, his long hair tucked behind his ears and his auburn mustache drooping down around his mouth. "If his faded blue levis and brilliant orange sweat shirt could have been exchanged for a cloak of woven camels' hair cloth," he ventured, "he easily could have been mistaken for Charlton Heston playing John the Baptist." The Wises and their gang of "turned on" Christians would "stroll like medieval mendicants along Haight street, strumming autoharps, playing harmonicas and passing out day-old doughnuts."[104]

From this combination of the hippie counterculture, neopentecostalism, and a general antiauthoritarian primitivism would come the Jesus people. Its young representatives, turned off by traditional churches, hungered for a more authentic and direct experience of Christianity. In the early 1970s, the movement that first took root in California branched out across the country and then spread to England, Norway, Germany, and beyond. A 1971 headline in the *Wall Street Journal* charted the movement's new visibility: "Hip Culture Discovers a New Trip: Fervent, Foot-Stompin' Religion."[105] That same year Archbishop Fulton J. Sheen editorialized in the *New York Times* about the "young crusaders" who stood "as an indictment of the church." They were, he thought, "picking up the Christ about Whom the church rarely preaches."[106] These Jesus people had first preached on the streets and beaches around San Francisco to eager listeners who did not quite know what to make of this unusually packaged gospel.

To the south, the former pentecostal pastor Chuck Smith took over the nondenominational Calvary Chapel in Costa Mesa in 1965. As a growing number of hippies began to move into the area, Smith and his family reached out to the new arrivals. Calvary Chapel became a hub for Jesus freaks as well as an incubator for the new Christian rock music.[107] The church catered to burnouts and runaways who were inspired by Calvary's house band, called Love Song. Other early Jesus rockers included the pentecostal and end-times popularizer Larry Norman, who attended Calvary Chapel. Christian labels like Maranatha and Zondervan Records chalked up early successes with the increasingly popular style. The music ran the gamut from plaintive folk to soft rock; from acid rock improvisations to fuzzed out garage rock; from Byrds-style country to Beatlesque, harmony-rich music. What might be called Jesus fever extended well beyond the walls of churches like Calvary Chapel.[108]

The pioneer Christian rock band Love Song plays at Robert E. Lee Park in Dallas, Texas. The concert was part of the Explo '72 festival, June 1972. Photo by and courtesy of Garry Slabaugh.

In Hollywood, Duane Pederson began publishing the *Hollywood Free Paper* in 1969, as a kind of counter to the underground radical press of the day. In fact, he styled it after the *Los Angeles Free Press.* Pederson, who coined the term "Jesus people" because he disliked "Jesus freaks," had come to the West Coast from Minnesota to pursue a career in entertainment. After his conversion, he worked in the city streets in and around LA. With his trademark suede fringed jacket, popularized by the actor Dennis Hopper in *Easy Rider* (1969), Pederson worked with youth, runaways, and the downtrodden. Pederson's *Hollywood Free Paper* would eventually achieve a circulation of over half a million.[109] The paper's articles were littered with the slang of the hippie and rock subculture, targeting "phonies" in the church, asking readers "Can You Dig It?," and urging "groovy people" to distribute the paper on their college campuses. Cartoons, drawn in the style of R. Crumb, poked fun at the establishment and the "hang ups" of the New Left. The paper drew together thousands of street Christians; advertised Jesus rock concerts and festivals; offered posters, T-shirts, and bumper stickers for sale; reviewed movies and records; and regularly featured columns by Christian rock musicians and earthy evangelists. Notices appeared for a local teen hangout on Yucca Street in Hollywood called the Salt Company.

In 1969, it hosted "folk, folk-rock, jazz, country Western, soul and hard rock" groups at live shows on Friday and Saturday nights. Larry Norman frequently played, as did guitarist Dennis Agajanian, the New Celebration, and the resident band the Salt Company Group.[110]

Similar centers of activity cropped up around the country. In New Milford, New Jersey, in 1969 and 1970 the Jesus movement took hold through the efforts of Paul Moore, a Nazarene pastor from the Midwest, and Charlie Rizzo, an Italian American hippie and one-time speed freak who was obsessed with the Beatles. The Maranatha Coffee House—and a house band also named Maranatha, led by Rizzo—drew in scores of countercultural youth. Other coffeehouses and newly formed Christian rock acts cropped up in Montclair, Morristown, and Plainfield in New Jersey and Ansonia, Danbury, and Norwalk in Connecticut.

The holiness Church of the Nazarene eventually embraced the movement.[111] Traveling Nazarene evangelist Chuck Millhuff—who, like many in the fold, had an air of straitlaced conformity—wrote a glowing report about the Jesus movement and its exciting new music. In the pages of the denomination's magazine, Millhuff recounted his firsthand experience of a 1971 New Milford, New Jersey, revival. He felt as though he had "walked in and out" of the pages of the New Testament book of Acts. Hundreds of youths thronged the tent where music blared and a service took place. "The Maranatha Band tuned up their guitars," he observed in wonder, "the drummer roared around his traps, the singer pulled his long hair from his eyes, and all heaven broke loose." The seasoned revivalist was stunned by it all. He had never seen or heard anything quite like this in his over ten years of ministry. "Bare feet, long hair, Afros, hippies, freaks . . . all turned on to Jesus." He tried to fit in, wearing bell-bottom jeans and a T-shirt. But he still felt out of place. Regardless, he was sure that the preaching and the hard rock music represented the work of the Holy Spirit.[112]

For all that pentecostal ferment, and the praise that Jesus rock received from those inside the church, the standard criticism of the music was that it was decidedly behind the latest trends. Youth pastors could tell their teen charges that if they liked the Beatles, they could listen instead to the sanctified rock of Phil Keaggy. Some who enjoyed the band Cream might fancy the hard, psychedelic Christian rock of Agape, from Azusa, California. Those who preferred the band Queen could be steered to the Christian alternative, 2nd Chapter of Acts. So widespread was the view that the music was hopelessly derivative that even some in evangelical circles poked fun at the genre. The San Diego–based satirical magazine the *Wittenburg Door* created a parody of a Christian rock star, Freddie "Fab" Frakowski, in the late 1970s. Asked about the highlights of his career, Freddie replies, "Well, it started in the 50s with my smash hit, 'Love Him Tender, Love Him Do.' Then came 'Jesus in the Tube' during the surfing craze, followed by 'I Want to Hold His Hand' when the Beatles were big." Several years after that, said the fictitious Freddie, he ventured into acid rock. Even within the Christian rock world there was some acknowledgment of the derivative or subpar nature of the music. The title of one of Larry Norman's most popular songs, a 1950s-style boogie-woogie called "Why Should the Devil Have All the Good Music?" (1972), hinted at the inauthenticity or poor quality of much evangelical pop.[113]

The tag of being second rate or inauthentic is not entirely accurate. That negative assessment paralleled cries of "inauthenticity" and "sellout" that critics shouted at 1970s soft rock groups, fine-tuned to middle-of-the-road tastes. The inauthentic label also smeared corporate stadium rock. The "music business today," rock critic Lester Bangs wrote in the *Village Voice* in 1978, "still must be recognized as by definition an enemy, if not the most crucial enemy, of music and the people who try to perform it honestly."[114] But in the case of early Christian rock, it was more complicated. Quite a few Christian rock performers actually did have major pop hits, garner critical acclaim, and first gain their popularity in the competitive secular market and on the music charts. The experiences of many of these early artists were similar. Their journey to faith, whether pentecostal or not, also bore resemblance to the experiences of the many hippies and countercultural youths who joined up with the Jesus people.[115] Some musicians achieved international fame before their conversion experiences. Others had played as backing musicians for well-known stars. Some rose up from relative obscurity to preach the hippie gospel through song.

Cliff Richard had already made his fortune and a name for himself as a star of the British pop scene in the early 1960s. His hit song "Move It" (1958) was one of the first British rock records. The teen-idol-styled

"Living Doll" (1959) won him the appellation "the British Elvis." Richard softened his image in the late 1950s and through the 1960s. By 1963, he and his backing group the Shadows had garnered twenty-nine top ten hits. After he became a born-again Christian in 1965, his UK chart success was never matched in the States. Still, American evangelicals marveled at the successful baby-faced singer who had given up the life of rock stardom to sing Christian-themed pop songs. Richard would join Billy Graham on the evangelist's crusades.[116]

Larry Norman, who would go on to perform with Richard, was the prime mover of Jesus rock and helped define the earnest, folkie genre in profound ways. Born in Corpus Christi, Texas, in 1947, Norman was an early, enthusiastic fan of Elvis Presley. "I started writing songs when I was nine," recalled Norman in 1979, "and I guess about the third or fourth song I wrote was the formulation of my idea for Christian rock music. Since then I haven't stopped."[117] In 1959, he appeared on Ted Mack's television program *The Original Amateur Hour.* He later styled himself as a kind of free-spirited Christian hippie. Fittingly, then, Norman began his adult musical career in San Francisco with a band called People! Unlike so many others who linked up with the Jesus movement, Norman had been a born-again Christian in the period before Christian rock emerged as a genre. His musical influences were secular, and he wore them on his sleeve. The Beatles, the Rolling Stones, and Bob Dylan were major sources of inspiration. People! recorded for Capitol Records, home of the Beatles and the Beach Boys, and opened for the Doors, Janis Joplin, the Who, Jimi Hendrix, and a host of others. The band received some chart success with their cover of the Zombies' "I Love You."[118] In 1969, Norman inked a solo contract with Capitol and released his first record, *Upon This Rock.* It included his memorable, haunting "I Wish We'd All Been Ready," a warning about the imminent return of Jesus and the rapture of true believers into heaven. He branched out into the record-label business as well after Pat Boone loaned him $3,000 to start Solid Rock Records. That influential label launched the careers of Mark Heard, Daniel Amos, Randy Stonehill, and other accomplished Christian performers.[119]

Like Norman, Chuck Girard achieved a degree of fame before the advent of Christian rock. Unlike Norman, Girard was not a Christian when he first recorded and performed. Others followed that same pattern. In the early 1960s, Girard made a name for himself in the pop music scene with his collegiate vocal quartet the Castells. They broke into the top forty three times, with hits like "Sacred" (1961) and "So This Is Love" (1962). In 1964, his new surf rock group the Hondells released "Little Honda," written by Brian Wilson and Mike Love of the Beach Boys. It climbed to number nine on the U.S. pop singles chart. Thereafter Girard went through a period of spiritual searching, a baby boomer rite of passage. Returning from a stint in Hawaii, he was arrested for drug possession.[120] "I became a regular LSD dropper and went through a lot of changes during my five years of the drug life," said Girard in the late 1970s. "I was really searching for God—trying to find spiritual fulfillment through my drug experiences. I was reading about all the eastern philosophies, all the different religions of the world including Christianity—and was trying to make ends meet." He attended Chuck Smith's Calvary Chapel in Costa Mesa and "realized this was what I had been looking for." He then decided to use his music for evangelism.[121]

Another early star of the genre, Barry McGuire, lived and moved in a similar countercultural world before his conversion. He was a successful solo artist and had a 1965 hit single with the apocalyptic "Eve of Destruction." The one-time front man of the New Christy Minstrels first encountered a street Christian while on his way to see Stanley Kubrick's cult classic *2001: A Space Odyssey* (1968). He was stoned when the evangelist approached him and told him about how Jesus would return to earth and rain down destruction on sinners. After that McGuire said he "couldn't get the name of Jesus out of my head." After his 1971 born-again experience, McGuire's circle of friends changed and the content of his songs did as well.[122] He was an imposing presence on stage. The burly, hirsute performer, one-time troubadour of the counterculture, said that he was bitter and resentful before his conversion. His transformation and the hope he now had, he would tell audiences, was tremendous. He subsequently relocated to Fresno, California, and joined up with an evangelical community outreach group called Agape Force.[123]

Like McGuire, other well-known pop celebrities—such as Johnny Cash, B. J. Thomas, Pat Boone, former member of Buffalo Springfield and Poco Richie Furay, and Noel Paul Stookey from Peter, Paul, and Mary—became important figures in the Christian rock world, too. To

Andraé Crouch performing with backing vocalists at Njårdhallen, Oslo, Norway, late 1976 or early 1977. Photo by and courtesy of Steinar Tyvand.

some extent, their fame in the secular realm lent them a credibility that lesser-known artists lacked.[124] These were just a handful of the dozens of solo artists, rock groups, and folk choirs that now filled evangelical and pentecostal churches and concert halls with new music. Other major performers and groups of the early days included black and white, male and female musicians, like Andraé Crouch and the Disciples, Randy Matthews, the Armageddon Experience, Agape, Sound Foundation, and Honeytree. The latter was the stage name of Nancy Henigbaum from Davenport, Iowa. The solo hippie folk singer, described as the Jesus movement's answer to Judy Collins, was a popular performer in the Midwest, where she toured coffee houses, churches, and small Christian colleges.[125]

As prominent ministers, like Billy Graham, and youth pastors cheered on such performers and adopted the dress, hairdos, and fashions of the young—and as critics wagged a finger at them for doing so—pop culture infiltrated the church in other ways as well. New Christian bookstores marketed T-shirts and knickknacks to young consumers and sold denim-covered Bibles. Starting in the 1950s, independent Christian bookstores had been established around the country. But between 1965 and 1975 their numbers skyrocketed from 725 to 1,850. Many of these were mom-and-pop operations. The Christian Booksellers Association (founded in 1950) professionalized the industry and established conventions for suppliers and merchants. In the early 1970s, the latest Christian rock records and eight-track tapes—by bands and solo artists like 2nd Chapter of Acts, Phil Keaggy, Randy Matthews, Love Song, and Children of the Day—were available at such stores and at music festivals.[126] Brightly colored bumper stickers with cheery Christian messages and dire warnings of the end of the world appeared in church parking lots.

Observers wanted to know what accounted for the sudden surge in Jesus's popularity and the rise of all this evangelical pop culture and God rock. Why were youngsters so enthralled with Christ in 1969 and 1970? they asked with some amazement. The lyrics of numerous Christian rock songs spoke of a soft Jesus who was as much a friend as a figure of judgment. Lyrics described being turned on to Jesus. One University of California professor thought he understood the nature of the Jesus people's appeal. Young Americans "[are rejecting] the configuration of symbols and gods in the 'head mysticism' of the 1960s and are focusing on one man—Jesus. They feel they are reaching the same kind of infinity consciousness—without drugs or meditation."[127] By contrast, the University of Southern California religion scholar Robert S. Ellwood judged that the movement owed much to its pop cultural appeal. "The ability of Jesus rock and gospel melodies to generate rich, powerful feelings in a mood and emotion-oriented age," claimed Ellwood, "has brought and held the movement together. It is largely music that has made the movement a part of pop culture, and it is the Jesus movement as pop culture that distinguishes it from what is going on in the churches."[128]

Certainly that pop cultural appeal and the baby boomer, seeker element were critical to the emergence of the Jesus people and Christian rock. But likely as important to their origins was pentecostalism. Two historians of that twentieth-century religious awakening note that the countercultural Jesus people "took a stream of pentecostalism out of its staid churches and presented it with a fresh face throughout the globe." The concerts and festivals the believers sponsored along with "Jesus marches, hippie Christian churches, coffeehouses, and communes" all helped create a new wave of the modern pentecostal movement.[129]

There is little doubt that pentecostalism, the religion of spirit abundance, had an enormous influence on the Jesus movement and helped usher in God rock. Since the early twentieth century, pentecostalism had grown tremendously in the states and abroad.[130] Believers claimed to have direct encounters with God. Adherents shrugged off religious convention, professed to heal the sick, foresee the future, and in some rare cases, handle deadly serpents as a sign of divine anointing.[131] In 1969, a UPI religious reporter highlighted the phenomenal growth of pentecostal churches. "Pentecostals," said Louis Cassels, "would be the first to acknowledge that their worship services are distinguished by a free expression of feelings and uninhibited exuberance not often encountered in other Protestant churches." Even more importantly, he noted, "the Pentecostal movement is growing much faster than any of the mainstream Protestant bodies."[132] It is difficult to generalize about pentecostals. Cassels and other commentators reported that some spoke in tongues; others did not. Many emphasized the imminent return of Jesus; some were not so concerned with the Second Advent. There were Unitarian and Trinitarian believers. There were some who thought that their small band of adherents held a monopoly on truth. And then there were others with a more ecumenical perspective.

Still, some generalizations applied to the movement as a whole. At this general level, it is easier to see how pentecostalism gave birth to Jesus rock. Put simply, pentecostals believed in the wonder-working power of the Holy Spirit. They held that the same gifts that the apostles received in the first century—speaking in tongues, healing the sick, reading the signs of the times—were still attainable. Pentecostals—members of the Assemblies of God, the Church of God in Christ, the Pentecostal Assemblies of the World, the Pentecostal Holiness Church, and hundreds of independent bodies—proclaimed that God empowered them to work his will in these last days. And their churches tended to welcome revved-up music and instrumental innovation that built to a climax.[133]

Leading lights of the Jesus movement like Chuck Smith came out of traditional pentecostal churches yet bristled at the conformity and restrictions of established denominations. Likewise, musicians looked back to the early church as a romantic model of community and untainted belief. The bearded saint of Calvary Chapel, a converted hippie named Lonnie Frisbee, foregrounded pentecostal practice during services he led. That was the norm among Jesus people, in fact, although many broke with traditional pentecostal churches—like the Assemblies of God that Elvis Presley and Jerry Lee Lewis called their spiritual home. Older pentecostal denominations struck many Jesus people and Christian rockers as too conformist or dogmatic, as Calvary Chapel's Chuck Smith had thought. Charismatic and pentecostal beliefs and worship practices still prevailed. Most memorably, Frisbee painted a cross on a deerskin cape he owned. He would occasionally drape the totem over tongues-speaking believers as he prayed for them.[134]

A *Time* magazine journalist detected this Holy Ghost emphasis: "'The Jesus revolution['s] . . . strong Pentecostalism emphasizes such esoteric spiritual gifts as speaking in tongues and healing by faith. For many, there exists a firm conviction that Jesus' Second Coming is literally at hand." That was confirmed over and over in firsthand accounts of concerts, revivals, and beachside baptisms. A group of researchers traveled up and down California in the early 1970s, asking Jesus people about their opinions on music, theology, politics, race, and more. Respondents were usually biblical literalists, had a favorable opinion of speaking in tongues and healing, and tended to believe in Bible prophecy. Would Jesus return to earth soon, they were asked. "Very shortly," said one respondent from Berkeley. "I think we are in the last days."[135] The neo-pentecostal millenarianism, and obsession with the rapture, so pervaded the Jesus movement that some observers thought it was at the core of the group's identity and a primary theme of its music. Early Jesus rockers sang lustily about the return of Jesus.[136] Apocalyptic guru Hal Lindsey's 1970, multimillion-selling book, *The Late Great Planet Earth,* informed the views of Jesus rock groups and their myriad fans. The movement as a whole could be summed up, as the subtitle of one popular treatment put it, "Old-Time Religion in the Age of Aquarius."[137]

At the peak of the Jesus people movement, followers eagerly shared their faith and their music with anyone who would listen, and even those who would not. Their songs and concerts were earnestly evangelistic. They warned of Armageddon, the futility of left-wing political activism, and the snares of drug and alcohol use. For all life's nettlesome problems, as Andraé Crouch phrased it in his 1973 song, "Jesus Is the Answer." There was a darker side at play, too. According to born-again believers' largely conservative, pentecostal outlook, the devil had immense powers over humankind. In 1971, the *Wall Street Journal* noted, "Though the Jesus People fashion their movement after the counter culture and share many of its accouterments—long hair, off-beat clothes, rock music—when they speak it sounds more like Billy Graham talking than Timothy Leary."[138] Converts proclaimed their evangelical message while busking on college campuses and handed out fundamentalist and pentecostal tracts and booklets on city streets to passersby. In the early 1970s, one such stalwart, who was also a fan of John Lennon, wrote to the celebrity former Beatle to offer an answer to Lennon's *Imagine* album. He mailed Lennon a standard fundamentalist tract called "The Four Spiritual Laws." Lennon fired back with an angry missive. "Listen, Brother," he wrote, pen dripping with bile, "why don't you Jesus Freaks get off peoples backs? It's been the same for *two thousand years*—will you ever learn?"[139]

Skeptics like Lennon might have wished that these "Bible thumpers" and "God botherers," with their ebullient anthems celebrating Jesus and clean living, would mind their own business. Yet in the coming decades Christian rock and the Jesus people movement would have an influence far beyond coffeehouses, Jesus music festivals, and West Coast Christian communes. In an April 2013 essay for *Harper's Magazine,* anthropologist T. M. Luhrmann sums up the importance of the Jesus people. She may be overstating the case when she writes that "the hippies changed what it meant to be a Christian in America." But she is right to point out that the Jesus people made speaking in tongues, among other innovations, far more commonplace within evangelicalism. Two years earlier, David W. Stowe made a similar argument in the pages of the *New York Times.* "The Jesus Movement and its music eventually found their way into churches," he notes, "helping them to rebrand themselves as youth-friendly and relevant, even groovy, attractive to the baby boomers moving out of their youth and into suburban family life." Congregations that adopted the new look and sound of the counterculture, says Stowe, also "helped incubate—sometimes intentionally, sometimes not—conservative views on emerging culture-war issues like school prayer, abortion, women's rights, gay marriage and aggressive foreign policy."[140]

The new songs evangelicals sang also helped popularize the idea of the rapture of believers into heaven before the end of the world and the reality of miracles and healing, just as adherents created new, nontraditional ways of being evangelical. Calvary Chapel congregations that popped up around the United States, along with the related charismatic Vineyard churches, both prime promoters of Christian rock, were instrumental in the growth of nondenominational Christianity. Nondenominational believers tended to look disparagingly on traditional, mainline churches—with their creeds, hymns, and dusty formalism—which seemed to them to be as dry as they were spiritually dead. Devotees felt their churches were especially alive to the workings of the spirit. That vibrancy, combined with the certainties of conservative theology, might help explain the enormous growth of pentecostalism and evangelicalism in the 1960s and 1970s. The Episcopal, Northern Baptist, Presbyterian, and American Lutheran churches, by contrast, were shrinking. One leading Methodist was observing that drastic change in the early 1970s. He pointed out the laxness and organizational weakness of the mainline and the guided, deliberate strictness of the evangelicals and pentecostals.[141] Whatever the reason, the conservatives were on the rise and were exercising greater religious influence. One scholar of the Jesus movement argues that the most significant contributions they made to the larger culture had to do with aesthetics, style, and media innovation. The resulting "evangelical popular media," suggests Shawn David Young, "contributed to the growth of both mega and new paradigm churches."[142]

Christian music, and rock in particular, would go on to reshape and even pentecostalize evangelicalism. After the early 1970s, many more evangelicals, especially in nondenominational churches, worshiped in a far more casual, free-form style then they had in earlier generations. The music, fashions, and neo-pentecostalism of Jesus rock had a wide-ranging impact.

In some quarters it all still came in for a stern rebuke. Not surprisingly, fundamentalist Christians—especially those in the American South who had ardently opposed the innovations of pentecostalism—became the most vocal critics of Jesus people and Christian rock. Fundamentalists furiously denounced the new movement and its new sound. In 1986, even the pentecostal televangelist Jimmy Swaggart was blasting his fellow believers. "You cannot proclaim the message of the anointed WITH THE MUSIC OF THE DEVIL!," he thundered. For fundamentalists, the innovations of both the countercultural Christians and associated pentecostalism were as biblically unsound as they were dangerous.[143] The strident reactions of white fundamentalists and the divisions within evangelicalism over the appropriateness of new music and theology tore at the fabric of conservative Protestantism from the 1970s forward.

• 5 •

The Fundamentalist Reaction to Christian Rock

You can't just sneak Jesus into music . . .
—Reverend Harry bruce, 1983

President Jimmy Carter was fond of country, jazz, and classical music. Shortly after his election in 1976, *Billboard* magazine observed that the evangelical commander in chief would be the first "since John Kennedy with pop music tastes." Fittingly, his 1977 inauguration festivities featured performances by Aretha Franklin, Linda Ronstadt, and Loretta Lynn. Invited guests included John Lennon and Yoko Ono, along with Paul Simon and Gregg Allman. The Carter White House hosted jazz, soul, and classical music concerts. Southern rockers, too, like the Allman Brothers Band, Charlie Daniels, and Willie Nelson would perform there.[1]

Late in his presidency, in early September 1979, Carter hosted an outdoor music festival on the White House lawn. The Old Fashioned Gospel Singin' concert drew together some of the best acts of the genre. A crowd of one thousand invited guests was on hand. In the picnic setting, they ate fried chicken and potato salad. It was as if Plains, Georgia, had been transported to Sixteen Hundred Pennsylvania Avenue.[2] The Old Fashioned Gospel Singin' event, rich with the romance and sentimentalism of southern religion, was different from other White House concerts. One of the performers bragged to reporters, "We have soul gospel, country gospel, Jesus rock and big band gospel." White gospel legends James Blackwood and Doug Oldham were on the bill. So were famous black performers like Shirley Caesar and Reverend James Cleveland. The black quartet Mighty Clouds of Joy appeared alongside the white quartet the Kingsmen. Joining these more traditional performers was Jesus rock icon Larry Norman. The founder of Christian rock spoke to the president about Bob Dylan's brand new, overtly Christian album *Slow Train Coming* on Columbia Records. Did the president have a copy? asked Norman. He did not. So Norman offered to send him one. Carter said he would place it in the presidential library. Dylan was not on hand, but other rock performers, like Barry McGuire, took part in the day's events.[3]

Earlier on that Sunday the Carters had attended the First Baptist Church on Sixteenth Street. The afternoon concert brought a relaxed church atmosphere to the stately White House South Grounds. The president, sporting a short-sleeve knit shirt with a wide collar and khaki pants, set the laid-back tone for the festivities. As he addressed the crowd, Carter was flanked by Norman, who had long, straight, light blond hair. The Christian rocker's radiating smile was as wide as the president's trademark, toothy grin. "What we want you to do," Carter said, "is just relax here on the White House grounds, enjoy yourself and listen to the delightful music." The president's daughter, eleven-year-old Amy, read comic books from her perch in a nearby tree. Others sat on woolen blankets and soaked up the music and the sunshine. The songs on offer, Carter noted, were "derived from deep within the heart of human beings." It was "a music of pain, a music of longing, a music of searching, a music of hope and a music of faith."[4]

Numerous conservative Christians might have had no problem with the close harmonies and rousing message of gospel quartets. But Christian rock, for fundamentalists especially, was anything but "a music of hope and a music of faith." Christian lyrics or evangelical messages could never redeem the loud, thumping beat or the droning of electric guitars. Rock music had far too many negative associations for them as well. The televangelist and linchpin of the new religious right Jerry Falwell thought Christian rock was blatantly outlandish. The Virginia Baptist, who would become one of Carter's harshest critics, said that, even when played by Christians, rock 'n' roll led to moral oblivion.[5] Falwell even included opposition to rock music as a defining principle of what it meant to be a fundamentalist. He, like millions of others, emphasized the imminent return of Jesus, the absolute authority of the Bible, and the deity and virgin birth of Jesus. "My definition of a fundamentalist," said Falwell in a 1981 interview with *Christianity Today,* "is one who, first, believes in the inerrancy of Scripture, and second, is committed to a biblical separation in the world and to the lordship of Christ." Offering specific, contemporary examples, Falwell continued, "I mean

Jerry Falwell and a member of the Georgia-based Davis Trio at a bicentennial religious meeting, Lynchburg, Virginia, July 4, 1976. "The Davis Trio & Jerry Falwell—July 4, 1976." Screenshot by the author from YouTube, Kayward Davis (http://www.youtube.com/watch?v=tUzzltszHxk).

separation from rock music, separation from immorality, separation from Hollywood culture."[6]

Falwell's opinions about music and politics looked almost moderate, though, when compared with those of fundamentalist firebrand Bob Jones III. When Jimmy Carter ran for the presidency in 1976, Jones upbraided the former Georgia governor from his South Carolina university. He certainly was no Christian, Jones reckoned. "We have a presidential candidate who seeks to ride the gospel train into the White House by deceiving gullible Christians with his talk about being born again," Jones griped. In that election year, Jones viewed the front-runner as an imposter who "speaks with a forked tongue, receives large sums of money from the dope-ridden rock culture . . . and replaces the Bible's teaching against homosexuality and women's lib with his own contrary opinions."[7] Jones's views might have been out of step with the majority of evangelicals, but his fear of the compromises he thought Carter and so many other Christians had made in the 1970s was likely shared by millions on the religious right.

There was much at stake in the debates and battles over Christian rock that swept through denominations and churches in the 1970s and 1980s. The controversy was never just about music—it never had been. The matter was anything but superficial, stalwarts on either side of the wide divide insisted. Believers were disagreeing over the basic relationship their faith should have to the larger culture. Numerous fundamentalists insisted on distancing themselves from all that was worldly. Accordingly, President Carter's acceptance of the new music looked like an utter capitulation to the dark powers of hell. Such tensions also pointed to a major split within the conservative Protestant world. Many had embraced the styles and sounds of pop culture and music. Others, especially fundamentalists, ardently rejected these. Quite a few of the latter angrily blamed pentecostals for embracing musical innovations and catering to the whims of teenagers.[8]

The historian George Marsden once pithily remarked that "a fundamentalist is an evangelical who is angry about something."[9] That is true enough, yet it leaves out much. Certainly fundamentalist anger burned hot against rock 'n' roll. But their ongoing crusade against the devil's music in the 1970s and 1980s reveals much about how they thought of themselves in relation to other Christians and to the world around them, mired in sin as it was. In the same years that numerous fundamentalists began to engage more publicly in politics, they drew lines between their communities and the sinful culture of America. They also set themselves off from fellow Christians. When they raised their voices in defiance against evangelicals and pentecostals who accepted rock 'n' roll, fundamentalists expressed their views about gender norms, propriety, and social order.

Such protests seemed to grow more desperate with each passing year. In the late 1970s, fewer and fewer conservative Christians considered Jesus rock an abomination. It was a time when, according to religion scholars, a fourth great awakening was under way. In 1976, in the first survey of its kind, a Gallup poll reported that 34 percent of American adults said that they were born-again Christians. Projecting from the agency's sample group, that meant that roughly seventy-four million Americans were devout Christians. Between the bicentennial year and 1984 "an average of 46% said they had tried to encourage others to believe," Gallup noted. In the latter year, when Reagan won his second term, 39 percent of respondents also thought that the "Bible is the actual word of God." More and more Americans would come to identify with the evangelical faith in the coming years. By 2005, nearly half the population of the country said that they had been born again.[10]

The once-laughed-at epithet "born again," said the Oxford University–trained historian Richard Quebedeaux, was now a term of respect. "Evangelical Christianity," he proclaimed just months after President Carter took office, "has finally emerged from its anticultural ghetto into the mainstream of American life." That was likely an exaggeration. But his claim that it was "now a force to be reckoned with" was indisputable.[11] In no small part, the evangelical venture into pop music had made that transformation possible. Adherents were visible now in ways they had never been in the 1950s and 1960s. Recent forays into partisan politics also drew national attention. Church attendance had already been on the rise in the early 1970s, and the Jesus people, Christian pop music, and feature stories about the influence of evangelicalism made it impossible to ignore the growing strength of a movement.

This was a movement that combined Age of Aquarius, baby boomer aesthetic sensibilities with the old-time certainties of traditional faith. Tongues speaking and healing services were now infused with electric guitars, drums, and loud, full-throated singing. "Only a few years ago," Ken Briggs quipped in 1972 in the Long Island *Newsday,* "a Jesus rock music concert would have seemed fairly incongruous if not totally sacrilegious." Times and tastes had changed. Rock music once "symbolized the profane in its blaring rebellion against form."[12] Another commentator in the *Dallas Morning News* sensed this changing spirit of the age, writing that "the stage has been set for a vast interdenominational evangelical revival in 1973." The Dallas Explo '72 music festival had recently swept the city into a hallelujah frenzy. Evangelicalism was now "fashionable" and "the fundamentalists who have been the keepers of the flame for the past century find themselves suddenly being joined by a host of unlikely companions—including Catholic bishops and former liberals of the peace movement."[13] The tent of the religious awakening was large. Still, fundamentalists overwhelmingly rejected much of the new cultural engagement as chasing after fads. Many adamantly opposed the bizarre innovations of rock music and neo-pentecotsal beliefs that seemed to be invading other churches.[14]

The rise of pentecostalism and the profusion of Jesus rock made the headlines during the presidencies of Richard Nixon, Gerald Ford, and Jimmy Carter. A 1975 article in the *Pittsburgh Press* observed that the "new Pentecostal movement" drew converts "from middle class Christians of all denominations." To the surprise of many traditionalists, even Roman Catholics and Episcopalians ranked among them. Adherents "feel a new joy of living," gushed the journalist. "They believe in miracles and 'expect the supernatural [at] any time.'" Some claimed to heal the sick. Many spoke in tongues: "Words they never heard before start flowing out of them."[15]

That pentecostal awakening was accompanied by chart-topping gospel music that was, for the first time, breaking into the mainstream. The all-time best-selling gospel single, the Edwin Hawkins Singers' version of "Oh Happy Day," shot up the charts in 1969. It was an international hit, climbing to number four on the American pop chart and number two on the rhythm and blues chart. The album-oriented station KSAN-FM in San Francisco helped launch the peppy single into the broader reaches of pop music. The trend continued to resonate for the next decade and went far beyond gospel music.[16] "This is no isolated incident," wrote one cultural observer in these years. "Religion has become a popular theme with performers and young devotees of pop and rock music."[17] In 1971, Judy Collins's rendition of "Amazing Grace," replete with a church choir singing backup, ranked at number sixteen among the nation's top-selling records. That same year, gospel legend Mahalia Jackson belted out the familiar hymn on Johnny Cash's musical variety show. The most well known performers and bands dabbled in religious and even Christian themes. By the end of April 1970, the best-selling single in America was the Beatles' somber, gospel-tinged "Let It Be," which called on Mary the mother of Jesus in dark times. Stalwarts like Larry Norman pushed back, saying that hits like this were "pseudo-Christian" songs. But such reactions did nothing to diminish their appeal. Hence, one journalist concluded, "We have definitely not reached the end of what some are calling 'Jesus rock.'"[18]

The new appeal of religious themes and evangelical Christianity was baffling to secular critics. It caught some in the mainstream media off guard. Why had not America become less, not more, religious? they asked with puzzled amazement. The popularity of Christian rock was just one aspect of the fourth great awakening in the 1970s.

The culmination of the trend might have been Carter's 1976 election to the highest office in the land. Even though there were seventy million American evangelicals in the 1970s who shared Carter's Christian views, the born-again former peanut farmer was thought, by some, to be too peculiar to lead the nation. Carter's campaign manager even described the candidate's faith as the "weirdo factor." *Newsweek* dubbed the bicentennial "the year of the evangelical."[19] Even Billy Graham got into the spirit of the Christian youth movement and peppered his preachments with an awkward paraphrase: "Tune in to God, then turn on . . . drop out—of the materialistic world."[20] Americans, in growing numbers, seemed to be doing just that.

Bob Dylan's late-1970s conversion gave even wider attention to the born again trend. The rock celebrity took courses at a California Bible school and became fascinated with end-times theology and the views of millennial popularizer and best-selling author Hal Lindsey. Dylan was connected to the Vineyard Christian Fellowship, a new offshoot of the charismatic movement. His *Slow Train Coming,* the record that Larry Norman recommended to President Carter, was the first in a trilogy of the famous troubadour's Christian albums. Themes of sin and salvation, the wrath of God, and the apocalypse animated these records. He took a special interest in the last days and the obscure matters that Lindsey explicated. At one concert during his born-again phase, Dylan asked his listeners, "You know what's happening right now, when you look at the Middle East?" He brought it all back to his earlier songs:

> They're headed for a war. That's right, they're headed for war. There's gonna be war over there. I'd say maybe five years, maybe 10 years, could be 15 years, I don't know, but remember I told you right here. I told you "The Times They Are A-Changin' " and they did! I said the answer was "Blowin' In The Wind" and it was! I'm telling you now, Jesus is coming back, and he is! There is no other way of salvation.[21]

Rolling Stone reported that Dylan now delivered this kind of "nightly sermon" to his captive audiences.[22]

It was too much for many longtime listeners.[23] Writing in *New York* magazine, Ron Rosenbaum figured that the sunshine state had addled

Dylan's brain. The countercultural Jesus revolution was to blame. The logo for Dylan's Vineyard church in Tarzana featured an image of Jesus that Rosenbaum thought looked "like a Marin County coke dealer, a late seventies smoothy, a quintessentially California Christ." In jest, he pleaded, "Bob, I don't necessarily want you to leave Christ and come back to your roots," but a return to the solid, secular ground of New York was in order.[24]

For others the prospect of a born-again Dylan was no laughing matter. Critics sneered at his doctrinaire LP *Slow Train Coming.* But the folk-rock icon and inscrutable cultural chameleon had long been challenging fans' expectations. Critic Greil Marcus—a contributor to *Creem,* the *Village Voice,* and *Rolling Stone*—groused, "What we're faced with here is really very ugly." The voice of a generation was now hawking "a prepackaged doctrine he's received from someone else." "Jesus is the answer," Marcus complained, "and if you don't believe it, you're fucked."[25]

For others, it was an instant classic and an artistic triumph. In the pages of *Rolling Stone,* Jann S. Wenner gave it fulsome praise: "The more I hear the new album—at least fifty times since early July—the more I feel that it's one of the finest records Dylan has ever made. In time, it is possible that it might even be considered his greatest." But Wenner was equally aware that "this claim will not go down easily, especially with all the 'born again' clamor."[26] Other encomiums followed. By October 1979, just a month after Jimmy Carter's Old Fashioned Gospel Singin', Dylan's evangelical LP had climbed fifty-four positions on the *Billboard* charts, landing at number three. On October 18, 1979, Dylan even appeared on the decidedly irreverent and satirical *Saturday Night Live,* alongside Monty Python star Eric Idle, to perform three tracks from the record: "I Believe in You," "When You Gonna Wake Up," and "Gotta Serve Somebody." The latter garnered Dylan a Grammy in 1980.[27]

Looking back from the vantage of 1980, a writer in the *Humanist* magazine took stock of this strange Christian turn. "Bob Dylan, Jennifer Warnes, Billy Preston, and Arlo Guthrie are now riding their rock-and-roll trains into Christian pastures," the reporter noted with awe. "To be 'born-again' Christian is now as popular as it was a few years ago to be a hard-rock music freak." This doubter could hardly believe that just so many years before there "were bonfires to burn albums of rock music" taking place across the Bible belt.[28] In the middle of the decade journalist and critic Tom Wolfe turned his skepticism into parody, with a send-up of the new evangelicalism. Wolfe sniffed,

> Today it is precisely the most rational, intellectual, secularized, modernized, updated, relevant religions—all the brave, forward-looking ethical culture, Unitarian, and Swedenborgian movements of only yesterday—that are finished, gasping, breathing their last. What the Urban Young People want from religion is a little *Hallelujah!* . . . and *talking in tongues!* . . . *Praise God!* . . . The Easter Christians still usually control the main Sunday-morning service—but the Charismatics take over on Sunday evening and do the holy roll.[29]

For Wolfe, latter-day holy rollers were as naïve as they were bizarre. The religious reawakening, of which the Jesus people and Christian rock acts were the most potent symbol, bothered Wolfe and a whole host of cultured despisers. But they were now ascendant and held a new kind of cultural power.

Wolfe's holy rollers were not the only ones caught up in the wave of spirituality in these years. The hallelujah trend continued to influence many far outside the domains of traditional Christianity. Reverend Eugene L. Smith, the executive secretary of the World Council of Churches, thought that Jesus rock fit right in with the temper of the times. A new interest in spirituality and the divine animated young people, many of whom traditional churches failed to reach. Said Smith, "Not since the 1st or 16th centuries has there been such a combination of interest in Christian faith and a disinterest in its institutional forms."[30]

By the early 1970s, that interest in Jesus and the vogue for religious-themed music was inspiring pop hits. It continued to find expression in top-selling records and on new FM radio stations far outside the explicitly religious realm. The pop charts in the late 1960s and early 1970s were filled with songs like Harry Nilsson's "I Guess the Lord Must Be in New York City" (1969), the Doobie Brothers' "Jesus Is Just Alright" (1972), and George Harrison's "My Sweet Lord" (1970). In 1971, the latter, with its alternating refrains of "Hallelujah" and "Hare Krishna," became the biggest-selling single of an increasingly post-

Christian Britain. Norman Greenbaum's jocular "Spirit in the Sky" (1969), replete with a driving fuzz guitar and heavy beat, would go on to become the best-selling single record in the United States in 1970. So pervasive was the trend that the 1950s revival group Sha Na Na even released a parody in 1971, "Top 40," which asked listeners if they were on the top forty of the Lord.[31] The national press also took notice. *Time* magazine reported that in "1966 Beatle John Lennon casually remarked that the Beatles were more popular than Jesus Christ; now the Beatles are shattered and George Harrison is singing 'My Sweet Lord.'" It was a surprising turn of events. "The new young followers of Jesus listen to Harrison," *Time* noted, "but they turn on only to the words of their Master."[32] With a flare for overstatement the London *Daily Mirror* proclaimed, "Suddenly, Jesus Christ Is More Popular than the Beatles."[33]

That was clearly hyperbolic. Still, the faith fad was everywhere. Christianity was now even the subject of Broadway fanfare. The stage success of musicals like *Joseph and the Amazing Technicolor Dreamcoat* (1968), *Godspell* (1971), and *Jesus Christ Superstar* (1971) reflected this new openness to, or cashing in on, religious topics. The latter seemed to capture the 1970s obsession with Jesus, although the King of Kings appeared in a decidedly earthy incarnation. In the *Chicago Tribune,* Thomas Willis enthused, "I am neither a theologian nor a rock critic, but if 'Jesus Christ Superstar' isn't the most important religious music of the year—and one of two or three significant recordings of the decade, I am sadly mistaken." It would not come as a shock, he wrote, echoing the *Daily Mirror's* exaggeration, if "John Lennon, who once suggested that the Beatles were bigger than Jesus Christ, may at this moment be eating his words."[34] Mainline Protestants, like many others in the national media, also heaped praise on the production. "Musically *Superstar* employs a variety of styles from blues to classical to English music hall to rock," remarked a Lutheran reviewer, "most of it [is] well done and surprisingly effective in expressing the wide range of emotions demanded by the text." He summarized, "The opera works to sensitize believers to the awesome fact that the word did become flesh and dwelt among us, that our redemption was won by the agony and bloody sweat of a real man, dying a real death on a terribly real cross."[35] An Episcopal church in Washington, DC, even opened up its doors and hosted a performance of the rock opera on Palm Sunday in 1971. The event was dedicated to

Martin Luther King Jr. "This is the first time I've been here," confessed one woman in attendance. "It was terrific," she judged. Even the older men and women in the pews admitted that they enjoyed the modern musical.[36]

Many other observers found it shallow or otherwise deficient. Anyone thinking the musical's kindergarten message was profound, sneered Dalton James in the *Village Voice,* "might want to invest in the Jesus Freak business."[37] But whether the attention was negative or positive, no one could deny that the success and reach of *Jesus Christ Superstar* was becoming one of the most important religious stories of the day. The media-hyped musical, written by the English duo Andrew Lloyd Webber and Tim Rice, proved to be a stunning international triumph. Jesus, in this retelling, was modern and surprisingly subversive. Judas was a sympathetic pragmatist. It amounted to a contemporary revamp of the passion play. But for millions of fans of *Jesus Christ Superstar,* the music itself was the big draw. A double-disc concept album of its songs came out in 1970 and charted success from Brazil to Thailand. The idea in itself was not entirely novel. The Who had already explored the rock opera in their 1969 opus *Tommy.* Venturing into the religious realm and the musical's mass audience appeal was what set *Jesus Christ Superstar* apart. The album quickly sold more than two million copies in the United States. Radio Vatican played it. In 1973, the musical was even adapted for the big screen.[38]

The evangelical reaction was mixed. Jesus people and other representatives of the new Christian counterculture were divided over what to make of it. On the one hand, the album and the musical seemed dismissive of the divine Christ that they worshipped. On the other, the record and the performance emphasized a personal and human Christ that they recognized.[39] Certainly, Jesus people welcomed the new interest in religious music. For that embrace of the counterculture and more, believers became a target for critics.

Representing the moderate, centrist part of the evangelical spectrum, the best-selling author and self-help prophet Norman Vincent Peale and the evangelist Billy Graham offered their verdicts. Peale thought it was a good sign of a return to Christianity. Drugs and hollow countercultural philosophies, he reasoned, were now losing ground to Jesus.[40] Graham thought that the musical was incomplete and theologically

Ted Neeley as Jesus Christ and Barry Dennen as Pontius Pilate in the 1973 film adaptation of *Jesus Christ Superstar*. Fundamentalists blasted the movie as blasphemous and profane. *Jesus Christ Superstar* (Universal Pictures, 1973), a Norman Jewison-Robert Stigwood production. Screenshot by the author from *Jesus Christ Superstar*, Special Edition (Universal Studios Home Entertainment, 2004), DVD.

problematic. Still, it shed a bright light on the son of God, he judged, and it revealed a new search for ultimate answers.[41] The television healing evangelist and college president Oral Roberts saw the performance in his hometown of Tulsa, Oklahoma. "I dug about 70 percent of it," he told those gathered at a Los Angeles Junior Chamber of Commerce prayer breakfast. Perhaps trying a little too hard to bridge the generation gap, the fifty-four-year-old Roberts then remarked, "I don't often dig that much of a church service."[42] At the very least, such evangelical leaders reasoned, young people were asking who Jesus Christ was. That was a step in the right direction.

Fundamentalists certainly could not admit as much. For such staunch conservatives, Christian themes just could not be set to rock and folk music. Such a fusion was unnatural, if not demonic. White southern fundamentalists offered stern warnings against the Jesus people, their hippie clothes, and their hideous music. The hippie counterculture was finally making inroads into the church. As far as defensive believers were concerned, the whole thing amounted to a troubling and dangerous turn of events. In the words of one doubter in 1971, Jesus freaks offered little more than Hollywood-type religion that was "turning on to Jesus!" The critic starkly concluded his diatribe with a King James flourish: "FUNDAMENTALIST: BEWARE that ye are not led astray. Examine every movement by the WORD OF GOD not the WONDER OF THE CROWD!!!!"[43]

In the same period another typical skeptic wrote, "Our Lord did not adopt the philosophies of the Greeks to reach the Greeks. He did not acquire the ways of the Romans to communicate to the Romans."[44] The fundamentalist preacher Jack Van Impe released a sermon on LP denouncing *Jesus Christ Superstar* in apocalyptic tones.[45] The *Biblical Evangelist* newspaper in Indiana gave its unvarnished opinion of the travesty. Expressing the opinion of numerous conservatives, it pronounced the rock opera an abomination. Lloyd Webber and Rice portrayed Jesus as "a vain, self-seeking man who really didn't know who He was, where He was going, or why He was here."[46] Another typical fundamentalist critic in Minneapolis was unwavering about the real trouble with the popular musical. "The 'Jesus Freaks' along with the rock-manic-freaks will leave no stone unturned to satisfy their ungodly appetites," he said. Surely the devil himself, he claimed, had made sure that the popular musical promoted a sinister, distorted doctrine.[47] Pastors and laypeople lined up to condemn the new sound of *Jesus Christ Superstar.*

Fundamentalists targeted any Christian compromisers who would dare to praise the musical or even play the hit album. In 1971, one program on the Moody Bible Institute's WMBI radio ran a segment on the rock opera. The response from fundamentalists was immediate and vociferous. A minister in Prospect Heights, Illinois, led the charge. In a circular letter he thrashed WMBI. "I ask you," fumed Paul Lindstrom, "how can you continue to support the station that misleads impressionable young people? . . . That speaks well of those who are haters of Jesus Christ and liars? . . . That promotes the tools of Satan?" Picketers descended on the station and organized protests at the Broadway musical's performances around the country.[48] The president of Moody Bible Institute, engulfed by the radio controversy, made the school's position on the musical absolutely clear. To prove that he was on the right side of the theological divide, the president wrote to Bob Jones III, claiming that the rock opera was indeed "blasphemous, Satanic, and of no evangelistic value."[49]

Few continued to crusade against rock music in the 1970s and 1980s as did Jerry Falwell. In the early and mid-1980s, he still found rock 'n' roll music an inappropriate carrier for the gospel. The Virginia television preacher even publicly criticized evangelical soft rock and pop. The chaotic, savage, and disruptive beat of the music, he said, was just one of the many things that made it problematic.[50] Such ministers continued to focus on the jungle rhythms that damned rock 'n' roll. Falwell's Thomas Road Baptist Church would stay segregated until 1968. The strident minister of the Baptist Bible Fellowship congregation had preached in favor of segregation a decade earlier. In 1971, the first African American was baptized in the church. By then, Falwell could no longer resist the inevitable.[51]

Constituents of Falwell's Moral Majority, a political action group that the televangelist founded in 1979, tended to remain steadfast in their rejection of rock and all its unholy bombast. Sanctified rock 'n' roll was still rock 'n' roll as far as they were concerned. The Moral Majority had brought the movement into the harsh glare of the national spotlight. It helped the GOP take the White House in 1980. Yet taking part in politics was one thing. Approving of church music that featured loud electric guitars and the steady banging of drums was another.

"Jerry Falwell would run us out of town," Dan Harrell, cofounder of the Nashville gospel label Reunion Records, told a reporter in 1982. "Some of our musicians have long hair. They're not clones" of the standard Christian, he said. Indeed, as of the late 1970s, Falwell's Liberty Baptist College maintained stringent rules for its two thousand students. Prohibitions seemed designed to hold back the currents of the countercultural revolution. Men were not allowed to have beards or mustaches. In the promiscuous and permissive "me decade," the student handbook banned women from wearing clothes that were "tight, scant, backless and low." It also prohibited "griping," because "a cynical attitude is destructive to Christian growth and fellowship." Rebellious rock music, religious or not, was positively out of the question. A Virginia radio announcer put it succinctly in the pages of *Christianity Today.* "Christian rock music," he observed in 1979, "is a bone in the throat" for those who detested the counterculture. But for the conservative faithful it was much more than just a matter of taste or politics. Fundamentalists looked to eternal truths to back them up. They pointed to passages in scripture like 2 Corinthians 6:14: "Be ye not unequally yoked together with unbelievers: for what fellowship hath righteousness with unrighteousness? and what communion hath light with darkness?" In these dark years, when music and pop culture reflected a new pessimism to match the outcomes of Watergate and the Vietnam War, Falwell's college promoted Christian nationalism and respect for authority.[52]

Under the aegis of Falwell's Moral Majority, a variety of conservative Christians united to fight off liberalism and what they assumed to be an insidious brand of secular humanism. Enthusiasts did not focus their energies just on external foes. Moderate and liberal Protestants and Catholics also came under fire. By the 1980s, Falwell's *Moral Majority Report* claimed it had one million subscribers and his *Fundamentalist Journal* boasted seventy thousand readers. Thirteen million viewers tuned in to his syndicated television program.[53]

Not all was well within the fundamentalist world, however. The movement was, as it had been for decades, rife with serious infighting. Laypeople and high-profile pastors across the spectrum might have been joined in opposition to permissiveness, rock music, and so much that they deemed worldly and reprobate. Still, they upbraided one another ferociously. For instance, Bob Jones II, and Bob Jones III, found much to criticize in Jerry Falwell's "pseudo-fundamentalism." They stood aghast that Falwell had built his political coalition with Mormons, Catholics, and Jews. Such rancor was not unusual. Numerous fundamentalists believed themselves to be set apart, or they claimed the title of the *true* remnant of believers. When they thumbed through their Bibles they saw as much in God's word: "I the Lord am holy, and have separated you from the peoples, that you should be mine" (Leviticus 20:26). Although the Joneses doubted Falwell's core values, Falwell was careful to spell out what it meant to be a separatist. Much of it had to do with shunning worldly amusements and pleasures. "Here at Liberty Baptist College," he lectured, "we require our faculty and students to abstain from the use of alcoholic beverages and tobacco." The small school in the foothills of the Virginia Blue Ridge mountains also forbade "attendance at dances or the Hollywood theater."[54]

Others might call themselves true believers who stood apart from a corrupting, evil culture, but the zealous Joneses did not believe them. In this way, denominations and independent churches disagreed with each other sharply about the specifics of ecclesiology, political activity, and theological subtleties. The faithful occasionally shouted down fellow fundamentalists with the kind of rage usually reserved for rock stars or liberal Protestants.[55]

The evangelical or pentecostal Christian rockers and their fundamentalist doubters were not entirely different, though. As scholar Heather Hendershot observes, "Separatist fundamentalists were never fully sheltered from secular forms of entertainment, for even as they attacked worldly mass culture as dangerous, they selectively drew from that culture when it suited their needs."[56] The promoter and Christian record executive Dan Harrell and others in the Christian rock industry wanted to reach out to the masses in much the same way that Falwell hoped to expand the Republican coalition. One set of conservative Christians looked to widen political participation. The other hoped that gospel music could infiltrate pop radio.

In late 1987, Billy Ray Hearn, president of the evangelical Sparrow Records in Tennessee, offered his thoughts on the subject to the *New York Times.* "Many evangelicals say that rock music is of the devil," he lamented. "But thousands of kids come to our concerts and get their lives straightened out."[57] Hearn, along with Ralph Carmichael and Kurt Kaiser, had already done much to fuse pop and folk music with Christian themes. Such pioneers even wrote early youth folk musicals—*Tell It Like It Is* (1969), *Good News* (1967), and *Natural High* (1970)—in the Jesus people mold.[58] Pop sensibilities, evangelicalism, and entrepreneurialism merged in such work.

Capitalizing on those early efforts, Amy Grant, one of the most popular new young artists, drew massive teenage crowds to her concerts in the 1980s and sold millions of records. Word Records released her self-titled debut when she was only sixteen. It sold a respectable fifty thousand copies. At twenty-one, Grant was being managed by Harrell. At the time, Grant, an Augusta, Georgia, native, was still a student at Vanderbilt University. In the coming years she would become a world-famous soft rock and pop star, crossing over into the realm of mainstream music. She sang ballads, country songs, and rock. In the early 1980s she performed on the nationally televised *Billy Graham Crusade*. Music critics and fans heard in her songs distinct echoes of Carole King, Carly Simon, or Whitney Houston. She also brought a new kind of sex appeal and stylishness into the world of contemporary

Christian music. In 1982, ten years after the Jesus people first made international headlines, Grant's album *Age to Age* did surprisingly well, eventually going gold. She even scored a Grammy Award nomination.[59] By the middle of the decade she was a well-known star. In December 1985, she joined President Reagan and the First Lady on stage for NBC's televised *Christmas in Washington* special, along with Tom Brokaw, Pat Boone, and Natalie Cole.[60]

For those who opposed the lurid innovations of Christian pop and rock music, such official recognition or worldly acclaim mattered little. Even rock music with its hard edges softened, like that performed by Amy Grant, was still rock music. Such music sounded nothing like what white fundamentalists like Falwell and others promoted. The new music violated the standards of decency. Staunch traditionalists approved of southern gospel music, hymns, and patriotic God-and-country standards. Falwell's Liberty Baptist College, for instance, sponsored vocal groups and soloists that harkened back to a pure America that never was. The college's performers—the men wearing matching, light-colored three-piece suits and the women sporting long colonial-style dresses that celebrated purity and bicentennial values—sang in dulcet tones about family, piety, church life, and the hereafter. The male performers kept their hair cropped short. They combined nostalgic barbershop harmonies with the lulling melodies of *The Lawrence Welk Show*. An antidote to punk and heavy metal music it was not. Falwell's campus community, school officials asserted, would promote Christian Americanism and moral values. In the early 1970s, the institution forbade any "demonstration, riot, or other act of violence." Students who circulated unauthorized petitions would "be expelled immediately." The school, like numerous fundamentalists and evangelical academies and colleges, intended to control almost every aspect of student life and entertainment.[61]

In her celebratory *Jerry Falwell: Man of Vision,* the popular Christian author Patricia Pingry describes one of the Lynchburg pastor's 1980 political rallies. No one could mistake this kind of activism for the sort that dominated headlines and disrupted college campuses in the 1960s. At the Charleston, West Virginia, "I Love America" rally in April, she recalls, the "crowd is modestly dressed; there are no protest signs. The singers are not from a rock group or a country and Western group or even from a popular vocal group . . . the young men have that freshly scrubbed look." A row of fluttering American flags provided a backdrop for the patriotic tableau. America was in trouble, Falwell typically announced at such gatherings. Dangerous influences were working their way into public schools. Women had entered the workforce and forsaken their God-given roles within the family. Bursts of cheers and loud amens punctuated Falwell's jeremiad. Perhaps to remind those gathered that the America they knew was fast fading, the choral group performed old-time hymns before finishing off with a crowd-pleasing rendition of Irving Berlin's "God Bless America."[62]

The Liberty Baptist College Singers and the I Love America Singers accompanied Falwell at such political rallies and college-related events. These and similar groups crisscrossed the nation with their message of salvation and patriotism, playing at the congressional prayer breakfast, Disneyland, and on the weekly TV show *Old-Time Gospel Hour with Dr. Jerry Falwell.* One Liberty Baptist College Singers music revue that toured in 1977, said Falwell, was meant "to awaken Americans to a deeper love for our country and to rekindle the love for God's precious word in the hearts of every citizen." Another multimedia music performance, of which Falwell was equally proud, was titled "America, You're Too Young to Die!"[63]

Perhaps the most successful of an array of prefab gospel and folk acts of this era was Up with People, which served as a kind of model for similar efforts on Christian college campuses across the nation. Evangelical magazines and denominational newspapers eagerly featured the bright, young, clean-cut singing group in their pages. In the late 1960s, Up with People relied on a staggering twenty thousand performers, young men and women from twenty nations. *Life* magazine called it the "latest manifestation of Moral Re-Armament, [a] quasi-religious, quasi-political group which has endeavored for 30 years to promote four absolute standards of behavior: honesty, purity, unselfishness, and love." The group's self-titled album sold nearly one million copies and their *Pace* magazine reached one hundred thousand readers each month. Up with People's "sugar-coated" songs were optimistic and patriotic, a conservative answer to protest music and antisocial rock. Not surprisingly, the group garnered financial support from major corporations and became a special cause for the Republican Party. Conservative pop icon Pat Boone hosted one of their first major TV specials. (Decades later, in a running gag on the critically acclaimed animated television program *The Simpsons,* Up with People would be parodied as the fresh-faced Hooray for Everything.)[64]

It all seemed to prove that not every young person was a political dissenter or a savage longhair with a rock 'n' roll addiction. The troupe performed at the Super Bowl and met with presidents and the pope. They also toured high school auditoriums, community centers, and county fairs. In the late 1960s, they played a Young Republicans–sponsored event at Harvard University. The *Harvard Crimson* took note of the 130 singers, who seemed to be bizarrely out of step with the era. "Their blue eyes gleamed and smiles wrapped all the way around their faces," wrote a suspicious student reporter. "Their hair was short and they wore yellow and tan and blue blazers or pastel jumpers with white blouses." On the Cambridge campus they performed songs like "You Can't Live Crooked (and Think Straight)" and "Which Way America?" to the hisses and catcalls of skeptical students. Another standard number, titled "Gee, I'm Looking Forward to the Future," contained the lyrics "I threw a wish afar / That the whole world could be better than before." A San Jose, California, student who sat through one of their performances at his high school thought their music was "sickening" and "preachy," "a cheap kind of propaganda."[65] Years later, a *Rolling Stone* writer cracked that the choral sensation was composed of "chipper castrati packed in ice."[66] Still, the show's leader, J. Blanton Belk Jr., said that Up with People sang beloved anthems for the silent majority. "Why should the only voice that is heard from youth be the pacifist, anti-patriotic protest of a minority?" he rhetorically asked a reporter.[67] President Richard Nixon agreed. The musical group supported Nixon on the campaign trail in 1968, belting out songs like "Freedom Isn't Free." In February 1971, the troupe performed alongside Bob Hope in the White House's East Room as part of a dinner honoring governors. By then, its male singers wore slightly longer hair and sideburns, in keeping with new fashion sensibilities. Even with the change in appearance, Up with People was exactly the kind of vibrant, obedient, and cheery group that conservatives hoped would be the cure for discordant, distasteful rock music.[68]

Conservative parents, Republican politicians, and corporate sponsors hoped that Up with People would lead a revolution in youth values.

Yet it would take more than that to change preferences and listening habits. Policing and controlling the musical tastes of young people proved especially difficult for fundamentalists, who held exacting standards. It was not just Liberty Baptist College that closely monitored student behavior. School officials at a variety of fundamentalist colleges told young men and women what clothes they could and could not wear, what hairstyles were unacceptable, who they could date, and what forms of entertainment were off limits. Ardent critics of Christian rock were not above making fun of the appearance of prominent performers. One minister charged that Larry Norman's "long, blond locks would allow him to fit unobtrusively into the Peter, Paul & Mary group (as Mary)."[69] Such criticisms along with codes of conduct set these fundamentalists off from their secular, liberal, or moderate evangelical counterparts. Still, the kinds of rules enforced were not static but changed with shifting values and cultural mores. At the Bible Institute of Los Angeles (Biola), for instance, school officials expanded regulations over the decades of the twentieth century. The regulations these schools set out reveal much about the boundary work and maintenance of gender norms that fundamentalists were engaged in. Biola regulated dating and banned blue jeans, Bermuda shorts, collarless shirts, and beach sandals for men. Women were required to wear dresses and "feminine clothing," unless they were involved in recreational activities. In the early 1970s, the student handbook laid down the law: "Men may not wear beards and sideburns must not extend below the bottom of the ear. Biola College does not approve of long hair for men." The countercultural revolution that surrounded the Los Angeles campus would be kept at bay.[70]

Biola, the Moody Bible Institute in Chicago, Liberty Baptist College, and Bob Jones University all forbade students from listening to rock, jazz, and other questionable styles of music. Bob Jones University maintained one of the strictest regimens of them all. They had the usual rules that constrained the behavior of the six thousand students on its sprawling Greenville, South Carolina, campus. The young men and women there were forbidden to smoke, drink alcohol, play cards, listen to rock music, and dance, and they were not allowed to hold hands or date those of a different race. Bob Jones continued to link rock music to savagery and racial drift in ways that other evangelicals had come to find disturbing, if not downright racist. The school's administration upheld these policies as a feature of social stability and good order. As one journalist put it, the rules guaranteed that "Bob Jones' students were not tempted to marry outside the race." The 1975 student handbook spelled out the details with razor-sharp clarity: "Students who date outside of their own race will be expelled." That regulation would remain in place until the year 2000. Facing greater public scrutiny, Bob Jones III tried to clarify the controversial matter in the early 1980s, remarking, "There's nothing in our religious beliefs that provides for the exclusion of blacks or any other races. We love all people." But then, as if to nullify what he had just said, Jones asserted, "The Bible clearly teaches, starting in the 10th chapter of Genesis and going all the way through, that God has put differences among people on the earth to keep the earth divided." God thwarted mankind's foolish efforts to unify the world, Jones declared. Moreover, the acceptance of interracial marriage played into the hands of "the antichrist and the one-world system." Not surprisingly, at that time Bob Jones University had only ten black students.[71]

Bob Jones University authorities even called on students to help the school police the behavior of other students. Upon seeing co-eds violate rules, they were to report the misconduct. Rock music, associated as it was with disorder, rebellion, and interracialism, was singled out for special rebuke. Even religious music set to a rock beat or melody or played in a folk style was not allowed. And whereas the school eventually eased up on mixed-race relationships, the ban on pop music remained. As of the 2015–2016 school year, Bob Jones University still advised students that "any music which, in whole or in part, derives from the following broadly defined genres or their subgenres: Rock, Pop, Country, Jazz, Electronic / Techno, Rap / Hip Hop or the fusion of any of these genres" conflicts "with our mission and is therefore excluded from performance, personal listening on and off campus, or use in student organizations, societies, student productions, outreach ministries or social media."[72]

Liberty Baptist College president Jerry Falwell believed that firm rules sharpened students' moral vision and gave them firm principles to live by. In the mid-1970s, Liberty even instituted a kind of moral tabulation system. Students would receive demerits for writing bad checks, leaving Lynchburg without permission, breaching the dress code, or having the wrong kind of haircut. Five demerits would result in a letter home to the student's parents. Ten triggered a minimum one-week suspension. For those few who reached fifteen, it meant suspension for a semester. Anyone caught listening to rock music received four demerits. Drinking alcohol or stealing resulted in fifteen.[73]

Nancy Tatom Ammerman embarked at Yale on a doctorate in sociology to understand the social world of fundamentalists in this era. She wanted to know how they saw themselves in relation to the world around them. She intended to avoid the limited, functionalist, reductive interpretation dominant in her field. Ammerman paid special attention to the ways the faithful marked themselves off from other Christians and from worldly people. Those she studied were certain that their faith was the only true path. Others, be they liberal Protestants or moderate evangelicals, were lost in a dark cloud of apostasy. Stalwarts guarded themselves from the wicked pop culture that surrounded them. They would not make compromises, as other wayward Protestants had. Ammerman observed that these fundamentalists were "unwilling to accept 'Christian' rock." The "music with a strong beat is inherently seductive, and no amount of good intentions can turn one of Satan's tools into something a believer should enjoy." One way to guarantee the purity of young people, then, was to shut them off from the larger world. "Students at Bible colleges," said Ammerman, "are protected from the evils of rock music by being forbidden to listen to any but Christian radio."[74]

But even Christian radio was now under some suspicion, as its format expanded to include an ever-widening array of Christian rock songs by Keith Green, John Michael Talbot, DeGarmo & Key, Amy Grant, or louder, heavier acts like Petra or Resurrection Band. A standard fundamentalist denunciation of Christian rock in these years focused on the unholy compromise it represented. A fundamentalist minister in Arizona condemned it as a "middle of the road" approach. "Christian rock uses the beat and sound which even the secular world associates with promiscuous sex!" shouted Reverend Harry Bruce in 1983. He took it upon himself to warn his community of this snake in the garden. His sermon on the subject was armed with exclamation points. "Christian rock is an attempt to give young people what they want rather than what they need!" Taking a clear shot at the Jesus hippies and their movement, he admonished them, "There is nothing groovy about Calvary. Jesus['s] death and resurrection isn't titillating hype! You can't just sneak Jesus into music, while the beat is so loud the people are hypnotized behind closed doors!" Surely, he pleaded with his church and the larger community, the ends in this case could never justify the means.[75]

The fundamentalist tract writer Jack Chick, whose cheaply printed cartoon pamphlets were ubiquitous on college campuses in the 1970s and 1980s, also focused on the extreme incongruousness of Jesus rock. One of Chick's cartoons from 1989 featured a fictional Christian rock group called the Green Angels. The band exemplified the moral compromises and hypocrisies of performers. Panels show them signing their contract in blood, being sexually "deviant," and complaining about not making enough money. At one point, a member of the Green Angels wonders why a pastor had criticized his band. "We were putting Jesus in it," he comments with exasperation, "just like all the other rock groups who play in churches."[76]

The itinerant crusader Bob Larson relied on some of these same themes and arguments. He would become the most well known minister in the United States to fulminate against rock 'n' roll. Like the anti-Beatles and anticommunist lecturer David Noebel, Larson would rise to fame in evangelical and fundamentalist circles by speaking at churches, summer camps, community centers, or anywhere else that would host him. Larson told his listeners that he had once fronted a rock band in the Midwest before undergoing a conversion experience. Part of the popular youth evangelist's pitch had to do with his own experience. He claimed to have written over a hundred rock songs and worked as a radio DJ. After being born again he had decided to commit himself to preaching on the evils of rock 'n' roll, dropping out of the University of Nebraska to do so.[77] Starting in the mid-1960s, Larson took to the road. He went onto local television and radio shows, demonstrating with vivid and lurid illustrations the "moral evils of rock 'n' roll." He toured the country, taking his self-professed insider knowledge to Youth for Christ rallies and high school assemblies. His lecture topics ranged over "Astrology and the Age of Aquarius," "Demonology and Jesus Christ Superstar," and "Drugs, Defilement, and Death." His own album, an alternative to the music he denounced from the pulpit so intensely, was titled *The Humorous Gospel Songs of Bob Larson.* It sold for five dollars.[78]

Larson, a consummate self-promoter, even won the attention of a snarky journalist at the *Village Voice,* who gleefully pilloried the square, itinerant evangelist. Years before, the big beat had been linked to juvenile delinquency. Larson, the writer cracked, traveled the land, "warning against the same old bugaboo." In Larson's "updated version, rock and roll leads innocent youth to stuff far more pernicious than ducktails and dual mufflers." After reading Larson's many pamphlets and books and interviewing him in person, the writer concluded that it "sounds as if Bob Larson is auditioning for a seat on Nixon's [Federal Communications Commission]."[79] Unfazed by doubters and scoffers, Larson went on to establish a kind of fundamentalist media empire. He set up Bob Larson Ministries in Denver, Colorado. He later ventured into exorcism and exposing the plots of Satanists. So successful were his heavily publicized campaigns, books, and radio show that by the late 1980s he was reportedly earning around $200,000 annually.[80]

Larson delivered one of his standard lectures in Portland, Oregon, in late October 1978. The rock performer turned evangelist always had plenty of sermonic material to work with. In the months before his lecture the hard rock band AC/DC issued its *If You Want Blood You've Got It,* punk rockers the Ramones put out *Road to Ruin,* and experimental art rocker David Bowie released his live *Stage* album. "David Bowie," Larson said to his Portland audience, "is an avowed homosexual and he is one of the most popular figures in the entertainment field today." The thirty-four-year-old evangelist, with modest sideburns and a 1970s-style swooped, short hairdo, had been fine-tuning such lectures for over a decade. Here in the Northwest he spoke to capacity crowds at George Fox College and a Foursquare Gospel church. Young people were emulating these flawed and sinful stars, Larson counseled. He listed a litany of vices and crimes that rock promoted: pornography, drugs, Satanism, and masochism. Yes, Larson concluded, "we still can rescue some of the kids and that is what we must work to do." The last thing believers should do was make any room for rock 'n' roll.[81] Good intentions about inclusivity and reaching out to youth could not mask the real harm of rock, he assured his listeners.

Late in the 1970s, the Christian satirical magazine the *Wittenburg Door* decided to pit Bob Larson against Dennis Benson, who argued avidly for rock 'n' roll. By then, Larson was well established as the chief anti-rock-'n'-roll apostle, having written his first major book on the topic in 1967. To the editors of the *Door*, Larson appeared slight, small, and clean-shaven. His hair was held down with hairspray. They thought he looked like a "Southern Baptist." Benson, a study in contrast, was a burly forty-two-year-old man with a large beard. The Pittsburgh native was a Presbyterian minister and a popular radio DJ on KQV AM in Pittsburgh. His program, *The Backstage Special*, was heard across the country on sixty-five stations. He had interviewed John Lennon, Elvis Costello, Alice Cooper, and the wildly popular jazz-rock and white soul group Chicago. Those were all, of course, reprobates, in the clutches of Satan, as far as Larson was concerned.[82]

Sardonic as ever, the editors of the San Diego–based magazine got the interview off to a rocky start. Turning to Larson, they asked, "What do you like about rock music?" Perhaps stunned, Larson fired back, "What do I like about it? That's a back-handed question." A veteran of church hall meetings and youth group question-and-answer sessions, Larson was ready with a standard response. Rock was basically sensual, he lectured. It was carnal. Beyond that, it delved into dangerous Eastern mysticism. The Beatles were pioneers in that regard, especially after their 1968 pilgrimage to an Indian retreat center under the tutelage of guru Maharishi Mahesh Yogi. Larson called rock a doorway to the occult. The interviewer asked, "Do you really feel that eastern religion and demon possession is a part of rock and rock musicians lead to the East?" Larson snapped back, "A sizable percentage do and some of the more important ones do. The most obvious example is George Harrison." Larson confessed that he subscribed to *Rolling Stone* magazine and *Billboard.* One must know thy enemy, he reasoned.[83]

There was little that Larson had to say on the subject that had not been said before. But he had a special Manichaean knack for painting a frightening picture, populated with demons and succubi, drug users, lunatics, and an assortment of delinquents. But other crusaders, too, were finding new ways to warn of the demonic influence of rock in the 1980s. The entrepreneurial traveling evangelist Billy Mayo; the youth minister who worked with Larson, Jacob Aranza; and a collection of others convinced church, radio, and television audiences in the early 1980s that popular rock acts placed secret messages on their LPs. These were, in their telling, delivered by "backward masking" and could be heard when teenagers played their records in reverse. Mayo claimed that Queen's song "Another One Bites the Dust," when played backward, enticed youth to "start to smoke marijuana." The Beatles' "Revolution 9" from their 1968 White Album entreated, "Turn me on, dead man." The state governments of Arkansas and California even debated legislation to warn against or prevent rock groups from delivering such secret messages to impressionable fans.[84]

In these years, Bob Larson led the charge. Echoing the arguments that David Noebel or the Southern Baptist leader W. A. Criswell made years before, he drove home his point about the genre. Rock music, he figured, completely surrounded and captivated fans: "A person becomes very psychologically vulnerable to any suggestion that the man on the stage wants to make. [Fans] are literally controlled by the sounds." Larson also drew on persistent racialized arguments that had once been so common, especially in the white South. "I think the black has to be honest about his African culture," mused the preacher. "His African culture," Larson went on, "was to a very large extent, a pagan, demonized culture." He added that "rhythms were used to a large extent in fertility and licentious rituals, and they were designed to induce trance states." Obviously, Larson knew that African Americans might not like to hear such unvarnished truths, but he had "to be very honest in pointing that out."[85]

Dennis Benson, Larson's opponent in the interview, had a sharply different take on the music. The *Door* editors wanted to know if, like Larson, Benson thought that rock musicians were "under the influence of Satan." Benson believed that rock music was a mere expression of the longings and the desires of the audience. He even saw some continuities with American Christianity. Remarked Benson, "The whole rock concert is really like what a revival meeting used to be." The music united fans in a common search for truth. Was the beat of the music peculiarly sinister? asked the *Door*'s editors. No, Benson answered. Black music, he observed, had much in common with Hebrew music. Perhaps most importantly, Benson, unlike Larson, saw rock music as a bridge to young people. He thought it was best for Christians to "have the kids bring the album that turns them on and give them a real hearing for why they love that Bruce Springsteen hit or that one from James Taylor. Let them explain." Bob Larson's unequivocal demonization of the genre was matched here by Benson's sympathy for and desire to understand teenagers.[86]

In San Diego, the fundamentalist preacher Tim LaHaye, much like Larson and others on the far right, spelled out his views forcefully and clearly. Rock music, whether Christian or not, was bad for young people. The music was simply irredeemable. In a 1982 book that targeted humanism, LaHaye classed rock 'n' roll with other looming threats and deviant activities. He wrote about its nature and impact alongside discussions of drugs, pornography, homosexuality, feminism, and women in the workforce. On the latter, LaHaye found it "gratifying that many young college women are seeing through the feminist movement, which has agitated careerism, regardless of the cost, based on a humanist commitment to self-actualization. When he made these observations in 1982 about 52.6 percent of American women over the age of sixteen were actively looking for work or were employed. Thirty years earlier that number was a mere 34.7 percent. Such creeping careerism eroded the Christian family in much the way that "rock music is a vicious enemy of the family and should have no place in a Christian home." He also drew on the expertise of Larson. LaHaye was certain that "the sound and beat of rock are capable of destroying the emotions" and inflaming lusts that "are so easily ignited in young people." Such pronouncements harkened back to the race-baiting rhetoric of an earlier generation of white believers. In LaHaye's estimation, teenagers, under the influence of the devil's theme music, would turn to the occult and all manner of perversions. LaHaye looked back all the way to the early days of rock 'n' roll. Elvis had started it, he lamented, with "a musical revolution that integrated aggressive music and aggressive sex."[87]

One Christian educator drew on the wisdom of these self-styled rock-'n'-roll experts. "Noted authorities such as Jack Wyrtzen, Bob Larson, Dr. David Noebel and Sketch Erickson all agree," he wrote with certainty. Each of them had shown that it was impossible for "a rock 'n' roll sound that is described by 'rock stars' as 'sex music' " to ever "be an appropriate medium for conveying the gospel of Christ." If that was not enough to convince, he offered in addition the words of the New Testament passage of 2 Corinthians 7:1: "Having therefore these promises, dearly beloved, let us cleanse ourselves from all filthiness of the flesh and spirit, perfecting holiness in the fear of God."[88]

The well-known pentecostal television evangelist Jimmy Swaggart spent a great deal of time and energy on that theme of purity. Long before Swaggart would suffer public humiliation from a sex scandal involving a prostitute, he used his pulpit to oppose the wickedness of rock 'n' roll. On television he warned off Christians from dabbling in the music. In the mid-1980s, he joined the likes of U.S. Attorney General Edwin Meese and popular evangelical family expert James Dobson in labeling heavy metal as pornographic. Swaggart preached against retail chains like Wal-Mart and Kmart for carrying objectionable records.[89]

After Elvis died in 1977, Swaggart used the star as an object lesson on the many troubles of rock. The televangelist wrote somberly, "I delayed writing this for some time after the premature death of Elvis Presley because I didn't want to speak out on this subject without much prayerful consideration." Now he was ready, and he was not holding back. Lucifer used the music as "a weapon in his cause" and "made rock and roll the anthem of the drug generation." Some well-known preachers, Billy Graham among them, Swaggart admitted, were certain that they would meet Elvis up in heaven. "I hope they're right," Swaggart remarked. The thought of Elvis burning for all eternity in hell unnerved him. At best, the Louisiana evangelist said, Elvis was a lukewarm believer. He did not pass the faith test.[90]

It was easy enough for Swaggart to pass judgment on the King of Rock 'n' Roll. But some wondered if Swaggart was so certain that the music itself was inherently bad. The Assemblies of God minister liked to comment on his deep familiarity with the pernicious effects of the genre. His cousin was Jerry Lee Lewis after all, he would tell interviewers. He knew of the travails of Jerry Lee, Elvis, Chuck Berry, and similar stars from the first generation. "I've seen it destroy my cousin and so many others," he remarked in 1985, "just totally wreck them." By extension, Swaggart was firm, arguing that "so-called Christian rock" was wrong and was leading believers astray. In part, argued the famous television minister, contemporary Christian music was troubling because of the "attitude, the atmosphere of trying to make a group *look* like a rock group. . . . I don't know why anyone would want to do that." It certainly was not leading youngsters to Jesus, he cautioned.[91]

Ironically, one of the most famous, and controversial, Christian rock groups of the era, called Stryper, owed much to Swaggart and his TV

The pentecostalist televangelist Jimmy Swaggart, cousin of Jerry Lee Lewis, preaching to a large crowd in Dallas, Texas, June 20, 1981. Swaggart was a fierce opponent of rock music and Christian rock. *Classic Crusades: Dallas, Texas* (Jimmy Swaggart Ministries, 1981), CR1022. Screenshot by the author from YouTube, Louis Calzada (https://www.youtube.com/watch?v=StLB1bZuNhE).

ministry. Guitarist Michael Sweet and his brother Robert Sweet, a drummer, claimed to have been converted while watching one of Swaggart's high-energy evangelistic campaigns on television. Swaggart, in turn, would later denounce with full force the Christian metal band the two formed.[92]

In the early 1980s, the Sweet brothers joined up with Oz Fox (guitar) and Tim Gaines (bass guitar) to form their Orange County, California, band. Stryper very quickly garnered media attention, loyal fans, and created a fair share of controversy. The group took its name from a passage in the Old Testament book of Isaiah 53:5: "But he was wounded for our transgressions, he was bruised for our iniquities: the chastisement of our peace was upon him; and with his stripes we are healed."[93] Their long hair was teased up, in the style of 1980s metal chart toppers. They wore yellow-and-black skintight suits, festooned with zippers and chains. The metal-studded armbands and gloves they put on, a fashion that had drifted from bikers and bondage mavens, were essential to the look of popular secular artists like Iron Maiden, Mötley Crüe, W.A.S.P., and Judas

Priest. "The Los Angeles–based groups that have made it nationally . . . offer the lures of dope, sex, cheap thrills, and Satanism," wrote rock critic Chris Morris in 1985. "But Stryper," he continued, heaping on the cynicism, "eschew the pro-Devil trappings." They combined heavy power chords with "the religious fervor of a Baptist tent show."[94] The band had been mocked and laughed at so much on the road and in gritty clubs that they had become almost immune to it.

Secular label Enigma Records in Los Angeles was certainly not deterred by sneering critics. They signed the group and released Stryper's first album, *Yellow and Black Attack!*, in 1984. There had been other hard rock and Christian metal bands before, like Barnabas or Daniel Band. But none had garnered the critical backing of a well-situated secular label, and none would win the kind of attention the Los Angeles foursome did.[95]

The same year of their first release they played the storied Calvary Chapel in Costa Mesa, California, an early base for the Jesus people and instrumental in the fusion of neo-pentecostalism and rock music. Stryper's music, of course, sounded nothing like the Jesus freak folk tunes of 1971. But their songs crossed new boundaries in much the way that Larry Norman's songs had a decade before. Stryper's chugging, squealing, and buzzing electric guitars were accompanied by the standard semioperatic and growling vocals of front man Michael Sweet. The group had the unmistakable sound of the UK's Def Leppard and the Los Angeles–based Quiet Riot. Subsequent albums like *Soldiers under Command* (1985), *To Hell with the Devil* (1986), and *In God We Trust* (1988) would sell millions of copies. On the heels of that success, Stryper played churches, youth hangouts, large auditoriums, stadiums, and festivals around the United States and launched world tours as well. *To Hell with the Devil* received a Grammy nomination and climbed up the top forty chart. At various times the bands Poison and Metallica opened up for them. In 1988, Stryper even performed on the long-running rock and dance television show *American Bandstand.* At the high point of their run, the group boasted two platinum and four gold records.[96]

Throughout their career, Stryper had two hostile camps arrayed against them. It was a turn of events that fit with the Christian metal band's black-and-white view of the universe. The group proved to be both enormously popular with fans and detested by their many critics in the rock press. Fundamentalists also reviled them. Or, as an Austra-

Christian heavy metal band Stryper's bassist Tim Gaines in the band's 1987 video for "Calling on You" (Enigma Music Video, 1987), from the album *The Hell with the Devil* (Enigma Records, 1986), distributed by Capitol Records, Inc. Screenshot by the author from YouTube, TMFC's Classic Rock Channel (http://www.youtube.com/watch?v=P9dVGThz1-E).

lian reporter put it, rock groups like "Stryper have conservative Christians and atheist rock fans alike shuddering."[97] Another savvy observer summed up the trouble with the band and its mission to reach youth: "True, God's Word doesn't have to be boring, but it doesn't have to be mediocre either."[98]

Rock journalists and music aficionados alike were immediately suspicious of what they thought were Stryper's gimmicks, schlocky music, and painfully sincere message. A writer in *Billboard* magazine caught a 1985 show at the Santa Monica Civic Auditorium. At such performances, the band hurled small Gideon Bibles into the crowd. On some nights, that added up to $1,000 worth of Good Books. Strobe lights, a yellow-and-black-striped set, and elaborate staging added to the drama. This observer thought the music was too derivative of other heavy metal groups. The band nonetheless seemed sincere, even though Stryper's "stage show is as manipulative as a Jimmy Swaggart fundraiser."[99] Another, more acerbic reviewer in *Spin* magazine dressed down the group for making "lousy records" and for being "boring." "If they played good metal," he sniped, perhaps their sanctimoniousness could be forgiven.[100] A Texas journalist, and a critical observer of all things evangelical, had made a similar comment several years before. "The irony of all this ruckus being raised about Christian rock," she quipped, "was that most of it was so dull it would have lulled any lurking demons."[101]

Fundamentalists had their own reasons for denouncing the popular Christian metal band. The group's fashion sensibilities, the makeup they wore, and their wailing guitars made them an easy target. Writing in Jerry Falwell's *Fundamentalist Journal,* a reporter from Pennsylvania reflected on the larger meaning of Stryper. The group seemed to him like a supposedly Christian version of the much-discussed glam metal band KISS. But true Christians, he reasoned, could easily see that Stryper was "a ridiculous contradiction that helps prove the medium must fit the message." To make things crystal clear, he continued, "Music cannot be prostituted to spread the gospel." Such fundamentalists applied the same kind of commonsense logic they used to interpret the Bible to the problem of musical style. There might not be such a thing as a Christian car, the writer in the *Fundamentalist Journal* reasoned; however, "there is a type of music that lifts the name of Christ." He concluded, "It is not the type that contains a throbbing rock 'n' roll beat."[102] Stryper, in this sense, were unwitting agents of Lucifer. As another fundamentalist put it, they were the "Devil's Disciples." Allowing teens to listen to heavy metal because of its Christian lyrics amounted to "the same deception that was used when 'Jesus Christ Superstar' came out."[103]

Heeding that wisdom, some religious groups took direct action. At the Assemblies of God's August 1987 convention, the denomination condemned Amy Grant and Stryper as well as oxymoronic Christian rock. Grant's overtly sexual performances, they admonished listeners, were disgraceful. Stryper's music and shows were antithetical to pentecostalism. "They dress like devils and wear Spandex costumes," declared church leaders, "their performance contradicted everything the Gospel stands for."[104] Reverend Joseph Pyott thought the matter was simple enough. "If you put the name Jesus on whiskey," he reasoned, "it would still make you drunk. Putting the label 'Jesus' on rock music doesn't change the essential nature of it. . . . It is still as bad as before."[105] Jimmy Swaggart, the most prominent member of the Assemblies of God, called it simply the "music of Satan."[106] It stung. Christians who boycotted their shows, drummer Robert Sweet confided to a reporter, "come out with picket signs and bullhorns and banners from TV, they've never seen us in concert." He thought it "just seems weird. Here we are standing

Amy Grant appearing on Jim and Tammy Faye Bakker's Christian television program *PTL*, on November 18, 1981. The singer spoke to the hosts about disobedient children and the signs of the times. Grant also performed her soft rock on the show. PTL Television Network, November 18, 1981, PTL Ministries Inc. Screenshot by the author from YouTube, Mansion Entertainment (http://www.youtube.com/watch?v=lo3RQJMe8WE).

up for Jesus and they are too. Yet they boycott us." Sweet told the *Washington Post* in November 1985 that Swaggart was still his "favorite evangelist," even though the affection was not mutual. Sweet said, "He and I are going to sit down one day. I predict after he gets to know us he'll hold up a Stryper album on television and say, 'Hey, these guys are okay.' "[107] But such a rapprochement was not meant to be.

Through all the handwringing, debates, and denunciations, Christian rock kept pace with the changing styles and tastes of the era. In truth, solo artists and bands tended to arrive a little late to a given scene. But there was rarely a subgenre that could not be colonized by Christian artists. Some heavy metal acts had been around long before Stryper formed; among those were Jerusalem from Sweden; Petra from Fort Wayne, Indiana; and the Resurrection Band, who were part of the Jesus People USA community in Chicago. Disco music, too—so associated as it was with nightlife, gay club culture, and cocaine—had an evangelical version in the band Seawind and in Reba Rambo.[108]

Disco and hard rock might appeal to those raised on 1970s FM radio. But for younger listeners, such music sounded rusty and out of touch. In 1978, Christian rock icon Larry Norman warned readers of *Christianity Today* of the new " 'punk rock' groups like The Dead Boys, The Damned, and Johnny Rotten and The Sex Pistols." These new bands—with their atonal, riotous music, dyed hair, and torn clothes—"claim to believe in absolutely nothing," he informed them.[109] In only a matter of years, Christian acts moved into this new sonic and stylistic territory. They replaced nihilism with born-again Christianity. For new wave and synthesizer pop, evangelical fans turned to The 77s, Steve Taylor, or Daniel Amos. There were even punk rock groups that an adventurous, progressive Baptist youth minister might recommend to his teens. Among these were the metal-punk fusionists One Bad Pig from Austin, Texas; Nobody Special and Undercover from Orange County, California; and Scattered Few from nearby Burbank. Alternative and art-rock bands formed, toured, and released records in the 1980s as well. Those included Lifesavers Underground, Adam Again, 4-4-1, the Altar Boys, and the Choir.[110] One entrepreneurial pastor and youth worker even published a handy guide to Christian rock in 1984. Fundamentalists might reject all this kind of music, but they were being impractical and bigoted, he reasoned. His chart allowed youngsters and their parents to find the artists or bands that sounded most like the secular performers they once had enjoyed. "What's *your* favorite style of music?" he asked. Perhaps with too much optimism he emphasized, "No matter what it is, there's probably some contemporary Christian music which will fit your tastes."[111]

Not surprisingly, *Billboard* magazine summed up the year 1985 by observing that it "was the year the rest of the world began to take Christian music seriously." During the Reagan and George H. W. Bush years, newspapers and magazines ran features on Amy Grant and Stryper, as well as the pop rock heartthrob Michael W. Smith. Sounding and looking like an evangelical version of George Michael or Richard Marx, Smith wrote albums that went gold and platinum. *Keyboard Magazine* praised Smith as one of the best rock keyboardists around. Stryper, said a critic, showed that "even headbangers could make a joyful noise." A select group of Christian artists were now selling records at nearly the rate that their mainstream counterparts were.[112]

The new, ubiquitous Christian rock music, the Christian bookstores that were popping up around the country, and the large, outdoor concerts that showcased the talents of the saved were hard to miss. Festival attendees, artists, and preachers inhabited a world that was losing some of its strangeness, its weird sectarianism. By the late 1970s and early 1980s, believers were out in public, blaring their sanctified rock in new ways. The Explo '72 festival in Dallas, headlined by Billy Graham and Johnny Cash, had set the tone for a range of highly coordinated and planned music events. Creation Festival in Pennsylvania, which began in the late 1970s, would eventually draw between fifty thousand and one hundred thousand festival goers. Other gatherings, like Cornerstone Music Fest, near Macomb, Illinois, boasted twenty-five thousand attendees in the mid-1990s. "Christian rock musicians may look like their secular colleagues—sporting Mohawk haircuts and punk outfits," said a reporter who braved the dusty, crowded, and loud, three-day Cornerstone festival in the summer of 1984, but those who gathered there had a higher calling and saw "themselves as 'music ministers,' using their sound to spread the gospel."[113]

For all that had changed, much remained the same. The theology and evangelism techniques of most performers placed them in the conservative camp, if not in an outright fundamentalist one. Musicians emphasized the rock-solid truths of an inerrant Bible and sang or preached about abstinence, upright middle-class values, and the imminent return of Jesus. Their lyrics lamented the banning of school prayer and the acceptance of homosexuality. Some songs took aim at secular humanism or the Supreme Court's *Roe v. Wade* decision that legalized abortion in 1973. Performers called America back to the country's presumed sacred roots.[114] In that sense, even the longhaired and leather-clad rocker was not so unlike Jerry Falwell. In 1972, the Southern Baptist seminary professor John W. Drakeford described the Jesus freaks as a "strange shotgun marriage of conservative religion and a rebellious counterculture."[115] That observation still held true in subsequent decades.[116] In 1991, one music critic described Steven Curtis Chapman's mixture of soft Christian rock with creationism and militarism: it was like "Lionel Richie meets Oral Roberts."[117]

Exceptions tended to prove the rule. There were some signs of a more moderate or even liberal outlook among some musicians and within select communities. Some alternative groups and solo artists from the 1980s to the early 2000s—like Mark Heard, T Bone Burnett, Sam Phillips, Over the Rhine, Bruce Cockburn, the Lost Dogs, Adam Again, Pedro the Lion, or Sufjan Stevens—were more open to social justice matters or championed progressive and liberal causes. Some were even vocal about their political leanings. Many of these, not surprisingly, would have complicated if not discomfited relations with the Christian rock industry and music scene. The Jesus People USA (JPUSA) commune in Chicago, for instance, kept alive an activist vision and an antimaterialist practice. The Christian rock group most closely attached to the community, the Resurrection Band, or Rez Band, sang and preached about poverty, discipleship, injustices, and the ethic of Jesus. Stalwarts' view of scripture was still markedly conservative, but one scholar of the movement places JPUSA squarely in the evangelical left camp. Shawn David Young observes that "as the 1980s wore on, any sort of 'religious left' became increasingly uncommon. And this is precisely what makes JPUSA so significant." Many other former Jesus hippies became Reaganites in the alchemy of politicized religion.[118]

In some ways this turn of events in the 1970s and 1980s paralleled the resistance to the Equal Rights Amendment campaign or the rising pro-life movement. Activists in those circles had learned valuable lessons of civil disobedience, nonviolent resistance, grassroots organizing, and persistent agitation from 1960s antiwar protesters and African American activists. This was also happening at a time when white conservatives and moderates were drawing on Martin Luther King's legacy for their own national purposes. President Ronald Reagan had opposed both the Civil Rights Act of 1964 and the Voting Rights Act of 1965. But in 1982, the Gipper supported the national holiday to commemorate Martin Luther King Jr.[119] Similarly, the music and the tactics that were once part of the liberal or leftist fringe were being reworked by evangelicals and Catholics for their own conservative ends.[120]

Fundamentalists, of course, adamantly rejected that logic when applied to popular music. Frank Garlock, director of Musical Ministries and a music teacher in the past, spoke forthrightly to the press about the problems of rock 'n' roll in the church. Like his fellow crusaders

David Noebel, Bob Larson, and Tim and Beverly LaHaye, Garlock viewed his ministry as an extremely important calling. Garlock was a faculty member at Bob Jones University throughout the turbulent 1960s. By the 1970s, the music minister and fundamentalist entrepreneur was certain that the unbridled big beat would lead to the demise of good, wholesome choral music. It deserved no place in the church. Rock music, he said, was of "poor quality," and its "words are unimportant." Even so, it had an enormous, destructive power.[121]

Bob Jones University was happy to endorse Garlock, who launched a new speaking ministry in the 1970s, which university officials described as "Symphony of Life seminars." Garlock designed these to "provide Christians with an understanding of the Biblical principles of music and their application to Christian living." Some of his tailored talks included "The Rock of Ages versus the Age of Rock" and "The Music Is the Message." Bob Jones University claimed his booklets, decrying the apostasies of Christian pop, had sold over a quarter of a million copies. The university extolled his success at saving souls in equal measure.[122]

Keeping to this theme, Garlock argued that the "Jesus" that showed up in Christian rock music was not the Christ of the Bible. Instead, he was a revolutionary, a superstar, or a strange mythic figure. The Jesus that Larry Norman sang of was no Son of God in Garlock's estimation. Jesus-rock stars, he said, dodged the difficult eternal truths of scripture. Loud guitars, drums, and caterwauling singers had no place within the walls of a church. Garlock even suspected that the trombone was not dignified enough for houses of worship. It sounded too much "like it comes straight from the nightclub." He reasoned that a simple truth should guide parents and impressionable youths. "The devil's music," he advised, "will eventually be accompanied by the devil's ideas and words."[123]

Garlock also had some unique ideas. In the mid-1970s, Garlock spoke about Christian rock music at the World Congress of Fundamentalists. To warn off fellow conservatives from accepting the new music, he inveighed against some of the music's deviant features. Christian rock artists were uniformly influenced by the liberal "social gospel." If that were not enough, he continued, "most Rock gospel people are effeminate." Perhaps even more damning for far-right fundamentalists, he charged, "The majority of Christian rock writers are charismatic." That slur against the genre appeared again and again in the 1970s and 1980s. Conservative ministers and laypeople reasoned that it was almost natural for Christian rock to have emerged from what they considered innovative, heretical pentecostal circles.[124]

Critics spied tongues speakers and other heretics among Christian rockers. So said a pastor of a Longview, Texas, fundamentalist Baptist church. He believed that rock music was just one trend among many ushering in the apocalypse. The ecumenical movement and charismatic Christianity, along with rock 'n' roll, would bring down a fiery judgment. An ally of the Texas pastor went a step farther. Had not rock music already infiltrated church choirs and the kind of music that neo-evangelicals assumed was harmless? In this reading, conservative Christians had been far too lax in allowing charismatic theology and worship styles into their churches.[125]

Fundamentalists had long adopted a position on pentecostalism that ranged between suspicion and outright condemnation. When pentecostals claimed that Christians did not have the full experience of the Holy Spirit unless they spoke in tongues, fundamentalists were quick to denounce these adversaries as backsliders. Fundamentalists and many evangelicals declared that the biblically pure message they preached and lived by *was* fully Christian. Such critics did not accept charismatics or pentecostals into the fold. Tongues-speaking groups that emphasized healing and other gifts of the spirit were beyond the pale of Christianity. Fears that charismatics especially were not doctrinally conservative enough raised significant doubts. One historian calls the ongoing tensions between these camps the "travail of a broken family."[126]

One of the most influential fundamentalist leaders, John F. MacArthur Jr., went on a kind of personal crusade against charismatics and pentecostals. The longtime pastor of Grace Community Church in Los Angeles and alum of Bob Jones University and the Bible Institute of Los Angeles, MacArthur composed sermons and books on the subject of what he called "Charismatic Chaos." Wayward souls were basing their doctrine on their own flimsy experiences, he said. Yet the Bible stood in judgment of experience. Tongues speaking was "not biblical." He wondered why such believers tried to "convince and intimidate others to start doing the same thing." MacArthur denounced the movement as reckless and silly, and he claimed it was without grounding. It did not surprise him that their glitzy TV preachers and loud radio ministers were caught up in "appalling sex scandals" and crooked financial schemes.[127]

Fundamentalists' misgivings about flashy gospel music and pentecostalism had a long history by the 1970s and 1980s. Some hardline critics thought that the religion of the spirit invited new styles and dangerous new ideas. It certainly did not help that Elvis Presley, Jerry Lee Lewis, Johnny Cash, and so many other early artists had been raised in tongues-speaking churches. Writing in the late 1950s, a Baptist preacher from Alton, Illinois, pointed his finger squarely at Elvis "and others of his ilk" who "have entered into league with the devil to corrupt the minds and souls and bodies of millions." But, for this minister, the blame did not end with shouting, shaking rock 'n' rollers. He also targeted those gospel groups that were so influential for the young Presley. Modern gospel music, he warned, did not "reverence God." It was too worldly.[128]

Later denunciations looked quite similar. "The Jesus People Movement is essentially an interdenominational Pentecostal youth movement," proclaimed an administrator at Piedmont Bible College in the early 1970s. Jesus people, stated the school official, might share with fundamentalists a literal interpretation of scripture, a belief in miracles, and a premillennial view of the end of the world, but that certainly did not mean that they were *true* fundamentalists. There was something galling about the movement. The administrator had spent some time counseling drug addicts. There was no "definable difference between the emotional experience of a young person who gives himself up to the control of another spirit when 'getting into' Rock 'n' Roll Music and that of a young person who gives himself up to another spirit to 'speak in tongues.'" In the end, he counseled, in "neither case can this power be shown to be the Holy Spirit of God."[129] In similar fashion, a conservative skeptic at a Bible institute in Montana said these young Jesus revolutionaries were overly emotional in their faith. That was a long-standing critique that fundamentalists leveled against their pentecostal foes. Tongues speakers, so went the argument, anchored their faith in subjective, unstable human experience rather than grounding it in rational, commonsense biblical principles. In agreement, Jerry Falwell said charismatics "have a tendency to overemphasize the emotional" over the "intellectual." The Montana educator also wondered if the Jesus freaks' son of God "may be very little more than a psychological substitute for LSD. If this is true, then whatever experience one has will be temporary and perhaps hurtful." That was also the thinking of a Missouri Baptist editor of a fundamentalist newspaper. Jesus freaks would not be able to maintain their Jesus high. "Will they eventually become as bored with Jesus as they were with sex and dope?" the editor asked with a rhetorical flourish. The music and ephemeral tastes of the movement had even started to taint Baptist churches. The editor wondered if some congregations should replace the word "Baptist" with "Holy Roller" or "Rock and Shake."[130]

Another fundamentalist Baptist in the Golden State, the preacher and rabble-rouser G. Archer Weniger, took it upon himself to expose the evils of the Jesus people and their sinister, worldly music. Weniger enthusiastically campaigned against Christian rock. He wrote editorials and sent letters to fellow conservatives in which he denounced all evangelicals who accepted the new trend. One accommodationist he targeted was the Ronald Reagan associate and clean-cut celebrity entertainer Pat Boone. Weniger liked to point out that the "Hollywood" singer performed in nightclubs and casinos. Boone, Weniger huffed, had also embraced the pentecostal heresies of tongues speech and Holy Spirit baptism. "Accounts of his having recently received the 'baptism' of the Holy Spirit," Weniger reported of Boone in the 1970s, "are now appearing in Pentecostal magazines."[131] Bob Jones III, not to be outdone in denouncing new trends and innovations, called the Jesus people and its cultural explorations "undeniably wicked—wicked because it speaks not according to the Word of God."[132]

Applying this logic, critics could find fault with just about any group or artist. In the late 1970s, in Jones's hometown of Greenville, South Carolina, one agitated fundamentalist preacher even laid blame at the feet of white southern gospel vocal groups. These performers cavorted with moderate evangelicals and borrowed from popular musical styles. A Praise Gathering musical revue, which was organized by the popular gospel singer and composer Bill Gaither, said the indignant Greenville evangelist, was "nothing less than ecumenical evangelism via the back door of music." Such concerts and festivals were guilty of the twin heresies of neo-pentecostalism and religious liberalism. When southern gospel performers like Bill and Gloria Gaither claimed to fuse popular styles like country-western and ballads, the minister thundered, true believers should not be deceived. It amounted to little more than "a worldly-sensual-sexually oriented rhythm-beat."[133]

Almost any borrowing from the world of pop music, no matter how conservative or tame, said far-right fundamentalists, equaled an unforgivable sellout. One angry believer said as late as 1990 that the inroads rock and pop had made into the church represented some of "the most unfortunate trends down towards slob culture, charismatic overtones, [and] soft rock."[134]

From his headquarters in Tulsa, Oklahoma, Billy James Hargis joined his voice with other fundamentalists who linked heretical pentecostalism with Christian rock. The advent of sanctified pop music was "a gigantic compromise with Satan," he blasted. He was sure that "charismatic ministers have certainly compromised their beliefs and have greatly sinned by allowing their churches to sponsor rock concerts by so-called Christian groups, as many have."[135] To the east of Hargis and his Christian Crusade organization, other groups were taking an official stand. An independent consortium of fundamentalist churches revealed how seriously the threat had become. "WHEREAS there is a growing religious youth movement, commonly referred to by the terms, 'Jesus People,' 'Jesus Freaks,' and 'Jesus Movement,'" declared the Ohio Bible Fellowship's general conference, "and being largely Pentecostal in its worship . . . we encourage the churches of the Ohio Bible Fellowship to warn their young people of the spiritual danger inherent in this movement."[136]

A fundamentalist Baptist minister in Newfoundland extended the blame to a new style of outreach and evangelicalism. With its most visible public face in Billy Graham and the magazine *Christianity Today*, this new movement watered down the gospel. It was responsible for "bridging the gap between Christianity and the world." Stalwarts like him, he said, were fighting a lonely battle. "Except in fundamental Bible churches," he announced with equal parts chagrin and wild exaggeration, "this type of music (and possibly straight rock) is the only music heard today in the religious world."[137]

Evangelicals, too, could be riled by pop music. But their response was typically more nuanced. In 1977, the year that punk broke and bands like the Sex Pistols were subject to a new wave of parental outrage, *Christianity Today* offered some advice to families about radio listening habits. With more than a hint of disgust the editor offered a sampling of rock song titles on the top forty: Carly Simon's "Nobody Does It Better"; Foghat's "I Just Wanna Make Love to You"; and Peter Brown's "Do You Wanna Get Funky with Me." Unlike fundamentalists, this writer did not advise parents to ban their children from listening to rock or country music entirely, regardless of how offensive it seemed to them. Instead, he hoped parents would "teach [their] children discernment." For their part, sons and daughters needed to "listen to the radio more closely and realize for themselves how disgusting most of it is." If that did not work, he suggested optimistically, parents should get their children to "spend more time reading."[138]

The Radio and Television Commission of the Southern Baptist Convention joined in the denunciatory chorus as well. It put together a press release in 1977, highlighting just how reprehensible and profane rock lyrics had become. Even the Southern Baptist Convention's own youth-oriented program *Powerline* came under pressure. The show needed to better police the popular music it played. The report warned that "the permissive use of four letter words and overemphasis on sexual oriented lyrics began as a creeping disease and now has infected the music industry in epidemic proportions." The study also drew on the words of civil rights campaigner and black minister Jesse Jackson, who called much of popular music "decadent." "I recently went to a live show," said Jackson with obvious consternation, "and heard kids in the audience singing, 'get up off your ass, smoke some grass, shit goddamn.' " Jackson was resolute: "This has gone too far and we must do something about it."[139]

At the same time that such outrage burned hot, even conservative believers slowly began to have second thoughts about Christian rock. Billy Graham made his peace with beat-driven, loud Christian pop music by at least the early 1970s. Following his lead, other conservative holdouts grudgingly admitted that Christian rock music might serve a useful purpose, even if it sounded atrocious to their ears. Older generations of believers had long scoffed at or denounced innovations in worship, music, and preaching. Maurice Irvin, an editor with the Christian and Missionary Alliance, a holiness and fundamentalist group, in

1973 admitted that "we all have different tastes." He recalled how a pastor had telephoned him to denounce faddish and misguided trends in Christian music. "I do not like Christian rock," Irvin admitted. The sheer "racket and dissonance" was hideous. "But we have better things to do than to call attention all the time to what we do not like," said Irvin. Christians should refrain from nattering on about "what in the Lord's work we dislike."[140]

Those who once confidently denounced pop music in the church gradually changed their minds on the matter. In the late 1970s, even Bob Larson began to doubt his blanket statements on rock 'n' roll. The radio personality and popular speaker still drew a line or two in the sand. For instance, he approved of Stryper's message, he said in 1985. "But I very strongly object to the whole heavy-metal frame of reference," he told *Christianity Today.* He was put off by "their stage presence, and the chains, leather, and studs."[141] Such subtle distinctions did not matter to the unbending. Any waffling on the matter seemed like a betrayal. One outraged conservative concluded that "pastors, Christian school administrators, and all others who might be planning to have Larson speak to their youth need to check with him personally about his position before giving him a platform."[142]

Like Larson, the pentecostal youth minister David Wilkerson had made crusading against rock central to his evangelistic work. When Elvis was still plaguing preachers and Sunday school teachers, Wilkerson thundered against rock, which he considered "Satan's pentecost."[143] But twenty years later he was not so sure that the mere rhythm, melody, or tone of the music made it evil. Not long after Larson changed his mind, Wilkerson made a similar about-face. In the early 1980s he admitted, "I preached against what I thought was compromised." Now, though, he wondered about "how many innocent young converts I hurt—those who were giving to Christ the only talent they had."[144]

Perhaps the most important fundamentalist reversal on rock music came in the early 1990s, when Jerry Falwell had a change of heart. By then the fires of controversy had long died out in many evangelical sectors. Even much of the earlier hostility to pentecostalism had faded as well. For fundamentalists, acceptance of the new music and the styles that went with it was slow. Some never would make the change. So much associated with deviance, race-mixing, and rebellion, rock music remained tainted for decades at places like Bob Jones University. Over three hundred miles to the northeast of Bob Jones University, Falwell's Liberty University upheld a stringent "Music Code." "Philosophy, tastes, and personal convictions concerning music vary greatly among Christians," the student handbook conceded. But the school, so closely identified with political and cultural conservatism, maintained a "standard conducive to a healthy Christian atmosphere on campus." Accordingly, its officials stipulated that students "refrain from listening to rock, disco, country and western, Christian rock, or any music that is associated closely with these types."[145] Students who brought to campus rock records, tapes, and paraphernalia would have to surrender them to the Office of Student Development. Listening to such music in dorm rooms or cars resulted in reprimands. Then, in the early 1990s, that categorical language changed, marking a major shift in one of the most visible fundamentalist bastions in the nation. Listening to certain kinds of Christian rock music, by this time, was permissible. Resident supervisors would do the adjudicating.[146]

The change in view was anything but random. Not long before the shift in policy two Liberty students formed a rap group, later a threesome, called DC Talk. The rock and rap fusion of Toby McKeehan and Kevin Smith, who were white, and Michael Tait, who was African American, was enormously popular with white, suburban evangelicals. The group sounded and looked a little like a scrubbed and profanity-free Beastie Boys or Run DMC. Some skeptics pegged them as an evangelical New Kids on the Block. DC Talk performed as part of Billy Graham Crusades, scored two gold records, twice won *Billboard*'s Contemporary Christian Artist of the Year, and in 1997 won a Grammy for Best Rock Gospel Album.[147] Falwell counted himself a convert, after decades of opposition to rock and pop music. "I'm for it," he enthusiastically told the *Wall Street Journal.* Now, as far as he was concerned, "young people will often attend . . . a concert or a rally—particularly if rap is involved—that would never attend a traditional church-type meeting."[148]

Falwell's turnaround signaled a larger shift within the world of fundamentalism and conservative evangelicalism. Long gone were the days when believers stood largely united in their opposition to rock music and its various offshoots. By the 1990s, the race-baiting rhetoric that once so powerfully damned the music had diminished, had been camouflaged, or was relegated to the fringes of the larger movement. Youth pastors, music ministers, and evangelists—pragmatic to the core—knew that Christian rock could draw in youngsters in ways that the standard, dusty hymns, quiet folk music, and organ solos could not. Perhaps in the last years of George H. W. Bush's presidency it was just too difficult, if not impossible, for the faithful to resist changing styles and tastes. In earlier decades holdouts had decided that feature films, radio, and television could proclaim the good news. Now, loud, beat-driven music could do the same. The growth in nondenominational churches, too, had something to do with the shift. As evangelicals rejected the trappings of institutionalism and rigid dogmatism, they embraced nontraditional music and outreach tools. Market forces were likely at play as well, because Christian pop music charted unimaginable commercial success. By the early 1990s, the Recording Industry Association of America was reporting that Christian music had an 11 percent share of the total market. Even with such success, evangelicals were not ready for complete capitulation. The acceptance of Christian rock did not mean that believers were ready and willing to make peace with its secular evil twin. In fact, the ubiquity of pop music—on the radio, on MTV, and in record stores and blasting from boom boxes in high school cafeterias—made it all the more necessary for a pastor-approved sanitized version. A *Chicago Tribune* reporter made sense of these changes in 1991. The conservative WMBI station of Chicago's Moody Bible Institute was now spinning the records of the middle of the road, soft rock band Harvest. "Indeed," the journalist concluded, "even the pastors who used to wage war against Christian rock seem to be coming around; if they don't enjoy it, they at least accept it." Now more than ever conservative Christians were making concessions to a wide range of new ideas and styles.[149]

In the same years that evangelicals publicly embraced politics and linked their denominations to the GOP in particular, they were also realizing that it was far better to borrow from and exploit popular culture than to reject and condemn it outright.[150] In the closing years of the century, America's conservative faithful rejected old taboos about music, rhythm, and comportment. In doing so, they followed the well-trod paths of their progenitors, who decades before had crafted catchy gospel music, used radio and television to reach massive audiences, and clothed the Gospel in contemporary garb. It had become entirely normal to set the message of sin and salvation, defeat and triumph to the music of the moment.

EPILOGUE

Bono, the lead singer of the acclaimed Irish postpunk and alternative rock band U2, had become one of the most influential celebrities in the world by the late 1990s. The group he fronted staged elaborate multimedia concerts. They sold out arenas around the world. U2's 1987 *Joshua Tree* album, replete with religious imagery, sold over fifteen million copies by 1995. Number-one hits from the record included the radio-friendly "I Still Haven't Found What I'm Looking For" and "With or Without You." Bruce Springsteen inducted U2 into the Rock and Roll Hall of Fame in 2005, culminating a career marked by fame, wealth, and touring success.[1]

Over the decades, Bono emerged as a leading voice of Christian social justice. In the late 1990s and first decade of the next century, he was a kind of peripatetic goodwill ambassador for African nations, poverty relief, and HIV / AIDS initiatives. He spoke repeatedly to reporters and church leaders about the ethic of Jesus and what God meant to him. The star even ventured that there was some larger religious significance in the hunger for fame and success. "You don't become a rock star unless you've got something missing somewhere," he proclaimed. "If you were of sound mind or a more complete person, you could feel normal without 70,000 people a night screaming their love for you." Bono chalked it up to a Pascalian "God-shaped hole" in one's life. "Everyone's got one," he believed, "but some are blacker and wider than others."[2]

U2 had long brought together the worlds of megastardom and industry success with Christianity and the quest for meaning. Bono might have been uncomfortable in churches and with the trappings of the institutional church; that did not keep the devout from heaping praise on him or the group. Wealthy philanthropists like Bill Gates and George Soros joined the Irish rock star's crusades for economic justice and world health. He wooed Hollywood celebrities, too, in the fight against poverty, for debt relief, and for humanitarian aid. In 1999, Bono met with Pope John Paul II to converse on debt relief in the third world. The meeting with the pontiff was not as unusual or jarring as it might have seemed. U2's songs were rich with Christian imagery, biblical references, and probing questions about life. Bono sang of temptation, prayer and supplication, discipleship, the kingdom of God, and Calvary. A 2010 headline in the *Guardian* asked if U2 was "rock 'n' roll's answer to the Book of Common Prayer."[3] The group's Christian commitments had set them apart from the very beginning.

At various times, Bono and his bandmates looked back on their early encounters with a new, countercultural style of Christianity. It was exciting for Bono, then known as Paul David Hewson, much as it had been for the Jesus freaks in California. Back in 1976, he reminisced, he "wasn't the only one going through a religious experience" at his school, Mount Temple, in Dublin. "It felt like the whole place was going off," he enthused. "It was the early days in what would become known as the 'Charismatic' movement, Catholics and Protestants in Ireland worshipping God together in a kind of hippy rave format, minus the beats per minute."[4] Students joined in earnest Bible studies and theological chat sessions. Bono, guitarist The Edge, and drummer Larry Mullin Jr., had even been part of an evangelical worship group called Shalom. Bono viewed it all as part of a major worldwide revival. The Jesus movement and Christian rock spread throughout the West in the 1970s and 1980s. Outposts, communes, and bands could be found in Norway and Sweden, Great Britain and Ireland, and on the Continent in Germany and Switzerland. Scholars would later call it the fourth great awakening.[5] Whatever it was, Bono reasoned, "it was happening to a great many people. Bob Dylan was at one end of the spectrum in LA and a little school in Clontarf, Dublin, was at the other."[6]

The influence and appeal of pioneer performers like Dylan remained strong. Christian rock stars and fans, along with artists like Bono, looked up to the inscrutable troubadour whose conversion experience lent much to the cause. They also venerated the 1950s-era innovators of the music who so seamlessly fused gospel, rhythm and blues, and country music. In 1995, Bono spoke about Elvis Presley, "the 'Big Bang' of Rock 'n' Roll."

> It all came from there, and what you had in Elvis Presley is a very interesting moment because, really, to be pretentious about it for a minute, you had two cultures colliding there. You had a kind of white, European culture and an African culture coming together—the rhythm, okay, of black music and the melody, you know, chord progressions of white music—just all came together in that kind of spastic dance of his. That was the moment. That's really, that's it.[7]

Elvis Presley was, for many, sui generis. Not surprisingly, a kind of religious movement developed around the fallen King of Rock 'n' Roll. It had been building even in the early days of his career. For some the devotion was half in jest. Others took it much more seriously. Graceland, his 13.8-acre Memphis estate that he bought in 1957 for $100,000, became a pilgrimage site immediately after his overdose death in August 1977. Since the house had opened its doors to tourists in 1982, an estimated twenty million visitors walked through its halls, marveling at the things he touched and the rooms he decorated so garishly. The tour ended at the gravesite of the star.[8] Visitors bought posters, bric-a-brac, plates and mugs, CDs, and other treasured memorabilia while at Graceland. "Elvis Lives" had become a kind of mantra for some of those fans, of which there were many. A Gallup 1997 survey revealed that 45 percent of Americans counted themselves fans of Elvis. It was little wonder that some among them believed that he was not, in fact, dead. When Gallup asked Americans about the star's death that same year, 4 percent said they believed he was still walking the earth.[9]

What some critics were calling the Cult of Elvis or the Church of Elvis drew together fans in fervid devotion. Baby boomers remained the truest acolytes. Southern studies scholar Charles Reagan Wilson describes it as a kind of populist civil religion. The cult incorporated "supernatural legend, marketed souvenirs, and other cultural forms to tie Elvis to a regional (as well as national) patriotism." Wilson notes that the image of Elvis "soon appeared in tandem with the Confederate battle flag, linked usually with other southern heroes, and on religious relics such as 'Elvis sweat.' "[10] At Elvis conventions aficionados and devotees shared stories about his music and their faith journeys. They traded and sold memorabilia and Elvis kitsch. They watched Elvis impersonators ply their trade. In the early 1990s, there were an estimated three thousand Elvis impersonators in America alone. By then, Elvis studies was a burgeoning field. Books and articles probed his religious life, his habits and relationships, his southernness, the cultural meaning of his celebrity, and on and on. For some years, the University of Mississippi even hosted an annual conference on all things Elvis related.[11]

On the tenth anniversary of his death, a reporter on the scene in Memphis figured that some other performers had achieved a saintlike status after death—James Dean, John Lennon, and Marilyn Monroe were among them, although "it is hard to imagine any of them inspiring the kind of memorial fiesta that will go on at and around Graceland this week." It seemed like the "high holy days of Elvis Presley."[12] The *New York Times* dispatched Ron Rosenbaum to Memphis in 1995 during Elvis commemoration ceremonies. It came to be known as Elvis Week, but Rosenbaum dubbed it "Death Week." For days, he reported, "a Canterbury-like fusion of carnival and spiritual impulses has been building toward the convergence on the grave in a climactic ceremony referred to simply as 'Candlelight.'" The key ritual was "a phenomenon that has lately transcended the familiar contours of a dead celebrity cult and has begun to assume the dimensions of a redemptive faith."[13] Paul Simon's wildly successful 1986 album *Graceland* brought such Elvis veneration into a larger public view, with its title track about a pilgrimage to the hallowed ground in Memphis. Elvis Week is still going strong. The 2016 schedule included a dizzying array of activities and events: the Ultimate Elvis Tribute Artist Contest, George Klein's Elvis Mafia Reunion, an Elvis Memorial Service, and the Gospel Music of Elvis Presley.[14]

Of course, Elvis was deeply uncomfortable with the religious adoration and the deification. One typically repeated story of Elvis's response to it has the singer saying, "There is only one King."[15] Elvis, who could be surprisingly humble, certainly endeared himself to many born-again Christians, especially when he performed the gospel songs and hymns of his pentecostal youth. So did Jerry Lee Lewis on albums like *In Loving Memories: The Jerry Lee Lewis Gospel Album* (1971). The record hit the shelves in the year that the Jesus people were making headlines and when evangelical rock music was just getting under way. On the album, the Killer sang standards like "I'll Fly Away" and "Old Rugged Cross," as well as, most fittingly, a newer number by Dottie Rambo titled "He Looked Beyond My Fault." Nearly a decade before, Mercury released Little Richard's *The King of the Gospel Singers.* Produced by Quincy Jones, the album featured a cover photo of Richard, his hair cropped close, singing passionately with a stained glass window behind him.

Little Richard, Jerry Lee, and Elvis—internationally successful artists on record, radio, the concert stage, and film—crossed back over to the sacred realm with their Christian albums. Christian rockers, too, would cross over in later years. But they would move from the confines of the Christian rock realm into the larger secular world. The cultural power and the appeal of U2, along with other major artists who ventured into mainstream success and won secular accolades, illustrated how complicated and varied the mix of religion and rock music had become. The days when thundering preachers in major Baptist or Methodist churches sermonized against the devil's music and the savage rhythms of Elvis Presley or Little Richard were mostly a distant memory. In the new century, the majority of evangelical churches used popular tunes and beat-driven, rock-style music as part of their worship and praise services. The pop music charts were populated with the occasional Christian artist, too.

New bands and artists garnered critical attention and enormous fame. At the turn of the century, a collection of groups and solo performers moved in and out of Christian circles and became the darlings of even hard-hearted critics. Indie, underground, and art-folk groups like Danielson Famile, Sufjan Stevens, Starflyer 59, Innocence Mission, Over the Rhine, Soul Junk, Half-handed Cloud, 16 Horsepower, Sunny Day Real Estate, Cold War Kids, Pedro the Lion, and Damien Jurado won the plaudits of journalists and calloused record reviewers. Releases on labels like Tooth & Nail in Seattle—along with smaller independents such as Velvet Blue Music in Huntington Beach, California; Asthmatic Kitty in Brooklyn; Sounds Familyre in Clarksboro, New Jersey; or Burnt Toast Vinyl in Lansdale, Pennsylvania—received heavy rotation on college and alternative radio as well as the critical attention of indie magazines and the national press.[16]

A handful of crossover artists went beyond mere critical acclaim and achieved large-scale fame and an international following. Bands like the alternative Switchfoot and Jars of Clay, the second-wave grunge

U2 perform their 1987 hit "I Still Haven't Found What I'm Looking For" to a sold-out crowd of seventy thousand fans, Soldier Field, Chicago, June 4, 2017. Tim Newell / Paper Dolling Films, 2017. Screenshot by the author from YouTube, Paper Dolling Films (http://www.youtube.com/watch?v=HIOv2mUjUW4).

group Creed, the melodic pop rock band Sixpence None the Richer, the alternative adult contemporary rock outfit Casting Crowns, and the heavy, abrasive genre-fusing rap metal and postgrunge of the foursome P.O.D. (Payable on Death) won fame and high sales figures that would have been unimaginable in earlier years. The latter's album *Satellite* (2001) garnered triple-platinum status.[17] Other, lesser-known bands, like the death metal Living Sacrifice from Arkansas, gained a devoted evangelical following. In the 1980s and 1990s, CBS and EMI would strike deals with smaller Christian labels. A *New York Times* observer of the scene even suggested that the mainstreaming of Christian rock should not be all that surprising. "In an overwhelmingly Christian country," wrote Kelefa Sanneh in 2006, "it may seem strange that Christian rock even exists as a niche genre; if rock better reflected American demographics, then secular rock would be the niche." The devil still might have had all the good music, but, asked Sanneh in jest, can "he match that business model." There was money to be made.[18]

There were also fans to cultivate, especially among evangelical youth. A 2004 Gallup poll revealed that 59 percent of Protestant teenagers surveyed said that they considered themselves "born-again or evangelical." Gallup also quoted the Republican National Committee chairman Ed Gillespie, who praised the good influence that Christian rock groups were having on teens. "We're also extremely pleased," he stated, "that popular bands like Third Day are using their influence in a positive way by encouraging young people to get involved in our electoral process."[19] Alternative bands like Third Day, which successfully broke into the secular market, were poised to reap souls as well as sell concert tickets, T-shirts, and records.

Things did not always go smoothly. Crossover success often came at a heavy cost. Church leaders and laypeople wondered if artists like Amy Grant, Michael W. Smith, Jars of Clay, U2, or DC Talk could even be called Christian, let alone evangelical. Wasn't worldly success incompatible with righteousness? asked skeptics. In the late 1990s, a veteran entertainer staked his career on a bizarre about-face and suffered the humiliating consequences.

In a twist that was stranger than fiction, the evangelical pop star and former teen idol Pat Boone released an album of heavy metal cover songs in early 1997. Almost forty years before, his hit song "Wonderful Time Up There" was an early million-selling gospel record. *In a Metal Mood: No More Mr. Nice Guy* featured the sixty-two-year-old grandfather accompanied by four classically trained Finnish musicians. On the album cover a bare-chested Boone—outfitted with a leather vest, gold chains, and an earring—wore a serious expression and had a twinkle in his eye. Songs by Ozzy Osbourne, Van Halen, Dio, Metallica, Guns N' Roses, and others received a big band, crooner treatment. It was all a strange lark for Boone. He hoped it might revive his flagging career. "I wanted to do a big-band album of great metal songs," he told the *New York Times*, "doing them for people who will never be into metal." He admitted that he had been a harsh critic of the music and its performers in the past. Now he had met some of them and found that they were "fine human beings." Besides, Boone said, he had become too predictable and boring.[20] The turn seemed to trigger the bad-pun instincts of journalists along with plenty of sarcasm. Headlines announced "Pat Boone Minus Those White Bucks," "Boone to Be Wild," and "Bad to the Boone." Many in the conservative Christian fold, however, were not amused. Pat Robertson's Christian Broadcast Network refused to play the record.[21] Christians just did not get pop culture and the music business, Boone groused to *Christianity Today.* "They don't understand that if you don't do something out of the ordinary—something truly eyebrow-raising—to an extent, you're not going to get heard."[22]

The singer faced even more ire after he appeared as a presenter, alongside metal legend Alice Cooper, at the American Music Awards in January 1997. Clad in black leather and wearing fake tattoos and a studded dog collar, Boone showed up to announce the Heavy Metal / Hard Rock Favorite Artist Award. The stunt made headlines and garnered attention from national television news. "A lot of our [prayer] 'partners' had a real problem with that, more than a lot," a representative of Trinity Broadcasting Network responded.[23] He had sold out, thought evangelical critics. The Santa Ana–based Christian television network promptly cancelled Boone's program, *Gospel America.* Hundreds of viewers had called in to register their complaints. Boone eventually apologized on air for his poor judgment. "Just because I wore some leather pants and fake tattoos and non-piercing earrings," he explained, "doesn't mean that I'm a fundamentally different person." But the damage had already been done.[24]

In certain circles, the prospect of Christian artists—whether old-timers like Boone or relatively new stars like Amy Grant—selling out to the market and caving in to secularism was a pressing concern. In 1998 the organizers of the Christian rock Jesus Northwest festival at the Clark Country Fairgrounds in Vancouver, Washington, decided to cancel their massive outdoor concert series because the music had lost its Christian edge. The previous year, the festival had drawn a record thirty thousand attendees. An area Assemblies of God pastor thought the "Christian emphasis has gotten so watered down on some fronts that you can't distinguish it from pop secular messages anymore." Fans had made idols of the performers, said concerned promoters and local ministers.[25]

Crossover controversies raged around a group of burning questions. Was an artist Christian enough? Did bands and performers hold the same values that other evangelicals did? Soft rock and pop star Amy Grant did an interview with an LGBT media company, PrideSource, in 2013. She faced a swift backlash from conservatives, who felt betrayed by her.[26] The contemporary Christian folk-rock musician Jennifer

Knapp revealed in 2010 that she was in a long-term same-sex relationship. Christian radio stations and retailers pulled her music from the shelves and out of rotation. A station manager in Houston, Texas, claimed, "We have a standard of ministry for the artists we play." The "lifestyle" of an artist mattered, he argued: "We view our artists as 'ministers' on the air. We want artists who love the Lord and live by Christian principles."[27]

There were indeed clear limits to what the audience and the market would accept. Crossover artists could easily run afoul of evangelical sensibilities. When the lead singer of alt-country band Vigilantes of Love, Bill Mallonee, sang too frankly about sex in a song titled "Love Cocoon," the group faced the ire of the Christian industry. Evangelical retailers pulled the offending album, *Slow Dark Train* (Capricorn, 1997), from their store shelves.[28] Jay R. Howard and John M. Streck assessed the nature of the controversy. When Vigilantes of Love tried "to negotiate a path that would include elements of both evangelical and mainstream industries," they reasoned, the group "wound up alienating elements of both."[29]

There were other trends in Christian rock that shook up prevailing norms. In recent years, some artists and labels had become uncomfortable with the easy alignment with right-wing politics and the Republican Party. In the new century there were more political options for younger evangelicals.[30] The religious and generational divide showed up sharply in the 2016 election. White born-again Christians cast their ballots overwhelmingly for Republican presidential candidate Donald Trump. He won 81 percent of their votes. The real estate mogul and reality television star also did best with those over age sixty-five. Franklin Graham, the son of Billy Graham, prayed at Trump's inauguration. Still, there were political divisions among the faithful. A wag at the *New Statesman* pointed out that the Republican victor should know how bad things were when "even the mediocre Christian rock bands won't play at your inauguration."[31]

Surveys of baby boomers who had been part of the Jesus people movement, and who were the early fans of Christian rock, revealed a telling picture. They tended to self-identify as Republican and conservative on a variety of issues, but younger evangelicals were breaking from their parents on a host of political and cultural matters. Millennials and generation X evangelicals held more liberal views about homosexuality, environmentalism, and biblical interpretation. Millennials (born between 1981 and 1996) also were becoming less religious in the second decade of the century.[32] The views of younger evangelicals who did remain in the fold were looking more like those held by Bono. The music historian David Stowe aptly observes that "abortion and homosexuality have been joined and, in some sectors, overshadowed by other issues of concern: environmental stewardship, healthcare, AIDS, human trafficking, and poverty in the developing world." Stowe wonders how new artists and performers will address themes of social and environmental justice in their songs.[33]

Even with the rising public profile of artists, a newfound political engagement, and crossover appeal, little has changed the negative image of the music in the broader culture. For the uninitiated, Christian rock would always be unhip, substandard, or bogus. It was a pale imitation of the original. Even with the worldwide success of U2 and a host of high-profile sensations, critics continued to poke fun at and mercilessly ridicule God rock. Few genres seemed more oxymoronic to doubters in the press and in the music magazines. In a 2004 article in *GQ*, John Jeremiah Sullivan wrote that "Christian rock is a musical genre, the only one I can think of, that has excellence-proofed itself." Jesus music, especially when performed by overly sincere suburbanites, so goes the logic, tended to be tragically uncool, devoid of subtlety and artistic value. Fittingly, Sullivan subtitled his article "Rock Music Used to Be a Safe Haven for Degenerates and Rebels. Until It Found Jesus."[34] Another critic put it like this: "Christian rock has an arguably deserved reputation as the least fashionable music on earth."[35]

In the public mind, a chasm still supposedly separated rock and Christianity. In the 1990s and early 2000s, doubters said the music was defined by bland conformity and mediocre talent. A syndicated columnist and humorist pegged contemporary Christian music as "bad songs written about God by white people."[36] The hit television sitcom *Seinfeld* even took aim at it in a 1998 episode called "The Burning." The character Elaine complains that she borrowed her boyfriend's car and was horrified to discover that "all the presets on his radio were Christian rock stations." The feckless and defensive George Costanza replies, "I like Christian rock. It's very positive. It's not like those real musicians who think they're so cool and hip."[37]

The sneering and mockery of comedians or music critics did little to blunt the success of the genre. Such negative opinions fit in with how evangelicals viewed their place in the country. In the age of Donald Trump's ascendance to the presidency, 42 percent of white evangelicals, according to a Pew report, felt that "it has become more difficult to be an evangelical Christian in the U.S. in recent years." Perceptions about secularization, moral drift and acceptance of homosexuality, and a sense of losing their ability to express their religious faith in public made them feel persecuted.[38]

Regardless of believers' fears of losing out, the music continued to grow and become an even greater cultural force within church communities, and, to a lesser extent, in the wider market. At a fundamental level rock music changed the way that millions of evangelicals, Catholics, and pentecostals experienced church life. Repetitive drum-piano-and-guitar-driven praise music, which pentecostals and charismatics popularized in the 1970s, was ubiquitous in evangelical churches by the 1980s and 1990s. Pentecostals helped other Low Church Protestants experience church worship in novel, open ways. At a University of Southern California academic symposium marking the hundredth anniversary of the pentecostal Azusa Street revival, a collection of scholars reflected on some of the distinctive features of the tradition and the larger influence the movement exerted. "Pentecostalism is oftentimes attracting a fairly young constituency," said one participant, "and my opinion is that it's because they are attracted initially to the music; that is one sort of porthole into this movement."[39]

Already by the 1970s, worship music bore the strong imprint of the charismatic movement. Yet it would be many more years before a drum, bass guitar, lead electric guitar, and keyboard setup would be so common that it was almost taken for granted. At the time of Woodstock and then the Dallas Explo '72 festivals, rock music was not popular with many Americans. A 1966 Harris survey found that 44 percent of the public "actively disliked rock." Much had changed in the intervening years. Forty years later, the Pew Research Center found that "rock and roll today is the most popular music in the country, with nearly two-thirds of the public . . . saying they often (35%) or sometimes (30%) listen to it." In some sense, then, it is little wonder that rock music would become one of the standard forms, along with hymns and gospel music, enlivening church worship in the new millennium.[40] A few concerned evangelicals worried that perhaps too much emphasis was being placed on rock and pop performances in church services. Wrote one pastor and church leader in *Christianity Today*, "Worship leaders are not rock stars, and worship is not a rock concert." True, participant-oriented worship music was quite different from commercial and mass-marketed contemporary Christian music. The lines seemed to be blurring, though. The worried pastor thought it was a shame that "the natural tendency for a young worship leader is to seek to meet the concert-like demands and give the people a great show."[41] But that was the state of things for many in the fold.

At the turn of the century, what came to be known as megachurches, with members of two thousand or more, became more prominent on the American religious landscape. Many of these evangelical churches used multimedia presentations and elaborate set designs. They also featured Christian rock and pop groups.[42] Writing in 2000, a professor at Christian Theological Seminary reckoned that the changes to church worship, aesthetics, and Christian self-expression were undergoing enormous transformation. "A number of churches in various parts of the world are undertaking," he observed, "a sort of Christian cultural revolution. . . . Many of the more remarkable trends are especially conspicuous in church life as experienced in the United States." Pop and rock music, so prominent in American congregations, figured large in his assessment.[43]

Other developments pushed evangelicals in new directions that pulled them away from standard beliefs, practices, worship, and music. The so-called emerging church movement, popular with generation Xers and millennials, also developed a distinct pattern in music and worship. These churches, many in or near urban areas, hoped to foster community and local identity, and they sought to free themselves of the tired debates that had dominated the evangelical scene for decades. Some of its adherents promoted social justice causes and a new, culturally and politically informed version of the faith. Bono was a kind of patron saint for them. Two professors at Fuller Theological Seminary offered a basic definition of the movement in 2005. In their view,

> Emerging churches are communities that practice the way of Jesus within postmodern cultures. This definition encompasses nine practices. Emerging churches (1) identify with the life of Jesus, (2) transform the secular realm, and (3) live highly communal lives. Because of these three activities, they (4) welcome the stranger, (5) serve with generosity, (6) participate as producers, (7) create as created beings, (8) lead as a body, and (9) take part in spiritual activities.[44]

Magazines like *Cornerstone*, *Prism*, *Relevant*, and *Sojourners* explored the underground sensibilities and the pop cultural and literary tastes of emerging Christians. Parodied in some circles as a strange brand of hipster Christianity, some wondered what it meant in these churches when "cool met Christ." In certain cases, those who attended emerging churches cultivated skepticism and cynicism about their parents' faith and middle-class values and aesthetics. Services occasionally took on a High Church tone, rich with liturgy. Said one critic, "How tradition, liturgy and hymns have become a fad baffles me, but I think the Christian hipster is partly to blame." Worship bands traded the anthemic, God-and-country ballads and love songs to Jesus, which their parents had so treasured, for earthy authenticity, liturgical music, and indie rock credibility.[45]

In the wider evangelical world, however, conservative religious beliefs continued to dominate, influencing not only political behavior but also cultural outlook and even consumer tastes. Believers shopped for a new, expanding market of Christian goods. Already by 1980, the faithful were buying up evangelical products like never before. Christian record companies pulled in $100 million a year. The sale of advertising on 1,400 Christian radio stations that had cropped up across the country amounted to $40 million. In 1980, there were five hundred Christian solo artists and bands touring around the nation. Their sales of merchandise and tickets alone brought in an impressive $50 million.[46] "Christian music is the fastest-growing form of popular music," proclaimed a 1995 headline in the *New York Times Magazine.* The once-obscure genre was now "driving its message home to the tune of $750 million a year." Christian pop and rock music later ranked as one of the most profitable entertainment industries in America.[47] Then in 2001, contemporary Christian music—an umbrella category for rock, rap, pop, worship, and related genres—reached $1 billion in sales. That figure represented an increase of 12 percent from the previous year.[48] The surge made the Christian music industry a contender with the nation's other most popular styles. For instance, at roughly the same time, domestic sales of country music records amounted to $2 billion. The entire recording industry accounted for $13.7 billion dollars in the same period.[49] Contemporary Christian and gospel music outsold jazz and classical music combined by the first decade of the twenty-first century and accounted for about 6.5 percent of record sales.[50] Nashville served as the industry's hub. In the 1980s and 1990s, publications like *HM Magazine* (formerly *Heaven's Metal*), *Harvest Rock Syndicate*, *CCM Magazine*, *7ball*, and *True Tunes News* catered to fans and artists alike. These outlets carried interviews, reviews of concerts and albums, and the latest news and gossip about tours and forthcoming releases.

Newsweek ran a cover story on Jesus rock in the summer of 2001, "The Glorious Rise of Christian Pop," just months after evangelical Republican president George W. Bush entered the Oval Office. Lorraine Ali noted that "alternative rock is just one pillar in the gigantic cathedral of Christian entertainment." The parallel culture of evangelicalism was on display in everything from the best-selling apocalyptic novel series *Left Behind*, "which sold 28.8 million copies, to the Grammy-winning singer Steven Curtis Chapman, who helped pack in 50,000 at the Freedom Live festival in Tulsa, Okla., last week."[51] Suburban evangelicals, Catholics, and fundamentalists were buying an ever-widening range of goods. American believers, who listened to Christian bands and artists across the spectrum of pop music, defined their faith not just by what they believed, how they lived, or how they voted. Their devotion was also grounded in materialism and the market. CDs, T-shirts, cassettes, and fan books were just some of the many items available for purchase in the bazaar of Christian commodities. Believers were also acquiring children's DVDs, religious jewelry, up-to-date Bible studies, evangelical sex manuals, homeschool curricula, wall art, and a never-ending supply of born-again baubles. Christian bookstores profited enormously from a robust evangelical consumer culture. Sales figures for the thousands of outlets across the United States jumped from $3 billion in the early 1990s to a staggering $4 billion in 2000.[52]

In the new millennium, the old debates seemed a distant memory. Scandals about the devil's music in the 1950s, battles over long hair and rock 'n' roll idolatry in the 1960s, and the startling rise and controversy of Jesus rock from the late 1960s and early 1970s now mostly looked quaint or were overshadowed by other issues. America's conservative evangelicals, and its minority of moderate and more liberal believers, accepted Christian gangsta rap, along with evangelical versions of goth, indie pop, death metal, grindcore, hip hop, and electronic dance music. Christian chain stores, a slowly fading phenomenon with the rise and dominance of online shopping, sold Elvis Presley's melodious and spirited *Peace in the Valley* (1957) next to the abrasive and violent Christian metal and posthardcore of Wolves at the Gate's *Flickering Flame* (2016).

In 2002, Mark Allan Powell noted that "the Christian music subculture is a microcosm of popular religion in America." For decades, pop music revealed the ways the faithful viewed race, gender, the problems of youth, and a whole variety of religious and social matters. Powell thought that Christian music was "also a laboratory within which various theological questions are engaged."[53] Some still worried that entertainment and ministry might be mutually exclusive. Was it possible for God to work through secular music? they anxiously asked. But the very success of evangelicalism and pentecostalism had much to do with a willingness to remain culturally relevant, to adapt to changing tastes and new ideas. Nonetheless, believers continued to grapple with the pressing questions of how they should best relate to the larger society around them. Evangelicals, Catholics, pentecostals, and many other Christian groups in the United States willingly accepted the styles of the age, even if those had once seemed so threatening, disruptive, and dangerous. Believers had made similar accommodations in the past. They had also entered the political arena with greater commitment and passion. Fitting that larger pattern, film and other forms of entertainment were no longer inherently deviant or sinful. Born-again Christians, accounting for about 25 percent of the population, continued to borrow from the secular culture around them as well as find new and innovative ways to worship, entertain themselves, and evangelize.

NOTES

Introduction

1. Peter Guralnick, "The Million Dollar Quartet," *New York Times*, March 25, 1979, SM7; Mitchell K. Hall, *The Emergence of Rock and Roll: Music and the Rise of American Youth Culture* (New York: Routledge, 2014), 21; Glenn C. Altschuler, *All Shook Up: How Rock 'n' Roll Changed America* (New York: Oxford University Press, 2003), 92, 97–98; "Wed Myra Before Divorce Final, Admits Jerry (Rock 'n' Roll) Lewis," *Boston Globe*, May 26, 1958, 20; Amanda Sharp, "Jerry Lee Lewis Was Acquitted of Income Tax Evasion," http://www.upi.com/Archives/1984/10/18/Jerry-Lee-Lewis-was-acquitted-of-income-tax-evasion/8262466920000/, October 18, 1984, accessed June 22, 2017.
2. Nick Tosches, *Country: The Twisted Roots of Rock 'n' Roll* (New York: Da Capo Press, 1985), 66. See also "Killer's Gospel," *Guardian*, February 16, 1980, 10.
3. Patrick Doyle, "The Killer at Peace: Jerry Lee Lewis' Golden Years," http://www.rollingstone.com/music/features/the-killer-at-peace-jerry-lee-lewis-golden-years-20141104, November 4, 2014, accessed June 22, 2017; Caroline Sullivan, "I Second That Devotion," *Guardian*, April 12, 1993, A4; John Rockwell, "Tracing Little Richard to the Source: Little Richard," *New York Times*, February 1, 1987, H29.
4. Simon Hattenstone, "Jerry Lee Lewis: 'I Worry about Whether I'm Going to Heaven or Hell,' " http://www.theguardian.com/music/2015/aug/08/jerry-lee-lewis-interview-heaven-hell, August 8, 2015, accessed June 22, 2017; Robert Palmer, "The Devil and Jerry Lee Lewis," http://www.rollingstone.com/music/news/the-devil-and-jerry-lee-lewis-19791213, December 13, 1979, accessed June 22, 2017 (italics in the original).
5. John Wigger, *PTL: The Rise and Fall of Jim and Tammy Faye Bakker's Evangelical Empire* (New York: Oxford University Press, 2017), 249; "Jerry Lee Lewis with Mickey Gilley Pop Goes Country Show 1978 Full Video High Quality," YouTube video, 20:47, posted by "Federico," December 27, 2014, https://www.youtube.com/watch?v=m4UR13SmeE8; Jimmy Swaggart, interview by John W. Styll, "Jimmy Swaggart: Christian Rock Wars, June 1985," in *The Heart of the Matter: The CCM Interviews*, ed. John Styll (Nashville, TN: Star Song Communications, 1991), 1:137–138.
6. "New Haven Connecticut 07-13-1985 - CR1140," YouTube video, 2:07:33, posted by "Louis Calzada," July 1, 2015, https://www.youtube.com/watch?v=cbftxyiDMMg.
7. For earlier Jimmy Swaggart pronouncements on rock and roll that follow a similar line, see Jimmy Swaggart, *To Cross a River*, with Robert Paul Lamb (Plainfield, NJ: Logos International, 1977), 85, 88, 239; Jimmy Swaggart, "The Death of Elvis Presley," *Evangelist* (Baton Rouge, LA), February 1, 1978, n.p.; and Jimmy Swaggart, "An Unexpected Reaction," *Evangelist*, February 15, 1978, n.p., "Rock Music," G. Archer Weniger Collection, Bob Jones University.
8. R. Serge Denisoff, *Tarnished Gold: The Record Industry Revisited* (New Brunswick, NJ: Transaction, 1997), 407; Tom Zito, "Witness of Fire: Putting the Torch to Thousands

of Rock Albums, Two Midwest Preachers Aim to Burn the Devil in America's Ears," *Washington Post*, December 3, 1980, D1.

9. Roman Kozak, "After 10 Rocking Years, Don't Kiss Them Off," Rock 'n' Rolling, *Billboard*, March 19, 1983, 44. See also Sean McCloud, *American Possessions: Fighting Demons in the Contemporary United States* (New York: Oxford University Press, 2015), 27–30. The rumors about the band's name were fabricated and denied by the group. See Brett Weiss, "Knight's in Satan's Service," in *Encyclopedia of KISS: Music, Personnel, Events and Related Subjects*, ed., Brett Weiss (Jefferson, NC: McFarland and Company, 2016), 119.
10. Zito, "Witness of Fire," D1.
11. Robert O. Self, *All in the Family: The Realignment of American Democracy since the 1960s* (New York: Hill and Wang, 2012), 352–355; David Snowball, *Continuity and Change in the Rhetoric of the Moral Majority* (New York: Praeger, 1991), 9–10, 43; Robert C. Liebman, "Mobilizing the Moral Majority," in *The New Christian Right: Mobilization and Legitimation*, eds., Robert C. Liebman and Robert Wuthnow (Hawthorne, NY: Aldine Publishing Company, 1983), 50–74; Oran P. Smith, "Baptists," in *The Encyclopedia of Politics and Religion, Vol. 1*, ed., Robert Wuthnow (London: Routledge, 1998), 66; Ellen MacGilvra Rosenberg, *The Southern Baptists: A Subculture in Transition* (Knoxville: University of Tennessee Press, 1989), 2–3. Nancy Tatom Ammerman, *Baptist Battles: Social Change and Religious Conflict in the Southern Baptist Convention* (New Brunswick, NJ: Rutgers University Press, 1995), 3, 14, 253, 264.
12. Darren Dochuk, *From Bible Belt to Sunbelt: Plain-Folk Religion, Grassroots Politics, and the Rise of Evangelical Conservatism* (New York: W. W. Norton, 2011); Daniel K. Williams, *God's Own Party: The Making of the Christian Right* (New York: Oxford University Press, 2010). For general reactions to rock 'n' roll, see Linda Martin and Kerry Segrave, *Anti-rock: The Opposition to Rock 'n' Roll* (New York: Da Capo Press, 1993).
13. Larry Eskridge, *God's Forever Family: The Jesus People Movement in America* (New York: Oxford University Press, 2013); David Stowe, *No Sympathy for the Devil: Christian Pop Music and the Transformation of American Evangelicalism* (Chapel Hill: University of North Carolina Press, 2011); Jay R. Howard and John M. Streck, *Apostles of Rock: The Splintered World of Contemporary Christian Music* (Louisville: University Press of Kentucky, 1999).
14. Barry Hankins, *American Evangelicals: A Contemporary History of a Mainstream Religious Movement* (Lanham, MD: Rowman & Littlefield, 2008); Barry Hankins, *Francis Schaeffer and the Shaping of Evangelical America* (Grand Rapids, MI: Eerdmans, 2008); Todd M. Brenneman, *Homespun Gospel: The Triumph of Sentimentality in Contemporary American Evangelicalism* (New York: Oxford University Press, 2014); Colleen McDannell, *Material Christianity: Religion and Popular Culture in America* (New Haven, CT: Yale University Press, 1995); R. Laurence Moore, *Selling God: American Religion in the Marketplace of Culture* (New York: Oxford University Press, 1995).
15. Greil Marcus, *History of Rock 'n' Roll in Ten Songs* (New Haven, CT: Yale University Press, 2014), 10.
16. Joel A. Carpenter, *Revive Us Again: The Reawakening of American Fundamentalism* (New York: Oxford University Press, 1997), 245, see also 3.
17. Stephen Hunt, "Going Back to Basics," *Third Way*, April 1999, 22.
18. Lesslie Newbigin, *Proper Confidence: Faith, Doubt, and Certainty in Christian Discipleship* (Grand Rapids, MI: Eerdmans, 1995), 1. For a focus on fundamentalists and evangelicals as sectarians who were cut off from larger social and cultural trends, see Marshall W. Fishwick, *Great Awakenings: Popular Religion and Popular Culture* (New York: Routledge, 1994), 87; Preston Shires, *Hippies of the Religious Right* (Waco, TX: Baylor

University Press, 2007), 41; David S. New, *Christian Fundamentalism in America: A Cultural History* (Jefferson, NC: McFarland, 2012), 164–165; and Maureen Dowd, "Didn't See It Coming, Again," *New York Times*, February 1, 2006, A25.

19. Kenneth Yu, "Relient K and CCM's Salvation," http://www.popmatters.com/feature/relient-k-050208/, February 8, 2005, accessed March 18, 2017.
20. R. Serge Denisoff and William D. Romanowski, *Risky Business: Rock in Film* (New Brunswick, NJ: Transaction, 1991), 283; Charlie Gillett, *Making Tracks: Atlantic Records and the Growth of a Multi-billion-dollar Industry* (New York: E. P. Dutton, 1974).
21. Lynn Van Matre, "Take That, Mr. Roboto: Styx Fires out at Zealots and Censorship," *Chicago Tribune*, April 17, 1983, D5 (italics in the original). Also see "Styx Bio," http://www.rollingstone.com/music/artists/styx/biography, accessed March 10, 2017; Konstantin Butz, *Grinding California: Culture and Corporeality in American Skate Punk* (Bielefeld, Germany: Transcript, 2014), 82, 141; and Dewar MacLeod, *Kids of the Black Hole: Punk Rock Postsuburban California* (Norman: University of Oklahoma Press, 2010), 103–105.
22. Roman Kozak, "Moral Majority in; What's in Future?" Rock 'n' Rolling, *Billboard*, November 15, 1980, 58.
23. "Interview with Richard M. Smith, Morton M. Kondracke, Margaret Garrard Warner, and Elaine Shannon of *Newsweek* on the Campaign against Drug Abuse, August 1, 1986," in *The Public Papers of the President of the United States: Ronald Reagan, June 28 to December 31, 1986* (Washington, DC: U.S. Government Printing Office, 1988), 1041–1042.
24. Marcia Eymann, "What's Going On?" in *What's Going On? California and the Vietnam Era*, ed. Marcia Eymann and Charles Wollenberg (Berkeley: University of California Press, 2004), 9. Also see Dochuk, *From Bible Belt to Sunbelt*, 295, 332.
25. "Interview with Richard M. Smith, Morton M. Kondracke, Margaret Garrard Warner, and Elaine Shannon," 1041–1042. For the music industry's response, see Patrick Goldstein, "Rock World Raps Reagan's Drug Stance," http://articles.latimes.com/1986-08-10/entertainment/ca-2084_1_drug-abuse, August 10, 1986, accessed February 25, 2017.
26. Zito, "Witness of Fire," D2.
27. Denisoff, *Tarnished Gold*, 407; *The Truth about Rock*, directed by Dan Peters and Steve Peters (St. Paul, MN: Peters Ministries, 1985), VHS; *Rock: It's Your Decision*, directed by John Taylor (Madison, AL: Olive's Film Productions, 1982), VHS; *Hells Bells: The Dangers of Rock and Roll*, directed by Eric Holmberg (Gainesville, FL: Reel to Real Ministries, 1989), VHS. For the pentecostal and fundamentalist focus, see Julia Cass, "Fiery Christians Burning Books to Banish Evil and Save the Kids," *Chicago Tribune*, June 16, 1982, C1. See also "Preacher's Record Smash Scores Hit with Followers," *Arizona Republic* (Phoenix), September 24, 1982, 23; "Evangelist Warns of Devil Message," *Ellensburg (WA) Daily Record*, September 24, 1982, 10; and Colin Nickerson, "To Purge Rock Music Is the Goal," *Boston Globe*, May 1, 1983, 47.
28. Laura A. Mercer, "Church Record-Burning Draws Mixed Reaction," *Wilmington (NC) Morning Star*, May 31, 1983, 2B.
29. June Bundy, "DJ's Dramatize R&R Sneer Campaign via Colorful Tactics," *Billboard*, April 21, 1958, 1, 4, 52; June Bundy, "Freed Replies to R&R Slurs," *Billboard*, April 28, 1956, 19, 22.
30. Allen A. Bassin to Hon. Senator Pastore, Philadelphia, March 20, 1958, in *Hearings before the Committee on Interstate and Foreign Commerce, United States Senate, Eighty-Fifth Congress* (Washington, DC: U.S. Government Printing Office, 1958), 949. Efforts to curb the negative effects of popular music continued in later decades as well. In the mid-1980s, Tipper Gore and Susan Baker formed the Parents Music Resource Center.

Congressional hearings that targeted themes of sex and violence in the music followed. The hearings resulted in warnings of explicit content being placed on select music releases. Kristin A. Bates and Richelle S. Swan, *Juvenile Delinquency in a Diverse Society* (Thousand Oaks, CA: Sage, 2018), 48; Quentin James Schultze et al., eds., *Dancing in the Dark: Youth, Popular Culture, and the Electronic Media* (Grand Rapids, MI: Eerdmans, 1991), 278–309.

31. Ann Landers, "More Comments on 'Rock and Roll,'" *Lawrence (KS) Daily Journal*, June 29, 1961, 6; "After-Hours Session: What's Your Yardstick for Screening Rock 'n' Roll Tunes?" *Billboard*, February 24, 1958, 9; Richard Aquila, *Let's Rock! How 1950s America Created Elvis and the Rock and Roll Craze* (Lanham, MD: Rowman and Littlefield, 2017), 12; W. T. Lhamon, *Deliberate Speed: The Origins of a Cultural Style in the American 1950s* (Cambridge, MA: Harvard University Press, 2002), 95. For contemporary controversies over the music, see Norman O'Connor, "If You Wish to Be 'Crazy' You Must Rock and Roll," *Boston Globe*, May 1, 1955, C67; Gertrude Samuels, "Why They Rock 'n' Roll—and Should They?" *New York Times*, January 12, 1958, SM16; and Phyllis Battelle, "Rock 'n' Roll Music Is Tops with Teen-Agers: Rock 'n' Rollers Still Mad for Crazy Music Fad," *Washington Post*, June 24, 1956, F1.
32. Eisenhower speech quotes from: Dwight D. Eisenhower, "Eisenhower Library Dedication, Abilene, Kansas, May 1, 1962," Dwight D. Eisenhower Presidential Library. See also Austin C. Wehrwein, "Eisenhower Discerns a Decline in Morality: Decries Modern Art and Twist in Talk at Library Dedication," *New York Times*, May 2, 1962, 1. "On Moral Standards of Nation: Eisenhower Remarks at Library Fete," *Washington Post*, May 3, 1962, A19. See also John Johnson, Jr., Joel Selvin, and Dick Cami, *Peppermint Twist: The Mob, the Music, and the Most Famous Dance Club of the '60s* (New York: Thomas Dunne Books, 2012), 138; and Ellis Amburn, *Buddy Holly: A Biography* (New York: St. Martin's Press, 2010), 179.
33. Allan Nevins, "What Has Happened to Our Morality?" *New York Times*, June 10, 1962, 203.
34. Andrew M. Greeley, *Religious Change in America* (Cambridge, MA: Harvard University Press, 1989), 38.
35. Richard E. Holz, "The Song Book of the Salvation Army," in *Historical Dictionary of the Salvation Army*, ed. John G. Merritt (Lanham, MD: Scarecrow Press, 2006), 541.
36. "Religious Music in America, a History," in *Encyclopedia of Contemporary Christian Music: Pop, Rock, and Worship*, ed. Don Cusic (Santa Barbara, CA: Greenwood Press, 2010), 373.
37. Reflecting on the advent of Christian rock, Larry Eskridge writes, "The rise of Jesus rock in the late 1960s was not something that many observers could have envisioned—evangelicals had been in the forefront of rock 'n roll's homegrown American critics during the 1950s." Eskridge, *God's Forever Family*, 210.
38. "'Live Clean,' Graham Tells Teen-Agers," *Washington Post*, June 26, 1960, D22. Also see Billy Graham, *The Mystery of Iniquity* (Minneapolis, MN: Billy Graham Evangelistic Association, 1957), n.p. Many thanks to Matthew Sutton for providing me with *The Mystery of Iniquity* pamphlet.
39. Mark Laver, *Jazz Sells: Music, Marketing, and Meaning* (New York: Routledge, 2015), 42–45.
40. Maud Cuney-Hare, *Negro Musicians and Their Music* (Washington, DC: Associated Publishers, 1936), 156.
41. N. Barrows, "Musical Smut," *Family Digest* (Huntington, IN) 13 (May 1958): 25–29; "What Is the Disease in Modern Popular Music?" *Liguorian* (Liguori, MO) 45 (July 1957): 13–15; David Wilkerson, "Rock and Roll: The Devil's Heartbeat," *Pentecostal Evangel* (Springfield, MO), July 12, 1959, 4; David A. Noebel, "Are the Beatles

Minstrels of the Antichrist?" *Christian Crusade*, October 1966, 26–27. A Southern Baptist minister's sermon on rock and roll illustrates the point well. In the sermon, which is likely from the late 1950s, the minister remarks on how psychiatrists and others explained the power of the music. "The answer for it is," he confidently intoned, "it is the work of the devil among those who do not yield to Christ." Jesse Murphy Hendley, "Sermons: Rock and Roll," n.p., n.d., 1, Jesse Murphy Hendley Collection, Southern Baptist Historical Library and Archives, Nashville, TN.

42. Martha Bayles, *Hole in Our Soul: The Loss of Beauty and Meaning in American Popular Music* (Chicago: University of Chicago Press, 1994), 127–142.
43. "Little Richard Gets the Call," *Billboard*, October 21, 1957, 22; Steve Morse, "Musical Legends: Jerry Lee Lewis, Whole Lotta Rockin' by Mr. Versatility," *Boston Globe*, May 1, 1983, B1.
44. Charles White, *The Life and Times of Little Richard: The Quasar of Rock* (New York: Da Capo Press, 1994), 121.
45. Timothy Moore, "Jerry Lee: Country Music," *Washington Post*, February 27, 1977, E5.
46. Nick Tosches, *Hellfire: The Jerry Lee Lewis Story* (New York: Dell, 1982), 57.
47. Wilkerson, "Rock and Roll," 4.
48. Lambert Schuyler and Patricia Schuyler, *Close That Bedroom Door!* (Winslow, WA: Heron House, 1957), 166. Also see "Lambert Schuyler-Local History," http://www.bainbridgepubliclibrary.org/Lambert-Schuyler.aspx, accessed February 8, 2017.
49. "Religion a la NAACP," *Citizens' Council* (Jackson, MS), September 1958, 3.
50. Neil R. McMillen, *The Citizens' Council: Organized Resistance to the Second Reconstruction, 1954–1964* (Urbana: University of Illinois Press, 1994), 54.
51. "Ray Brock Answers Your Personal Questions," *C. A. Herald* (Springfield, MO), July 1962, 25.
52. Jessie Funston Clubb, "What about Rock 'n' Roll?" *Home Life* (Nashville, TN), April 1957, quote on 42; 43. For more on the racist element in anti-rock, see Brian Ward, *Just My Soul Responding: Rhythm and Blues, Black Consciousness, and Race Relations* (London: UCL Press, 1998), 100.
53. Altschuler, *All Shook Up*, 161.
54. Carl F. H. Henry, "The Road to Freedom," *Christianity Today* (Carol Stream, IL), February 28, 1964, 27.
55. Billy Graham, *World Aflame* (New York: Doubleday, 1965), 22.
56. Dick Sutcliffe, "Ideal Man of the Year," *Biblical Recorder* (Raleigh, NC), January 7, 1967, 2.
57. Richard Connolly, "Billy Graham Talks of Youth," *Boston Globe*, September 18, 1964, 1. For Graham's comments on the Beatles following their *Ed Sullivan Show* appearance, see "Trends," *Moody Monthly* (Chicago), April 1964, 8. See also R. O. Denton, "News of the Churches: Windsor, N.C.," *Pentecostal Evangel* (Springfield, MO), August 29, 1965, 30.
58. "Ten Commandments for Teen-Agers," *Bridegroom's Messenger* (Atlanta, GA), December 1964, 6. The original is "Ten Commandments for Teen-agers," *King's Business* (Los Angeles), December 1957, 31.
59. Claudia M. Higgins, "Let's Break Down the Bed," *Pentecostal Evangel* (Springfield, MO), October 17, 1965, 24.
60. "Can Name 20 Beatle Songs, But Only 2 Apostles," *Biblical Recorder* (Raleigh, NC), January 30, 1965, 2. For more on Beatle hero worship, see "Young People See Hazards in Ministry," *Biblical Recorder*, February 22, 1964, 4.
61. For more on the baby boom, see Doug Owram, *Born at the Right Time: A History of the Baby Boom Generation* (Toronto: University of Toronto Press, 1997), 84, 146, 186–188, 209; and Elaine Tyler May, *Homeward Bound: American Families in the Cold War Era*

(New York: Basic Books, 2008), 130–132. For more on youth rebellion, see Gerard J. DeGroot, *The Sixties Unplugged: A Kaleidoscopic History of a Disorderly Decade* (Cambridge, MA: Harvard University Press, 2008), 208–242.

62. *Chicago Magazine*, March 1955, 42.
63. H. Peter Kuiper, "Free Church Communication Techniques: An Analysis of Communication Approaches Used by the Free Church in Its Ministry to Berkeley's Hippies" (master's thesis, Fresno State College, 1968), 19–20.
64. Originally published as Harvey Cox, "God and the Hippies," *Playboy* 15, no. 1 (January 1968): 94. Republished as "Playboy USA-January 1968," https://archive.org/stream/USPlayboy196801/US_Playboy_1968_01_djvu.txt, accessed March 20, 2017.
65. "The Jesus People," in *The Religious Reawakening in America*, ed. Joseph Newman (Washington, DC: U.S. News and World Report, 1972), 26.
66. T. M. Luhrmann, "Blinded by the Right? How Hippie Christians Begat Evangelical Conservatives," *Harper's Magazine*, April 2013, 40.
67. Robert Palmer, "The Pop Life; Rock: No Longer 'Devil's Music'?" *New York Times*, September 16, 1981, C23.
68. Carl F. H. Henry, *The Uneasy Conscience of Modern Fundamentalism* (1947; reprint, Grand Rapids, MI: Eerdmans Publishing Company, 2003), 39. For the evangelical fear of becoming too isolated and irrelevant, see John Goodwin, "Separate but Equal," *Eternity* (Philadelphia), August 1964, 16–18. The historian David Swartz claims that evangelicals who were associated with Wheaton College in Wheaton, Illinois, and Fuller Theological Seminary in Pasadena, California, "articulated a more comprehensive evangelical agenda for the twentieth century that proposed increased political, scholarly, and social activity. Henry himself emerged as the preeminent prophet and theologian of the emerging neo-evangelical movement." David R. Swartz, *Moral Minority: The Evangelical Left in an Age of Conservatism* (Philadelphia: University of Pennsylvania Press, 2012), 20, see also 21–25.
69. See the "Contemporary Christian Music," and "Jesus People" folders in the G. Archer Weniger Collection, Bob Jones University.
70. "Religious Landscape Study," http://www.pewforum.org/religious-landscape-study/, 2008, accessed December 14, 2013.

Chapter 1

1. Elvis Presley, interview by Dolores Diamond, "Presley," *Dig Magazine*, June 1958, 8, 10.
2. Davin Seay and Mary Neely, *Stairway to Heaven: The Spiritual Roots of Rock 'n' Roll* (New York: Ballantine Books, 1986); Teresa L. Reed, *The Holy Profane: Religion in Black Popular Music* (Lexington: University of Kentucky Press, 2003); Gene Santoro, *Highway 61 Revisited: The Tangled Roots of Jazz, Blues, Rock, and Country Music* (New York: Oxford University Press, 2004), 93–98. In its first stage, rock 'n' roll might best be defined as singles-based, black-rooted, mostly vocal music that could be found on the rhythm and blues as well as country and western charts. See Charlie Gillett, *The Sound of the City: The Rise of Rock and Roll* (New York: Pantheon, 1983), viii–xii; and Dave Marsh, *The Heart of Rock and Soul: The 1001 Greatest Singles Ever Made* (New York: Penguin, 1989), xv–xvi.
3. Charles Reagan Wilson, "'Just a Little Talk with Jesus': Elvis Presley, Religious Music, and Southern Spirituality," in *Southern Crossroads: Perspectives on Religion and Culture*,

ed. Walter H. Conser Jr., and Rodger M. Payne (Lexington: University of Kentucky Press, 2008), 16–18; Craig Mosher, "Ecstatic Sounds: The Influence of Pentecostalism on Rock and Roll," *Popular Music and Society* 31, no. 1 (February 2008): 95–112; Martha Bayles, *Hole in Our Soul: The Loss of Beauty and Meaning in American Popular Music* (Chicago: University of Chicago Press, 1994), 127–142; Stephen R. Tucker, "Pentecostalism and Popular Culture in the South: A Study of Four Musicians," *Journal of Popular Culture* 16 (Winter 1982): 68–78. For religion, pop culture, and secularism, see David Chidester, "The Church of Baseball, the Fetish of Coca-Cola, and the Potlatch of Rock 'n' Roll: Theoretical Models for the Study of Religion in American Popular Culture," *Journal of the American Academy of Religion* 64, no. 4 (1996): 743–765; Robert A. Orsi, *Between Heaven and Earth: The Religious Worlds People Make and the Scholars Who Study Them* (Princeton, NJ: Princeton University Press, 2006); Kathryn Lofton, *Oprah: The Gospel of an Icon* (Berkeley: University of California Press, 2011); and "Varieties of Secularism in a Secular Age," https://tif.ssrc.org/tif/secular_age/, accessed April 4, 2012.

4. "U.S. Religious Landscape Survey: Religious Beliefs and Practices," http://www.pewforum.org/religious-landscape-study/, 2008, accessed September 2, 2010.
5. Flannery O'Connor, "Some Aspects of the Grotesque in Southern Fiction," in *Mystery and Manners: Occasional Prose*, ed. Sally Fitzgerald and Robert Fitzgerald (New York: Farrar, Straus and Giroux, 1969), 44. See also "To Maryat Lee," November 14, 1959, in *The Habit of Being: Letters of Flannery O'Connor*, ed. Sally Fitzgerald (New York: Farrar, Straus, and Giroux, 1988), 358–359.
6. Samuel S. Hill Jr., *Southern Churches in Crisis Revisited* (Tuscaloosa: University of Alabama Press, 1999), 25, 26–27.
7. For a clear, detailed definition of evangelicalism, see James Davidson Hunter, *Evangelicalism: Conservative Religion and the Quandary of Modernity* (New Brunswick, NJ: Rutgers University Press, 1983), 7–9.
8. George F. Ketcham, ed., *Yearbook of American Churches* (New York: National Council of the Churches of Christ in the USA, 1951), 234.
9. Bret E. Carroll, *The Routledge Historical Atlas of Religion in America* (New York: Routledge, 2000), 115.
10. William James, *The Varieties of Religious Experience* (Cambridge, MA: Harvard University Press, 1985), 86.
11. Mark Twain, "A Singular Episode: The Reception of Rev. Sam Jones in Heaven," in *The Bible According to Mark Twain: Writings on Heaven, Eden, and the Flood,* ed. Howard G. Baetzhold and Joseph B. McCullough (Athens: University of Georgia Press, 1995), 199, 200, 201. For a summary of the prohibitions and behavioral codes of the Church of God of Anderson, Indiana, see Valorous Bernard Clear, "The Church of God: A Study in Social Adaptation" (Ph.D. diss., University of Chicago, 1953), 220–228.
12. For pentecostalism, see Roger G. Robins, *A. J. Tomlinson: Plainfolk Modernist* (New York: Oxford University Press, 2004); Grant Wacker, *Heaven Below: Early Pentecostals and American Culture* (Cambridge, MA: Harvard University Press, 2001); Matthew Avery Sutton, *Aimee Semple McPherson and the Resurrection of Christian America* (Cambridge, MA: Harvard University Press, 2007); Anthea D. Butler, *Women in the Church of God in Christ: Making a Sanctified World* (Chapel Hill: University of North Carolina Press, 2007); and Randall J. Stephens, *The Fire Spreads: Holiness and Pentecostalism in the American South* (Cambridge, MA: Harvard University Press, 2008).
13. "Letter of a Baptist Preacher to His Wife Describing a Pentecostal Meeting at Durant, Fla.," *Evening Light and Church of God Evangel,* July 1, 1910, 2.

14. Wallace P. Blackwood, "Pentecost," *Christianity Today* (Carol Stream, IL), February 15, 1963, 25.
15. Elaine J. Lawless, *God's Peculiar People: Women's Voices and Folk Tradition in a Pentecostal Church* (Lexington: University of Kentucky Press, 2005), 38.
16. "The Third Force in Christendom: Gospel-Singing, Doomsday-Preaching Sects Emerge as a Mighty Movement in World Religion," *Life*, June 9, 1958, 122.
17. Robins, *A. J. Tomlinson*, 5. See also David Martin, "Pentecostalism: An Alternative Form of Modernity and Modernization?" in *Global Pentecostalism in the 21st Century*, ed. Peter L. Berger (Bloomington: Indiana University Press, 2013), 37–62; Sutton, *Aimee Semple McPherson and the Resurrection of Christian America*; Wacker, *Heaven Below*; Kate Bowler, *Blessed: A History of the American Prosperity Gospel* (New York: Oxford University Press, 2013); and Shayne Lee and Phillip Luke Sinitiere, *Holy Mavericks: Evangelical Innovators and the Spiritual Marketplace* (New York: New York University Press, 2009), 22.
18. H. L. Mencken, "Yearning Mountaineers' Souls Need Reconversion Nightly, Mencken Finds," *Baltimore Evening Sun*, July 13, 1925, 1–2; William A. Clark, "Sanctification in Negro Religion," *Social Forces* 15 (May 1937): 546, 549; Will Herberg, *Protestant-Catholic-Jew: An Essay in American Religious Sociology* (Chicago: University of Chicago Press, 1983), 123; Norman G. Eddy, "Store-Front Religion," *Religion in Life* 28, no. 1 (1958–1959): 68–85; J. Paul Williams, *What Americans Believe and How They Worship* (New York: Harper and Row, 1962), 434–436. See also Deidre Helen Crumbley, *Saved and Sanctified: The Rise of a Storefront Church in Great Migration Philadelphia* (Gainesville: University Press of Florida, 2012), 17–27.
19. Anton T. Boisen, "Religion and Hard Times: A Study of the Holy Rollers," *Social Action* (New York), March 15, 1939, 28.
20. Ira E. Harrison, "The Storefront Church as a Revitalization Movement," *Review of Religious Research* 7, no. 3 (1966): 161.
21. James Baldwin, *Go Tell It on the Mountain* (New York: Random House, 2000), 7–8.
22. Jack Conroy, *A World to Win* (Urbana: University of Illinois Press, 2000), 36, 37, 38. For additional context, see also Douglas Wixson, introduction in Conroy, *A World to Win*, xxiii.
23. V. E. Daniel, "Ritual and Stratification in Chicago Negro Churches," *American Sociological Review* 7, no. 3 (June 1942): 354–355.
24. Ibid., 358, 359, and see 360; block quote on 357.
25. Ibid., 355, block quote on 358.
26. James Bright Wilson, "Religious Leaders, Institutions and Organizations among Certain Agricultural Workers in the Central Valley of California" (Ph.D. diss., University of Southern California, 1944), 273. For a description of a 1942 Pentecostal Holiness Church service, see 273–288.
27. William Alexander Percy, *Lanterns on the Levee: Recollections of a Planter's Son* (Baton Rouge: Louisiana State University Press, 2006), 149.
28. Leo G. Mazow, *Thomas Hart Benton and the American Sound* (University Park: Pennsylvania State University Press, 2012), 76–79; Thomas Hart Benton, *An Artist in America* (Columbia: University of Missouri Press, 1968), 97–98, 100–101; Annett Claudia Richter, "Fiddles, Harmonicas, and Banjos: Thomas Hart Benton and His Role in Constructing Popular Notions of American Folk Music and Musicians" (Ph.D. diss., University of Minnesota, 2008), 188–189.
29. Benton, *An Artist in America*, 106, 110–111.
30. Bill C. Malone and David Stricklin, *Southern Music/American Music* (Lexington: University of Kentucky Press, 2003), 104, see also 102.

31. Shayne Lee, *T. D. Jakes: America's New Preacher* (New York: New York University Press, 2007), 1–3, 158–177.
32. Jon Hartley Fox, *King of the Queen City: The Story of King Records* (Urbana: University of Illinois Press, 2009), 119–120.
33. Jerma Jackson, "Sister Rosetta Tharpe and the Evolution of Gospel Music," in *Religion in the American South: Protestants and Others in History and Culture*, ed. Beth Barton Schweiger and Donald G. Mathews (Chapel Hill: University of North Carolina Press, 2004), 219–222, 230–232; Paul Oliver, *Songsters and Saints: Vocal Traditions on Race Records* (Cambridge: Cambridge University Press, 1984), 170–171, 188–189, 197–198; Reed, *The Holy Profane*, 35–38; Larry Birnbaum, *Before Elvis: The Prehistory of Rock 'n' Roll* (Lanham, MD: Scarecrow Press, 2013), 19, 226, 303, 349.
34. Don Cusic, "Cash, Johnny," in *Encyclopedia of Contemporary Christian Music: Pop, Rock, and Worship*, ed. Don Cusic (Santa Barbara, CA: ABC-CLIO, 2010), 42.
35. Johnny Cash, *Man in Black* (Grand Rapids, MI: Zondervan, 1975), 25.
36. Tammy Wynette, *Stand by Your Man*, with Joan Dew (New York: Simon and Schuster, 1979), 23–24. Also see Tucker, "Pentecostalism and Popular Culture in the South," 68–78.
37. B. B. King, *B. B. King: The Autobiography*, with David Ritz (London: Hodder and Stoughton, 1997), 16–18.
38. Bruce Pegg, *Brown Eyed Handsome Man: The Life and Hard Times of Chuck Berry* (New York: Routledge, 2005), 22, 26.
39. Marc Myers, "A Cultural Conversation with Little Richard: Richard, the First," *Wall Street Journal*, August 10, 2010, D5. See also Preston Lauterbach, *The Chitlin' Circuit: And the Road to Rock 'n' Roll* (New York: W. W. Norton, 2011), 152; "Little Richard Bio," *Rolling Stone*, http://www.rollingstone.com/music/artists/little-richard/biography, accessed March 25, 2017.
40. Charles White, *The Life and Times of Little Richard: The Quasar of Rock* (New York: Da Capo Press, 1994), 16, and see 17. See also Charles Sawyer, *The Arrival of B. B. King* (Garden City, NY: Doubleday, 1980), 39–40. Myra Lewis, *Great Balls of Fire: The Uncensored Story of Jerry Lee Lewis*, with Murray Silver (New York: William Murrow, 1982), 34–35, 308–311. Marvin Gaye and Dolly Parton also attended pentecostal churches in their youth.
41. Jimmy Swaggart, *To Cross a River*, with Robert Paul Lamb (Plainfield, NJ: Logos International, 1977), 28, and see 26, 27.
42. Swaggart, *To Cross a River*, 100. See also Jerry Lee Lewis Subject Folder, Center for Popular Music, Middle Tennessee State University; and Ann Rowe Seaman, *Swaggart: The Unauthorized Biography of an American Evangelist* (New York: Continuum, 1999).
43. Peter Guralnick, *Last Train to Memphis: The Rise of Elvis Presley* (Boston: Little, Brown, 1994), 39, 75. James E. Hamill, Memphis, TN, to Ralph M. Riggs, Springfield, MO, August 1, 1956, Flower Pentecostal Heritage Center, Springfield, MO.
44. See, for instance, Michael T. Bertrand, "Elvis Presley and the Politics of Popular Memory," *Southern Cultures* 13, no. 3 (2007): 62–86; Brian Ward, *Just My Soul Responding: Rhythm and Blues, Black Consciousness, and Race Relations* (London: UCL Press, 1998), 6, 120; Louie Robinson, "The Blackening of White America," *Ebony*, May 1980, 158–162; "B. B. King Hears How Presley Copied Style," *Chicago Defender*, February 2, 1957, 14; Amiri Baraka, *Digging: The Afro-American Soul of American Classical Music* (Berkeley: University of California Press, 2009), 97, 114, 135; Langston Hughes, "Highway Robbery Across the Color Line in Rhythm and Blues," *Chicago*

Defender, July 2, 1955, 9; and Ralph Matthews, "Thinking Out Loud," *Baltimore Afro-American*, March 16, 1957, 16.

45. Michael T. Bertrand, *Race, Rock, and Elvis* (Champaign: University of Illinois Press, 2000), 220.
46. Elvis Presley, interview by Pierre Adidge and Robert Abel, March 31, 1972, in *Elvis: Word for Word: What He Said, Exactly as He Said It*, ed. Jerry Osborne (New York: Harmony Books, 2000), 243. See also Rose Clayton and Dick Heard, *Elvis up Close: In the Words of Those Who Knew Him Best* (Atlanta, GA: Turner Publishing, 1994), 13–17; interview with Elvis about religion in Jack Carrell, "I Like Elvis Presley," *Ottawa Citizen*, September 8, 1956, 11; and Elvis's 1966 interview with May Mann quoted in Peter Guralnick, *Careless Love: The Unmaking of Elvis Presley* (Boston: Back Bay Books, 2000), 223.
47. Vince Staten, *The Real Elvis: Good Old Boy* (Dayton, OH: Media Ventures, 1978), 47–48. Also see Van K. Brock, "Assemblies of God: Elvis and Pentecostalism," *Bulletin of the Center for the Study of Southern Culture and Religion* 3 (June 1979): 9–15. For Elvis's relationship with the Blackwood Brothers, see James R. Goff Jr., *Close Harmony: A History of Southern Gospel* (Chapel Hill: University of North Carolina Press, 2002), 237–238. For more on Elvis, see Saul Pett, "Why Do the Girls Love Elvis?" *Richmond Times-Dispatch*, July 22, 1956, L-7; "Elvis Says Jumping 'Arown' Comes Natural When He Sings"; Saul Pett, "'It's Just the Way Ah Feel,' Says Young Elvis"; Louella O. Parsons, "What Makes Elvis Rock?"; and Saul Pett, "I Don't Feel Sexy When I Sing, Pleads Diamond Loaded Elvis," newspaper clippings, Flower Pentecostal Heritage Center, Springfield, MO. Also see Guralnick, *Last Train to Memphis*, 17, 67, 75. See the *Elvis Answers Back* magazine interview with Elvis on "My True Religion." Elvis was clearly bothered by claims that he had given up on religion after he became famous. Elvis Presley, "My True Religion," August 28, 1956, *Elvis: Word for Word*, ed. Jerry Osborne (New York: Harmony Books, 2000), 70.
48. Don Cusic, "Singing with the King: The Groups That Performed with Elvis," *Rejoice! The Gospel Music Magazine*, Summer 1988, 13. See also Guralnick, *Careless Love*, 233; and J. D. Sumner, *Elvis: His Love for Gospel Music and J. D. Sumner*, with Bob Terrell (Nashville, TN: W. C. I. Publishing, 1991), 5–19.
49. Don Cusic, "Southern Gospel and Contemporary Christian Music," in *Encyclopedia of Contemporary Christian Music*, 410.
50. Jennifer Harrison, *Elvis as We Knew Him: Our Shared Life in a Small Town in South Memphis* (Lincoln, NE: iUniverse, 2003), 16–17. See also Elvis Presley Subject Folder, Center for Popular Music, Middle Tennessee State University; Charles Wolfe, "Elvis Presley and the Gospel Tradition," in *The Elvis Reader: Texts and Sources on the King of Rock 'n' Roll*, ed. Kevin Quan (New York: St. Martin's Press, 1992), 13–27; and Joe Moscheo, *The Gospel Side of Elvis* (New York: Center Street, 2007), 27–36.
51. Elvis Presley, interview by Paul Wilder, in Osborne, *Elvis: Word for Word*, 52–53.
52. James Brown, *James Brown: The Godfather of Soul*, with Bruce Tucker (New York: Thunder's Mouth Press, 1986), 18, and see 19.
53. "Bishop Grace Is Welcomed by Fervid Followers Here," *Augusta (GA) Chronicle*, September 21, 1938, 5.
54. "'Daddy' Grace Seeks Permit for Church," *Augusta (GA) Chronicle*, July 3, 1941, 2; Marie W. Dallam, *Daddy Grace: A Celebrity Preacher and His House of Prayer* (New York: New York University Press, 2007); Dudley K. Brewer, "Bishop Grace Is Austere Ruler and 'Daddy' to All House of Prayer Members," *Augusta (GA) Chronicle*, November 15, 1935, 6; "Baptizes 200 with Hose and Asks for Cash," *Springfield (MA) Republican*,

August 20, 1945; and "Daddy Grace: Grandiloquent Negro Preacher Has a Half-Million Faithful Followers," *Life*, October 1, 1945, 51.

55. Alex Poinsett, "Farewell to Daddy: Both Praised and Condemned, Prelate Is as Much an Enigma in Death as He Was in Life," *Ebony*, April 1960, 25.
56. Brown, *James Brown*, 18, 19. See also George Lipsitz, *Footsteps in the Dark: The Hidden Histories of Popular Music* (Minneapolis: University of Minnesota Press, 2007), xix–xx; and Timothy White, "Searing Fires vs. Sounds of Faith," *Billboard*, June 29, 1996, 5.
57. Hamill to Riggs, Flower Pentecostal Heritage Center, Springfield, MO.
58. Linda Martin and Kerry Segrave, *Anti-rock: The Opposition to Rock 'n' Roll* (New York: Da Capo Press, 1993), 27–29; Paul Henry Lang, "Music and Musicians: The Riot in Asbury Park," *Herald Tribune* (New York), July 22, 1956, D5; James Nelson Goodsell, "Rock 'n' Roll Opposition Rises," *Christian Science Monitor*, May 8, 1958, 3; "Little Richard Fined in Texas," *Dallas Morning News*, August 28, 1956, 5; " 'Rock' Movie Banned for Fear of Rioting," *Boston Globe*, September 13, 1956, 7.
59. Martin and Segrave, *Anti-rock*, 31, 32–35. For more on anti-rock campaigns, see Bertrand, *Race, Rock, and Elvis*, 181–184; and Glenn C. Altschuler, *All Shook Up: How Rock 'n' Roll Changed America* (New York: Oxford University Press, 2003), 105–112.
60. Milton Bracker, "Experts Propose Study of 'Craze,' " *New York Times*, February 23, 1957, 12; "Presley Termed Passing Fancy: Minister in Village Asserts Singer Gives Teen-Agers 'a Vicarious Fling,' " *New York Times*, December 17, 1956, 28. For other critical accounts, see "Rock 'n' Roll Called a Disease," *Catholic Choirmaster* 42 (Summer 1956): 121; Kate Dooley, "Why Elvis?—Or, I Remember Rudolph," *Ave Maria*, November 17, 1956, 22; Martin "Butch" Hardman, "Rock 'n' Roll: Music or Madness?" *Youth for Christ* (Wheaton, IL), October 1958, 10–12; Norman King, "Teen-Age Idol Worship," *Youth for Christ*, March 1959, 6–7; and "Rock 'n' Roll," *Alabama Baptist* (Birmingham), November 1, 1956, 3.
61. Martin and Segrave, *Anti-rock*, 50–53.
62. Verna B. Gordon, letter to the editor, *Life*, September 17, 1956, 19. Other, similar criticisms include "Stritch Urges Catholics: Ban Rock and Roll," *Chicago Daily Tribune*, May 1, 1957, 4; "Rock 'n' Roll Hurting Teens, CYO Head Tells Police League," *Boston Globe*, May 16, 1960, 4; and Phyllis Battelle, "Rock 'n' Roll Beat Irks People the Nation Over," *Journal and Guide* (Norfolk, VA), June 30, 1956, 15.
63. Tony Zoppi, "Presley Thrills Crowd of 26,500," *Dallas Morning News*, October 12, 1956, 2.
64. "Music: Teeners' Hero," *Time*, May 14, 1956, 55.
65. Erika Lee Doss, *Elvis Culture: Fans, Faith, and Image* (Lawrence: University Press of Kansas, 1999), 129.
66. "What Is the Disease in Modern Popular Music?" *Liguorian* (Liguori, MO), 45, July 1957, 14.
67. "Zion Body Hits Elvis Presley," *Baltimore Afro-American*, December 8, 1956, 7.
68. "Rock-and-Roll Religion," *Christian Herald* (New York), September 1956, 12. See also a screed against "juke-box religion" in A. Roy Eckhardt, "Down with this *New* Religion," *Baptist Student* (Nashville, TN), April 1956, 19.
69. W. G. Vorpe, "As the Parade Passes By," *Cleveland Plain Dealer*, 1938, 2. Other concerned churchmen were far more specific.
70. Don Cusic, *The Sound of Light: A History of Gospel and Christian Music* (Milwaukee, WI: Hal Leonard, 2002), 191.
71. Chaeryl A. Kirk-Duggan, "African American Hymnody," in *Encyclopedia of Women and Religion in North America*, eds., Rosemary Skinner Keller and Rosemary Radford

Ruether (Bloomington: Indiana University Press, 2006), 992; "Clara Ward Denies She 'Rocks 'n Rolls,'" *Baltimore Afro-American*, November 26, 1955, 6. See also "Blast on Gospel Singers' Style Pits Baker against Ward," *Chicago Defender*, November 26, 1955, 7; "Clara and LaVern Argue Origin of the R & B Beat," *New Journal and Guide* (Norfolk, VA), December 3, 1955, B20; "Rhythm and Blues Not Stolen—Baker," *Philadelphia Tribune*, October 15, 1955, 11; and see an interview with Clara Ward in Ren Grevatt, "On the Beat," *Billboard*, March 9, 1959, 8. For a similar debate, see "Is There Too Much Rock 'n' Roll in Religion?" *Color* 11, no. 14 (January 1957): 12–13. Pearl Bailey claimed to have sung rocking music at her "Holy Roller" brush arbor church in Virginia, which her father pastored, decades before. Larry Grove, "Pearl Says Not Everybody Eatin' Beatle Jelly Beans," *Dallas Morning News*, September 18, 1964, 10.

72. William Ward Ayer, "Are Demon Forces at Work in the World Today?" *Baptist Standard*, October 27, 1956, 7.
73. David Ritz and Ray Charles, *Brother Ray: Ray Charles' Own Story* (Cambridge, MA: Da Capo Press, 2004), 149, 150. See also Dave Headlam, "Appropriations of Blues and Gospel in Popular Music," in *The Cambridge Companion to Blues and Gospel Music*, ed. Allan Moore (Cambridge: Cambridge University Press, 2002), 173–175. Ray Charles attended a Baptist church with his mother, and these services seemed to feature some pentecostal elements. See Ray Charles Robinson Jr., *You Don't Know Me: Reflections of My Father*, with Mary Jane Ross (New York: Harmony Books, 2010), 51–53. For Milt Jackson's words on the influence of the sanctified church on black soul music in the 1950s, see Lerone Bennett Jr., "The Soul of Soul," *Ebony*, December 1961, 116. On the popularity of Charles and other early black soul artists, see, "Most Played in Juke Boxes," *Billboard*, March 26, 1955, 138; "The Billboard Music Popularity Charts," *Billboard*, March 26, 1955, 142; Horace C. Boyer, "Black Music Comes of Age," *Black World*, November 1973, 43.
74. "Remarks at a White House Reception for the Kennedy Center Honorees, December 7, 1986," in *The Public Papers of the President of the United States: Ronald Reagan, June 28 to December 31, 1986* (Washington, DC: U.S. Government Printing Office, 1988), 1610.
75. Ralph J. Gleason, "Ray Charles' Motto—'Singing Is Believing,'" *Cleveland Plain Dealer*, December 27, 1959, 6H. See also Rick Coleman, *Blue Monday: Fats Domino and the Lost Dawn of Rock 'n' Roll* (Cambridge, MA: Da Capo Press, 2006), 4–5; and Michael Lydon, *Ray Charles: Man and Music* (New York: Routledge, 2004), 114.
76. Ritz and Charles, *Brother Ray*, 151.
77. Hollie I. West, "Mixing Gospel and the Blues," *Washington Post*, July 9, 1972, BW10. See also Francis Davis, *The History of the Blues: The Roots Music of the People* (Cambridge, MA: Da Capo Press, 2003), 227. For the introduction of the "holy roller" theme in a review of Jackie Wilson's music and TV performance style, see "Channel Time," *Los Angeles Tribune*, May 30, 1958, 18.
78. Gerri Hirshey, *Nowhere to Run: The Story of Soul Music* (London: Macmillan, 1984), 26–27; Michael W. Harris, *The Rise of Gospel Blues: The Music of Thomas Andrew Dorsey in the Urban Church* (New York: Oxford University Press, 1994), 148–150; Ross Laird, *Brunswick Records: Chicago and Regional Sessions* (Westport, CT: Greenwood Press, 2001), 1045, 1083, 1163, 1174, 1183; "Prominent Visitors," *Chicago Defender*, September 13, 1930, 13; Edward Moore, "Recent Disk Recordings Will Please Ravel, Schumann Fans," *Chicago Daily Tribune*, November 30, 1930, F5. For more on the interplay of African American blues and gospel music, see Paul Harvey, *Through the Storm, through the Night: A History of African American Christianity* (Lanham, MD: Rowman & Littlefield, 2011), 102–105; Burton William Peretti, *Lift Every Voice: The*

History of African American Music (Lanham, MD: Rowman & Littlefield, 2009), 129–138; and Jeff Todd Titon, "Labels: Identifying the Categories of Blues and Gospel," in *The Cambridge Companion to Blues and Gospel Music*, 13–19.

79. Charles D. Beck, "Rock and Roll Sermon" (1956), *Fire in My Bones: Raw+Rare+Otherworldy African-American Gospel, 1944–2007* (New York: Tompkins Square, 2009), CD. Also see Evelyn M. E. Taylor, "Beck, Elder Charles D.," in *Encyclopedia of American Gospel Music*, ed. W. K. McNeil (New York: Routledge, 2010), 33–34.
80. Milton Perry, "A Minister in Defense of Elvis," *Cleveland Call and Post*, January 19, 1957, 7A. See also the remarks of songwriter Samuel "Buck" Ram in Hal Boyle, "Rock 'n' Roll Defended as Descendant of Gospel Hymn," *Ocala (FL) Star-Banner*, August 23, 1956. See also "Minister Says Rock-n-Roll True U.S. Art," *Chicago Daily Tribune*, February 17, 1957, SW16; and "It Can't Be That Bad!" *Baltimore Afro-American*, July 28, 1956, 4.
81. Letters to the editor, *Life*, September 17, 1956, 19.
82. Phyllis Battelle, "Rock 'n' Roll Music Is Tops with Teen-Agers: Rock 'n' Rollers Still Mad for Crazy Music Fad," *Washington Post*, June 24, 1956, F1.
83. William Leonard, "You Can Have Rock 'n' Roll!" *Chicago Tribune*, February 3, 1957, F21.
84. "Letters from Readers," *Chicago Tribune*, March 24, 1957, F6.
85. "Letters from Readers," *Chicago Tribune*, March 10, 1957, D2.
86. Joan Beck, "Sour to Parents, Perhaps: But This Rock 'n' Roll Is Sweet to Our Teens," *Chicago Tribune*, July 15, 1959, B1. "Teen Talk: Mothers, Please Try to Understand Elvis," *Boston Globe*, November 11, 1956, C23. See also "Teen Talk: Freshman Thinks Elvis 'the Mostest,'" *Boston Globe*, July 2, 1956, 22.
87. Mrs. Earl H. Clements, Richmond, VA, to Ralph M. Riggs, Springfield, MO, August 4, 1956. Mrs. George Arnold, Macon, GA, to Ralph M. Riggs, Springfield, MO, September 29, 1956. See also G. P. Hertweck, Hattiesburg, MS, to Ralph M. Riggs, Springfield, MO, Flower Pentecostal Heritage Center, Springfield, MO.
88. David Wilkerson, *The Cross and the Switchblade*, with John Sherrill and Elizabeth Sherrill (New York: Pyramid Books, 1962).
89. David Wilkerson, "Rock and Roll: The Devil's Heartbeat," *Pentecostal Evangel* (Springfield, MO), July 12, 1959, 4.
90. David R. Wilkerson, "The Devil's Heartbeat Rock and Roll! Teenage Sins Exposed!" (Philipsburg, PA: Teen-Age Evangelism, n.d.), 3, 8.
91. Homer Tomlinson, *The Shout of a King* (Queens, NY: Church of God, 1968), 21.
92. Elvis Presley, interview by Jim Stewart, in *Elvis Presley: The Complete Interviews from 1955–1977*, vol. 2 (n.p.: Synergie OMP, 2011), CD.
93. Barbara Lee Fridinger, "His Singing Causes Demolition," *Youth for Christ* (Wheaton, IL), November 1956, 18; Nancy Astinger, "He Needs Christ," in "Special Panel: What about Elvis Presley?" *Youth for Christ*, November 1956, 19. For how the controversy from such articles played out, see the magazine's letters to the editor, "Presley, Pro and Con," *Youth for Christ*, January 1957, 6–7; "More Patter on Presley," *Youth for Christ*, February 1957, 6–7; "Elvis Is Back," *Youth for Christ*, March 1957, 6–7; and "Elvis Is Back," *Youth for Christ*, May 1957, 4–5.
94. Bill Sachs, "Folk Talent and Tunes," *Billboard*, August 13, 1955, 24; *RCA Victor Country and Western Attraction Presents the Caravan Souvenir Folio* (Madison, TN: Jamboree Attractions, circa 1953–1954), 15, Rare Books and Scores, souvenir booklets, Center for Popular Music, Middle Tennessee State University; "Second Generation—a Family That Picks Together . . ." *Billboard*, October 18, 1969, 38; Otto Fuchs, *Bill Haley: Father of Rock 'n' Roll* (Gelnhausen, Germany: Wagner, 2011), 356.

95. Guralnick, *Last Train to Memphis*, 447. See also "Jimmy [*sic*] Snow Smears R&R; Presley's Ex-Aid, Now an Evangelist, Calls It Sinful," *Variety*, March 2, 1960, 1, 54; Jack Castleman, "That 'Evil Beat' of Rock Rapped," *Dallas Morning News*, September 25, 1961, 1; "Evangelist Jimmie Snow Files for Divorce," *Fort Scott Kansas Tribune*, August 15, 1972, 5; and "Snow's Son Intense at Pulpit: Preacher Broadcasts from Opry Stage," *Lawrence (KS) Journal-World*, September 22, 1976, 34.
96. Jimmie Snow, "Called from 'Show Biz,'" *C. A. Herald* (Springfield, MO), January 1961, 5, 7. For a report on Snow's early evangelism and media exposure, see "Savannah, GA," *Pentecostal Evangel* (Springfield, MO), June 26, 1960, 28.
97. David Jeffries, "Billy Adams," http://www.allmusic.com/artist/billy-adams-mn0000081806, accessed February 27, 2017; "Preacher's Record Smash Scores Hit with Followers," *Arizona Republic* (Phoenix), September 24, 1982, 23; "Evangelist Warns of Devil Message," *Ellensburg (WA) Daily Record*, September 24, 1982, 10; William Harwood, "The Rev. Billy Adams Told His Followers Thursday Night . . . ," http://www.upi.com/Archives/1982/09/23/The-Rev-Billy-Adams-told-his-followers-Thursday-night/1616401601600/, September 23, 1982, accessed February 2, 2017.
98. "Studio Discussion between Sam Phillips, Jerry Lee Lewis, James Van Eaton and Billy Riley," in *Good Rockin' Tonight* (Netherlands: Bopcat Records, 1974), LP.
99. For the struggles rockers experienced between secular and sacred lives, see James M. Curtis, *Rock Eras: Interpretations of Music and Society, 1954–1984* (Bowling Green, OH: Bowling Green State University Popular Press, 1987), 61.
100. Myers, "A Cultural Conversation with Little Richard," D5.
101. June Bundy, "Vox Jox," *Billboard*, May 27, 1957, 54.
102. "Most Played R&B in Juke Boxes," *Billboard*, April 27, 1957, 60. See also Deena Weinstein, *Rock'n America: A Social and Cultural History* (Toronto: University of Toronto Press, 2015), 68; and Roger Baker, *Drag: A History of Female Impersonation in the Performing Arts* (New York: New York University Press, 1994), 259.
103. Jack Davey interview with Little Richard, Macquarie Auditorium, Sydney, Ampol Show, from *Rock 'n' Roll Radio: Australia 1957* (Woodford Green, UK: Rockstar Records, 2003), CD.
104. David Kirby, *Little Richard and the Birth of Rock 'n' Roll* (New York: Continuum, 2009), 154.
105. "Little Richard Gets the Call," *Billboard*, October 21, 1957, 22.
106. Altschuler, *All Shook Up*, 162–163.
107. White, *The Life and Times of Little Richard*, 197.
108. Don Cusic, "Cash, Johnny," in *Encyclopedia of Contemporary Christian Music*, 42; Bill C. Malone, *Don't Get Above Your Raisin': Country Music and the Southern Working Class* (Champaign: University of Illinois Press, 2002), 110–111.
109. Guralnick, *Careless Love*, 209, 223, 231, 657. See also Mosher, "Ecstatic Sounds," 100–101; Wilson, "Just a Little Talk with Jesus," 16–18; James R. Goff Jr., "Conflicted by the Spirit: The Religious Life of Elvis Presley," *Assemblies of God Heritage* 28 (2008): 22–31; and Alanna Nash, ed., *Elvis and the Memphis Mafia* (London: Autumn Press, 2005), 19.
110. Kevin Crouch and Tanja Crouch, *The Gospel According to Elvis* (London: Bobcat Books, 2007), 120; Guralnick, *Careless Love*, 189.
111. Timothy Leary, Ralph Metzner, and Richard Alpert, *The Psychedelic Experience: A Manual Based on the* Tibetan Book of the Dead (New York: University Books, 1964); Joseph Benner, *The Impersonal Life* (New York: Penguin, 2017).

112. Wilson, "Just a Little Talk with Jesus," 18; Goff, "Conflicted by the Spirit," 22–31; Guralnick, *Careless Love*, 173–225; Jess Stearn and Larry Geller, *Elvis' Search for God* (Murfreesboro, TN: Greenleaf Publications, 1998); Larry Geller, *Leaves of Elvis' Garden: The Song of His Soul* (Beverly Hills, CA: Bell Rock, 2007); Nash, *Elvis and the Memphis Mafia*, 333–344; Priscilla Beaulieu Presley, *Elvis and Me*, with Sandra Harmon (New York: Putnam, 1985), 195–207.
113. Billy Graham, *The Mystery of Iniquity* (Minneapolis, MN: Billy Graham Evangelistic Association, 1957), n.p. See also George Burnham, "Billy Graham Talks to Teens," *C. A. Herald* (Springfield, MO), October 1957, 29; and William G. McLoughlin Jr., *Billy Graham: Revivalist in a Secular Age* (New York: Ronald Press, 1960), 128, 218.
114. "Two Popular Heroes," *Hartford Courant*, May 20, 1957, 10. For a rebuttal, see William A. Webb, "Dr. Graham's Appeal Is to the Intellect," *Hartford Courant*, June 3, 1957, 10. "Graham Crusade Like Circus, Cleric Asserts," *Washington Post*, June 10, 1957, B6; John Steinbeck, "Bryan and Sunday Would Be Proud of Clement's Talk," *Washington Post*, August 15, 1956, 8.
115. Samuel A. Floyd, *The Power of Black Music: Interpreting Its History from Africa to the United States* (New York: Oxford University Press, 1995), 64–65.
116. Alastair McKay, "New Day Rising: How the Sound of Rock 'n' Roll Was Invented in Sun Studio, 60 Years Ago—by a Lucky Hillbilly Who Became Music's Thomas Edison," *Uncut*, April 2012, 46.
117. Earl Calloway, "Gospel Music: The Basis for Rock an' Roll Pop," *Chicago Defender*, September 4, 1969, 18.
118. Benson Saler, *Conceptualizing Religion: Immanent Anthropologists, Transcendent Natives, and Unbounded Categories* (New York: Oxford University Press, 1999), 25; Charles Taylor, *A Secular Age* (Cambridge, MA: Belknap Press of Harvard University Press, 2007), 86, 79, 266, 446.

Chapter 2

1. Maury Dean, *Rock and Roll: Gold Rush* (New York: Algora, 2003), 46.
2. Linda Martin and Kerry Segrave, *Anti-rock: The Opposition to Rock 'n' Roll* (New York: Da Capo Press, 1993), 42; "Council Shunned," *Washington Afro-American*, April 17, 1956, 2.
3. *Toronto Star* quoted in Jamie Bradburn, "Haley," https://torontoist.com/2011/11/a-gardens-gallery/20111130haley7213/, November 30, 2011, accessed September 16, 2017.
4. Glenn T. Askew, *But for Birmingham: The Local and National Movements in the Civil Rights Struggle* (Chapel Hill: University of North Carolina Press, 1997), 129, 142; Edward Shannon LaMonte, *Politics and Welfare in Birmingham, 1900–1975* (Tuscaloosa: University of Alabama Press, 1995), 268n14.
5. Michael T. Bertrand, *Race, Rock, and Elvis* (Champaign: University of Illinois Press, 2000), 181. The protesters' use of "bebop" as an epithet likely reveals something about their misunderstanding of the genre or their simple confusing of it with jazz. " 'Jungle Music' Cry at Randall US Show," *Melody Maker*, May 26, 1956, 1. See also "Programs Heavily Guarded: Some 2,500 Ignore White Citizens' Pickets to Attend Rock-and-Roll Show Concert in Birmingham," *Florence (AL) Times*, May 21, 1956, 2; "Council Picks White," *Baltimore Afro-American*, June 2, 1956, 6; "Whites Picket Rock-'n'-Roll Concert Stars," *Miami News*, May 21, 1956, 11A; and Eskew, *But for Birmingham*, 116–118.

6. Otto Fuchs, *Bill Haley: The Father of Rock & Roll* (Gelnhausen, Germany: Wagner, 2011), 391.
7. William D Romanowski, *Pop Culture Wars: Religion and the Role of Entertainment in American Life* (Eugene, OR: Wipf and Stock, 2008), 210–213.
8. Jack Hamilton, "Rubber Souls: Rock and Roll and the Racial Imagination" (Ph.D. diss., Harvard University, 2013), 3.
9. Askew, *But for Birmingham*, 117. See also "White Citizens Councils vs. Rock and Roll," *Newsweek*, April 23, 1956, 32.
10. Edward F. Haas, *Mayor Victor H. Schiro: New Orleans in Transition, 1961–1970* (Jackson: University Press of Mississippi, 2014), 3.
11. "White Citizens Council Notice," in *Brown v. Board of Education: A Brief History with Documents*, ed. Waldo E. Martin, Jr. (Boston: Bedford / St. Martin's Press, 1998), 222.
12. Sydney E. Ahlstrom, "The Traumatic Years: American Religion and Culture in the '60s and '70s," in *Critical Issues in American Religious History*, ed. Robert R. Mathisen (Waco, TX: Baylor University Press, 2001), 634–636; "Church Membership in U.S. Rising; 62% Are Church-Goers," *Living Church* (Milwaukee, WI), September 1, 1957, 7–8; Ross Gregory, *Cold War America, 1946 to 1990* (New York: Facts on File, 2003), 222–226.
13. Martin Marty, *The New Shape of American Religion* (New York: Harper, 1959), 7.
14. Gibson Winter, *The Suburban Captivity of the Churches: An Analysis of Protestant Responsibility in the Expanding Metropolis* (Garden City, NY: Doubleday, 1961).
15. Phyllis Battelle, "That Rock 'n' Roll Craze: It Started Three Years Ago and It's Stronger than Ever," *St. Petersburg Times*, June 17, 1956, 10E; George E. Sokolsky, "Our Crude Era of Non-Conformity," *Milwaukee Sentinel*, June 11, 1956, 8.
16. "The War on Rock 'n' Roll," *Pittsburgh Courier*, October 6, 1956, A5.
17. *Charlotte Observer* interview with Elvis Presley, June 26, 1956, B1, excerpted in *Music in the USA: A Documentary Companion*, ed. Judith Tick and Paul Beaudoin (New York: Oxford University Press, 2008), 585.
18. Ren Grevatt and Merrill Pollack, "It All Started with Elvis," *Saturday Evening Post*, September 26, 1959, 27. See also Louis Cantor, *Dewey and Elvis: The Life and Times of a Rock 'n' Roll Deejay* (Urbana: University of Illinois Press, 2005), 145; Simon Frith, *Sound Effects: Youth, Leisure, and the Politics of Rock 'n' Roll* (New York: Pantheon Books, 1981), 15–23; and Paul Harvey, *Freedom's Coming: Religious Culture and the Shaping of the South from the Civil War through the Civil Rights Era* (Chapel Hill: University of North Carolina Press, 2005), 158–168.
19. Religion News Service: "Dixieland Bands Distort Sacred Music Is Charge," *Baptist Record* (Jackson, MS), January 24, 1957, 3. The Alabama segregationist Southern Baptist editor Leon Macon pointed out much the same regarding "When the Saints Go Marching In." "Jazzed Up Hymns," *Alabama Baptist* (Birmingham), March 7, 1957, 3. See also "Religious Leaders Criticize 'Jukebox' Gospel Jazz," *Conquest* (Kansas City, MO), April 1957, 56. For a similar complaint about an August 1959 Nat King Cole concert at the Hollywood Bowl in which the star sang Negro spirituals, see Chestyn Everett, "Nat Cole, St. Paul Choir Complete Fiasco at Bowl," *Los Angeles Tribune*, August 28, 1959, 19.
20. Thaddeus Russell, "The Color of Discipline: Civil Rights and Black Sexuality," *American Quarterly* 60, no. 1 (March 2008): 122; Martin and Segrave, *Anti-rock*, 18, 23.
21. W. G. Vorpe, "As the Parade Passes By," *Cleveland Plain Dealer*, June 26, 1938, 2. For earlier ideas about black rhythmic music, see Ronald Radano, "Hot Fantasies: American Modernism and the Idea of Black Rhythm," in *Music and the Racial Imagination*,

ed. Ronald Radano and Philip V. Bohlman (Chicago: University of Chicago Press, 2000), 459–480.

22. John Lear, "'God' Shakes Hands, Will Not Talk; How Does Father Divine Do It?" *Milwaukee Journal*, August 14, 1938, 10. For a description of the musical revue titled "From Spirituals to Swing," which ran at Carnegie Hall, in an African American newspaper, see Sallye Bell, "On the Air," *Plaindealer* (Kansas City, KS), November 25, 1938, 3.
23. T. F. P., "Daddy Grace Dies," *Baltimore Afro-American*, January 26, 1960, 4.
24. "Actors under Provisions of Immigration Laws: Statement of Ralph Errole, Director American Institute of Arts and Drama, Director of the Montclair Opera Co., and Director of the American Grand Opera Co., Montclair, N.J.," *Committee on Immigration and Naturalization, House of Representatives, 72nd Congress, First Session on H.R. 8877* (Washington, DC: U.S. Government Printing Office, 1932), 122.
25. "Back to the Jungle," *Biblical Recorder* (Raleigh, NC), March 8, 1922, 6.
26. Nicholas M. Evans, *Writing Jazz: Race, Nationalism, and Modern Culture in the 1920s* (New York: Garland, 2000), 209–210, and see 293–294. See also Lawrence W. Levine, *Black Culture and Black Consciousness: Afro-American Folk Thought from Slavery to Freedom* (New York: Oxford University Press, 1977), 293–294; Kevin Gaines, "Duke Ellington, *Black, Brown and Beige*, and the Cultural Politics of Race, in *Music and the Racial Imagination*, ed. Ronald Radano and Philip V. Bohlman (Chicago: University of Chicago Press, 2000), 585–602; and "Jungle or Jehovah," *Globe and Mail*, January 27, 1932, 2. On the use of "jungle" themes in black art and music in the 1920s, see James Edward Smethurst, *The African American Roots of Modernism: From Reconstruction to the Harlem Renaissance* (Chapel Hill: University of North Carolina Press, 2011), 13–14; and Jonathan Kamin, "Parallels in the Social Reactions to Jazz and Rock," *Black Perspective in Music* 3, no. 3 (October 1975): 278–298.
27. Matthew F. Delmont, *The Nicest Kids in Town: American Bandstand, Rock 'n' Roll, and the Struggle for Civil Rights in 1950s Philadelphia* (Berkeley: University of California Press, 2012), 138. See also "Charlotte School Dance Changed to Ban a Negro," *Milwaukee Journal*, May 2, 1959, 2; and "Louisiana Governor Asked for Mixed Sports Bill Veto," *Sarasota (FL) Herald-Tribune*, July 13, 1956, 11. For an atypical story of dance bans, see "Negro Legion Ends Spot for Whites at Dances," *Dispatch* (Lexington, NC), September 11, 1956, 1.
28. "Integration Ban—Chattanooga, Tenn.," *Seattle Daily Times*, February 1, 1956, 7. See also "Chattanooga Officials Probe Negro-White Dance Brawl," *Atlanta Constitution*, February 1, 1956, 23; "Rock 'n Roll Riot Jails 9," *New York Amsterdam News*, February 4, 1951, 1; and Martin and Segrave, *Anti-rock*, 27–39.
29. Martin and Segrave, *Anti-rock*, 48–50. See also Brian Ward, *Just My Soul Responding: Rhythm and Blues, Black Consciousness, and Race Relations* (London: UCL Press, 1998), 95–105.
30. Martin Luther King Jr., *Why We Can't Wait* (Boston: Beacon Press, 2010), 11.
31. James T. Patterson, *Grand Expectations: The United States, 1945–1974* (New York: Oxford University Press, 1996), 385; David Levering Lewis, "The Origins of the Civil Rights Movement," in *The Civil Rights Movement in America*, ed. Charles W. Eagles (Jackson: University of Mississippi Press, 1986), 3–17.
32. Dennis McNally, *On Highway 61: Music, Race, and the Evolution of Cultural Freedom* (Berkeley, CA: Counterpoint, 2014), 274. See also Michael J. Stiavnicky, "'Stop! Hey! What's That Sound!' A Critical Re-examination of the Socio-political Functions of 1960s Popular Music in America" (Ph.D. diss., York University, 2010), 54, 62.

33. Elizabeth Wilson, *Bohemians: The Glamorous Outcasts* (London: Tauris Parke, 2003), 145.
34. Norman Mailer, "The White Negro: Superficial Reflections on the Hipster," *Dissent*, July 1957, 278–279. See also Francesco Adinolfi, *Mondo Exotica: Sounds, Visions, Obsessions of the Cocktail Generation* (Durham, NC: Duke University Press, 2008), 54–56; and Jason C. Bivins, *Spirits Rejoice! Jazz and American Religion* (New York: Oxford University Press, 2015), 164–166.
35. Senator James Eastland, "The Supreme Court, Segregation, and the South," May 27, 1954, *Congressional Record, 83rd Congress, 2nd Session* 100, no. 6 (Washington, DC: U.S. Government Printing Office, 1954), 1255.
36. "The Decision of the Supreme Court in the School Cases—Declaration of Constitutional Principles," March 12, 1956, *Congressional Record, 84th Congress, 2nd session* 102, no. 4 (Washington, DC: U.S. Government Printing Office, 1956), 4460.
37. *Western Recorder* (Louisville, KY) excerpted in "The Rock and Roll Craze," *Alabama Baptist* (Birmingham), April 11, 1957, 5.
38. Jack Wyrtzen, "Rock and Roll," *C. A. Herald* (Springfield, MO), November 1957, 6, 7. See also Dave Peters, "Tuned Heavenward," *C. A. Herald*, March 1961, 8–9; and "Your Questions," *Pentecostal Evangel* (Springfield, MO), April 9, 1961, 15. For descriptions of integrated and segregated rock 'n' roll dancing, see Leonard Courtney Archer, "The National Association for the Advancement of Colored People and the American Theatre: A Study of Relationships and Influences" (Ph.D. diss., Ohio State University, 1959), 242–243, 246. For a later fundamentalist denunciation of Elvis, interracial dancing, and rock shows, see Hugh F. Pyle, "The Beatle Plague," *Sword of the Lord* (Murfreesboro, TN), April 30, 1965, 10.
39. On race, rock, and integrated dances, see Lisa Jo Sagolla, *Rock 'n' Roll Dances of the 1950s* (Santa Barbara, CA: Greenwood Press, 2011), 34–35; and "Integrated Houston Dance Draws 4,000," *Pittsburgh Courier*, August 25, 1956, 21.
40. Freed in the April 1955 issue of *Down Beat*, quoted in Christopher Small, *Music of the Common Tongue: Survival and Celebration in African American Music* (Hanover, NH: Wesleyan University Press, 1998), 386. See also "City Bans 'Rock and Roll' Dancing," *Pentecostal Evangel* (Springfield, MO), July 8, 1956, 7.
41. Herm Schoenfeld, "Teenagers Like 'Hot Rod' Tempo," *Variety*, January 19, 2015, 49, 54.
42. Rick Coleman, *Blue Monday: Fats Domino and the Lost Dawn of Rock 'n' Roll* (Cambridge, MA: Da Capo Press, 2006), 97, quote on 98.
43. "Rock 'n' Riot," *Time*, May 19, 1958, 50. See also Deena Weinstein, *Rock'n America: A Social and Cultural History* (Toronto: University of Toronto Press, 2015), 78–79; Karen Sternheimer, *Pop Culture Panics: How Moral Crusaders Construct Meanings of Deviance and Delinquency* (New York: Routledge, 2015), 114–115; and "Letters to the Editor: Cause of Riots," *Augusta (GA) Chronicle*, July 18, 1956, 4. For a debate between two clergymen, an Episcopalian and a Catholic, following the Boston riot, see Jane Gerard, "Does the Bell Toll for Rock 'n Roll? The Big Beat's Death Rattle," *Newsday* (Long Island, NY), June 15, 1958, 10c–11c.
44. "Teen Talk about Rock and Roll" (Christian Life Commission of the Baptist General Convention of Texas, 1960), 1, Southern Baptist Historical Library and Archives, Nashville, TN.
45. Pat MacAdam, "Famed Southern Evangelist Stood Test of Time," *Ottawa (Canada) Citizen*, June 27, 1998, C3.
46. Ibid., C3. For more on Freed's misfortunes, see Martin and Segrave, *Anti-rock*, 98–102.

47. "Is There a 'Spiritual Recession?'" *Biblical Recorder* (Raleigh, NC), October 29, 1960, 3.
48. For an example of one such sermon, see the Southern Baptist evangelist Jesse Murphy Hendley's "Rock and Roll," delivered circa late 1950s, 1–24, "Sermons: Rock and Roll," Jesse Murphy Hendley Collection, Southern Baptist Historical Library and Archives, Nashville, TN.
49. Harvey J. Graff, *The Dallas Myth: The Making and Unmaking of an American City* (Minneapolis: University of Minnesota Press, 2008), 94. See also "Background Info," DISD [Dallas Independent School District] Desegregation Litigation Archives, http://library.law.smu.edu/Collections/DISD/Background-Info, accessed August 11, 2015.
50. "25 Collapse in Rock-Roll Traffic Jam," *Dallas Morning News*, March 26, 1957, 1. In early July 1956, Domino and his group found themselves in the middle of a teenage riot in San Jose, California. The hour-long fight took place after someone hurled a beer bottle into the middle of the dance floor. "Ten Arrested in California Teen-Ager Riot," *Augusta (GA) Chronicle*, July 9, 1956, 2. For a similar outbreak of violence at a Fats Domino show two months later, see "1500 in Rioting at Naval Base," *Springfield (MA) Union*, September 19, 1956, 1.
51. Coleman, *Blue Monday*, 162. Alleged quote from "6 Dallas Youths Hurt: Attacks Erupt as 6,000 Fans Leave Rock 'n' Roll Show," *New York Times*, July 17, 1957, 23; "Rock 'n' Roll Riot: 4 Stabbed, 20 Jailed, in Race Clash," *Trenton (NJ) Evening Times*, 2; and "Drunk Disturbances for Rock 'n' Roll Fight," *Daily Defender* (Chicago), July 17, 1957, 19. For a follow-up story on the riot, see "Fats Domino Gets Lotsa Mola, Riot Unsolved," *Plaindealer* (Kansas City, KS), August 2, 1957, 6.
52. Helen Bullock, "Exciting? Inciting? or Both?" *Dallas Morning News*, July 29, 1957, 1. See also Helen Bullock, "Rock 'n' Roll: Harmless Tunes or Evil Beat?" *Dallas Morning News*, July 29, 1957, 1, 3; and Carroll Griggs, "Three Eds Knifed following Dallas Rock and Roll Show," *Campus Chat* (Denton, TX), July 19, 1957, 1. For the staunch segregationist stance on dances, see "Race Mixing Sets Off Wild Disorder," *Citizens' Council* (Jackson, MS), February 1956, 2.
53. "Part Three: Violence, Texas," in *Civil Rights—1959: Hearings before the Subcommittee on Constitutional Rights of the Committee on the Judiciary, United States Senate, Eighty-Sixth Congress* (Washington, DC: U.S. Government Printing Office, 1959), 1602.
54. Ibid., 1600.
55. Helen Bullock, "Adult Opinion Ranges Wide on Effects of Music Craze," *Dallas Morning News*, July 30, 1957, 1, 4.
56. For more on Criswell and First Baptist, see Nathan Andrew Finn, "The Development of Baptist Fundamentalism in the South, 1940–1980" (Ph.D. diss., Southeastern Baptist Theological Seminary, 2007), 105–114; and "Editorial Brevities," *Biblical Recorder* (Raleigh, NC), September 1, 1956, 2.
57. "An Address by Dr. W. A. Criswell, Pastor, First Baptist Church, Dallas, Texas, to the Joint Assembly," February 22, 1956, 8, Southern Baptist Historical Library and Archives, Nashville, TN. See also Curtis W. Freeman, "'Never Had I Been So Blind': W. A. Criswell's 'Change' on Racial Segregation," *Journal of Southern Religion* 10 (2007): 1–4; and Bill Minutaglio and Steven L. Davis, *Dallas 1963* (New York: Twelve, 2013), 12–14, 37–38.
58. Patrick Allitt, *Religion in America since 1945: A History* (New York: Columbia University Press, 2003), 53.
59. David Halberstam, "The White Citizens Councils," *Commentary*, October 1956, 301.
60. "A Manual for Southerners," Citizens' Council (Jackson, MS), February 1957, 1. See also Renee C. Romano, *Racial Reckoning: Prosecuting America's Civil Rights Murders*

(Cambridge, MA: Harvard University Press, 2014.), 29; and Jeanette Keith, *The South: A Concise History* (Upper Saddle River, NJ: Prentice Hall, 2002), 2:170.

61. "Criswell Talk Stirs Comment," *Dallas Morning News*, February 24, 1956, 1.
62. For more on Criswell's segregationist views, see his sermon notes, "The Second Letter to Corinth," First Baptist Church, Dallas, Texas, February 26, 1956, https://wacriswell.com/Media/PDFs/S/Second%20Letter%20to%20Corinth.pdf, accessed August 11, 2015. On segregated cemeteries, see Terry G. Jordan, *Texas Graveyards: A Cultural Legacy* (Austin: University of Texas Press, 2004), 30–33; and Donald Lee Grant, *The Way It Was in the South: The Black Experience in Georgia*, ed. Jonathan Grant (Athens: University Press of Georgia, 2001), 221.
63. W. A. Criswell, "The Facts of Embryology Repudiate the Theory of Evolution," sermon preached at First Baptist Church in Dallas, Texas, January 27, 1957, https://www.wacriswell.com/sermons/1957/the-facts-of-embryology-repudiate-evolution/, accessed August 11, 2015.
64. W. A. Criswell, "Christ Beyond Crises," sermon preached at First Baptist Church, Dallas, Texas, May 4, 1958, https://www.wacriswell.com/sermons/1958/christ-beyond-the-crises/, accessed August 11, 2015. See also W. A. Criswell, "The Defense of the Faith," sermon preached at First Baptist Church, Dallas, Texas, July 31, 1960, https://www.wacriswell.com/sermons/1960/the-defense-of-the-faith/, accessed August 11, 2015. For Billy Graham's similar comments about rock 'n' roll in a sermon he delivered at Ebbets Field, home of the Brooklyn Dodgers, see George Burnham, "40,000 Dodger Fans Flock to Hear Billy," *Tuscaloosa (AL) News*, May 23, 1957, 26.
65. "Pastor Says Bible Orders Color Line," *Citizens' Council* (Jackson, MS), May 1956, 4. See also "Who Has God's Word on Integration?" *Citizens' Council*, April 1956, 1; Henry Knox Sherrill, "Does Church Favor Race Mongrelization?" *Citizens' Council*, November 1956, 4; and Joseph Crespino, *In Search of Another Country: Mississippi and the Conservative Counterrevolution* (Princeton, NJ: Princeton University Press, 2007), 69–70.
66. Benson Y. Landis, ed., *Yearbook of American Churches* (New York: Office of Publication and Distribution, National Council of the Churches of Christ in the USA, 1964), 253–259. A tabulation of the membership numbers of thirty predominately white denominations in the evangelical and fundamentalist camp for 1964 comes to 26,229,317. For growth from the 1950s to the late 1970s, see Constant H. Jacquet, ed., *Yearbook of American and Canadian Churches* (New York: Office of Publication and Distribution, National Council of the Churches of Christ in the USA, 1980), 219–227.
67. "Wrongs Do Not Make Civil Rights," *Eternity* (Philadelphia), June 1964, 4. Also see Randall J. Stephens "'It has to come from the hearts of the people': Evangelicals, Fundamentalists, Race, and the 1964 Civil Rights Act," *Journal of American Studies* 50, no. 3 (August 2016): 559–585.
68. Landis, *Yearbook of American Churches*, 23.
69. "Timeline of Polling History: Events That Shaped the United States, and the World," http://news.gallup.com/poll/9967/timeline-polling-history-events-shaped-united-states-world.aspx, accessed September 3, 2015.
70. John Lee Eighmy, *Churches in Cultural Captivity: A History of the Social Attitudes of the Southern Baptists* (Knoxville: University of Tennessee Press, 1972), 190, and see 191.
71. Numan V. Bartley, *The Rise of Massive Resistance: Race and Politics in the South during the 1950's* (Baton Rouge: Louisiana State University Press, 1997), 295–305.

72. "The Convention and Integration," *Alabama Baptist* (Birmingham), November 28, 1957, 3.
73. Samuel S. Hill, *Southern Churches in Crisis Revisited* (Tuscaloosa: University of Alabama Press, 1999), lxvi, and see 106–107, 114–115. See also Charles Marsh, *God's Long Summer: Stories of Faith and Civil Rights* (Princeton, NJ: Princeton University Press, 1997), 113. For more on white southern evangelical responses to integration and the civil rights movement, see James W. Silver, *Mississippi: The Closed Society* (Jackson: University of Mississippi Press, 2012), 53–60.
74. Religion News Service, "Race Relations Principles Given in Statement," *Baptist and Reflector* (Nashville, TN), November 21, 1957, 12.
75. John C. Neville Jr., "Let's Be Prejudiced," *Presbyterian Journal* (Weaverville, NC), February 26, 1964, 16. See also Carolyn Renée Dupont, *Mississippi Praying: Southern White Evangelicals and the Civil Rights Movement, 1945–1975* (New York: New York University Press, 2013), 63, 214–216; and Jane Dailey, "Sex, Segregation, and the Sacred after Brown," *Journal of American History* 91, no. 1 (June 2004): 119–144.
76. "Alabama Baptist Officials Hit Lay White Supremacy Group," *Alabama Baptist* (Birmingham), June 27, 1957, 6. See also "Ministers, Churches Uphold Segregation," *Citizens' Council* (Jackson, MS), April 1959, 4.
77. Alan Scot Willis, *All According to God's Plan: Southern Baptist Missions and Race, 1945–1970* (Louisville: University of Kentucky Press, 2005), 149–151; Thomas S. Kidd and Barry Hankins, *Baptists in America: A History* (New York: Oxford University Press, 2015), 211–226.
78. Andrew M. Manis, "'Dying from the Neck Up': Southern Baptist Resistance to the Civil Rights Movement," *Baptist History and Heritage* 34, no. 1 (Winter 1999): 34. See also Mark Newman, *Getting Right with God: Southern Baptists and Desegregation, 1945–1995* (Tuscaloosa: University of Alabama Press, 2001), 63, 83, 125, 185, 206; and "Sou. Baptists Chided to Be More Active in Politics, Public Life," *Biblical Recorder* (Raleigh, NC), April 4, 1964, 9. For an earlier hardcore segregationist stance, see Leon Macon, "The Segregation Problems," *Alabama Baptist* (Birmingham), March 8, 1956, 3; "Racial Tensions," *Baptist and Reflector* (Nashville, TN), May 16, 1957, 3; "Churches Must Decide College Race Issue," *Baptist and Reflector*, February 14, 1957, 3; Leon Macon, "Integration," *Alabama Baptist*, May 3, 1956, 3; and Julian Williams, "In Defense of the White South," *Christian Crusade* (Oklahoma City), May 1961, 12. For the southern Presbyterian Church, see Dupont, *Mississippi Praying*, 63, 214–216. For a counterview, see Matthew Petway, "Report of the Panel on Social Action," *A.M.E. Zion Quarterly Review* 74, no. 3 (Fall 1962): 140–143.
79. "What Did the Convention Say about the Race Problem," *Baptist Record* (Jackson, MS), July 4, 1957, 4.
80. David Hynd, *Africa Emerging* (Kansas City, MO: Nazarene Publishing House, 1959), 24–35.
81. H. K. Bedwell, *Black Gold* (Kansas City, MO: Beacon Hill Press, 1953), 18. For more of the same, see Bedwell, "African Religion," in *Black Gold*, 33–39, 48–53.
82. Willis, *All According to God's Plan*, 5, 7–8.
83. Excerpt from the *Baptist Record* (Jackson, MS) quoted in Silver, *Mississippi*, 54.
84. Molly Worthen, *Apostles of Reason: The Crisis of Authority in American Evangelicalism* (New York: Oxford University Press, 2014), 136, 137.
85. Raymond T. Brock, "The Blue Caribbean," *Pentecostal Evangel* (Springfield, MO), June 10, 1962, 17. See also Carol Gish, *The Magic Circle of the Caribbean* (Kansas City, MO: Nazarene Publishing House, 1954), 9–17. For warnings about the sensuality of

dancing, see the Southern Baptist Convention's youth magazine, "I've Been Wondering," *Upward* (Nashville, TN), January 11, 1959, 31; and "I've Been Wondering," *Upward*, April 5, 1959, 31.

86. Don Argue, "Chapel at the Devil's Pit," *Pentecostal Evangel* (Springfield, MO), September 2, 1962, 16, 17. For parallel later developments, see John Haines, "The Emergence of Jesus Rock: On Taming the African Beat," *Black Music Research Journal* 31, no. 2 (Fall 2011): 235–236.
87. "Obituaries: William Ward Beecher Ayer, Pioneer Gospel Radio Broadcaster," *St. Petersburg Times*, November 19, 1985, 7B.
88. William Ward Ayer, "Jungle Madness in America," *Youth for Christ* (Wheaton, IL), November 1956, 20. Ayer's story unleashed a barrage of pro and con letters. See "Presley, Pro and Con," *Youth for Christ*, January 1957, 6–7; "More Patter on Presley," *Youth for Christ*, February 1957, 6–7; "Elvis Is Back," *Youth for Christ*, March 1957, 6–7; and "Elvis Is Back," *Youth for Christ*, May 1957, 6–7.
89. Ken Sharp, "Voodoo and the Calypso Craze," *Youth for Christ* (Wheaton, IL), March 1958, 14–15. For the exoticization of black music in the late 1950s and early 1960s, see Francesco Adinolfi, *Mondo Exotica: Sounds, Visions, Obsessions of the Cocktail Generation* (Durham, NC: Duke University Press, 2008), 54–56.
90. "Swing Music Gnaws at Moral Fiber of Youth, Catholic Women's Meeting Told by Archbishop," *Dallas Morning News*, October 26, 1938, 1. See also David W. Stowe, *Swing Changes: Big-Band Jazz in New Deal America* (Cambridge, MA: Harvard University Press, 1994), 23–24.
91. "Rock 'n' Roll Likened by Cleric to Jungle Tomtoms," *Variety*, September 5, 1956, 33.
92. "Stritch Urged Catholics: Ban Rock and Roll," *Chicago Daily Tribune*, March 1, 1957, 4.
93. "Voodoo Rites in Hollywood!" *Alabama Baptist* (Birmingham) October 24, 1957, 16. See also Norman E. King, "Teen-Age Idol Worship," *Youth for Christ* (Wheaton, IL), March 1959, 6–7. For a firsthand evangelical account of Elvis idolatry, see "The Last Time I Saw Elvis," *Youth for Christ*, March 1960, 4–5.
94. Patterson, *Grand Expectations*, 374, and see 312. See also David Halberstam, *The Fifties* (New York: Random House, 1993), 506–507.
95. Patterson, *Grand Expectations*, 312–333, 240. John Kenneth Galbraith, *The Affluent Society* (New York: Houghton Mifflin, 1998), 109.
96. Thomas Hine, *The Rise and Fall of the American Teenager* (New York: Perennial, 2000), 237.
97. "Adults 19–70 Dislike R&R, Ohio U. Finds," *Billboard*, December 14, 1959, 12. See also Halberstam, *The Fifties*, 473. A fairly extensive 1958 doctoral dissertation found a high teenage preference for rock 'n' roll. It also showed a stronger affection for the music among lower socioeconomic groups. Victor H. Baumann, "Socio-economic Status and the Music Preferences of Teen-Agers" (Ph.D. diss., University of Southern California, 1958), 183, 187, 198. For other surveys of youth and rock 'n' roll, see Eugene Gilbert, "What Young People Think," *Schenectady (NY) Gazette*, August 10, 1956, 5; Phyllis Battelle, "Teen-Agers Say It Is Beat Not Words That 'Sends 'Em,'" *Ottawa (Canada) Citizen*, September 29, 1956, 32; "Bobby-Soxers' Gallup," *Time*, August 13, 1956, 72–73; and Eugene Gilbert, "Rock'n Roll Is Here to Stay," *Montreal Gazette*, April 12, 1958, 36. See also Eugene Gilbert, "Why Today's Teen-Agers Seem So Different," *Harper's Magazine* 219 (November 1959): 76–79.
98. "In U.S., 87% Approve of Black-White Marriage, vs. 4% in 1958," http://news.gallup.com/poll/163697/approve-marriage-blacks-whites.aspx, July 25, 2013, accessed August 19, 2015.

99. "Ask Edith," *Window*, June 1961, 42. See also "Mixed Marriage Gaining Notice," *Citizens' Council* (Jackson, MS), December 1957, 2; and a fairly moderate Nazarene view in "Your Questions Answered," *Eternity* (Philadelphia), December 1963, 37.
100. "Rock and Rollers Strike Sour Note," *Citizens' Council* (Jackson, MS), August 1959, 4. See also "Black Cats Find Mixed Cincy Nite Means Biz Gone," *Citizens' Council*, October 1959, 3; and "Four Members of Singing Group Freed on Bond," *Lewiston (ME) Evening Journal*, August 11, 1959, 13. The four were eventually acquitted of wrongdoing, though the incident hurt the group's career. On race mixing, see "Methodists Meet, Issue More Call for More Mixing," *Citizens' Council*, September 1959, 3; "Church Women Seek Continued Segregation," *Citizens' Council*, October 1959, 3; and "Denominational Split Possible; Unit Fights Church Race Mixing," *Free Lance-Star* (Fredericksburg, VA), October 14, 1958, 2.
101. "What a Twisted Scale of Values," *Christian Century*, May 25, 1960, 630.
102. William Stephenson, "From Bawdy Houses to Parlor, via Nat'l Council of Churches," *Citizens' Council* (Jackson, MS), January 1956, 4.
103. Kathryn T. Long, "In the Modern World, but Not of It: The 'Auca Martyrs,' Evangelicalism, and Postwar American Culture," in *The Foreign Missionary Enterprise at Home*, ed. Daniel H. Bays and Grant Wacker (Tuscaloosa: University of Alabama Press, 2003), 223–231. See also the race-baiting in "Time Magazine Offers a Note on African Culture," *Citizens' Council* (Jackson, MS), February 1956, 4; "Riot Squad Halts Rock 'n Roll Show," *Tuscaloosa (AL) News*, October 19, 1959, 2; and "Rock 'n' Roll Riot; 14 Hurt," *Milwaukee Sentinel*, March 11, 1963, 4.
104. The book was *Through Gates of Splendor*, and the advertisement appeared in "The Whole Incredible Story of the Jungle Missionary Martyrs," *Biblical Recorder* (Raleigh, NC), June 29, 1957, 17. See also Elisabeth Elliot, *The Savage My Kinsman* (New York: Harper, 1961), 10–14.
105. Dallas Mucci, "Jim Elliot, a Martyr," *Conquest* (Kansas City, MO), November 1966, 25, 26, 27.
106. "Five Young Missionaries Become Mid-century Martyrs," *Youth for Christ* (Wheaton, IL), March 1956, 10. See also "Five Evangelical Missionaries Slain by Savage Indians," *Conquest* (Kansas City, MO), May 1956, 58.
107. Marg Jones, "I Don't Like Him," *Youth for Christ* (Wheaton, IL), November 1956, 18. See also the photo essay, Russell T. Hitt, "Cannibal Valley," *Youth for Christ*, November 1962, 38–41.
108. Vic Erickson, "Jungle to Jukebox" (Oradell, NJ: American Tract Society, n.d.), n.p., "Rock Music," Papers of G. Archer Weniger, Bob Jones University.
109. David Wilkerson, "Juvenile Jungle," *C. A. Herald* (Springfield, MO), January 1961, 8. See also Ruth Lyon, "Teen-Age Evangelism—a New Dimension in Home Missions Activity," *Pentecostal Evangel* (Springfield, MO), June 5, 1960, 18–19.
110. For a 1958 survey of four hundred teachers, ranging from kindergarten to high school, that highlights the perception of rock 'n' roll's negative impact, see Eugene Gilbert, "What Teachers Think—Teachers Express Views on Teen-Agers," *Spokane Daily Chronicle*, April 10, 1958, 28. See also "Catholic Parley Blasts Current Rock 'n Roll Fad," *Springfield (MA) Union*, May 15, 1956, 37; and Damon Runyon Jr., "Not Entirely Opposed: Ministers Weighing Rock-'n'-Roll Craze," *Miami News*, June 4, 1956, 1.
111. Robert Wallace, "Crime in the U.S.," *Life*, September 9, 1957, 47, and see 48–50, 59–60, 62, 67–68, 70. See also "Bad Boys in the Schoolroom," *Life*, March 28, 1955, 49–50, 52. For linkages of violence and early rock 'n' roll, see "Yeh-Heh-Heh-Hes, Baby," *Time*, June 18, 1956, 54; Arlene Skolnick, *Embattled Paradise: The American Family in*

an Age of Uncertainty (New York: Basic Books, 1991); and James Bennett, *Oral History and Delinquency: The Rhetoric of Criminology* (Chicago: University of Chicago Press, 1981), 62–64.

112. J. Edgar Hoover, "Trade Softness for Firmness," *Youth for Christ* (Wheaton, IL), August 1957, 12. See also "J. Edgar Hoover Blames Juvenile Crime on Lack of Respect for God," *Baptist Record* (Jackson, MS), April 5, 1956, 1; J. Edgar Hoover, "Spiritual Priorities: Guidelines for a Civilization in Peril," *Christianity Today* (Carol Stream, IL), June 22, 1962, 3–4; and quotes from Hoover on dancing and teenage violence in "Should Christians Dance?" *King's Business* (Los Angeles), October 1965, 16. For Hoover's writing in *Christianity Today*, see David E. Settje, *Faith and War: How Christians Debated the Cold and Vietnam Wars* (New York: New York University Press, 2011), 31.
113. Billy Graham, "God's Juvenile Delinquent," *Youth for Christ* (Wheaton, IL), November 1959, 10–11. See also J. V. James, Atlanta, GA, to fellow Baptist, April 25, 1960, "Juvenile Delinquency" file, 1960–64, Southern Baptist Historical Library and Archives, Nashville, TN.
114. Martin and Segrave, *Anti-rock*, 23; Dennis McNally, *On Highway 61: Music, Race, and the Evolution of Cultural Freedom* (Berkeley, CA: Counterpoint, 2014), 276. Contemporary studies pointed out the ethnic and black dimensions of delinquency. See, for example, S. Kirson Weinberg, "Sociological Processes and Factors in Juvenile Delinquency," in *Juvenile Delinquency*, ed. Joseph S. Roucek (New York: Philosophical Society, 1958), 118–120.
115. "Youth Nabbed in Theft Case," *Spokane Daily Chronicle*, January 26, 1960, 1. "Roy Campanella's Son Nabbed in Gang Fight," *Miami News*, February 24, 1959, 1. "Roy Campanella's Son Makes First Recording," *Jet*, November 19, 1959, 62.
116. Jack Wyrtzen, "Rock and Roll," *C. A. Herald* (Springfield, MO), November 1957, 8, and see 6, 7. See also Marlin "Butch" Hardman, "Rock 'n' Roll: Music or Madness," *Youth for Christ* (Wheaton, IL), October 1958, 10–12; and Marlin "Butch" Hardman, "The Real Scoop on Rock 'n Roll," *Youth for Christ*, October 1959, 10–12.
117. James Gilbert, *A Cycle of Outrage: America's Reaction to the Juvenile Delinquent in the 1950s* (New York: Oxford University Press, 1988), 18. See also Harry M. Shulman, *Juvenile Delinquency in American Society* (New York: Harper and Row, 1961).
118. "Rock 'n Roll," *Alabama Baptist* (Birmingham), November 1, 1956, 3. See also "Juvenile Delinquency and the Home," *Moody Monthly* (Chicago), February 1956, 20–21. For similar Catholic outrage directed specifically at Elvis, see "Beware Elvis Presley," *America*, June 23, 1956, 294–295; and Glen Jeansonne, David Luhrssen, and Dan Sokolovic, *Elvis Presley, Reluctant Rebel: His Life and Our Times* (Santa Barbara, CA: Praeger, 2011), 122–124.
119. George Burnham, "Billy Graham Talks to Teens," *C. A. Herald* (Springfield, MA), October 1957, 29.
120. "A Youth Rally with a Rock 'n' Roll Beat," *Life*, May 20, 1957, 51.
121. Advertisement in *Youth for Christ* (Wheaton, IL), October 1959, 1.
122. *Youth for Christ* (Wheaton, IL), July 1957 cover; "Do You Know These Christian Recording Artists?" *Youth for Christ*, March 1963, 17. See also Thurlow Spurr, "Mr. Music," *Youth for Christ*, October 1960, 47.
123. "Editorial Brevities," *Biblical Recorder* (Raleigh, NC), March 9, 1957, 4; W. Lloyd Cloud, "Should I Dance?" *Baptist Standard* (Dallas, TX), October 1, 1955, 7–8; *Manual of the Church of the Nazarene* (Kansas City, MO: Nazarene Publishing House, 1956), 36–38. See also "A Resolution Protesting Dancing," *Alabama Baptist* (Birmingham),

June 5, 1958, 2; Bud Lyles, "No More Dancing Lessons," *Sword of the Lord* (Murfreesboro, TN), May 7, 1962, 7; and "Juvenile Delinquency and the Home," *Moody Monthly* (Chicago), February 1956, 20–21. For more on "savagery," "sex appeal," and dancing, see "The Dance," *Herald of Holiness* (Kansas City, MO), January 29, 1958, 2.

124. "Students Pan a Dancing Ban," *Life*, December 2, 1957, 32–33; "Hot Foot in North Carolina," *Biblical Recorder* (Raleigh, NC), January 18, 1958, 20; David Fyten, "Pilgrim's Progress," *Wake Forest Magazine*, http://archive.magazine.wfu.edu/archive/wfm.2006.09.pdf, September 2006, accessed August 11, 2015.

125. Sasha Frere-Jones, "A Paler Shade of White: How Indie Rock Lost Its Soul," *New Yorker*, October 22, 2007, 176.

126. John Earl Haynes, *Red Scare or Red Menace? American Communism and Anticommunism in the Cold War Era* (Chicago: Ivan R. Dee, 1996), 184; Ward, *Just My Soul Responding*, 106, 225. For Elvis's answer to the charge of rock as communist subversion, see Jerry Osborne, ed., *Elvis: Word for Word* (New York: Harmony Books, 2000), 101, 111; Bertrand, *Race, Rock, and Elvis*, 163.

127. Paul Robert Kohl, "Who Stole the Soul? Rock and Roll, Race, and Rebellion" (Ph.D. diss., University of Utah, 1994), 139–150.

128. Ward, *Just My Soul Responding*, 115, 139–140.

129. *Down Beat*, May 30, 1956, 10.

130. David Anderson, "For the Defense of Rock 'n' Roll," *New York Amsterdam News*, April 19, 1958, 13.

131. Young also believed that "basically the important cultural bridge between the Negro world and the white world was bridged by Elvis Presley and the rock and roll movement." Andrew Young, "SCOPE Orientation, June 18, 1965. Discussion of Problems of Understanding," 0099–6. KZSU Project South Interviews (SC0066). Department of Special Collections and University Archives, Stanford University Libraries, Stanford, CA, https://stacks.stanford.edu/file/druid:sh283zt0821/sh283zt0821.pdf, accessed October 1, 2017. Thanks to Paul Harvey for alerting me to this source.

132. "'Rock 'n' roll Church Singing Must Go,' Says Dr. Brewster," *Cleveland Call and Post*, February 9, 1957, 6B. See also George E. Pitts, "Rock 'n' Roll Department: A Churchman Speaks . . . ," *Pittsburgh Courier*, September 22, 1956, A22; George E. Pitts, "Religious Assembly Cracks Down on Jazzy Spirituals," *Pittsburgh Courier*, October 25, 1958, 20; "Ministers Still Protest 'Swinging' Gospel Tunes," *Chicago Defender*, August 31, 1960, 17; and Harvey, *Freedom's Coming*, 158–168.

133. Martin Luther King Jr., "Advice for Living," *Ebony*, April 1958, 392. See also Ward, *Just My Soul Responding*, 189.

134. Mrs. Claude Rhea Jr., "Music and Morality," *Baptist Young People* (Nashville, TN), (third quarter, 1959): 27.

135. "Is Rock 'n Roll on the Way Out?" *Youth for Christ* (Wheaton, IL), March 1960, 14–15.

136. "Crash Kills Rock-Roll Threesome," *Dallas Morning News*, February 4, 1959, 2; "Singer Sentenced," *Dallas Morning News*, March 13, 1960, 18; Glenn C. Altschuler, *All Shook Up: How Rock 'n' Roll Changed America* (New York: Oxford University Press, 2003), 171–176.

137. "R&R Still Beams Plenty of Life," *Billboard*, January 18, 1960, 6.

138. Hamilton, "Rubber Souls," 2. For early obituaries for rock 'n' roll, see "Banana Boat Takin' Elvis for Long, Lonesome Ride?" *Springfield (MA) Republican*, January 13, 1957, 13A; and Jane Gerard, "Does the Bell Toll for Rock 'n Roll? The Big Beat's Death Rattle," *Newsday* (Long Island, NY), June 15, 1958, 10c–11c. For a contrary view on

the viability of rock after 1959, see the 1961 Gilbert Youth Research survey of 994 teenagers: "Only a small minority felt rock 'n' roll was on the way out, and most of them said they personally were getting tired of it." Eugene Gilbert, "Rock 'n' Roll Still Alive, Kicking," *Tuscaloosa (AL) News*, December 7, 1961, 11.

139. "Teen-Ager Rocks Teen-Agers," *Life*, December 1, 1958, 123. See also Marcel Danesi, *Cool: The Signs and Meanings of Adolescence* (Toronto: University of Toronto Press, 1994), 20–22; Richard A. Peterson and David G. Berger, "Cycles in Symbol Production: The Case of Popular Music," in *On Record: Rock, Pop and the Written Word,* ed. Simon Frith and Andrew Goodwin (London: Routledge, 1990), 126; George McKinnon, "Retreat to Squaresville? Rock 'n' Roll Discs Losing Their Spin," *Boston Globe*, September 6, 1959, 1; and Lloyd Shearer, "Goodbye, Rock 'n' Roll: As Teenagers Swing Back to Dreamy Tunes and Love Songs, Moody Rod Lauren Gets Build-Up as Their New Singing Idol," *Boston Globe*, December 20, 1959, B8.
140. Keith Richards, *Life* (New York: Little, Brown, 2010), 159.
141. Shana Alexander, "Love Songs to the Carburetor," *Life*, November 6, 1964, 33. See also Paul Friedlander, *Rock and Roll: A Social History* (Boulder, CO: Westview Press, 1996), 70–76.
142. David Sheff, *All We Are Saying: The Last Major Interview with John Lennon and Yoko Ono* (New York: Macmillan, 2000), 84. See also Hunter Davies, *The Beatles: The Only Authorized Biography* (London: Ebury Press, 2009), 95–97.
143. Klaus Voorman quoted in Philip Norman, *John Lennon: The Life* (New York: Harper Collins, 2008), 210.
144. Lewis quoted in Jon Wiener, *Come Together: John Lennon in His Time* (Urbana: University of Illinois Press, 1991), 267. Also see Paul Lester, "Jerry Lee Lewis: 'Without Great Balls of Fire, Rock 'n' Roll Would Be Boring,'" https://www.theguardian.com/music/2015/jul/09/jerry-lee-lewis-30-minutes-interview, July 9, 2015, accessed October, 12, 2015.

Chapter 3

1. Maureen Cleave, "How Does a Beatle Live? John Lennon Lives Like This," *Evening Standard* (London), March 4, 1966, 10.
2. Hugh J. Schonfield, *The Passover Plot: New Light on the History of Jesus* (New York: Random House, 1966).
3. "Obituaries: Scholar H. J. Schonfield; Wrote 'Passover Plot,'" *Chicago Tribune*, January 28, 1988, 10.
4. Godfrey Anderson, "Scholar Questions Authority of Church," *Morning Record* (Meriden, CT), July 5, 1969, 7.
5. "The Crucifixion Plot," *Newsweek*, August 8, 1966, 51. For a negative evangelical reaction to the book, see Alan Johnson, "Credibility Gap in 'The Passover Plot,'" *Moody Monthly* (Chicago), June 1968: 17–19; James Megivern, "If Jesus Was a Fraud, Maybe Lee Was a Yankee," *Star-News* (Wilmington, NC), August 1, 1981, 4A; and Albert L. Winseman, "Britons Lack American Cousins' Piety," http://news.gallup.com/poll/13990/britons-lack-american-cousins-piety.aspx, November 9, 2004, accessed October 13, 2015. See also Hugh McLeod, *The Religious Crisis of the 1960s* (New York: Oxford University Press, 2007), 17–27; and Callum G. Brown, *The Death of Christian Britain: Understanding Secularisation, 1800–2000* (London: Routledge, 2009), 1–2, 5.
6. Cleave, "How Does a Beatle Live?," 10.

7. Hunter Davies, *The Beatles: The Only Authorized Biography* (London: Ebury Press, 2009), 314–315; Bob Spitz, *The Beatles: The Biography* (New York: Little, Brown, and Company, 2005), 627–637; Devin McKinney, *Magic Circles: The Beatles in Dream and History* (Cambridge, MA: Harvard University Press, 2003), 140–153; Steven D. Stark, *Meet the Beatles: A Cultural History of the Band That Shook Youth, Gender, and the World* (New York: Harper Paperbacks, 2006), 191–192; Michael R. Frontani, *The Beatles: Image and the Media* (Jackson: University of Mississippi Press, 2007), 99–104; Brian Ward, "'The "C" Is for Christ': Arthur Unger, *Datebook* Magazine and the Beatles," *Popular Music and Society* 35, no. 4 (October 2012): 541–560; Philip Norman, *Shout! The Beatles in Their Generation* (New York: Simon and Schuster, 2003), 298–301; Steve Turner, *The Gospel According to the Beatles* (Louisville, KY: Westminster John Knox Press, 2006), 15–36.
8. Ward, "The 'C' Is for Christ," 3, 12.
9. "Blues for the Beatles," *Newsweek*, August 22, 1966, 94. See also "Rock and Roll according to John," *Time*, August 12, 1966, 38.
10. "Beatles' Manager Flies to Defense," *Pittsburgh Press*, August 5, 1966, 8; Claude Hall, "Beatles Running Strong—with Powerhouse Stations' Blessing," *Billboard*, August 20, 1966, 34, 39.
11. "Magazine Quote Sets off Furor against Beatles," *Spartanburg (SC) Herald-Journal*, August 4, 1966, 1.
12. "Comment on Jesus Spurs a Radio Ban against the Beatles," *New York Times*, August 5 1966, 20; "More Critics Board Beatle 'Ban Wagon,'" *Chicago Tribune*, August 6, 1966, D11; "Beatle Crisis: Lennon Remark—Growing Furor," *San Francisco Chronicle*, August 5, 1966, "Rock Music," G. Archer Weniger Collection, Bob Jones University. For an estimate on the number of radio bans, see Linda Martin and Kerry Segrave, *Anti-rock: The Opposition to Rock 'n' Roll* (New York: Da Capo Press, 1993), 179.
13. "More Critics Board Beatle 'Ban Wagon,'" D11; Martin and Segrave, *Anti-rock*, 179; "Beatle Discs Will Be Shot," *Leader-Post* (Regina, Saskatchewan), August 6, 1966, 16.
14. "Senator Wants Beatle Ban," *Reading (PA) Eagle*, August 9, 1966, 2.
15. "Blues for the Beatles," 94. "Foursome Wary of U.S. Welcome: 'Jesus' Quote Mars Beatle Visit," *Pittsburgh Press*, August 9, 1966, 9. "Jesus - John Lennon Controversy (Part 3 of 4)," YouTube video, 4:23, posted by "tunenito," December 15, 2007, http://www.youtube.com/watch?v=rN3wvY4alDU. This Shelton interview is from the ITN documentary *Reporting 66: The Beatles across America* (1966).
16. Radio bans of the Beatles music and demonstrations spread across the United States and were especially strong in the Bible Belt South. Ward, "The 'C' Is for Christ," 552; Leroy Aarons, "'Can't Express Myself Very Well,' Beatle Apologizes for Remarks," *Washington Post*, August 15, 1966, A1; "Baptist Minister Makes Issue of Beatle Remark," *St. Joseph (MO) News-Press*, August 14, 1966, 3A; "Bible Class Holds Beatle Burning," *Reading (PA) Eagle*, August 27, 1966, 1. Still, the scandal did little to harm the Beatles' popularity as ministers and laypeople had hoped it would. Lawrence Margasak, "Lennon's Comments on Jesus Didn't Affect Beatle Fans," *St. Paul Dispatch*, August 17, 1966, 2; Claude Hall, "Beatles Running Strong," 1966, 34, 39; "Banning the Beatles," *Alabama Baptist* (Birmingham), August 11, 1966, 2.
17. Mary Norris, "Sister Mary Paul McCartney," in *The Beatles Are Here! 50 Years After the Band Arrived in America, Writers, Musicians, and Other Fans Remember*, ed. Penelope Rowlands (Chapel Hill, NC: Algonquin Books, 2014), 92. "Baptist Minister Makes Issue of Beatle Remark," 3A. Leroy F. Aarons, "Beatle Tells How Religion Got into the Act," *Tuscaloosa (AL) News*, August 16, 1966, 5; and Aarons, "'Can't Express Myself

Very Well,' 1, A16. See Babb's photo and a description of his sermon in "Fans, 'Brimstone' Await the Beatles," *Plain Dealer* (Cleveland, OH), August 14, 1966, 18A.

18. Dick Sutcliffe. "Ideal Man of the Year," *Biblical Recorder* (Raleigh, NC), January 7, 1967, 2.
19. "Los Angeles Press Conference, Los Angeles International Airport, Los Angeles, California, December 27, 1968," Billy Graham's News Conferences, Records: 1963–1977, Archives of the Billy Graham Center, Wheaton, IL, 4; "New York City Press Conference for WFME, Craig Hulsebos, June 23, 1969," Billy Graham's News Conferences, Records: 1963–1977, Archives of the Billy Graham Center, Wheaton, IL, 7. See also John Turner, *Bill Bright and Campus Crusade for Christ: The Renewal of Evangelicalism in Postwar America* (Chapel Hill: University of North Carolina Press, 2008), 129.
20. Wilfred J. Martin, "Parents and Rock Music," *Eternity* (Philadelphia), April 1971, 23. For instances of young evangelicals embracing the left and the protest movement, see Molly Worthen, *Apostles of Reason: The Crisis of Authority in American Evangelicalism* (New York: Oxford University Press, 2014), 181; and David R. Swartz, *Moral Minority: The Evangelical Left in an Age of Conservatism* (Philadelphia: University of Pennsylvania Press, 2012).
21. R. Judson Carlberg, "Ferment in the Christian College," *Eternity* (Philadelphia), June 1967, 18.
22. Joel Carpenter, *Revive Us Again: The Reawakening of American Fundamentalism* (New York: Oxford University Press, 1997), 55–56, 58–59; Randall Balmer, *Mine Eyes Have Seen the Glory: A Journey into the Evangelical Subculture in America* (New York: Oxford University Press, 1989), x–xi; "Worldliness" in *Encyclopedia of Evangelicalism*, ed. Randall Balmer (Waco, TX: Baylor University Press, 2004), 642. For the conservative Christian response to the 1960s, see Robert Booth Fowler, *A New Engagement: Evangelical Political Thought, 1966–1976* (Grand Rapids, MI: Eerdmans, 1982), 27–28, 71, 214; Edward B. Fiske, "There Are Those Who Think It Is Imminent," *New York Times*, October 8, 1972, E8; and "A Biblical Response to America's Emergency," http://www.pe.ag.org/Articles2001/4564_davis.cfm, accessed on April 27, 2008. See also William C. Martin, *With God on Our Side: The Rise of the Religious Right in America* (New York: Broadway Books, 2005), 33–34; and Mark Taylor Dalhouse, *An Island in a Lake of Fire: Bob Jones University, Fundamentalism, and the Separatist Movement* (Athens: University of Georgia Press, 1996), 105–106.
23. For more on the evangelical encounter with the budding 1960s counterculture, see Barry Hankins, *Francis Schaeffer and the Shaping of Evangelical America* (Grand Rapids, MI: Eerdmans, 2008), 62, 102–103.
24. James C. Dobson, *Parenting Isn't for Cowards* (Dallas: Word Publishing, 1987), 13, 14.
25. Andrew Hartman, *A War for the Soul of America: A History of the Culture Wars* (Chicago: University of Chicago Press, 2015), 4. See also Rick Perlstein, *Before the Storm: Barry Goldwater and the Unmaking of the American Consensus* (New York: Nation Books, 2009), 125–126.
26. Vinson Synan, *Old Time Power: A Centennial History of the International Pentecostal Holiness Church* (Franklin Springs, GA: LifeSprings Resources, 1998), 256–257; "Assemblies of God Opposes Kennedy," *Leader and Press*, n.p., Flower Pentecostal Heritage Center, Springfield, MO; Mickey Crews, *Church of God: A Social History* (Knoxville: University of Tennessee Press, 1990), 161. For an earlier view, see C. Stanley Lowell, "Will a Roman Catholic Be President," *Christian Herald* (New York), November 1958, 22–23, 40–43. For the perceived intrusion of the federal government into racial matters, see Mark A. Noll, *God and Race in American Politics: A Short History* (Princeton, NJ:

Princeton University Press, 2009), 157–159; J. Edgar Hoover, "The Danger of Civil Disobedience," *King's Business* (Los Angeles), February 1966, 14; Frank Farrell, "NCC Pleads for Racial Justice," *Christianity Today* (Carol Stream, IL), January 3, 1964, 34–36; and Axel R. Schäfer, "The Great Society, Evangelicals, and the Public Funding of Religious Agencies," in *American Evangelicals and the 1960s*, ed. Axel R. Schäfer (Madison: University of Wisconsin Press, 2013), 167–169.

27. "Engel v Vitale," *New Republic*, July 9, 1962, 3, 5. See also John Morton Blum, *Years of Discord: American Politics and Society, 1961–1974* (New York: W. W. Norton, 1991), 187–217.
28. "Prayer Ban Shocks Billy Graham, Cardinal Cushing," *Evening Independent* (St. Petersburg, FL), June 19, 1963, 3A.
29. "Supreme Court Curb of School Prayer Arouses Vigorous Protests, Support," *Toledo Blade*, June 30, 1962, 8; "Constitution Change Sought to Kill School Prayer Ban," *Spokesman-Review* (Spokane, WA), June 27, 1962, 2. See also Robert Murray Thomas, *God in the Classroom: Religion and America's Public Schools* (Westport, CT: Praeger, 2007), 116–117; and Thomas S. Kidd and Barry Hankins, *Baptists in America: A History* (New York: Oxford University Press, 2015), 206–207.
30. "The Schoolyard Becomes a New Battleground," *Christianity Today* (Carol Stream, IL), September 13, 1963, 29. See also Loren E. Schaffer, "The Tyranny of the Minority," *Herald of Holiness* (Kansas City, MO), October 9, 1962, 9–10; George W. Long, "One Nation, Under God," *Christianity Today*, July 3, 1964, 14–15; John M. Stewart, "Give Me Back My Child!" *Christianity Today*, August 30, 1963, 9–10; and James V. Panoch, "Is Prayer in Public Schools an Illegal Maneuver?" *Christianity Today*, September 30, 1966, 3–6.
31. Linda Lyons, "The Gallup Brain: Prayer in Public Schools," http://news.gallup.com/poll/7393/gallup-brain-prayer-public-schools.aspx, December 10, 2002, accessed October 1, 2015. See also Emma Long, "Making Lemonade from *Lemon:* Evangelicals, the Supreme Court, and the Constitutionality of School Aid," in Schäfer, *American Evangelicals and the 1960s,* 141–144; and Robert Mason, *Richard Nixon and the Quest for a New Morality* (Chapel Hill: University of North Carolina Press, 2004), 17–23.
32. Matthew Avery Sutton, *American Apocalypse: A History of Modern Evangelicalism* (Cambridge, MA: Belknap Press of Harvard University Press, 2014), 326–339.
33. Stanley C. Baldwin, "Sodom and America," *Christianity Today* (Carol Stream, IL), October 25, 1963, 14–15. See also David L. McKenna, "Morals Revolution Hits Campus," *Christian Reader* (Wheaton, IL), August–September 1964, 11–13; Russell J. Fornwalt, "Pollution of the Moral Waters," *Christianity Today*, September 5, 1965, 11–12; Daniel K. Williams, "Sex and the Evangelicals: Gender Issues, the Sexual Revolution, and Abortion in the 1960s," in Schäfer, *American Evangelicals and the 1960s*, 97–118; and Darren Dochuk, *From Bible Belt to Sunbelt: Plain-Folk Religion, Grassroots Politics, and the Rise of Evangelical Conservatism* (New York: W. W. Norton, 2010), 259–274.
34. James T. Patterson, *Grand Expectations: The United States, 1945–1974* (New York: Oxford University Press, 1996), 355–361; Sharon Monteith, *American Culture in the 1960s* (Edinburgh: Edinburgh University Press, 2008), 51–52.
35. Quoted in Dewitt Whistler Jayne, "'Pop Art' Is No Joke," *Christian Reader* (Wheaton, IL), April–May 1965, 61.
36. "Toward a Hidden God," http://content.time.com/time/subscriber/article/0,33009,835309,00.html, April 8, 1966, accessed September 23, 2017.

37. David Aikman, *One Nation without God? The Battle for Christianity in an Age of Unbelief* (Grand Rapids, MI: Baker Books, 2012), 160–161. See also Christopher J. Richmann, "'Is God Dead?' (*Time* magazine, 1966)," in *Encyclopedia of the Sixties: A Decade of Culture and Counterculture*, ed. James S. Baugess and Abbe A. DeBolt (Santa Barbara: ABC-CLIO, 2012), 1:311–313; and Andrew S. Finstuen, *Original Sin and Everyday Protestants: The Theology of Reinhold Niebuhr, Billy Graham, and Paul Tillich in an Age of Anxiety* (Chapel Hill: University of North Carolina Press, 2009), 45–46.
38. "Letters," *Time*, April 22, 1966; "Letters," *Time*, ebscohost, April 15, 1966, accessed on September 22, 2015.
39. Billy Graham, Bernard Ramm, Vernon C. Grounds, and David Hubbard, *Is God "Dead"?* (Grand Rapids, MI: Zondervan Publishing, 1966).
40. Harold H. Martin, "Doomsday Merchants of the Far Right," *Saturday Evening Post*, April 28, 1962; Travis Hughs, "Hargis Loves a Revival," *Palm Beach (FL) Daily News*, December 22, 1964, 4.
41. Billy James Hargis, "Please Act Immediately," fund-raising letter, April 15, 1967, Wilcox Collection of Contemporary Political Movements, Spencer Library, University of Kansas.
42. Robert S. Ellwood, *The Fifties Spiritual Marketplace: American Religion in a Decade of Conflict* (New Brunswick, NJ: Rutgers University Press, 1997), 103–106.
43. For evangelical reactions to cultural and social changes in the 1960s and 1970s, see David Harrington Watt, *A Transforming Faith: Explorations of Twentieth-Century American Evangelicalism* (New Brunswick, NJ: Rutgers University Press, 1991), 67–71. Watt notes, "In the early 1960s, evangelicals began to comment frequently and anxiously on a series of developments that . . . ranged from the increasing 'lawlessness' of American society (by which evangelicals meant chiefly race riots in the cities and antiwar demonstrations on college campuses) to a general decline in America's power and prestige in the international realm." Believers' concerns about society centered on three issues, says Watt: "the decline of the American family, America's rejection of family values, and America's drift away from its Christian moorings" (67). See also Leonard Sweet, "The 1960s: The Crises of Liberal Christianity and the Public Emergence of Evangelicalism," in *Evangelicalism and Modern America*, ed. George Marsden (Grand Rapids, MI: Eerdmans, 1984), 29–45.
44. Bill Crandall, "CBS News Reports on the Beatles in 1963," http://www.cbsnews.com/news/cbs-news-reports-on-the-beatles-in-1963/, January 21, 2014, accessed September 23, 2017.
45. Tom Wolfe, "Beatles! More than Just a Word to the Wild," *Herald Tribune* (New York), February 8, 1964, 1, 4. See also McKinney, *Magic Circles*, 54.
46. Bill Whitworth, "Plaza Is Dazed by Beatles," *Boston Sunday Globe*, February 9, 1964, 45.
47. "YEAH-YEAH-YEAH! Beatlemania Becomes a Part of U.S. History," *Life*, February 21, 1964, 34B.
48. "George, Paul, Ringo, and John," *Newsweek*, February 24, 1964, 54. Editorial from *Milwaukee Sentinel* quoted in Richard F. Whalen, "Who, Besides Teenagers Likes Britain's Beatles?" *Day* (New London, CT), February 11, 1964, 13.
49. Frontani, *The Beatles*, 56–58. For an interesting take on the band's success, fans, and head-shaking skeptics, see James Morris, "The Monarchs of the Beatle Empire," *Saturday Evening Post*, August 27, 1966, 22–27; and "Enterprise: Blue-Chip Beatles," *Newsweek*, October 4, 1965, 82.
50. "Beatles' Boodle—a Cool Million for 30 Days in U.S. . . . Yeah," *Boston Globe*, September 20, 1964, 22; "Beatles Sign to Appear in Kansas City, Will Get $150,000 for

One Show," *Chicago Tribune*, August 24, 1964, 3; Darryl Levings, "50 Years Ago: The Beatles Played for 31 Minutes in Kansas City," http://www.kansascity.com/living/star-magazine/article2127287.html, September 17, 2014, accessed March 27, 2017.

51. Jonathan Gould, *Can't Buy Me Love: The Beatles, Britain, and America* (New York: Three Rivers Press, 2008), 249–252.
52. Michael S. Willis, "Lo! The Beatles Descend from Sky for Apotheosis in Frisco," *Variety*, August 26, 1964, 45.
53. "Of Many Things," *America*, September 26, 1964, 335.
54. Bernard Saibel, "Beatlemania Harmful to the Teen-Aged Mind?" *Boston Globe*, August 26, 1964, 1, 2. See also "Beatlemania Frightens Child Expert," *Seattle Daily Times*, August 22, 1964, 1.
55. Gail Savage, "Beatles Fans Know What They Like," *Boston Globe*, September 2, 1964, 8. For a teenager's positive response to Saibel's comments, see Heather Winters, "Fans Won't See or Hear the Beatles," *Boston Globe*, September 11, 1964, 14.
56. Michael Ray Fitzgerald, "Boss Jocks: How Corrupt Radio Practices Helped Make Jacksonville One of the Great Music Cities," *Southern Cultures* 17, no. 4 (Winter 2011): 11.
57. "Beatles Boston September Concert Already Sellout," *Boxoffice*, June 15, 1964, SE6.
58. Larry Kane, *Ticket to Ride: Inside the Beatles' 1964 and 1965 Tours That Changed the World* (New York: Penguin, 2004), 116.
59. "I Just Have to Have Something They Touched," *Boston Globe*, September 13, 1964, 1.
60. James Calogero, "Beatles Arrive in Hub Unseen by Followers," *Nashua (NH) Telegraph*, September 12, 1964, 7. See also Robert J. Anglin, "Girls Start 24-Hour Beatles Vigil," *Boston Globe*, September 12, 1964, 1–3.
61. Calogero, "Beatles Arrive in Hub Unseen by Followers," 7.
62. "Teens Flip Wigs for Beatles," *Boston Sunday Globe*, September 13, 1964, 1, 67.
63. Gloria Negri, "Teen-Agers Answer Call to Christ," *Boston Globe*, September 22, 1964, 1.
64. George M. Collins, "Billy Graham Has Rare Talent for Drawing Crowds," *Boston Sunday Globe*, September 20, 1964, 52.
65. Richard Connolly, "Billy Graham Talks of Youth," *Boston Globe*, September 18, 1964, 1. James M. Johnston, "Chapter and Verse: Billy Graham on Beatles," *Milwaukee Sentinel*, September 5, 1964, 6. For Graham's comments on the Beatles following their *Ed Sullivan Show* appearance, see "Trends," *Moody Monthly* (Chicago), April 1964, 8; "Dr. Graham Crusade Here in 1966?" *Guardian*, March 20, 1964, 5; "Billy Graham Doesn't Dig the Beatles," *Owosso (MI) Argus-Press*, February 11, 1964, 3; and "Notes and Quotes," *Lutheran Witness* (St. Louis, MO), March 17, 1964, 23.
66. Billy Graham, "Youth of Today Searching for Security, Houston Crusade, 1965," in *The Wit and Wisdom of Billy Graham*, ed. Bill Adler (New York: Random House, 1967), 150.
67. Reinhold Niebuhr, "Heroes and Hero Worship," *Nation*, February 23, 1921, 293.
68. William F. Buckley Jr., "How Globe Columnists See It: Why Do We Deserve the Beatles? Ear of Younger Group Has Gone Sour Musically," *Boston Globe*, September 13, 1964, A3.
69. Jeff Nilsson, "Why Early Critics Hated the Beatles," http://www.saturdayeveningpost.com/2014/01/31/history/post-perspective/why-the-beatles-bugged-the-critics.html, January 31, 2014, accessed September 24, 2015.
70. Betty Jane West, "What about the BEATLES," *Tell* (Nashville, TN), February 1965, 14.
71. Joanne Kay Junger, "I Hate the Beatles," *Conquest* (Kansas City, MO), July 1966, 20.
72. Rhonda Markowitz, *The Greenwood Encyclopedia of Rock History: Folk, Pop, Mods, and Rockers, 1960–1966* (Westport, CT: Greenwood Press, 2005), 2:100.

73. Burl Ratzsch, "Sounds off on Music," *Pentecostal Evangel* (Springfield, MO), January 23, 1966, 28.
74. Warren L. Vinz, "*Sword of the Lord*, 1934–," in *The Conservative Press in Twentieth-Century America*, ed. Ronald Lora and William Henry Longton (Westport, CT: Greenwood Press, 1999), 132.
75. Derek Taylor quoted in Alfred G. Aronowitz, "The Return of the Beatles," *Saturday Evening Post*, August 8, 1964, 28.
76. *Sword of the Lord* quoted in "The Beatles and Religion," *Sawdust Trail*, November 1, 1964, 2. Also see Jack Daniel, "Is Beat Music Eroding Our Youth?" *Moody Monthly* (Chicago), May 1966, 26–28.
77. Carl F. H. Henry, "The Passing Parade," *Christianity Today* (Carol Stream, IL), September 11, 1964, 32.
78. Norman, *Shout!*, 190.
79. Jann S. Wenner, "John Lennon, Part 1: The Working Class Hero," *Rolling Stone*, January 7, 1971, 42. See also McKinney, *Magic Circles*, 144–146.
80. Aronowitz, "The Return of the Beatles," 28.
81. M. D., San Francisco, "The Playboy Adviser," *Playboy*, March 1965, 38.
82. Elizabeth Fraterrigo, *Playboy and the Making of the Good Life in Modern America* (New York: Oxford University Press, 2009), 65–69.
83. Eddie Wagner, "What's Behind the Beatle Craze?" *King's Business* (Los Angeles), May 1965, 16.
84. Hugh F. Pyle, "The Beatle Plague," *Sword of the Lord* (Murfreesboro, TN), April 30, 1965, 1.
85. "Letters: Demon Possession," *Alliance Witness* (New York), November 23, 1966, 18.
86. Bernice Buresh, "The Beatle Worshippers," *Milwaukee Sentinel*, August 31, 1964, 1, 5. In 1964, one savvy entrepreneur published a collection of fan notes titled *Love Letters to the Beatles*, reviewed in "An Aid to the Study of Beatlemania," *Ottawa Citizen*, December 12, 1964, 16. See also Barbara Ehrenreich, Elizabeth Hess, and Gloria Jacobs, "Beatlemania: Girls Just Want to Have Fun," in *The Adoring Audience: Fan Culture and Popular Media*, ed. Lisa A. Lewis (London: Routledge, 1992), 84–106.
87. "One of America's Great Feminists, Betty Friedan, CBC," YouTube video, 3:00, posted by "CBC," March 24, 2010, http://www.youtube.com/watch?v=qfgxHKli9CU&t=37s.
88. "Effeminate Boys' Fashions 'Bug' American Girls," *C. A. Herald* (Springfield, MO), September 1966, 31. For bans of Beatle haircuts in schools, see "Banned," *Spokane (WA) Daily Chronicle*, February 12, 1964, 2; and Hal Cooper, "Teachers, Pupils Still at Battle," *Daytona Beach (FL) Morning Journal*, December 3, 1965, 1. For a moderate Catholic response to the issue of long hair, see "The Long-Hair Controversy," *America*, November 12, 1966, 578.
89. David Noebel summarized Hargis's 1964 trip to London in a reel-to-reel recording, "Communism Hypnotism and the Beatles—Presented by Testimony Press Publications," YouTube video, 1:19:08, posted by "Testimony Press," November 3, 2014, https://www.youtube.com/watch?v=IGg5QADoQhU.
90. "Schools Can Ban Beatle Haircuts," *Gettysburg (PA) Times*, September 25, 1965, 8. For more on similar bans of the hairstyle in Florida, see "Haircut," *Ocala (FL) Star-Banner*, September 4, 1966, 5.
91. "Fads: The Short & the Long of It," *Time*, October 1, 1965, 60. See also "The Unbarbershopped Quartet," *Time*, February 21, 1964, 48.

92. Stark, *Meet the Beatles*, 133–137, 177–178. For a contemporary take on the Beatles and sex, see M. M. Carlin, "Love on Film," *Transition* 17 (1964): 37–38.
93. *The Making of the Beatles First U.S. Visit*, directed by Albert Maysles and David Maysles (Hollywood: Capitol Records, 2003), DVD.
94. Amy Vanderbilt, *New Complete Book of Etiquette: The Guide to Gracious Living* (Garden City, NY: Doubleday, 1963), 155. See also Stark, *Meet the Beatles*, 177.
95. Bob Thomas, "Beatle-Type Hair Styles Prompt Filmland Comment," *Reading (PA) Eagle*, November 26, 1965, 24. See also "Problem: How to Un-lock Teenagers," *Fort Scott (KS) Tribune*, November 11, 1964, 4; and Russell Baker, "Ferment Concerning Hair Causes Odd Conclusions," *Pittsburgh Post-Gazette*, August 6, 1964, 8. For the influence of the Beatle cut among African Americans, see "Bouffants Are Out, Beatle Cuts Are In," *Ebony*, February 1965, 118.
96. Billy Graham, *World Aflame* (New York: Doubleday, 1965), 22.
97. "Humanity Not Drifting to Unisex, Expert Says," *Toledo (OH) Blade*, May 4, 1966, 16. See also Hal Cooper, "Teachers, Pupils Still at Battles," *Daytona Beach (FL) Morning Journal*, December 3, 1965, 1.
98. For the cultural politics of hair, see Mark Hamilton Lytle, *America's Uncivil Wars: The Sixties Era from Elvis to the Fall of Richard Nixon* (New York: Oxford University Press, 2006), 145–146, 199; Martin King, *Men, Masculinity, and the Beatles* (Farnham, UK: Ashgate, 2013); and Gael Graham, "Flaunting the Freak Flag: *Karr v. Schmidt* and the Great Hair Debate in American High Schools, 1965–1975," *Journal of American History* 91, no. 2 (September 2004): 522–543.
99. "'64 Mood: Soul-Searching among Pastors, Churches," *Biblical Recorde*r (Raleigh, NC), February 22, 1964, 2. See also California gubernatorial candidate Ronald Reagan's flub when he misidentified a young man with a Beatle haircut as a woman while stumping at Claremont College, "Beatle Haircut Was Not on Woman," *Gettysburg (PA) Times*, April 2, 1966, 7.
100. "Don't Blame the Beatles!" *Baptist Bulletin* (Schaumburg, IL), July 1964, 24, in "Rock Music," G. Archer Weniger Collection, Bob Jones University.
101. "It Was the First Time in 48 Years That Parson Jones' Church Booted Out Anyone," *Biblical Recorder* (Raleigh, NC), September 9, 1967, 20.
102. Ibid.
103. "Hair Warfare," *Bridegroom's Messenger* (Atlanta), June 1966, 2, 8.
104. Bill Goetz, "Are You a Beatle Bug?" *AYF Compass*, n.d., 26–27, "Rock Music," G. Archer Weniger Collection, Bob Jones University.
105. Eddie Wagner, "What's Behind the Beatle Craze?" *King's Business* (Los Angeles), May 1965, 16.
106. David Riesman, *The Lonely Crowd: A Study of the Changing American Character* (New Haven, CT: Yale University Press, 1950).
107. The February 24, 1964, *U.S. News and World Report* interview with David Riesman republished as "What the Beatles Prove about Teen-Agers: Interview with a Leading Educator and Sociologist," https://www.usnews.com/news/national/articles/2008/05/16/what-the-beatles-prove-about-teen-agers, May 16, 2008, accessed October 6, 2015.
108. R. O. Denton, "News of the Churches: Windsor, N.C.," *Pentecostal Evangel* (Springfield, MO), August 29, 1965, 30. See also Charles E. Shepard, *Forgiven: The Rise and Fall of Jim Bakker and the PTL Ministry* (New York: Atlantic Monthly Press, 1989), 17–20.
109. Robert O. Self, *All in the Family: The Realignment of American Democracy since the 1960s* (New York: Hill and Wang, 2012), 342–344.

110. Sydney E. Ahlstrom, "The Traumatic Years: American Religion and Culture in the '60s and '70s," in *Critical Issues in American Religious History*, ed. Robert R. Mathisen (Waco, TX: Baylor University Press, 2001), 636–637.
111. George Sokolsky, "These Days: The John Birch Society," *Times-News* (Hendersonville, NC), April 10, 1961, 2.
112. "Billy Graham Aiding Reds, Bob Jones Says," *Spartanburg (SC) Herald*, April 16, 1958, 1.
113. Grant Wacker, *America's Pastor: Billy Graham and the Shaping of a Nation* (Cambridge, MA: Belknap Press of Harvard University Press, 2014), 231–239.
114. Andrew Preston, "Evangelical Internationalism: A Conservative Worldview for the Age of Globalization," in *The Right Side of the Sixties: Reexamining Conservatism's Decade of Transformation*, ed. Laura Jane Gifford and Daniel K. Williams (New York: Palgrave Macmillan, 2012), 229. Sutton, *American Apocalypse*, 160, 186–187, 312, 316, 331–332.
115. J. F. Ter Horst, "College Survey Shows Liberalism Increases," *Sunday Herald* (Bridgeport, CT), October 20, 1963, 14.
116. "Christian Crusade Youth University," *Christian Crusade* (Tulsa, OK), June 1962, 12.
117. Billy James Hargis, "Operation: Campus Awakening," Christian Crusade fund-raising letter, February 15, 1967, Wilcox Collection of Contemporary Political Movements, Spencer Library, University of Kansas.
118. *In Assembly: Journal of Proceedings of the Seventy-Sixth Session of the Wisconsin Legislature, 1963* (Wisconsin Legislature Assembly, 1964), 159; William D. Romanowski, *Pop Culture Wars: Religion and the Role of Entertainment in American Life* (Eugene, OR: Wipf and Stock, 2008), 213; David A. Noebel, "ACLU Activities," As You See It, *Milwaukee Sentinel*, January 7, 1962, B2; David A. Noebel, "Reds in the Churches," As You See It, *Milwaukee Sentinel*, June 10, 1960, 16; David A. Noebel, "Clergy and Reds!" As You See It, *Milwaukee Sentinel*, December 10, 1960, 16; and David A. Noebel, "Human Dignity," As You See It, *Milwaukee Sentinel*, August 26, 1960, 12; William R. Bechtel, "Kindschi, Noebel Fight to Face Kastenmeier," *Milwaukee Journal*, September 5, 1962, 2.
119. "Anti-Communist Group Speakers to Be in Eugene," *Eugene Register-Guard*, October 16, 1964, 4B. See also "Beatles Called a Red Menace," *San Francisco Chronicle*, January 28, 1965, "Rock Music," G. Archer Weniger Collection, Bob Jones University; "Dr. Hargis Set for Address on 'The Far Left,'" *Sarasota (FL) Herald Tribune*, April 8, 1964, 7; "'Psycho-Politics': Beatle Music Said Communist Tool," *Sarasota Herald Tribune*, February 21, 1965, 14B; "Beatles Part of a Red Plot, Former State Pastor Says," *Milwaukee Journal*, February 20, 1965, 7; and David A. Noebel, "Columbia Records: Home of Marxist Minstrels," *Christian Crusade* (Tulsa, OK), March 1967, 18–20.
120. David A. Noebel, *Communism, Hypnotism, and the Beatles: An Analysis of the Communist Use of Music, the Communist Master Music Plan* (Tulsa, OK: Christian Crusade Publications, 1965), 1. See also David Hitchcock, "Stop the Communist Use of Music," *Christian Crusade* (Tulsa, OK), October 1966, 26.
121. Ron Theodore Robin, *The Making of the Cold War Enemy: Culture and Politics in the Military-Intellectual Complex* (Princeton, NJ: Princeton University Press, 2001), 168–171; William Brinkley, "Valley Forge GIs Tell of Their Brainwashing Ordeal," *Life*, May 25, 1953, 108–110, 113–116, 121–122, 124.
122. Noebel, *Communism, Hypnotism, and the Beatles*, 11, 15. For more on Noebel's race-baiting, see John Haines, "The Emergence of Jesus Rock: On Taming the 'African Beat,'" *Black Music Research Journal*, 31, no. 1 (Spring 2011): 232–238.

123. "Beware, the Red Beatles," *Newsweek*, February 15, 1965, 89.
124. "Noebel and the Beatles," *Newsweek*, March 8, 1965, 6.
125. Billy James Hargis, *Newsletter*, September 1965, 1, Wilcox Collection of Contemporary Political Movements, Spencer Library, University of Kansas.
126. See, for example, David A. Noebel, "The Beatles: Minstrels of the Antichrist," *Christian Crusade* (Tulsa, OK), October 1966, 26–27; David A. Noebel, *Rhythm, Riots, and Revolution: An Analysis of the Communist Use of Music, the Communist Master Plan* (Tulsa, OK: Christian Crusade Publications, 1965); David A. Noebel, *The Beatles: A Study in Drugs, Sex, and Revolution* (Tulsa, OK: Christian Crusade Publications, 1971); and David A. Noebel, *The Marxist Minstrels: A Handbook on Communist Subversion of Music* (Tulsa, OK: American Christian College Press, 1974).
127. "Christian Crusade Rally Presents David Noebel's 'Communism, Hypnotism, and the Beatles,'" Christian Crusade flyer, 1965, Wilcox Collection of Contemporary Political Movements, Spencer Library, University of Kansas.
128. Billy James Hargis, letter to Christian Crusade members, n.d., Wilcox Collection of Contemporary Political Movements, Spencer Library, University of Kansas. See also "From Ringo to Revolution? Rightist Exposes Beatles as Part of Communist Plot," *Daily News* (Charlotte Amalie, Virgin Islands), September 1, 1965, 10. For a reader's letter supporting Noebel's efforts, see Ruth Horsh, "Ban the Beatles," *Deseret News* (Salt Lake City, UT), August 17, 1966, A18. For more on Noebel and his anti-Beatles, anticommunist crusading, see R. Serge Denisoff, *Tarnished Gold: The Record Industry Revisited* (New Brunswick, NJ: Transaction Books, 1986), 382–384, 386, 420.
129. Bernard L. Hughes, "Of Christ and the Beatles," *Boston Globe*, November 1, 1966, 14.
130. Norman Vincent Peale, *The Power of Positive Thinking* (New York: Fireside, 2003), 1. See also Carol V. R. George, *God's Salesman: Norman Vincent Peale and the Power of Positive Thinking* (New York: Oxford University Press, 1993).
131. Norman Vincent Peale, "Confident Living: Jesus and the Beatles," *Lewiston (ME) Daily Sun*, October 29, 1966, 6.
132. Ibid.
133. "Beatle Ban Is Gaining Momentum," *Rome (GA) News-Tribune*, August 4, 1966, 1.
134. Quoted in Martin and Segrave, *Anti-rock*, 179.
135. "Beatles at Astor Tower Hotel Interview 1966," YouTube video, 21:07, posted by "Godzzzila69," June 4, 2014, https://www.youtube.com/watch?v=WhI9D7qLSqA; and Leroy F. Aarons, "What John Lennon Really Said," *Milwaukee Journal*, August 16, 1966, 1. See also Aarons, "'Can't Express Myself Very Well,'" 1, A16; and Geoffrey Giuliano and Brenda Giuliano, eds., *The Lost Beatles Interviews* (London: Virgin, 1995), 62–65. For David A. Noebel's comments on the influence of Schonfield's *The Passover Plot*, see David A. Noebel, no title, *Christian Crusade* (Tulsa, OK), November 1966, n.p., "Rock Music," G. Archer Weniger Collection, Bob Jones University.
136. Martin and Segrave, *Anti-rock*, 180; "Birmingham Station Ends Beatles Ban," *Herald-Tribune* (Sarasota, FL), August 13, 1966, 10; "Sorry—Yeah, Yeah, Yeah!" *Moody Monthly* (Chicago), October 1966, 12.
137. "John Lennon Interview in Almería, Spain (1966)," YouTube video, 13:55, posted by "lennonista9," March 1, 2012, http://www.youtube.com/watch?v=-lYgo0z7lto.
138. Tony Barrow, *John, Paul, George, and Me* (New York: Thunder's Mouth Press, 2005), quote on 204, see also 208.
139. *The Beatles Anthology* (San Francisco: Chronicle Books, 2000), 227.

140. "What Lennon Really Meant: The Misunderstood Beatle," press clipping, August 6, 1966, "Rock Music," G. Archer Weniger Collection, Bob Jones University. For fears about security, see "Beatles Will Keep U.S. Tour Schedule," press clipping, August 6, 1966, "Rock Music," G. Archer Weniger Collection, Bob Jones University.
141. See, for example, the relatively tame take on the Beatles in Rachel Conrad Wahlberg, "Analyzing the Beatles," *The Lutheran* (Minneapolis), September 23, 1964, 18–20.
142. "Lively Liverpudlians," *America*, February 22, 1964, 245.
143. "Beatlemania and the Fast Buck," *Christian Century*, February 24, 1965, 230. For the Quaker civil rights activist Chuck Fager's glowing review of the Beatles' *Abbey Road*, see Charles E. Fager, "Massive Impact," *Christian Century*, January 14, 1970, 54, 56. For a similar laid-back approach on the Beatles from the United Methodists, see Richmond Barbour, "Teens Together," *Together*, May 1965, 48.
144. Wahlberg, "Analyzing the Beatles," 19.
145. Ibid., 20.
146. Ibid, 20.
147. Robert L. White, "Some Reflections on Beatle-ese," *Motive* (Nashville, TN), November 1965, 34–37; Robbie Mason, "The Beatles: Aesthetic of the Absurd," *Motive*, March 1966, quote on 42.
148. William Stringfellow, "The Beatles and the Unpopularity of Jesus," *Presbyterian*, November 15, 1966, 36. See also Ken Caunce, "Beatles 'Help': Cleric Lands Lesson," *Windsor (Ontario) Star*, June 3, 1966, 1.
149. John R. Sampey, "Question for the Beatles to Answer," *Western Recorder* (Louisville, KY), September 1, 1966, 12. The Southern Baptist critic would likely have been shocked by the development of Beatles studies and the steady stream of books, academic articles, and conferences dedicated to the group's output. Whereas the Beatles charged $4.50 to $6.50 for tickets, Billy Graham rallies were free of charge. Adjusted for inflation, those Beatles tickets amount to approximately $35 and $50 in 2016. For further remarks, by Alabama teenagers, about the Beatles and Lennon's statement, see Lucille Prince, "Shoals Teen-Agers Take Issue with Beatle John for Remarks," *Florence (AL) Times*, August 9, 1966, 2. Few critics would go as far as a Washington Seventh-day Adventist minister, who, commenting on Lennon's remark, told a reporter that "according to scripture, this is just another sign that Christ is soon to come back to earth. He will return because it mentions in the last days scoffers will appear right before Christ does." "Most Condemn Statement by Beatle about Christ but Feel Record Ban Is Overdoing It," *Lewiston (ID) Morning Tribune*, August 5, 1966, 16.
150. Peale, "Confident Living," 6.
151. Billy Graham, "Rich, Famous Owe a Debt to Public," *Palm Beach (FL) Post*, September 14, 1966, 6.
152. Steven P. Miller, *Billy Graham and the Rise of the Republican South* (Philadelphia: University of Pennsylvania Press, 2009), 37. See also W. A. Criswell, "The Wounds of Jesus," sermon preached at First Baptist Church in Dallas, Texas, August 7, 1966, https://www.wacriswell.com/sermons/1966/the-wounds-of-jesus-3/, accessed August 11, 2015.
153. C. Wright Mills, *The Sociological Imagination* (New York: Oxford University Press, 1959), 32–33. See also William H. Swatos and Daniel V. A. Olson, eds., *The Secularization Debate* (Lanham, MD: Rowman and Littlefield, 2000); David Martin, *On Secularization: Towards a Revised General Theory* (Aldershot, UK: Ashgate, 2005); Charles Taylor, *A Secular Age* (Cambridge, MA: Harvard University Press, 2007); C. John Sommerville, "Secular Society / Religious Population: Our Tacit Rules for Using the Term

'Secularization,'" *Journal for the Scientific Study of Religion* 37, no. 2 (June 1998): 249–253; Alan Aldridge, *Religion in the Contemporary World: A Sociological Introduction* (Cambridge: Polity Press, 2013), 66–96; and Peter L. Berger, ed., *The Desecularization of the World: Resurgent Religion and World Politics* (Grand Rapids, MI: Eerdmans, 1999).

154. "A Bleak Outlook Is Seen for Religion," *New York Times*, February 25, 1968, 3. See also Peter Berger, *The Sacred Canopy: Elements of a Sociological Theory of Religion* (Garden City, NY: Doubleday, 1967).
155. "Vatican Accepts Lennon's Apology," *New York Times*, August 14, 1966, 13.
156. "I Just Have to Have Something They Touched," 1; Timothy Leary, "Thank God for the Beatles," in *The Beatles Book*, ed. Edward Davis (New York: Cowles Education, 1968), 44; David T. Courtwright, *Forces of Habit: Drugs and the Making of the Modern World* (Cambridge, MA: Harvard University Press, 2001), 88.
157. Ehrenreich, Hess, and Jacobs, "Beatlemania," 85. For more on the Beatles as revolutionary, see Ward, "The 'C' Is for Christ," 548.
158. "The Beatles—Why?" *Lutheran Witness* (Concordia, MO), March 3 1964, 4. For a Catholic examination of the Beatles' 1965 hit song "Help!" and what it meant to its teen listeners, see Pauline Mulligan, "Can We Understand Present-Day Adolescents through Their Songs?" *Lumen Vitae: International Review of Religious Education* 21, no. 3 (September 1966): 389–404.
159. "Beatles and Beagles Are Baptist Topic," *Washington Post*, June 16, 1964, B2. See also "C. W. Cranford, Baptist Minister, Dies of Cancer," *Washington Post*, October 26, 1983, C8.
160. Ahlstrom, "The Traumatic Years," 642.
161. Daniel, "Is Beat Music Eroding Our Youth?," 26–28. For the most severe criticism of the Beatles from Billy James Hargis's anticommunist, fundamentalist publication *Christian Crusade*, see *Christian Crusade*, November 1966, "Rock Music," G. Archer Weniger Collection, Bob Jones University; David Hitchcock, "The Communist Use of Music," *Christian Crusade*, July 1966, 26; and David A. Noebel, "Are the Beatles Minstrels of the Antichrist?" *Christian Crusade*, October 1966, 26–27. Also see Frontani, *The Beatles*, 95.
162. Margaret L. Bendroth, *Growing Up Protestant: Parents, Children and Mainline Churches* (New Brunswick, NJ: Rutgers University Press, 2002), 125; J. Terry Todd, "Mainline Protestants and News Narratives of Declension," in *The Oxford Handbook of Religion and the American News Media*, ed. Diane Winston (New York: Oxford University Press, 2012), 186–187.

Chapter 4

1. Alistair Cooke, "Grooving on the Sounds," *Guardian*, August 19, 1969, 9. See also Simon Warner, "Reporting Woodstock: Some Contemporary Press Reflections on the Festival," *Remembering Woodstock*, ed. Andy Bennett (Aldershot, UK: Ashgate, 2004), 69–72.
2. "The Big Woodstock Rock Trip," *Life*, August 29, 1969, 14B.
3. David Stowe, *No Sympathy for the Devil: Christian Pop Music and the Transformation of American Evangelicalism* (Chapel Hill: University of North Carolina Press, 2011), 59.
4. One year before, Brian Vachon of *Look* magazine wrote about the new musical phenomenon. "The Jesus movement seems to be springing up simultaneously in a

miscellany of places," said Vachon, "and often in the last places you would think to look. But maybe, because this is California, this should be the first place to look. In Orange County, an entire motorcycle gang converted. In Anaheim, a huge entertainment complex called Melodyland has been taken over by a nondenominational, solidly middle-class religious group. Dozens of go-go clubs throughout the state have been turned into religious coffeehouses, where kids go to sing and pray. . . . Young volunteers from all over are being invited to high school assemblies, singing rock/religious songs and giving testimony." Brian Vachon, "The Jesus Movement Is upon Us," *Look*, February 9, 1971, quote on 16. See also Robert S. Ellwood, *One Way: The Jesus Movement and Its Meaning* (Englewood Cliffs, NJ: Prentice Hall, 1973), 63, 64.

5. For early speculation about right-wing political engagement, see "Youth in Sects on Coast Registering Republican," *New York Times*, April 16, 1972, quote on 36; Ellwood, *One Way*, 132; and Jay R. Howard and John M. Streck, *Apostles of Rock: The Splintered World of Contemporary Christian Music* (Louisville: University Press of Kentucky, 2004), 150, 199. For an early journalistic treatment, see Wayne King, "'Jesus Rock' Now a New Musical Industry," *New York Times*, June 10, 1977, 16.
6. Steven Félix-Jäger, *With God on Our Side: Towards a Transformational Theology of Rock and Roll* (Eugene, OR: Wipf and Stock, 2017), 26–49; Shawn David Young, *Gray Sabbath: Jesus People USA, the Evangelical Left, and the Evolution of Christian Rock* (New York: Columbia University Press, 2015), 142–143; Stowe, *No Sympathy for the Devil*, 246–248; Kathy Sawyer, "Fundamentalism, the New Old-Time Religion: Christian Right Takes Its Place at Center Stage," *Washington Post*, December 25, 1984, A1, A14; Jonathan Yardley, "Religion Revival: A Look at the Rise of Evangelicals," *Washington Post*, October 3, 1984, B1, B13; Larry Eskridge, *God's Forever Family: The Jesus People Movement in America* (Oxford: Oxford University Press, 2013), 281–282.
7. Eskridge, *God's Forever Family*, 134–137;"Rallying for Jesus: 80,000 Jam Dallas for a Crusade Called Explo '72," *Life*, June 30, 1972, quote on 40, 41. See Graham's form letter summing up the event: "Dear Friend," November 1971, "Jesus Movement," G. Archer Weniger Collection, Bob Jones University.
8. Billy Graham's changing views about youth and rebellion were evident in press conferences he held from 1967 to 1970. In a 1967 question-and-answer session, Graham excoriated hippies as dropouts and naïve youths. In 1970, he lauded the kinds of questions young people were asking and remarked that the younger generation seemed to be more interested in the gospel. "Press Conference: Regency Hyatt House, Atlanta, Georgia, December 29, 1967," 7; and "Press Conference: Knoxville Tennessee, May 21, 1970," 4, Billy Graham Center Archives, Wheaton, IL. See also Larry Eskridge, "'One Way': Billy Graham, the Jesus Generation, and the Idea of an Evangelical Youth Culture," *Church History* 67, no. 1 (March 1998): 83–106.
9. "Evangelist Wants to Chat with Elvis," *Lakeland (FL) Ledger*, October 4, 1956, 4; "Teen-Agers Urged to Accept Christ," *Lewiston (ME) Daily Sun*, May 1, 1958, 14; Billy Graham, *The Mystery of Iniquity* (Minneapolis: Billy Graham Evangelistic Association, 1957), n.p.
10. Linda Martin and Kerry Segrave, *Anti-rock: The Opposition to Rock 'n' Roll* (New York: Da Capo Press, 1993), 27, 30, 48, 52–53, 62, 64; Margaret McManus, "Educator Sees No Menace in Presley. Elvis Rankles? Ignore Him, Says Savant," *Miami News*, October 6, 1956, 3A. For a local take, see "Will Not Ban Rock, Roll Music in Santa Cruz," *Robesonian* (Lumberton, NC), June 7, 1956, 10.
11. "Lovin' Spoonful," *Newsweek*, September 5, 1966, 80.

12. Jesse Murphy Hendley, "Rock and Roll," n.p., n.d., Jesse Murphy Hendley Collection, 1, "Sermons: Rock and Roll," Southern Baptist Historical Library and Archives, Nashville, TN.
13. "Billy Graham Says He'll Meet Elvis in Short Time," *Ocala (FL) Star-Banner*, October 8, 1977, 12A.
14. Bruce J. Schulman, *The Seventies: The Great Shift in American Culture, Society, and Politics* (New York: Free Press, 2001), 9–10; John Morton Blum, *Years of Discord: American Politics and Society, 1961–1974* (New York: W. W. Norton, 1991), 92–101; Kirse Granat May, *Golden State, Golden Youth: The California Image in Popular Culture, 1955–1966* (Chapel Hill: University of North Carolina Press, 2002), 67–75; James T. Patterson, *Grand Expectations: The United States, 1945–1974* (New York: Oxford University Press, 1996), 447–450; Dick West, "Ready Remedy for the Generation Gap," *Dispatch* (Lexington, NC), May 22, 1967, 6; Brittany Bounds, "Youth Culture," in *Encyclopedia of the Sixties: A Decade of Culture and Counterculture*, ed. James S. Baugess and Abbe Allen Debolt (Santa Barbara, CA: ABC-CLIO, 2012), 1:735–738.
15. *The Port Huron Statement (1962)* (Chicago: C. H. Kerr, 1990), 11. See also Christopher Bone, *The Disinherited Children: A Study of the New Left and the Generation Gap* (New York: Schenkman, 1977), 1–10.
16. "Activist Answers Columbia Prexy," *Plumed Horn*, July 1968, 169, 168. See also Mark Kurlansky, *1968: The Year That Rocked the World* (London: Vintage Books, 2004), 194–208; David Farber, *The Age of Great Dreams: America in the 1960s* (New York: Hill and Wang, 1994), 156–160; May, *Golden State, Golden Youth*, 139–156; and David Bruner, *Making Peace with the 60s* (Princeton, NJ: Princeton University Press, 1996), 136.
17. Jeff Tamarkin, *Got a Revolution! The Turbulent Flight of Jefferson Airplane* (New York: Atria Books, 2003), 206–207.
18. Elijah Wald, *How the Beatles Destroyed Rock 'n' Roll: An Alternative History of American Popular Music* (New York: Oxford University Press, 2009), 230.
19. Roy Shuker, *Understanding Popular Music Culture* (London: Routledge, 2008), 77–78; Theodore Roszak, "The Counter Culture: Part I—Youth and the Great Refusal," *Nation*, March 25, 1968, 405.
20. Andy Neill and Matt Kent, *Anyway, Anyhow, Anywhere: The Complete Chronicle of the Who, 1958–1978* (London: Virgin Books, 2007), 69, 177–178.
21. Richard Goldstein, "The New Rock: Wiggy Words That Feed Your Mind," *Life*, June 28, 1968, 68. See also "Psychedelic Generation Gap," KRON- TV News (San Francisco), https://diva.sfsu.edu/collections/sfbatv/bundles/189594, circa 1968, accessed October 29, 2015; Bob Stanley, *Yeah Yeah Yeah: The Story of Modern Pop* (London: Faber and Faber, 2013), 223–236; and George Lipsitz, "Who'll Stop the Rain? Youth Culture, Rock 'n' Roll, and Social Crises," in *The Sixties: From Memory to History*, ed. David Farber (Chapel Hill: University of North Carolina Press, 1994), 206–234.
22. "There Will Never Be a Gap Gap," *Life*, June 7, 1968, 6.
23. William Safire, *Safire's Political Dictionary* (New York: Oxford University Press, 2008), 274. Also see Grace Hechinger and Fred Hechinger, *Teen-Age Tyranny* (New York: Crest Books, 1964), 191–194.
24. Because rock as a relatively distinct genre dates to the mid-1950s, the late 1960s emergence of Christian rock came after waves of development: the southern dominance of early rock, the teen crooners of the late 1950s, the surf craze, girl groups, the British invasion, and Motown and soul. For more on the generation gap, see Enid A. Haupt,

"Friends Bridge Generation Gap," *Washington Post*, January 10, 1965, F27; Richard Lorber and Ernest Fladell, "The Generation Gap," *Life*, May 17, 1968, 81–82, 85–86, 88–92; Ralph E. Prouty, "Teenese, Anyone?" *Columbia*, March 1966, 31–32; Bone, *The Disinherited Children*; Rebecca E. Klatch, *A Generation Divided: The New Left, the New Right, and the 1960s* (Berkeley: University of California Press, 1999); Peter Braunstein, "Forever Young: Insurgent Youth and the Sixties Culture of Rejuvenation," in *Imagine Nation: The American Counterculture of the 1960s and 1970s*, ed. Peter Braunstein and Michael William Doyle (New York: Routledge, 2002), 243–274; Axel R. Schäfer, *Countercultural Conservatives: American Evangelicalism from the Postwar Revival to the New Christian Right* (Madison: University of Wisconsin Press, 2011), 99; and Eileen Luhr, *Witnessing Suburbia: Conservatives and Christian Youth Culture* (Berkeley: University of California Press, 2009), 75–77. The historian Thomas E. Bergler writes, "The sixties first revealed what would be the consequences of various Christian approaches to youth culture. Some ways of managing juvenilization were nimble enough to adapt to the seismic shifts of the sixties; others were overly dependent upon the old era that was rapidly disappearing. The times revealed who would be the winners and losers when it came to motivating teenage religious commitment in the decades to come." Thomas E. Bergler, *The Juvenilization of American Christianity* (Grand Rapids, MI: Eerdmans, 2012), 177, and see 176.

25. Ed Tywoniak, "The Whole World Is Watching: The SDS and the Student Movement of the 1960s," in *Baby Boomers and Popular Culture: An Inquiry into America's Most Powerful Generation*, ed. Brian Cogan and Thom Gencarelli (Santa Barbara, CA: ABC-CLIO, 2015), 17–18.
26. Bruner, *Making Peace with the 60s*, 136.
27. Theodore Roszak, *The Making of a Counter Culture: Reflections on the Technocratic Society and Its Youthful Opposition* (Garden City, NY: Doubleday, 1969).
28. Henry Fairlie, "How Is Youth to Be Served?" *New Republic*, April 8, 1967, 12.
29. Roszak, "The Counter Culture: Part I," 404.
30. "Twenty-Five and Under, Man of the Year," *Time*, January 6, 1967, 17–18. See also John Poppy, "The Generation Gap," *Look*, February 21, 1967, 26–32; and Kenneth Crawford, "Generation Gap," *Newsweek*, March 13, 1967, 48.
31. Clayton Fritchey, "Generation Gap Is Always with Us, But Now It Is Much More Pronounced," *Toledo (OH) Blade*, April 18, 1967, 14.
32. Phil Landrum, "Today's Teenagers . . . Another Lost Generation?" *Moody Monthly* (Chicago), June 1965, 16.
33. "The Generation Gap," *Lawrence (KS) Journal-World*, November 22, 1966, 4. See also Margaret Mead's comments on the generation gap in Marian McBride, "Generation Gap Explored," *Milwaukee Sentinel*, October 9, 1969, 7.
34. W. T. Purkiser, "Editorially Speaking: Generation Gap—Not One but Two," *Herald of Holiness* (Kansas City, MO), January 29, 1969, 10.
35. Richard Nixon, "425—Address to the Nation on the War in Vietnam," http://www.presidency.ucsb.edu/ws/index.php?pid=2303&st=&st1=, November 3, 1969, accessed October 28, 2015.
36. David Farber, "The Silent Majority and Talk about Revolution," in Farber, *The Sixties*, 291–316.
37. Daniel K. Williams, "Richard Nixon's Religious Right," in *The Right Side of the Sixties: Reexamining Conservatism's Decade of Transformation*, ed. Laura Jane Gifford and Daniel K. Williams (New York: Palgrave Macmillan, 2012), 151. Also see Steven

P. Miller, *Billy Graham and the Rise of the Republican South* (Philadelphia: University of Pennsylvania Press, 2009).

38. Willis Snowbarger, "Campus Commentary: Generation Gap," *Herald of Holiness* (Kansas City, MO), December 6, 1967, 16.
39. Leslie Parrott, "A Look at the Generation Gap," *Herald of Holiness* (Kansas City, MO), April 3, 1968, 12–13. See also Mary H. Augsbury, "On Narrowing the Generation Gap," *Herald of Holiness*, August 7, 1968, 3–4; and Eugene L. Stowe, "Bridging the Generation Gap," *Herald of Holiness*, January 29, 1969, 2.
40. W. A. Criswell, "Our Acceptance before God," sermon preached at First Baptist Church in Dallas, Texas, October 26, 1969, https://www.wacriswell.com/sermons/1969/our-acceptance-before-god/, accessed December 2, 2015.
41. Billy James Hargis, *Billy James Hargis Speaks Out on the Issues!* (Tulsa, OK: Christian Crusade Publications, 1971), 3, and see 4–9.
42. W. T. Purkiser, "Editorially Speaking: The *Now* Generation," *Herald of Holiness* (Kansas City, MO), April 19, 1967, 15–16.
43. John D. Black, "U.S. 'Generation Gap' Widened by Conflicts in Modern Society," *Los Angeles Times*, November 20, 1966, F1, 3. See also Walt Dutton, "Attempt to Bridge the Generation Gap," *Los Angeles Times*, August 30, 1967, 14.
44. Karl H. Brevik, "A Generation of Gaps," *Baptist Student* (Nashville, TN), October 1969, 32.
45. Newman Cryer, "New Study Materials for Switched-On Youth," *Together* (Nashville, TN), September 1968, 47–48. For similar discussions, see Harry C. Meserve, "The Generation Gap," *Journal of Religion and Health* 6, no. 4 (October 1967): 255–258; Joseph T. Bayly, "A Word to the Now Generation," *Eternity* (Philadelphia), March 1967, 45–46; Merton P. Strommen, "I Can't Get Close to My Young People," *Eternity*, October 1966, 20–22; "Letters: On Youth," *Eternity*, December 1966, 4; Thomas J. Mullen, "New-Breed vs. Old-Breed Christians: Can We Bridge the Gap?" *Together*, April 1969, 18–23; Marilou Jacobsen, "There Is Supposed to Be a Generation Gap," *Home Life* (Nashville, TN), January 1969, 24–25; Marlene A. Hess, "Let's Span the Generation Gap," *Moody Monthly* (Chicago), June 1969, 30–31; James H. Jackson, "The Church and Its Youth: A Crisis of Alienation," *Herald of Holiness* (Kansas City, MO), April 16, 1969, 3–4; and Gordon R. McClean, "The Generation Gap," *King's Business* (Los Angeles), February 1970, 14–15.
46. Gerard J. DeGroot, "The Culture of Protest: An Introductory Essay," in *Student Protest: The Sixties and After*, ed. Gerard J. DeGroot (London: Routledge, 1998), 8.
47. Anthony J. Dosen, *Catholic Higher Education in the 1960s: Issues of Identity, Issues of Governance* (Charlotte, NC: Information Age, 2009), 226, 235; Philip G. Altbach, Robert O. Berdahl, and Patricia J. Gumport, eds., *American Higher Education in the Twenty-First Century: Social, Political, and Economic Challenges* (Baltimore, MD: Johns Hopkins University Press, 2005); Julie A. Reuben, "Reforming the University: Student Protests and the Demand for a Relevant Curriculum," in DeGroot, *Student Protest*, 153–168.
48. David A. Hubbard, "Big Smoke, No Fire: Why the Younger Generation Is Coughing," *Eternity* (Philadelphia), November 1966, 20. See also *Methodist Laymen of North Hollywood Newsletter* no. 72, August 22, 1967, "Jesus Movement," G. Archer Weniger Collection, Bob Jones University.
49. Marshall McLuhan, *Understanding Media: The Extension of Man* (London: Routledge, 2005), 366 (italics in the original).

50. Stephen L. Talbott, "Pop Music: What's It Really Saying," *Eternity* (Philadelphia), June 1968, 21, 41.
51. "Can the Church Reach the Teens of '65? An Interview with Bill Eakin," *Moody Monthly* (Chicago), June 1965, 18, 19, 20.
52. *Methodist Laymen of North Hollywood Newsletter*, "The Church's Guilt in the Generation Gap," no. 109, September 1970, "Jesus Movement," G. Archer Weniger Collection, Bob Jones University.
53. Stephen R. Kandall, *Substance and Shadow: Women and Addiction in the United States* (Cambridge, MA: Harvard University Press, 1996), 161. George Gallup, "The Gallup Poll: Today's Student New Breed in 6 Respects," *Los Angeles Times*, May 26, 1969, A6; "U. of Md. Study Finds Use of Marijuana Up," *Washington Post*, December 6, 1971, B1, B8; George Gallup, "The Gallup Poll: 51% of U.S. College Students Have Tried Marijuana," *Baltimore Sun*, February 6, 1972, A13; "Gallup Finds Rise in Marijuana Use: 51% of College Students Say They Have Tried It," *New York Times*, February 6, 1972, 36N; Linda Charlton, "Gallup Finds a Continued Rise in Use of Marijuana and LSD on Campuses," *New York Times*, February 10, 1972, 16.
54. L. Dana Gatlin, "Crackdown Points Up U.S. Drug-Abuse Increase," *Christian Science Monitor*, March 24, 1966, 18. See also Fred M. Hechinger, "Education: Drugs Threat on Campus," *New York Times*, April 10, 1966, 151; James D. Dilts, "A Cheap 'High': Pep Pills 'Way of Life' to Thousands," *Baltimore Sun*, February 27, 1966, D1; Klaus P. Fischer, *America in White, Black, and Gray: A History of the Stormy 1960s* (New York: Continuum, 2006), 302–312; Samuel Grafton, "Our New Drug Addicts," *Christian Reader* (Wheaton, IL), August–September 1965, 16–20; David Wilkerson, "Marijuana—High Road to Nowhere," *Christian Reader*, June–July 1968, 5–8; and John Mann, *Turn On and Tune In: Psychedelics, Narcotics, and Euphoriants* (London: Royal Society of Chemistry, 2009), 86–92.
55. Raymond L. Cox, "The Great Delusion," *Christian Life* (Chicago), November 1966, 54, 68–70.
56. Thomas Howard, "Christ and the Psychedelic Vision," *Eternity* (Philadelphia), May 1967, 26–28. See also Bruce A. Baker, "LSD and the Christian Mind," *Eternity*, December 1966, 25–26, 38; and Iris Michele, "I Tried LSD," *Christian Reader* (Wheaton, IL), October–November 1966, 9–12.
57. "The New Far-Out Beatles: They're Grown Men Now and Creating Extraordinary Musical Sounds," *Life*, June 16, 1967, 105.
58. Jesse Birnbaum and Christopher Porterfield, "Pop Music: The Messengers," *Time*, September 22, 1967, 60–61, 68.
59. "Beatle McCartney Admits Taking LSD," *Washington Post*, June 18, 1967, D10; Paul McCartney's LSD Tell-All Stirs Brouhaha," *Variety*, June 28, 1967, 1, 60; "Paul McCartney's LSD Caper Draws Blast," *Los Angeles Times*, June 20, 1967, D11; "Beatle Says He Took LSD Four Times: McCartney Feels Drug Helped Him, Refuses to Advocate Use," *Baltimore Sun*, June 19, 1967, A3; Harry Golden, "Only in America: The Beatles Prophecy," *Chicago Daily Defender*, December 20, 1967, 15; William D. Romanowski, *Pop Culture Wars: Religion and the Role of Entertainment in American Life* (Eugene, OR: Wipf and Stock, 2008), 218–220.
60. W. J. Rorabaugh, *American Hippies* (Cambridge: Cambridge University Press, 2015), 68; "Berkeley Hips Warm," *Berkeley Barb*, April 14, 1967, 4.
61. Billy Graham, "My Answer," *Cincinnati Enquirer*, December 9, 1967, 10.
62. Lauren F. Winner, "From Mass Evangelist to Soul Friend," http://www.christianitytoday.com/ct/2000/october2/7.56.html, October 2, 2000, accessed December 3, 2015;

Lane Smith, "Pro Gridder Calls for Christian Goal," *Seattle Times*, May 24, 1967, 63. "LSD Prophet to Appear at Circus," *Times Advertiser* (Trenton, NJ), June 25, 1967, 4.

63. Ronald Reagan, "Cow Palace Speech," May 12, 1966, in "Berkeley in the Sixites [*sic*] Transcript," 32, http://www.newsreel.org/transcripts/berkeley-in-the-60s-transcript.pdf, accessed August 3, 2016.
64. Richard Nixon, "123-Statement on Campus Disorders, March 22, 1969," http://www.presidency.ucsb.edu/ws/?pid=1968, accessed October 1, 2017. See also "An Epidemic of 'Acid Heads,'" http://content.time.com/time/subscriber/article/0,33009,899088,00.html, March 11, 1966, accessed August 3, 2009; "At War with War," *Time*, May 18, 1970, 6–8; and R. Jeffrey Lustig, "The War at Home: California's Struggle to Stop the Vietnam War," in *What's Going On? California and the Vietnam Era*, ed. Marcia A. Eymann and Charles Wollenberg (Berkeley: University of California Press, 2004), 75.
65. Billy Graham, "Billy Graham on Teen-Age Immorality," *Eternity* (Philadelphia), June 1965, 9, 10. For a denunciation of the immorality of rock music, see Vic Erickson, "Stop Look, and Listen to the Words," *Christian Reader* (Wheaton, IL), October–November 1966, 13–16.
66. Preston Shires, *Hippies of the Religious Right* (Waco, TX: Baylor University Press, 2007), 120; "The 'Free' Church of Berkeley's Hippies," *Christian Century*, April 10, 1968, 464–468.
67. Scottie Lanahan, "Swinging Episcopal Pastors Going after What's Happening," *Oregonian* (Portland, OR), June 15, 1967, 11. See also James A. Haught, "Swing: Youth Music Sounds Pour out of Church," *Sunday Gazette-Mail* (Charleston, WV), February 13, 1966, 8A, "Contemporary Christian Music," G. Archer Weniger Collection, Bob Jones University.
68. Francis A. Schaeffer, *How Should We Then Live: The Decline of Western Thought and Culture* (Westchester, IL: Crossway Books, 1976), 163–165, 205, 258. See also Frank Schaeffer, *Crazy for God: How I Grew Up as One of the Elect, Helped Found the Religious Right, and Lived to Take All (or Almost All) of It Back* (New York: Carroll and Graf, 2007), 211, 260; and "L'Abri Fellowship," and "Schaeffer, Francis August," in *Encyclopedia of Evangelicalism*, ed. Randall Balmer (Louisville, KY: Westminster John Knox Press, 2002), 326, 507–508.
69. Roland F. Chase, "Christian Colleges: Isolated or Involved," *Christianity Today* (Carol Stream, IL), September 2, 1966, 13.
70. David Neff, "Remembering Francis Schaeffer," http://www.christianitytoday.com/news/2009/may/remembering-francis-schaeffer.html, May 8, 2009, accessed December 14, 2015. See also Bob Micklin, "Jesus Rock: It's a New Trip for Kids, Musicians," *Tuscaloosa (AL) News*, February 27, 1971, 3.
71. Barry Hankins, *Francis Schaeffer and the Shaping of Evangelical America* (Grand Rapids, MI: Eerdmans, 2008), 62–63, 78; Jeff Sharlet, "Holy Fools," *New Statesman*, October 29, 2007, 52–53. For the cultural changes shaping conservative Protestants in these years, see Mitchell Morris, "Kansas and the Prophetic Tone," *American Music* 18, no. 1 (Spring 2000): 14–18.
72. Preston Rockholt, "Creative Tensions in Church Music," paper presented at the Scholastic Honors Society Convocation, Wheaton College, IL, March 7, 1969, 2, quoted in Donald Paul Ellsworth, *Christian Music in Contemporary Witness: Historical Antecedents and Contemporary Practices* (Grand Rapids, MI: Baker Book House, 1979), 148.
73. Charles W. Keysor, "What Is Pop Music Really Saying?" *Christianity Today* (Carol Stream, IL), December 23, 1966, 24, 25. See also Jesse Burt, "Why Do Youngsters Like

That Music?" *Home Life* (Nashville, TN), April 1969, 23–24; "Dear Vonda Kay," *Christian Life* (Chicago), September 1969, 20; and Wilfred J. Martin, "Parents and Rock Music," *Eternity* (Philadelphia), April 1971, 22–24.

74. Lincoln B. Justice, "Prophets with Guitars," *Hymn* 19 (January 1968): 13–14. See also David W. Music, *Christian Hymnody in Twentieth-Century Britain and America: An Annotated Bibliography* (Westport, CT: Greenwood Press, 2001), 6, 37–40; and "Rock Gets Boost from 3 Stations," *Billboard*, September 19, 1970, 46.

75. James H. Vail, "Values in Church Music: A Reassessment," *Choral Journal* 12, no. 2 (October 1971): 10. See also Phillip Landgrave, "Church Music and the 'Now Generation,'" *Review and Expositor* (Spring 1972): 195–198. On the changing shape of pentecostal worship music, see Margaret M. Poloma, *Main Street Mystics: The Toronto Blessing and Reviving Pentecostalism* (Walnut Creek, CA: AltaMira Press, 2003), 37–48.

76. Howard D. McKinney, "Winds of Change," in *Opinions on Church Music: Comments and Reports from Four-and-a-Half Centuries*, ed. Elwyn Arthur Wienandt (Waco, TX: Markham Press Fund of Baylor University Press, 1974), 183.

77. On the Jesus movement and the generation gap, see Sean McCloud, *Making the American Religious Fringe: Exotics, Subversives, and Journalists, 1955–1993* (Chapel Hill: University of North Carolina Press, 2004), 117–122. For cover designs and illustrations for 1966–1973, see *Moody Monthly, Herald of Holiness, Home Life, Christian Life, Together, Baptist Student*, and *Motive*.

78. Cover of *Lutheran Witness* (St. Louis, MO), December 1966; "Letters: Circus Clown," "Deplorable and Vulgar," and "Grotesque and Offensive," *Lutheran Witness*, February 1967, 23.

79. Billy Graham, *The Jesus Generation* (Grand Rapids, MI: Zondervan, 1971).

80. "Billy Graham," *St. Petersburg Independent*, September 21, 1972, 8A. See also "Graham Goes Long Hair," *Eugene (OR) Register-Guard*, June 23, 1970, 4A; and Louis Cassels, *Haircuts and Holiness: Discussion Starters for Religious Encounter Groups* (Nashville, TN: Abingdon Press, 1972), 13–15.

81. For the marketing of Christian products with late 1960s and 1970s design sensibilities, see Colleen McDannell, *Material Christianity: Religion and Popular Culture in America* (New Haven, CT: Yale University Press, 1995), 248–256; and Paul C. Gutjahr, "The Bible-zine *Revolve* and the Evolution of the Culturally Relevant Bible in America," in *Religion and the Culture of Print in Modern America*, ed. Charles L. Cohen and Paul S. Boyer (Madison: University of Wisconsin Press, 2008), 338, 340.

82. Richard Groves, "The Message in Modern Pop Music: Are Christians Alert to a New Avenue of Witness?" *Christianity Today* (Carol Stream, IL), June 23, 1967, 5–6.

83. William J. Petersen, "O, What a Fantastic New Day for Christian Music," *Eternity* (Philadelphia), April 1971, 12, 13.

84. Don Cusic, *The Sound of Light: A History of Gospel and Christian Music* (Milwaukee, WI: Hal Leonard, 2002), 274–275; Mark Oppenheimer, "Folk Music in the Catholic Mass," in *Religions of the United States in Practice*, ed. Colleen McDannell (Princeton, NJ: Princeton University Press, 2001), 2:103–111; Mark S. Massa, *The American Catholic Revolution: How the Sixties Changed the Church Forever* (New York: Oxford University Press, 2010), 26–27; Michael P. Hornsby-Smith, *The Changing Parish: A Study of Parishes, Priests, and Parishioners after Vatican II* (London: Routledge, 1989), 111; Stephen Marini, *Sacred Song in America: Religion, Music, and Public Culture* (Urbana: University of Illinois Press, 2003), 251–253; Don Cusic, "Catholics and Contemporary Christian Music," in *Encyclopedia of Contemporary Christian Music: Pop, Rock, and Worship*, ed. Don Cusic (Santa Barbara, CA: Greenwood Press, 2010), 45–47.

85. Paul Baker, "Setting the Good Word to Modern Music," *Billboard*, July 28, 1979, R4.
86. "Bach, Folk Guitar for Mass," *Catholic Voice*, January 31, 1968, 2; "A Jazz Messiah," n.p., November 22, 1967; Russ Wilson, "'Jazz Mass' Rule Raises Question," *Oakland (CA) Herald Tribune*, March 12, 1967, 7EN, "Contemporary Christian Music," G. Archer Weniger Collection, Bob Jones University. See also Don Hustad, "Gospel Folk Music Is 'In,'" *Eternity* (Philadelphia), August 1967, 35–36; and circular letter, "Dr. Billy Graham's Observations . . . More Jazz Masses," circa 1967, "Contemporary Christian Music," G. Archer Weniger Collection, Bob Jones University; "Preacher and Wife in Night Clubs While Youth Jazzes up Church Hymns," *Western Voice* (Fort Worth, TX), April 4, 1968, 1.
87. "Quiet Revolt in Gospel Music," *Christianity Today* (Carol Stream, IL), November 5, 1965, 52–54; Bryan Gilbert, "Folk Singing: Are You with It?" *Christian Life* (Chicago), July 1967, 22, 42; Bob Flood, "The New Folk Uprising," *Moody Monthly* (Chicago), March 1967, 90–93.
88. Mary Reed Newland, "Rock, Music, Books, the Draft," *Ave Maria* (Notre Dame, IN), March 21, 1970, 23.
89. "Religion and Jazz," *Alabama Baptist* (Birmingham), October 22, 1959, 3. See also "An Abomination," *Alabama Baptist*, November 8, 1956, 3; and Donald P. Hustad, "Jazz in the Church," *Eternity* (Philadelphia), April 19, 1966, 36–38. For disagreements and debates among Methodists, see William C. Rice, "To Worry or Not to Worry: The Question about Jazz," *Christian Advocate* (Nashville, TN), April 25, 1963, 13; "Jazz Communion Services," *Together* (Nashville, TN), June 1966, 10; Helen Johnson, "Worship in the Round," *Together*, August 1966, 26–28; and "Worship in Round: Ridiculous," *Together*, November 1966, 71–72.
90. Lester Kinsolving, "The Jazz Mass Movement," *San Francisco Chronicle*, March 26, 1966, n.p., "Contemporary Christian Music," G. Archer Weniger Collection, Bob Jones University.
91. Jason C. Bivins, *Spirits Rejoice! Jazz and American Religion* (New York: Oxford University Press, 2015), 11, 156–164.
92. "Putting It on Record," *Crusade*, July 1965, 18–19; "Onward Christian Soldiers," *Crusade*, May 1965, 14–15; "Juke Box to Quiet Choir," *Milwaukee Sentinel*, December 8, 1959, 1; Tom A. Cullen, "British Churches Using Gimmicks," *Victoria (TX) Advocate*, October 4, 1961, 4.
93. The Crusaders, *Make a Joyful Noise with Drums and Guitars* (Hollywood, CA: Tower, 1966), LP. Zondervan Records issued a Christian pop, rock, and folk record by a group called Sons of Thunder in 1968. John Joseph Thompson, *Raised by Wolves: The Story of Christian Rock and Roll* (Toronto: ECW Press, 2000), 43.
94. "'Rock Mass' Premiere at Church Here," *San Francisco Chronicle*, May 30, 1967, n.p., "Contemporary Christian Music," G. Archer Weniger Collection, Bob Jones University.
95. Brock Lucas, "Florida's Youth Ranches Roundup for Religion," *St. Petersburg Times*, August 14, 1965, 6–7; Alpha LaForce, "Holy Rock 'n' Rollers!" *Independent Star-News* (Pasadena, CA), October 23, 1966, 22, "Contemporary Christian Music," G. Archer Weniger Collection, Bob Jones University; Loren Chudy, "Religion Has a Teen's Touch," *St. Petersburg Independent*, July 16, 1966, 7A. For more on 1960s and 1970s experiments with sacred pop music, see Ellsworth, *Christian Music in Contemporary Witness*, 123–145. For similar developments, see Leslie Stobbe, "Hootenanny with a Twist," *Christian Life* (Chicago), March 1964, 44; "A Club for Teens," *Together* (Nashville, TN), December 1964, 51–53; Mary Fortson, "'Coffee House' in Church's Gym a Beatnik

Haven for a Night," *Atlanta Constitution*, March 5, 1966, 7; and "In Atlanta . . . a Coffeehouse," *Together*, October 1968, 38–39.

96. "Rebels with a Cause," *Bremerton (WA) Sun*, July 23, 1966, n.p., "Contemporary Christian Music," G. Archer Weniger Collection, Bob Jones University. On early fusions of folk and evangelicalism, see Eskridge, *God's Forever Family*, 211–212.

97. "5th Sunday after Trinity," Riffs, *Village Voice*, July 24, 1968, http://www.mindgarage.com/voice.html, accessed May 11, 2016.

98. "Demonstration Pilot: Powerline," "Powerline, 1–29, 1969," n.p., Southern Baptist Historical Library and Archives, Nashville, TN; Jim Anderson, *Powerline* pamphlet (Fort Worth, TX: Southern Baptist's Radio and Television Commission, n.d.), "Powerline: Radio and TV, 1970," n.p., Southern Baptist Historical Library and Archives, Nashville, TN. See also Alvin L. Reid, "The Impact of the Jesus Movement on Evangelism among Southern Baptists" (Ph.D. diss., Southwestern Baptist Theological Seminary, 1991), 12–37.

99. Clarence Duncan, "The Radio and Television Commission," in *Encyclopedia of Southern Baptists*, ed. Davis Collier Woolley (Nashville, TN: Broadman Press, 1971), 3:1933; Patsy Guenzel, "Powerline," *Ambassador Life*, December 1970, 8–10; Nat Freedland, "Top Show Ties Rock, Religion," *Billboard*, April 15, 1972, 20. For a similar Catholic radio effort, see "Radio Priest Uses 'Rock-Chat-Roll,'" *Sarasota (FL) Herald Tribune*, February 1, 1973, 5B.

100. John Wigger, *PTL: The Rise and Fall of Jim and Tammy Faye Bakker's Evangelical Empire* (New York: Oxford University Press, 2017), 30–31; Stowe, *No Sympathy for the Devil*, 182; Paul Baker, *Why Should the Devil Have All the Good Music?* (Waco, TX: Word Books, 1979), 76; "Religious Radio Programs," *Billboard*, April 15, 1972, 23. For an advertisement for *The Scott Ross Show*, see *Billboard*, August 18, 1973, 23. Also see "Letters to the Editor: Love Lines," *Billboard*, May 27, 1972, 6; Gil Faggen, "Vox Jox," *Billboard*, April 3, 1965; and Scott Ross, *Scott Free*, with John L. Sherrill and Elizabeth Sherrill (Lincoln, VA: Chosen Books, 1976); and "Religion on 130 Stations: Black New Ross Show Host," *Billboard*, January 29, 1977.

101. "'Hallelujahs' Resound at the Assemblies' Session," *Milwaukee Journal*, August 27, 1953, 1. See also "Melody Makers to Sing at Two Services of First Pentecostal," *Ocala (FL) Star-Banner*, October 2, 1959, 6. "The music which arose from and which reflects the Pentecostal environment and belief of necessity is less liturgical in its style," reflected one insider in the late 1960s. "It is more personal in its expression and is emphatically spirited and spiritual in its attitude of performance. Consequently, it is somewhat different in sound and concept from musical expressions of other areas of church history." Delton L. Alford, *Music in the Pentecostal Church* (Cleveland, TN: Pathway Press, 1967), 18.

102. Carl Brumback, *Suddenly . . . from Heaven* (Springfield, MO: Gospel Publishing House, 1961), 136. See also Frank Chester Masserano, "A Study of Worship Forms in the Assemblies of God Denomination" (master's thesis, Princeton Theological Seminary, 1966), 66–67; and Darrel Keith Johnson, "A Study of the Present-Day Music Practices in the Assemblies of God" (master's thesis, University of Southern California, 1972), 2–7.

103. The cultural history and religious studies scholar David Stowe put it quite simply, "To save hippies, inspiring music was needed." Stowe, *No Sympathy for the Devil*, 26.

104. Maurice Allan, "God's Thing in Hippieville," *Christian Life* (Chicago), January 1968, 21, 37. See also David DiSabatino, "The Spiritual Sixties and the Jesus People Move-

ment," *Refleks* 4, no. 2 (2005): 17–48; and David DiSabatino, "The Birth of Jesus Music," *Refleks* 4, no. 2 (2005): 49–52.

105. Earl C. Gottschalk, "Hip Cultures Discover a New Trip: Fervent, Foot-Stompin' Religion. 'Jesus Freaks' Quit Revolution, Drugs for Fundamentalism; They Offend & Anger Some," *Wall Street Journal*, March 2, 1971, 1.

106. Fulton J. Sheen, "Jesus People and the Churches," *New York Times*, August 8, 1971, E11.

107. Randall Stephens, "The Genesis of Jesus Rock: An Interview with David W. Stowe," http://usreligion.blogspot.co.uk/2011/12/genesis-of-jesus-rock-interview-with.html, December 28, 2011, accessed July 18, 2013. For early Christian rock music and Calvary Chapel, see Eskridge, *God's Forever Family*, 218–220.

108. Eskridge, *God's Forever Family*, 218–229; Baker, *Why Should the Devil Have All the Good Music?*, 23–29. For Mormon explorations of rock music in the late 1960s and early 1970s, see Stephen A. Marini, *Sacred Song in America: Religion, Music, and Public Culture* (Urbana: University of Illinois Press, 2003), 235–236.

109. Kelly Muhonen, "Guide to the Pederson, Duane, Jesus People International, and *Hollywood Free Paper* Collection," 2012, David Allan Hubbard Library Archives, Fuller Theological Seminary, http://pdf.oac.cdlib.org/pdf/cpft/pederson_duane_jesus_people_international_and_hollywood_free_paper_collection.pdf, accessed May 28, 2015.

110. Shires, *Hippies of the Religious Right*, 105; John Dart, "'Jesus People' Adopt Underground's Tactics: Free Newspaper with Circulation of 200,000 Promotes Youth Evangelism," *Los Angeles Times*, January 2, 1971, 26. For more on the *Hollywood Free Paper* and Christian rock concerts, see the *Hollywood Free Paper*, November 18, 1969; December 2, 1969; December 16, 1969; and January 6, 1970; "Duane Pederson Jesus People Collection," collection 66, box 4, Archives and Special Collections, Fuller Theological Seminary. See also Duane Pederson, *Larger than Ourselves: The Early Beginnings of the Jesus People*, with Mark Dixon (Hollywood, CA: Hollywood Free Paper, 2014).

111. Eskridge, *God's Forever Family*, 111–113; W. T. Purkiser, "Editorially Speaking: The Jesus Revolution," *Herald of Holiness* (Kansas City, MO), September 15, 1971, 15–16.

112. Charles Millhuff, "A Firsthand Account of the New Milford Revival," *Herald of Holiness* (Kansas City, MO), September 29, 1971, 23.

113. "Door Chat: Freddie 'Fab' Frakowski," *Wittenburg Door* (San Diego, CA), April–May 1979, 39; William D. Romanowski, "Roll Over Beethoven, Tell Martin Luther the News: American Evangelicals and Rock Music," *Journal of American Culture* 15, no. 3 (September 1992): 79–88.

114. Quoted in Schulman, *The Seventies*, 151–152.

115. For more on early Christian rock artists, see Mark Joseph, *The Rock and Roll Rebellion: Why People of Faith Abandoned Rock Music and Why They're Coming Back* (Nashville, TN: Broadman and Holman, 1999), 22–46; Andrae Crouch, *Through It All*, with Nina Ball (Waco, TX: Word Books, 1974); and Howard and Streck, *Apostles of Rock*, 24–31.

116. Cliff Richard, "Pop Singer Finds the Answer," *Christian Reader* (Wheaton, IL), April–May 1969, 37–40; Stanley, *Yeah Yeah Yeah*, 78, 124–125.

117. "God, Me, and My Guitar: Insights from Five Christian Musicians," *His*, January 1979, 17, "Entertainers, Christian," G. Archer Weniger Collection, Bob Jones University.

118. Steve Turner, *Hungry for Heaven: Rock 'n' Roll and the Search for Redemption* (Downers Grove, IL: InterVarsity Press, 1995), 164; "About Larry Norman," http://www.larrynorman.com/about.html, February 25, 2008, accessed December 11, 2015;

Don Cusic, "Larry Norman," in Cusic, *Encyclopedia of Contemporary Christian Music*, 311–313.

119. Howard and Streck, *Apostles of Rock*, 162–163; Stowe, *No Sympathy for the Devil*, 34–40.
120. Joseph, *The Rock and Roll Rebellion*, 57–58.
121. "God, Me, and My Guitar," 18.
122. Lee Burton, "Barry McGuire: Pied Piper to Kids," *Christian Life* (Chicago), November 1977, 32–33, "Entertainers, Christian," G. Archer Weniger Collection, Bob Jones University.
123. "Meet Barry McGuire," *Wittenburg Door* (San Diego, CA), April–May 1971, 3–5.
124. Joseph, *The Rock and Roll Rebellion*, 58–59. Howard and Streck, *Apostles of Rock*, 31.
125. "Honeytree," in *Encyclopedia of Contemporary Christian Music*, ed. Mark Allan Powell (Peabody, MA: Hendrickson, 2002), 421–422.
126. For a description of one festival—the 1971 Jesus, the Solid Rock festival—see Cal Farnham, Mission Department, First Presbyterian Church, Berkeley, CA, promotion letter, April 12, 1971, "Jesus Movement," G. Archer Weniger Collection, Bob Jones University. For the rise of Christian bookstores, see McDannell, *Material Christianity*, 246–247; Heather Hendershot, *Shaking the World for Jesus: Media and Conservative Evangelical Culture* (Chicago: University of Chicago Press, 2004), 21–25; and Todd M. Brenneman, *Homespun Gospel: The Triumph of Sentimentality in Contemporary American Evangelicalism* (New York: Oxford University Press, 2014), 83, 87.
127. "The Jesus People," in *The Religious Reawakening in America*, ed. Joseph Newman (Washington, DC: U.S. News and World Report, 1972), 31.
128. Ellwood, *One Way*, 63–64.
129. Margaret M. Poloma and John C. Green, *The Assemblies of God: Godly Love and the Revitalization of American Pentecostalism* (New York: New York University Press, 2010), 3. See also Young, *Gray Sabbath*, 139–141.
130. "Spirit and Power: A 10-Country Survey of Pentecostals," http://www.pewforum.org/2006/10/05/spirit-and-power/, October 5, 2006, accessed September 25, 2017.
131. Grant Wacker, *Heaven Below: Early Pentecostals and American Culture* (Cambridge, MA: Harvard University Press, 2001); Edith Blumhofer, *Restoring the Faith: The Assemblies of God, Pentecostalism, and American Culture* (Urbana: University of Illinois Press, 1993); Grant Wacker, "The Functions of Faith in Primitive Pentecostalism," *Harvard Theological Review* 77, no. 3 (1984): 355, 356, 363; D. William Faupel, "The Restoration Vision in Pentecostalism," *Christian Century*, October 17, 1990, 938; D. William Faupel, *The Everlasting Gospel: The Significance of Eschatology in the Development of Pentecostal Thought* (Sheffield, UK: Sheffield Academic Press, 1996); Donald Dayton, *Theological Roots of Pentecostalism* (Metuchen, NJ: Scarecrow Press, 1987).
132. Louis Cassels, "Pentecostals Have Fast Growth Rate," *Lodi (CA) News-Sentinel*, April 26, 1969, 4.
133. Roger G. Robins, *A. J. Tomlinson: Plainfolk Modernist* (New York: Oxford University Press, 2004), 5; Tona J. Hangen, *Redeeming the Dial: Radio, Religion and Popular Culture in America* (Chapel Hill: University of North Carolina Press, 2001); Shayne Lee and Phillip Luke Sinitiere, *Holy Mavericks: Evangelical Innovators and the Spiritual Marketplace* (New York: New York University Press, 2009).
134. The historian of pentecostalism R. G. Robins observes that although the Jesus people movement had many sources, "like the charismatic movement before it, the Jesus People movement attested to the growing ability of Pentecostalism to influence its

wider culture. In its frank supernaturalism, its primitivist urges to restore apostolic Christianity, its millenarian expectation, and its Spirit-centered openness to tongues, healing, and other charismatic gifts, the Jesus People movement bore the telltale imprint of Pentecostalism." R. G. Robins, *Pentecostalism in America* (Santa Barbara, CA: Greenwood Press, 2010), 99, and see 96–99. See also Eskridge, *God's Forever Family*, 76–80; Stowe, *No Sympathy for the Devil*, 25; and Poloma and Green, *The Assemblies of God*, 2–3.

135. "The New Rebel Cry: Jesus Is Coming!" *Time*, June 21, 1971, 59. Also see Mike Goodman, "'Jesus People' Protest Drug Use, Register as Republicans," *Los Angeles Times*, April 11, 1972, D1; and Ruben Ortega, ed., *The Jesus People Speak Out! What Do They Really Believe?* (London: Hodder and Stoughton, 1972), 38–54, 65–76, 98–99, 124.
136. Glenn D. Kittler, *The Jesus Kids and Their Leaders* (New York: Warner Paperback Library, 1972), 71. See also Eskridge, *God's Forever Family*, 85–86; Thompson, *Raised by Wolves*, 49; Randall J. Stephens and Karl Giberson, *The Anointed: Evangelical Truth in a Secular Age* (Cambridge, MA: Belknap Press of Harvard University Press, 2011), 153–155.
137. Ronald M. Enroth, Edward E. Ericson, and C. Breckinridge Peters, *The Jesus People: Old-Time Religion in the Age of Aquarius* (Grand Rapids, MI: Eerdmans, 1972), 194–206. For the prevalence of end-times popular theology in early Jesus rock, see Young, *Gray Sabbath*, 141–143. Hal Lindsey, *The Late Great Planet Earth* (Grand Rapids, MI: Zondervan, 1970).
138. Gottschalk, "Hip Cultures Discover a New Trip," 1.
139. "Letter 158: to Thomas Bonfield, 1971?" in *The John Lennon Letters*, ed. Hunter Davies (New York: Little, Brown, 2012), 230.
140. T. M. Luhrmann, "Blinded by the Right? How Hippie Christians Begat Evangelical Conservatives," *Harper's Magazine*, April 2013, 40; David W. Stowe, "Jesus Christ Rock Star," http://www.nytimes.com/2011/04/24/opinion/24Stowe.html, April 23, 2011, accessed June 30, 2017.
141. Dean M. Kelley, *Why Conservative Churches Are Growing: A Study in Sociology of Religion* (Macon, GA: Mercer University Press, 1986), xviii, xxii, 78–81 109–111, 117–124. See also Hugh McLeod, *The Religious Crisis of the 1960s* (Oxford: Oxford University Press, 2007), 137–140, 207–212.
142. Young, *Gray Sabbath*, 174. For more on changes to music and practice in evangelical churches, see Stella Sai-Chun Lau, *Popular Music in Evangelical Youth Culture* (New York: Routledge, 2012), 28–40; and Jon Bialecki, "After the Denominozoic: Evolution, Differentiation, Denominationalism," *Anthropological Research* 55, no. S10 (December 2014): S193–S204.
143. "Rockin' with the First Amendment," *Nation*, October 24, 1987, 444. See also the "Contemporary Christian Music," and "Jesus People" folders of the G. Archer Weniger Collection, Bob Jones University; and Anna Nekola, "'More than Just a Music': Conservative Christian Anti-rock Discourse and the U.S. Culture Wars," *Popular Music* 32, no. 3 (October 2013): 407–426.

Chapter 5

1. "No. 1 Hi Fi Buff," *Billboard*, November 20, 1976, 49; Jimmy Carter, *A Full Life: Reflections at Ninety* (New York: Simon and Schuster, 2015), 62–63.

2. "Carter Hosts Sing at White House; Top Acts Join Picnic," *Variety*, September 12, 1979, 93; Donnie Radcliffe and Hollie I. West, "For the President, an Afternoon of Gospel, a Night on the Emmys," *Washington Post*, September 10, 1979, B1, B9.
3. "The Daily Diary of President Jimmy Carter, September 9, 1979," https://www.jimmycarterlibrary.gov/assets/documents/diary/1979/d090979t.pdf, accessed September 29, 2017. Dave Boyer quoted in "Carter Asks Friends to White House for Afternoon of Gospel Music," *Lakeland (FL) Ledger*, September 10, 1979, 5B; "Joyful Noise at White House," *Pittsburgh Press*, September 10, 1979, 1; "Carters Hosts to 1,000 Gospel Folk," *Billboard*, October 6, 1979, 59; "Carters Play Host to Old-Fashioned Gospel Sing-In," *Montreal Gazette*, September 11, 1979, 49; James R. Goff Jr., *Close Harmony: A History of Southern Gospel* (Chapel Hill: University of North Carolina Press, 2002), 26.
4. "Carter Asks Friends to White House for Afternoon of Gospel Music," 5B. See also David W. Stowe, *No Sympathy for the Devil: Christian Pop Music and the Transformation of American Evangelicalism* (Chapel Hill: University of North Carolina Press, 2011), 190–193; and Janice D. Terrell, "The Growth of Contemporary Christian Music in the Last Ten Years (1973–1983)" (master's thesis, American University, 1984), 81–89.
5. Ray Ruppert, "There's a Message in Today's Music, but Is It Good or Bad?" *Seattle Times*, October 25, 1980, A6.
6. "An Interview with the Lone Ranger of American Fundamentalism," *Christianity Today* (Carol Stream, IL), September 4, 1981, 23. See also "Doctrinal Position," in *Liberty Baptist College Catalog* (Lynchburg, VA: Liberty Baptist College, 1977), 7, Archives and Special Collections, Liberty University. For further defining features and a general background, see Nancy T. Ammerman, "North American Protestant Fundamentalism," in *Media, Culture, and the Religious Right*, ed. Linda Kintz and Julia Lesage (Minneapolis: University of Minnesota Press, 1998), 55–113.
7. "Bob Jones III Says Carter Is No Christian," *Atlanta Constitution*, September 10, 1976, 20A. For the Georgia-based Capricorn Records' support of the Carter campaign, see Larry Rohter, "Rock on the Band Wagon," *Washington Post*, January 21, 1976, B1, B3.
8. For debates about the use of popular music in church that took place among evangelicals and fundamentalists, see Donald Paul Ellsworth, *Christian Music in Contemporary Witness: Historical Antecedents and Contemporary Practices* (Grand Rapids, MI: Baker Book House, 1979), 148, 147–172.
9. George Marsden, *Understanding Fundamentalism and Evangelicalism* (Grand Rapids, MI: Eerdmans, 1991), 1.
10. Frank Newport, "Who Are the Evangelicals?" http://news.gallup.com/poll/17041/who-evangelicals.aspx, June 24, 2005, accessed September 29, 2017; Albert L. Winseman, "U.S. Evangelicals: How Many Walk the Walk?" http://news.gallup.com/poll/16519/US-Evangelicals-How-Many-Walk-Walk.aspx, May 31, 2005, accessed September 29, 2017. Also see "We Poll the Pollster: An Interview with George Gallup Jr."; and "The Christianity Today–Gallup Poll: An Overview," *Christianity Today* (Carol Stream, IL), December 21, 1979, 10–12, 12–15.
11. Richard Quebedeaux, *The Worldly Evangelicals* (New York: Harper and Row, 1978), xi.
12. Ken Briggs, "Jesus Wins, Music Loses," *Newsday* (Long Island, NY), April 11, 1972, 9A.
13. "Religion and Youth," *Dallas Morning News*, September 4, 1972, 2.

14. For the fears harbored about the pentecostal and charismatic dimensions of Christian rock and Jesus people in one religious community in Missoula, Montana, see Charles Wesley Briggs, "Evangelical Transformations: A Historical Study of the Community Covenant Church of Missoula, Montana" (master's thesis, University of Montana, 1978), 1, 41, 114, 157–159, 167, 180.
15. "Bill Bright and the Campus Crusade: The Jesus Movement Spreads," *Atlanta Journal and Constitution*, June 27, 1971, 7D; George R. Pagenz, "Baptism of the Spirit Sneaks up on Many Skeptical Christians," *Pittsburgh Press*, February 22, 1975, 5. See also George W. Cornell, "Charismatic Renewal at Notre Dame: Small Church Order Is Growing Rapidly," *Montreal Gazette*, July 8, 1972, 43.
16. "Oh Happy Day (1969)—Edwin Hawkins Singers," in *Encyclopedia of Great Popular Song Recordings*, ed. Steve Sullivan (Lanham, MD: Scarecrow Press, 2013), 1:409–410.
17. "Religion Now Popular Theme with Devotees of Rock Music," *Sarasota (FL) Herald-Tribune*, February 13, 1971, 10A.
18. Larry Norman, "Who Leads the Arts?" *Christianity Today* (Carol Stream, IL), May 5, 1978, 9. "Religion Now Popular Theme with Devotees of Rock Music," 10A.
19. Paul Boyer, *When Time Shall Be No More: Prophecy Belief in Modern American Culture* (Cambridge, MA: Harvard University Press, 1992), 5; Christian Smith, *Christian America? What Evangelicals Really Want* (Berkeley: University of California Press, 2000), 1; Leo P. Ribuffo, "'Malaise' Revisited: Jimmy Carter and the Crisis of Confidence," in *The Liberal Persuasion: Arthur Schlesinger, Jr., and the Challenge of the American Past*, ed. John Patrick Diggins (Princeton, NJ: Princeton University Press, 1997), 164; Mark A. Noll, Nathan O. Hatch, and George M. Marsden, *The Search for Christian America* (Westchester, IL: Crossway Books, 1983), 14; *Newsweek*, October 26, 1976.
20. Stowe, *No Sympathy for the Devil*, 65. See also Steven P. Miller, *The Age of Evangelicalism: America's Born-Again Years* (New York: Oxford University Press, 2014), 17–31.
21. "The Evolution of Bob Dylan," http://www.rollingstone.com/music/pictures/the-evolution-of-bob-dylan-20110509/born-again-1979-1981-0025636, May 10, 2011, accessed March 15, 2017.
22. Ibid. See also R. Clifton Spargo and Anne K. Ream, "Bob Dylan and Religion," in *The Cambridge Companion to Bob Dylan*, ed. Kevin J. H. Dettmar (Cambridge: Cambridge University Press, 2009), 87–99.
23. Anthony Varesi, *The Bob Dylan Albums: A Critical Study* (Toronto: Guernica, 2004), 147–159; Christopher Ricks, *Bob Dylan's Visions of Sin* (New York: HarperCollins, 2003), 281, 379; Michael J. Gilmour, *Tangled Up in the Bible: Bob Dylan and Scripture* (New York: Continuum, 2004), 79.
24. Ron Rosenbaum, "Born-Again Bob: Four Theories," *New York*, September 24, 1979, 80.
25. Greil Marcus, "Amazing Chutzpah, New West, September 24, 1979," in *Bob Dylan by Greil Marcus: Writings 1968–2010* (New York: Public Affairs, 2010), 95. See also Charles Shaar Murray, "Bob Dylan: Slow Train Coming (CBS)," *New Musical Express*, August 25, 1979.
26. Jann S. Wenner, "Bob Dylan: Slow Train Coming," http://www.rollingstone.com/music/albumreviews/slow-train-coming-19790920, September 20, 1979, accessed March 15, 2017.
27. Jeff Taylor and Chad Israelson, *The Political World of Bob Dylan: Freedom and Justice, Power and Sin* (New York: Palgrave Macmillan, 2015), 84–85; Nigel Halliday, "What Are Dylan's Priorities?" *Third Way* (London), December 1979, 24; David Seay, "With

Spirit and Sales, Rock Gets That Old-Time Religion: A Host of Rock Stars Joins 'Musical Ministries,'" *Chicago Tribune*, October 21, 1979, E12.

28. "Passing Scene," *Humanist*, January–February 1980, 65; "Entertainers, Christian," G. Archer Weniger Collection, Bob Jones University. See also Wayne King, "'Jesus Rock' Now a New Musical Industry," *New York Times*, June 10, 1977, "Contemporary Christian Music," G. Archer Weniger Collection, Bob Jones University. For more on Bob Dylan's born-again phase, see Steve Turner, *Hungry for Heaven: Rock 'n' Roll and the Search for Redemption* (Downers Grove, IL: InterVarsity Press, 1995), 165–172.
29. Tom Wolfe, "The 'Me' Decade and the Third Great Awakening," in *The Purple Decades* (New York: Farrar, Straus and Giroux, 1982), 282–283. See also "Rock Music Held Immoral, Records Burned at Church," newspaper clipping, n.d., n.p., "Rock Music," G. Archer Weniger Collection, Bob Jones University.
30. John Dart, "Jesus Rock Called Clue to Our Time," *Tuscaloosa (AL) News*, February 12, 1971, 3.
31. "The Jesus People," in *The Religious Reawakening in America*, ed. Joseph Newman (Washington, DC: U.S. News and World Report, 1972), 39–40; Miller, *The Age of Evangelicalism*, 18; Tom McNichol, "A 'Spirit' From the '60s That Won't Die," http://www.nytimes.com/2006/12/24/fashion/24norman.html?mcubz=0, December 24, 2006, accessed September 25, 2017.
32. "The New Rebel Cry: Jesus Is Coming!" *Time*, June 21, 1971, 56.
33. Quote from John Smith, "Are You Listening John Lennon?" *Daily Mirror*, September 1, 1971, 14–15. See also "John Penrose, Turn On to Jesus," *Daily Mirror*, September 3, 1971, 5.
34. Thomas Willis, "Records: It Could Be the 'Rock' of Ages," *Chicago Tribune*, November 8, 1970, F1.
35. Richard E. Koenig, "A New 'Star' Has Risen," *Lutheran Witness* (St. Louis, MO), April 1971, 8, 9. See also Larry Eskridge, *God's Forever Family: The Jesus People Movement in America* (Oxford: Oxford University Press, 2013), 126–128; Don Heckman, "Rock, Religion, Jesus Christ and the Moneylenders," *New York Times*, December 26, 1971, D27.
36. Lurma Rackley, "Jesus Christ Superstar: Rock Opera Moves Church Audience," *Evening Star* (Washington, DC), April 5, 1971, n.p.
37. Dalton James, "'Jesus Christ Superstar': Jesus the Freak Meets Black Judas," *Village Voice*, September 16, 1971, 7. See also Stanley Kauffmann, "Jesus Crisis," *New Republic*, November 6, 1971, 24.
38. "The Wrenching Rock Opera, *Jesus Christ Superstar*," *Life*, May 28, 1971, 21; Ron Berler, "The 'Truth' of It Is It's God's Wrath Wrought," *Chicago Tribune*, December 26, 1971, 17.
39. Stowe, *No Sympathy for the Devil*, 41–42; Paul Baker, *Why Should the Devil Have All the Good Music?* (Waco, TX: Word Books, 1979), 53–58.
40. Norman Vincent Peale, "Jesus Christ Superstar," *Lewiston (ME) Daily Sun*, September 11, 1971, 6; Norman Vincent Peale, "Religious Fervor Beats Drug Kicks," *Bangor Daily News*, September 10, 1971, 14.
41. Billy Graham, "Parts of 'Superstar' Seem Sacrilegious," *Atlanta Constitution*, August 21, 1971, 5A. See also "'Superstar': Haunting Questions," *Christianity Today* (Carol Stream, IL), December 4, 1970, 38–39; and James M. Riccitelli, "Testing for Orthodoxy in Our Contemporary Society," *Alliance Witness* (New York), February 16, 1972, 8. For the questions the musical raised, see Steve Renicks, "What Kind of Graduate School?"

Alliance Witness, April 12, 1972, 9; and Herbert Henry Ehrenstein, "'Jesus Christ, Superstar,'" *Eternity* (Philadelphia), January 1971, 35.

42. "'Digs' Rock Opera," *Reading (PA) Eagle*, January 20, 1972, 31.
43. Rodney Bell, "Fundamentalist: Beware of the 'Jesus Movement,'" *Maranatha Baptist Watchman* (Elkton, MD) 6, no. 5 (September 1971): 1–2, "Jesus Movement," G. Archer Weniger Collection, Bob Jones University.
44. N. A. Woychuk, "The New Sound and the New Song" (St. Louis, MO: Bible Memory Association International, circa 1971), 11–12, "Contemporary Christian Music," G. Archer Weniger Collection, Bob Jones University. Also see "Two Ways—Light vs. Darkness," *Presbyterian Journal* (Asheville, NC), March 5, 1969, 12.
45. Jack Van Impe, *The Holy Bible Exposes Jesus Christ Superstar* (Grand Rapids, MI: Diadem Records, 1971), LP. See also Linda Martin and Kerry Segrave, *Anti-rock: The Opposition to Rock 'n' Roll* (New York: Da Capo Press, 1993), 180–184. For the evangelicals' new openness to culture, see Quebedeaux, *The Worldly Evangelicals*, 14–15; John W. Biggert, "Are Ministers Working to Beat the Devil?" (Memphis, TN: John W. Biggert, n.d.), "Jesus Christ Super Star," G. Archer Weniger Collection, Bob Jones University.
46. Paul Dixon, "Jesus Christ: 'Superstar' or 'Bright and Morning Star,'" *Biblical Evangelist* (Brownsburg, IN), November 1971, 8, "Jesus Christ Super Star," G. Archer Weniger Collection, Bob Jones University. See also "Church States Opposition to Christ Opera," *Washington Post*, December 12, 1971, A31; "Jesus Christ Superstar" (Collingswood, NJ: International Christian Youth, n.d.), "Jesus Christ Super Star," G. Archer Weniger Collection, Bob Jones University.
47. "Ballentine's Bulletins: Satan, the Superstar (for a Season)," *Plymouth Baptist Church Bulletin* (Minneapolis, MN), n.d., n.p., "Jesus Christ Super Star," G. Archer Weniger Collection, Bob Jones University.
48. Paul Lindstrom, "WMBI and 'Jesus Christ-Superstar,'" n.d., Prospect Heights, IL, 2, "Jesus Christ Super Star," G. Archer Weniger Collection, Bob Jones University. See also George Sweeting, Moody Bible Institute, Chicago, IL, to E. Loren Pugsley, Minneapolis, MN, December 7, 1971, "Jesus Christ Super Star," G. Archer Weniger Collection, Bob Jones University. Earlier rumors that John Lennon would portray Jesus in a BBC production only added to conservatives' white-hot outrage: "The Role of Christ 'Not for a Beatle,'" *Guardian*, March 24, 1969, 20.
49. George Sweeting to Bob Jones III, Chicago, IL, February 2, 1972, "Jesus Christ Superstar," G. Archer Weniger Collection, Bob Jones University.
50. Frank Spotnitz, "Sings Christian Music with a Beat: Amy Grant Sees No Contradiction between Religion, Rock 'n' Roll," *Schenectady (NY) Gazette*, August 1, 1985, 7; Bob Olmos, "Minister Aims Radio Rock Show at Young Adults," *Oregonian* (Portland, OR), April 17, 1984, 4M; Jerry Crowe, "At Falwell's College, They Stress Fundamentals," *Los Angeles Times*, December 19, 1985, C1, 15; Clint Confehr, "Jerry Falwell's Marching Orders: Washington Is Taking Note of Jerry Falwell and His Army of Followers—Whose Political Clout Is Growing," *Saturday Evening Post*, December 1980, 58–59, 99.
51. William Martin, *With God on Our Side: The Rise of the Religious Right in America* (New York: Broadway Books, 1997), 57–58.
52. Dan Harrell quoted in Mark Schwed, "New Breed of 'Gospel' Music Criticized," *Times Daily* (Florence, AL), May 2, 1982, 14. Liberty Baptist College handbook quoted in George Vecsey, "College of 'Born-Again' Christians," *Ocala (FL) Star-Banner*, June 23, 1979, 11A. See also "Christian Rock Music," *Standard Bearer*, February 15, 1980, 232,

"Contemporary Christian Music," G. Archer Weniger Collection, Bob Jones University. For Falwell's college and rock music, see "Diversions," in *Lynchburg Baptist College Student Handbook, 1972–1973* (Lynchburg, VA: Lynchburg Baptist College, 1972), n.p., Archives and Special Collections, Liberty University. Jim Pennington, "Christian Radio: Breaking Out of the Gospel Ghetto," *Christianity Today* (Carol Stream, IL), June 29, 1979, 33.

53. Sally Jenkins, "Falwell's Players Hit Hard, Praise Lord," *Houston Chronicle*, October 13, 1985, 12.
54. Jerry Falwell, "We Are Separatists," *Faith Aflame* (Lynchburg, VA), May–June 1977, 2, Archives and Special Collections, Liberty University. See also Susan Friend Harding, *The Book of Jerry Falwell: Fundamentalist Language and Politics* (Princeton, NJ: Princeton University Press, 2000), 10, 17, 77, 126, 165, 219; and Pete Daniel, *Standing at the Crossroads: Southern Life in the Twentieth Century* (Baltimore, MD: Johns Hopkins University Press, 1996), 224–225.
55. Mark Taylor Dalhouse, *An Island in the Lake of Fire: Bob Jones University, Fundamentalism and the Separatist Movement* (Athens: University of Georgia Press, 1996), 88–90; Douglas James Curlew, "They Ceased Not to Preach: Fundamentalism, Culture, and the Revivalist Imperative at the Temple Baptist Church of Detroit" (Ph.D. diss., University of Michigan, 2001), 159–195.
56. Heather Hendershot, *Shaking the World for Jesus: Media and Conservative Evangelical Culture* (Chicago: University of Chicago Press, 2004), 39.
57. Andrew L. Yarrow, "Christian Pop Is Gaining Fans: New Age, Gospel and Punk Become Evangelical Styles," *New York Times*, December 1, 1987, C17.
58. Earl Paige, "Word Expansion Worldwide in Religious and Pop as Well," *Billboard*, September 7, 1974, 38; Stowe, *No Sympathy for the Devil*, 179; Robert Darden, *People Get Ready! A New History of Black Gospel Music* (London: Bloomsbury, 2015), 295.
59. Mark Schwed, "New Breed of 'Gospel' Music Criticized," *Times Daily* (Florence, AL), May 2, 1982, 14; Richard Harrington, "Joyful Noise: Amy Grant, Queen of Christian Rock," *Washington Post*, June 9, 1985, F1; "A Billboard Spotlight: Gospel Music, Bridging the Secular Waters," *Billboard*, September 27, 1980, G1–G38; Alma Tuchman, "Gospel Singer Combines Ministry, Entertainment," *Lakeland (FL) Ledger*, October 16, 1982, 12A; Darren E. Grem, *The Blessings of Business: Corporate America and the Rise of Conservative Christianity* (New York: Oxford University Press, 2016), 186.
60. "Reagans Attend Benefit Concert," *Eugene (OR) Register-Guard*, December 16, 1985, 3A.
61. "Demonstrations," in *Lynchburg Baptist College Student Handbook, 1972–1973* (Lynchburg, VA: Lynchburg Baptist College, 1972), n.p., Archives and Special Collections, Liberty University.
62. Patricia Pingry, *Jerry Falwell: Man of Vision* (Milwaukee, WI: Ideals Publishing, 1980), 5, and see 12; " 'I Love America' Rally Held," *Sarasota (FL) Herald-Tribune*, March 4, 1980, 12B; C. Christopher Ross, " 'I Love America' Scheduled at Virginia," *Journal Champion* (Lynchburg, VA), August 17, 1979, 1, Archives and Special Collections, Liberty University.
63. "Liberty Baptist College Singers to Perform Locally Monday Night," *Kingman (AZ) Daily Miner*, April 16, 1982, A6; "Baptist Singers on Tour," *Citizen* (Ottawa, CA), July 31, 1976, 95; John Schlesinger and Carole Smith, "Ten Years Growing," in *Selah*, student yearbook (Lynchburg, VA: Liberty Baptist College, 1981), 14–19; "Dr. Falwell to Speak at Foster," *Tuscaloosa (AL) News*, March 11, 1977, 11. "Fundamentalist Sets Morals Rally," *Milwaukee Journal*, September 12, 1980, 5.

64. "Clean Cut, Sugar Coated," *Life*, July 26, 1968, 69, 70. See also "Up with People in Hernando Show Tonight," *St. Petersburg Times*, February 6, 1976, 3; and Daniel Sack, *Moral Re-Armament: The Reinventions of an American Religious Movement* (New York: Palgrave Macmillan, 2009), 175–176, 181–188. On corporate funding of Up with People, see Jennifer L. Robinson, "The Other Side of Up with People," *Philadelphia Lawyer*, Spring 2010, 45; *Giving USA: The Annual Report on Philanthropy for the Year 1991* (New York: AAFRC Trust for Philanthropy, 1992), 84, 96.
65. James K. Glassman, "Moral Rearmament: Its Appeal and Threat," http://www.thecrimson.com/article/1967/3/28/moral-rearmament-its-appeal-and-threat/, March 28, 1967, accessed September 29, 2017; Bill Learned, "To the Editors: 'Up with People!'" *Life*, August 16, 1968, 18B.
66. Rob Sheffield, "Super Bowl Halftime Shows Ranked: From Worst to Best," http://www.rollingstone.com/music/pictures/super-bowl-halftime-shows-ranked-from-worst-to-best-20140128, February 4, 2016, accessed September 29, 2017.
67. Claire Cox, "The Jesus Revolution: Youth Rediscovers Religion," *San Francisco Examiner*, December 1, 1970, 11, "Jesus Movement," G. Archer Weniger Collection, Bob Jones University.
68. "Nixon Promises Help for Farmer," *Tuscaloosa (AL) News*, September 15, 1968, 2; "President Richard Nixon's Daily Diary, February 23, 1971," 3, http://nixontapes.org/pdd/1971-02-12_28.pdf, accessed August 25, 2016.
69. John Ballentine, "Rock Music Is Basic to This Irrationalistic Movement," *Plymouth Crusader*, October 1971, 2, "Jesus Movement," G. Archer Weniger Collection, Bob Jones University.
70. Handbook quoted in Richard W. Flory, "Development and Transformation within Protestant Fundamentalism: Bible Institutes and Colleges in the U.S., 1925–1991, vol. 1" (Ph.D. diss., University of Chicago, 2003), 264, and see 245–246, 257, 259–260.
71. Christopher Connell, "Uniqueness Caused Bob Jones University to Lose Tax Status," *Times-News* (Hendersonville, NC), November 24, 1982, 10; Robert Reid, "At Bob Jones University: Disciplined Life Stressed," *Daily News* (Bowling Green, KY), June 4, 1974, 11; Flory, "Development and Transformation within Protestant Fundamentalism," 267, 330; Bob Jones University 1975 student handbook, 337, 347; "Bob Jones University Drops Interracial Dating Ban," http://www.christianitytoday.com/ct/2000/marchweb-only/53.0.html, March 1, 2000, accessed September 29, 2017.
72. Flory, "Development and Transformation within Protestant Fundamentalism," 267, 330; *Student Handbook, 2015–2016* (Greenville, SC: Bob Jones University, 2015), 27.
73. *The Way: Lynchburg Baptist College, 1974–75*, student handbook (Lynchburg, VA: Lynchburg Baptist College, 1974), 20, 23, Archives and Special Collections, Liberty University.
74. Nancy Tatom Ammerman, "The Fundamentalist Worldview: Ideology and Social Structure in an Independent Fundamental Church" (Ph.D. diss., Yale University, 1983), 3, 152. Also see Richard D. Barnet and Larry L. Burriss, *Controversies of the Music Industry* (Westport, CT: Greenwood Press, 2001), 92–94.
75. Harry Bruce, "Pastor's Corner: Rock and Roll in the Church?" *Kingman (AZ) Daily Miner*, April 28, 1983, 6; "300 Concerts a Year: Roadwork Pays off for Petra," *Billboard*, December 18, 1982, 36. Don Cusic, *The Sound of Light: A History of Gospel and Christian Music* (Milwaukee, WI: Hal Leonard, 2002), 195–198; Bob Lochte, *Christian Radio: The Growth of a Mainstream Broadcasting Force* (Jefferson, NC: McFarland and Company, 2006), 41–47, 64, 115; "Christian Rock Music Conference Held," *Back*

Stage, November 2, 1984, 53. On local churches using Christian rock as a way to attract youth and make some concessions to the counterculture, see Briggs, "Evangelical Transformations," 154–160;

76. "Angels?" (Chino, CA: Jack T. Chick, 1989), 2, http://www.chick.com/reading/tracts/0034/0034_01.asp, accessed March 28, 2017.
77. Jason C. Bivins, *Religion of Fear: The Politics of Horror in Conservative Evangelicalism* (New York: Oxford University Press, 2008), 20, 90, 93–94, 109–116; Jon Trott, "Bob Larson's Ministry Under Scrutiny," https://web.archive.org/web/20060610035955/http://cornerstonemag.com/features/iss100/larson.htm 21, no. 100 (1993), accessed September 26, 2017.
78. Kenneth D. Barney, "Houston, Tex.," *Pentecostal Evangel* (Springfield, MO), October 26, 1969, 30; Valeria Stratton, "Bob Larson Is a Man Who Speaks Out," *Bryan (OH) Times*, 8.
79. "Scenes," *Village Voice*, October 28, 1971, 60.
80. "Larson, Bob (1944–)," *Encyclopedia of Evangelicalism*, ed. Randall Balmer (Waco, TX: Baylor University Press, 2004), 396; Timothy C. Morgan, "Personnel Woes Persist at Larson Ministries," *Christianity Today*, September 13, 1993, 62.
81. Velma Clyde, "Music, Drugs, Sex: Former Rock Artist Warns of Threats," *Oregonian* (Portland, OR), October 28, 1978, A19.
82. "Door Interviews: Bob Larson, Dennis Benson," *Wittenburg Door* (San Diego, CA), April–May 1979, 7–32. For an interview with Benson about religion and rock music, see "Modern Song Lyrics Said Telling Truth," *Free-Lance Star* (Fredericksburg, VA), April 12, 1969, 2.
83. "Door Interviews," 8.
84. Becky Watson, "Billy Mayo Looks Behind Rock's Image," *Ocala (FL) Star-Banner*, March 15, 1983, 1C; Jay R. Howard and John M. Streck, *Apostles of Rock: The Splintered World of Contemporary Christian Music* (Louisville: University Press of Kentucky, 2004), 32; Bivins, *Religion of Fear*, 75, 94–95, 102, 105, 254; Sean McCloud, *American Possessions: Fighting Demons in the Contemporary United States* (New York: Oxford University Press, 2015), 29; "California Bill Would Require Record Warning," *Victoria (TX) Advocate*, May 24, 1982, 5D; Paul Greenberg, "Backward Masking Blathers in Arkansas," *Fort Scott (KS) Tribune*, February 4, 1983, 4; Jacob Aranza, *Backward Masking Unmasked: Backward Satanic Messages of Rock and Roll Exposed* (Shreveport, LA: Huntington House, 1983); Dan Peters, Steve Peters, and Cher Merrill, *Rock's Hidden Persuader: The Truth about Backmasking* (Minneapolis, MN: Bethany House, 1985); *Hells Bells: The Dangers of Rock and Roll*, directed by Eric Holmberg (Gainesville, FL: Reel to Real Ministries, 1989), VHS.
85. "Door Interviews," 10, 17. See also Richard D. Mountford, "Does the Music Make Them Do It," *Christianity Today* (Carol Stream, IL), May 4, 1979, 20–23; McCloud, *American Possessions*, 27–30.
86. "Door Interviews," 25, 26, 27, 31.
87. Tim LaHaye, *The Battle for the Mind* (Old Tappan, NJ: Fleming H. Revell, 1982), 176, 194, 195, 196; "Labor Force Participation Rate by Sex, Race and Hispanic Ethnicity, 1948–2015 annual averages," http://www.dol.gov/wb/stats/facts_over_time.htm#labor, accessed March 28, 2017. Also see Phil Stringer and Dan Ondra, "Is the Devil Behind Rock Music?" *Concept* (Indianapolis, IN) 3, no. 4; "Rock Music," G. Archer Weniger Collection, Bob Jones University; and Jeff Godwin, *The Devil's Disciples: The Truth about Rock* (Chino, CA: Chick Publications, 1985).

88. Paul A. Kienel, "Should Christian School Students Listen to Rock 'n' Roll Music?" *Christian School Comment*, n.d., 1, "Rock Music," G. Archer Weniger Collection, Bob Jones University.
89. "Swaggart, Meese Attack Rock," *Bryan (OH) Times*, August 23, 1986, 16; Tony Seideman, "Adult Vid Firms: Business as Usual. Reese Report 'Just a Lot of Smoke,'" *Billboard*, July 19, 1986, 1, 81.
90. Jimmy Swaggart, "The Death of Elvis Presley," *Evangelist* (Baton Rouge, LA), February 1, 1978, n.p.; and Jimmy Swaggart, "An Unexpected Reaction," *Evangelist* (Baton Rouge, LA), February 15, 1978, n.p., "Rock Music," G. Archer Weniger Collection, Bob Jones University. See also "Presley, Elvis," G. Archer Weniger Collection, Bob Jones University. For an account of Elvis's December 1976 meeting with the charismatic television preacher Rex Humbard—in which the two allegedly spoke about the return of Jesus, theology, and the struggles of fame—see E. L. Bynum, "Elvis Presley and Rex Humbard," *Cedar Chest* (Kingsport, TN) 1, no. 6 (July 1978): 1–2, "Presley, Elvis," G. Archer Weniger Collection, Bob Jones University.
91. John W. Styll interview with Jimmy Swaggart, "Jimmy Swaggart: Christian Rock Wars, June 1985," in *The Heart of the Matter: The CCM Interviews*, ed. John Styll (Nashville, TN: Star Song Communications, 1991), 1:137–138. See also "Stryper," in *Encyclopedia of Contemporary Christian Music*, ed. Mark Allan Powell (Peabody, MA: Hendrickson Publishers, 2002), 892–894.
92. Jimmy Swaggart, *Religious Rock 'n' Roll: A Wolf in Sheep's Clothing*, with Robert Paul Lamb (Baton Rouge, LA: Jimmy Swaggart Ministries, 1987), 7, 97–98; Glenn O'Brien, "Platter du Jour: Jimmy Swaggart," *Spin*, April 1987, 35.
93. Thom Granger, "Taking Stryper Seriously," in *The Heart of the Matter*, 1:129.
94. Chris Morris, "Heavenly Metal," *Spin*, May 1985, 55. Also see Richard Harrington, "Come-Ons, Comebacks & Comedowns; Rocking the Industry: Springsteen, Righteousness & Revivals," *Washington Post*, December 28, 1986, G6; Randy Lewis, "Stryper's Hard Rock Is Soft Sell," *Los Angeles Times*, January 2, 1987, 221; and Lynn Van Matre, "Stryper Is Out to Change the Evil Ways of Rock," *Chicago Tribune*, October 17, 1985, D9A.
95. Steve Rabey, "Christian 'Heavy-Metal' Band Makes Its Mark on the Secular Music Industry," *Christianity Today* (Carol Stream, IL), February 15, 1985, 45–46.
96. Don Cusic, "Stryper," in *Encyclopedia of Contemporary Christian Music: Pop, Rock, and Worship*, ed. Don Cusic (Santa Barbara, CA: Greenwood Press, 2010), 418–419; Bob Gersztyn, "Stryper," in *Encyclopedia of American Gospel Music*, ed. W. K. McNeil (New York: Routledge, 2010), 379; Eileen Luhr, *Witnessing Suburbia: Conservative and Christian Youth Culture* (Berkeley: University of California Press, 2009), 116–130; Bob Darden, "Gospel Lectern: Stryper Mixes a Heavy Metal Sound with Lyrics about Jesus," *Billboard*, March 30, 1985, 40; Charles M. Brown, "Apocalyptic Unbound: An Interpretation of Christian Speed / Thrash Metal Music," in *Religious Innovation in a Global Age: Essays on the Construction of Spirituality*, ed. George N. Lundskow (Jefferson, NC: McFarland, 2005), 122–125; Michael Sweet, *Honestly: My Life and Stryper Revealed*, with Dave Rose and Doug Van Pelt (St. Petersburg, FL: Big3 Records, 2014).
97. Richard Conrad, "Religion and Rock: Strange Bedmates," *Sunday Mail* (Brisbane, Australia), November 16, 1986, n.p.
98. Lucky Lara, "Record Review: Stryper, To Hell with the Devil," *Manila (Philippines) Standard*, January 5, 1988, 11.

99. "Stryper, Autograph," *Billboard*, January 26, 1985, 42.
100. George Smith, "Heavy Metal Heretic: The Blasphemy of Stryper," *Spin*, December 1988, 22. See also Jon Pareles, "Christian Rock in Tight Leather Pants," *New York Times*, October 20, 1990, 14.
101. Carol Flake, *Redemptorama: Culture, Politics, and the New Evangelicalism* (Garden City, NY: Anchor Press, 1984), 182.
102. Michael R. Smith, "In the 'Christian Rock' Sound . . . Can You Hear God Whisper?" *Fundamentalist Journal* (Lynchburg, VA), February 1986, 22, 33.
103. Godwin, *The Devil's Disciples*, 280–281.
104. Assemblies of God proceedings quoted in Erling T. Jorstad, *Holding Fast/Pressing On: Religion in America in the 1980s* (New York: Praeger, 1990), 124.
105. Pyott quoted in *Northwestern Lutheran* (Milwaukee, WI), vols. 74–75, 373.
106. Roy Livesay, *Understanding Deception* (Chichester, UK: New Wine Press, 1987), 47.
107. Mike Joyce, "Alloying Heavy Metal and God," *Washington Post*, November 12, 1985, B7.
108. Don Cusic, "Petra," and Don Cusic, "Resurrection Band," in *Encyclopedia of Contemporary Christian Music*, 330–334, 383–385; "The World of Gospel Music: Together for a Cause," *Billboard*, October 19, 1985.
109. Norman, "Who Leads the Arts?," 9.
110. Luhr, *Witnessing Suburbia*, 68–110.
111. J. Brent Bill, *Rock and Roll, Proceed with Caution: A Balanced Christian Response to the Music and Its Message* (Old Tappan, NJ: Fleming H. Revell, 1984), 143, 144–149. Also see Kenneth L. Woodward, Elisa Williams, Karen Springen, and Janet Huck, "The New Christian Minstrels," *Newsweek*, August 19, 1985, 70; Lynn Van Matre, "Christian Singers, Bands Rocking the Music Industry," *Evening Independent* (St. Petersburg, FL), April 20, 1985, 5A.
112. Parry Gettelman, "Christian Musicians Broaden Their Appeal: From Gospel to Rap, Industry Makes Room," *Washington Post*, October 26, 1991, B6. Sandra Brennan, "Michael W. Smith," http://www.allmusic.com/artist/michael-w-smith-mn0000466759/biography, accessed June 30, 2017; Bob Darden, "Gospel Lectern," *Billboard*, November 16, 1985, 53. Bob Darden, "Gospel Lectern," *Billboard*, November 15, 1986, 70; "Gospel '85," *Billboard*, December 28, 1985, T52. Jay R. Howard, "Contemporary Christian Music: Where Rock Meets Religion," *Journal of Popular Culture* 26, no. 1 (Summer 1992): 123–130; Steve Rabey, *The Heart of Rock and Roll* (Old Tappan, NJ: F. H. Revell, 1986).
113. John J. Thompson, *Raised by Wolves: The Story of Christian Rock & Roll* (Toronto: ECW Press, 2000), 147, 151, 234; "Creation Festival Returns to the Gorge This Weekend," *Ellensburg (WA) Daily Record*, July 22, 1999, 2; "Christian Rockers Gather Together for Music Festival," *Montreal Gazette*, August 4, 1984, H11. See also "Cornerstone Festival 1984 pt1," YouTube video, 8:18, posted by "paulcornerstone," February 7, 2009, https://www.youtube.com/watch?v=MN-fu5b08cM; and Henry Allen, "Almost Heaven, in Virginia: The Believers, Rocking to the Lord at Fishnet Fest," *Washington Post*, July 14, 1990, C1, C2.
114. Andrew L. Yarrow, "Christian Pop Is Gaining Fans: New Age, Gospel and Punk Become Evangelical Styles," *New York Times*, December 1, 1987, C17; Gail Pellett, "Christian Rock: The $100 Million Music That's Bigger Than Jazz, Classical, Soul, and Gospel," *Washington Post*, November 3, 1985, 27–29; David R. Dietrich, "Rebellious Conservatives: Social Movements in Defense of Privilege" (Ph.D. diss., Duke University, 2011), 119, 128.

115. John W. Drakeford, *Children of Doom: A Sobering Look at the Commune Movement* (Nashville, TN: Broadman Press, 1972), 36.
116. Shawn David Young, "Apocalyptic Music: Reflections on Countercultural Christian Influence," in *Countercultures and Popular Music*, ed. Sheila Whiteley and Jedediah Sklower (London: Routledge, 2014), 114–118; Preston Shires, *Hippies of the Religious Right* (Waco, TX: Baylor University Press, 2007).
117. Geoffrey Himes, "Christian Musicians Make Career Moves," *Washington Post*, June 7, 1991, 16.
118. Shawn David Young, *Gray Sabbath: Jesus People USA, the Evangelical Left, and the Evolution of Christian Rock* (New York: Columbia University Press, 2015), 109, and see 101–102; Howard and Streck, *Apostles of Rock*, 209–210; Thompson, *Raised by Wolves*, 55–56, 147; Lloyd Sachs, *T Bone Burnett: A Life in Pursuit* (Austin: University of Texas Press, 2016), 85–88, 107–108. For more insightful analysis of progressive and evangelical left Christian rock, see the music critic J. Edward Keyes's website, http://jedwardkeyes.tumblr.com, accessed March 15, 2017.
119. Lilia Fernandez, "Ronald Reagan, Race, Civil Rights, and Immigration," in *A Companion to Ronald Reagan*, ed. Andrew L. Johns (Malden, MA: Wiley Blackwell, 2015), 186–189; Terence Hunt, "Reagan Signs Martin Luther King Holiday Bill," *Schenectady (NY) Gazette*, November 1, 1983, 1; Doug Rossinow, "It's Time We Face the Fact That Ronald Reagan Was Hostile to Civil Rights," http://historynewsnetwork.org/article/158887, April 20, 2015, accessed September 1, 2016.
120. Stowe, *No Sympathy for the Devil*, 244–245; Luhr, *Witnessing Suburbia*, 5–8, 12–13, 35–36, 68–69, 156–157, 160–165; Howard and Streck, *Apostles of Rock*, 10, 15, 55–56; Mark Allan Steiner, *The Rhetoric of Operation Rescue: Projecting the Christian Pro-life Message* (New York: T. and T. Clark, 2006), 180–181.
121. Frances Evans, "Changing Their Tune: Musician Stresses Quality Music Education for the Young," newspaper clipping, no title, n.d., n.p., "Garlock, Frank," G. Archer Weniger Collection, Bob Jones University; David W. Cloud, "A Salute to Frank Garlock," newspaper clipping, 2003, n.p., "Garlock, Frank," G. Archer Weniger Collection, Bob Jones University; " 'Rock Music' Topic," *Sarasota (FL) Herald-Tribune*, February 20, 1972, 2B; Frank Garlock, *Can Rock Music Be Sacred?* (Greenville, SC: Musical Ministries, 1974), 2.
122. "News Release from Bob Jones University," n.d., 1–2, "Rock Music," G. Archer Weniger Collection, Bob Jones University.
123. Garlock, *Can Rock Music Be Sacred?* 28, 30, and see 4–5, 8, 10.
124. "Music—Frank Garlock," *Australian Beacon*, June–July 1976, 10, "Rock Music," G. Archer Weniger Collection, Bob Jones University.
125. Dorothy Jacquat, "Are We Really Neo-evangelical in Our Music?" *Fundamental Baptist Crusader* (Virginia Beach, VA), February 1979, 1, 3, "Contemporary Christian Music," G. Archer Weniger Collection, Bob Jones University; Joseph B. Tamney, *The Resilience of Conservative Religion: The Case of Popular, Conservative Protestant Congregations* (Cambridge: Cambridge University Press, 2002), 249–250.
126. Grant Wacker, "Travail of a Broken Family: Evangelical Responses to Pentecostalism in America, 1906–1916," *Journal of Ecclesiastical History* 47, no. 3 (July 1996): 505–528.
127. John F. MacArthur Jr., *Charismatic Chaos* (Grand Rapids, MI: Zondervan, 1992), 17, 19, 21, 244, 291.
128. Howard K. Miller, Contemporary Music: Is It Just a Harmless Fad? Or Does It Involve Moral and Spiritual Values?" *Baptist Bulletin* (Schaumburg, IL), March 1957, 12.

Indeed, even Jimmy Swaggart admitted that there were undeniable links between rock and pentecostalism, links that he pointed out in his thundering jeremiads. "I sat at the table the other day with two Baptist brethren," he preached at a mass revival meeting in the summer of 1985, "and you listen to me what I'm about to tell you. I had to bow my head in shame. My heart ached and hurt when I had to admit to those two Baptist brethren that not all, thank God, but most, most of the so-called Christian rock musicians come from pentecostal ranks!" he yelled as he pointed at his thousands of listeners. "That makes it even worse! . . . It's wrong. It's of the devil. It's of the powers of darkness. It's not of God!" "New Haven Connecticut 07-13-1985 - CR1140," YouTube video, 2:07:33, posted by "Louis Calzada," July 1, 2015, https://www.youtube.com/watch?v=cbftxyiDMMg.

129. Donald E. Nelson, Piedmont Bible College, unpublished position paper, "The Jesus People," circa 1972, 5, 6, "Jesus Movement," G. Archer Weniger Collection, Bob Jones University.
130. Harold L. Longnecker, "The Jesus People . . ." *Sawdust Trail* (Sioux City, IA), February 20, 1972, n.p., "Jesus Movement," G. Archer Weniger Collection, Bob Jones University; Jerry Falwell, Ed Dobson, and Ed Hinson, eds., *The Fundamentalist Phenomenon: The Resurgence of Conservative Christianity* (Garden City, NY: Doubleday–Galilee Original, 1981), 137–138; Noel Smith, "Churches and the Jesus People," *Baptist Bible Tribune*, July 30, 1971, 5, "Jesus Movement," G. Archer Weniger Collection, Bob Jones University; Dan Morgan, "Falwell and the Fundamentalists' Family Fight," *Newsday* (Long Island, NY), April 19, 1987, 5; C. E. Hershey, "Is Christian Rock Music Christian?" circular letter, n.d., Clovis, CA, 1, "Contemporary Christian Music," G. Archer Weniger Collection, Bob Jones University.
131. G. Archer Weniger, "New Evangelicals on the College Campus," *Sword of the Lord* (Murfreesboro, TN), n.d., n.p., "Jesus Movement," G. Archer Weniger Collection, Bob Jones University.
132. News release from Bob Jones University, Greenville, SC, circa 1972, 2, "Jesus Movement," G. Archer Weniger Collection, Bob Jones University.
133. Don Jasmin, "Bill Gaither's 'Praise Gathering' Features Apostates, Charismatics & Ecumenists!" *Voice of Fundamentalism* (Greenville, SC), December 1978–January 1979, 1–3, "Contemporary Christian Music: Conferences and Festivals," G. Archer Weniger Collection, Bob Jones University.
134. "News of Interests to Fundamentalists," *Projector*, Spring 1990, 5, "Garlock, Frank," G. Archer Weniger Collection, Bob Jones University.
135. Billy James Hargis, "'Christian Rock' Is a Compromise with Satan," *Christian Crusade* (Tulsa, OK), n.d., n.p., "Presley, Elvis," G. Archer Weniger Collection, Bob Jones University.
136. "Resolution on the Jesus People," *Ohio Bible Fellowship Visitor*, October 1971, 1–2, "Jesus Movement," G. Archer Weniger Collection, Bob Jones University.
137. A. Raske, "Electronically Induced Drug Abuse," *First Baptist Light House* (St. John's, Newfoundland), November 1978, 8, "Rock Music," G. Archer Weniger Collection, Bob Jones University.
138. "X-Rating Rock Radio," *Christianity Today* (Carol Stream, IL), November 18, 1977, 24.
139. Claude Cox, "Research and Development: Lyrics of Contemporary Music," Radio and TV Commission, Southern Baptist Convention, 1977, "Obscenity: Music," 36–38, Southern Baptist Historical Library and Archives, Nashville, Tennessee. Larry E. Par-

rish, Memphis, TN, to Foy Valentine, Nashville, TN, March 28, 1979, "Obscenity: Music," Southern Baptist Historical Library and Archives, Nashville, TN.

140. Maurice R. Irvin, "When Paul Returned to Jerusalem," *Alliance Witness* (New York), September 12, 1973, 4.

141. Steve Rabey, "Christian 'Heavy-Metal' Band Makes Its Mark on the Secular Music Industry," *Christianity Today* (Carol Stream, IL), February 15, 1985, 47.

142. "Larson Endorses Rock," *Biblical Evangelist* (Brownsburg, IN), August 1979, n.p., "Rock Music," G. Archer Weniger Collection, Bob Jones University.

143. David Wilkerson, "Rock and Roll: The Devil's Heartbeat," *Pentecostal Evangel* (Springfield, MO), July 12, 1959, 4. See also David R. Wilkerson, "The Devil's Heartbeat Rock and Roll! Teenage Sins Exposed!" (Philipsburg, PA: Teen-Age Evangelism, n.d.), 3, 8.

144. Paul Baker, *Contemporary Christian Music: Where It Came from, What It Is, Where It's Going* (Westchester, IL: Crossway Books, 1985), 179. See also David R. Wilkerson, *Confessions of a Rock n Roll Hater!* (Lindale, TX: Last Days Ministries, 1983).

145. "Music Code," in *The Liberty Way, 81/82, Liberty Baptist College*, student handbook (Lynchburg, VA: Liberty Baptist College, 1981), 38, Archives and Special Collections, Liberty University. See also *The Liberty Way* handbooks for 1987–1989, 40, and 1989–1990, 44.

146. "Policies: Music," in *The Liberty Way, 1991–1993* (Lynchburg, VA: Liberty University, 1991), 19, Archives and Special Collections, Liberty University.

147. "DC Talk," *Encyclopedia of Evangelicalism*, 206–207; "DC Talk" folder, Center for Popular Music, Middle Tennessee State University; Jon Pareles, "The Word of God with an MTV Beat," *New York Times*, February 6, 1996, C15.

148. Amy Gamerman, "Born-Again Rap: A New Medium for the Message," *Wall Street Journal*, April 9, 1991, A20. Also see Anjetta McQueen, "Devoted to Rap," http//www.philly.com, February 23, 1991, accessed October 7, 2016.

149. Geoffrey Himes, "Christian Musicians Make Career Moves," *Washington Post*, June 7, 1991, 16; Bill Carpenter, "DC Talk, a Group on a Mission to Spread Gospel," *Washington Post*, May 1, 1993, G10; Robert Wuthnow, *All in Sync: How Music and Art Are Revitalizing American Religion* (Berkeley: University of California Press, 2005), 9–11, 58, 136, 237; Richard A. Bustraan, *The Jesus People Movement: A Story of Spiritual Revolution among the Hippies* (Eugene, OR: Pickwick Publications, 2014), 181; Patrick Kampert, "Hearing Is Believing: Have You Listened to Christian Rock Lately?" *Chicago Tribune*, April 21, 1991, M20.

150. Mathew Brady, "WWJD Raises Many Questions," *Star-News* (Wilmington, NC), August 1, 1998, 7D; Randall Balmer, *The Making of Evangelicalism: From Revivalism to Politics and Beyond* (Waco, TX: Baylor University Press, 2010), 43–54; Colleen McDannell, *Material Christianity: Religion and Popular Culture in America* (New Haven, CT: Yale University Press, 1995), 222–266; Todd M. Brenneman, *Homespun Gospel: The Triumph of Sentimentality in Contemporary American Evangelicalism* (New York: Oxford University Press, 2014), 91–99.

Epilogue

1. "Biography," Rock and Roll Hall of Fame, http://www.rockhall.com/inductees/u2, accessed March 18, 2017.

2. Neil McCormick, *U2 by U2* (New York: HarperCollins, 2006), 14. See also "Bono: Who Is Jesus?" YouTube video, 2:45, posted by "God Inspirations," March 24, 2014, http://www.youtube.com/watch?v=kOQClgNRoPc.
3. Laura Barnett, "U2: Rock 'n' Roll's Answer to the Book of Common Prayer?" http://www.theguardian.com/music/musicblog/2010/jan/06/u2-book-common-prayer, January 6, 2010, accessed March 14, 2017. Also see Jeremy Weber, "Six Surprises from Bono's Interview with Focus on the Family," http://www.christianitytoday.com/gleanings/2013/june/bono-interview-with-focus-on-family-jim-daly.html, June 21, 2013, accessed March 18, 2017; "Bono & Eugene Peterson on THE PSALMS," Fuller Studio video, 21:43, April 26, 2016, http://fullerstudio.fuller.edu/bono-eugene-peterson-psalms/; and "It's Not Around the Clock, but Rockers Find Religion," *Chicago Tribune*, July 12, 1991, DC8.
4. McCormick, *U2 by U2*, 20.
5. Richard A. Bustraan, *The Jesus People Movement: A Story of Spiritual Revolution among the Hippies* (Eugene, OR: Pickwick Publications, 2014), 49–55; Jan-Åke Alvarsson, "The Development of Pentecostalism in Scandinavian Countries," in *European Pentecostalism*, ed. William Kay and Anne Dyer (Leiden, Netherlands: Brill, 2011), 33; "Various Artists: Rock Around the World," *Billboard*, March 23, 1985, 66; Robert William Fogel, *The Fourth Great Awakening and the Future of Egalitarianism* (Chicago: University of Chicago Press, 2002); Geoffrey Corry, *Jesus Bubble or Jesus Revolution: The Growth of Jesus Communes in Britain and Ireland* (London: British Council of Churches, Youth Department, 1973), 12, 49.
6. McCormick, *U2 by U2*, 20.
7. *The History of Rock 'n' Roll*, episode 2 of 10 (Burbank, CA: Warner Home Video, 1995), VHS.
8. Associated Press, "Elvis Presley Fans Make Pilgrimage to His Gravesite at Graceland," http://www.billboard.com/articles/news/7469710/elvis-presley-fans-pilgrimage-gravesite-graceland, August 16, 2016, accessed March 20, 2017; "About: The Estate of Elvis Presley / The Elvis Presley Trust," http://www.graceland.com/about/, accessed March 20, 2017.
9. Chris Chambers, "August 16 is 23rd Anniversary of Elvis' Death; Americans Still Consider Him the King of Rock and Roll," http://www.gallup.com/poll/2638/august-23rd-anniversary-elvis-death-americans-still-conside.aspx, August 16, 2000, accessed March 20, 2017. Also see Andrew M. Brown, "How Did Elvis Presley Become Our New Messiah?" http://www.telegraph.co.uk/books/what-to-read/how-did-elvis-presley-become-our-new-messiah—review/, August 22, 2016, accessed March 20, 2017.
10. Charles Reagan Wilson, *Judgment and Grace in Dixie: Southern Faiths from Faulkner to Elvis* (Athens: University of Georgia Press, 2007), 138.
11. Stephen Hinerman, " 'I'll Be Here with You': Fans, Fantasy and the Figure of Elvis," in *The Adoring Audience: Fan Culture and Popular Media*, ed. Lisa A. Lewis (London: Routledge, 1992): 119; Gilbert B. Rodman, *Elvis After Elvis: The Posthumous Career of a Living Legend* (London: Routledge, 2013), 1–29; David Di Sabatino, "And a Morbidly Obese Man Shall Lead Them," *Alberta Report* (Edmonton, Canada), September 1, 1997, 38; Greil Marcus, *Dead Elvis: A Chronicle of a Cultural Obsession* (Cambridge, MA: Harvard University Press, 1999); N. J. Girardot, "Ecce Elvis: 'Elvis Studies' as a Postmodernist Paradigm for the Academic Study of Religions," *Journal of the American Academy of Religion* 68, no. 3 (September 2000): 603–614; Becca Walton, "Ted Ownby on Elvis Presley as a Southern Studies Student," http://southernstudies.olemiss.edu/ted-ownby-elvis-presley-southern-studies-student/, No-

vember 11, 2014, accessed March 21, 2017; "Conference on Elvis Opens at Ole Miss," http://articles.latimes.com/1996-08-04/travel/tr-31110_1_elvis-week, August 04, 1996, accessed March 21, 2017.

12. Mary Schmich, "Pop: And the Beat Goes On: Memphis Prepares for the High Holy Days of Elvis Presley," *Chicago Tribune*, August 9, 1987, L4.
13. Ron Rosenbaum, "Among the Believers: The Elvis Presley Culture Has Gone Beyond Rock and Beyond Ridicule," *New York Times Magazine*, September 24, 1995, SM50. See also "Presley Fans Remember Their Hero," *Spartanburg (SC) Herald-Journal*, August 17, 1983, A10.
14. Bob Mehr, "Your Day-by-Day Guide to Elvis Week 2016 Activities," http://archive.commercialappeal.com/entertainment/elvis/your-day-by-day-guide-to-elvis-week-2016-activities-39048cf0-8358-0142-e053-0100007f6826-389009351.html, August 4, 2016, accessed March 20, 2017.
15. Ted Harrison, *The Death and Resurrection of Elvis Presley* (London: Reaction, 2016), 151.
16. Jessica Suarez, "The Love Ship: Danielson's Daniel Smith Says Come Aboard, He's Expecting You," *CMJ New Music Monthly* no. 139 (2005): 28–29; Jillian Mapes, "Sufjan Stevens: Carrie & Lowell," http://www.rollingstone.com/music/albumreviews/sufjan-stevens-carrie-lowell-20150331, March 31, 2015, accessed March 20, 2017; Andrew Beaujon, *Body Piercing Saved My Life: Inside the Phenomenon of Christian Rock* (Cambridge, MA: Da Capo Press, 2006); Eric Rephun, "I Know My Way from Here: Walking the Hutterite Mile with David Eugene Edwards," *The Counter-narratives of Radical Theology and Popular Music: Songs of Fear and Trembling*, ed. Mark Grimshaw (Springer, 2014), 95–118; Eileen Luhr, *Witnessing Suburbia: Conservative and Christian Youth Culture* (Berkeley: University of California Press, 2009), 192.
17. Mary Jenkins, "Creed's True Calling: Band Says It's about Rock, Not Religion," *Washington Post*, September 28, 1999, C1; Marcus Moberg, *Christian Metal: History, Ideology, Scene* (London: Bloomsbury, 2015), 38–39; Mark Moring, "P.O.D. Rocking Again," http://www.christianitytoday.com/ct/2012/julyweb-only/pod-rocking-again.html, July 10, 2012, accessed March 18, 2017; Lorne Behrman, "Like I Should: P.O.D. Rocks for God," *CMJ New Music Monthly*, June 2000, 43–47; Barbara Claire Freeman, "Practicing Christian Rock," in *One Nation under God? Religion and American Culture*, ed. Marjorie Garber and Rebecca L. Walkowitz (New York: Routledge, 1999), 222–223; Tanja N. Morgan, Cheryl A. Hampton, Shanise Davenport, Ellen Young, Diane M. Badzinski, Kathy Brittain Richardson, and Robert H. Woods, "Sacred Symbols with a Secular Beat? A Content Analysis of Religious and Sexual Imagery in Modern Rock, Hip Hop, Christian, and Country Music Videos," *Journal of Religion and Popular Culture* 24, no. 3 (Fall 2012): 432–448; Lisa Gubernick and Robert La Franco, "Rocking with God," *Forbes*, January 2, 1995, 40–41.
18. Kelefa Sanneh, "Christian Rock and Mainstream Music Move Closer Together," http://www.nytimes.com/2006/04/27/arts/music/christian-rock-and-mainstream-music-move-closer-together.html, April 27, 2006, accessed March 20, 2017. Also see Silvia Giagnoni, "Christian Rock Goes Mainstream: Youth Culture, Politics, and Popular Music in the U.S." (Ph.D. diss., Florida Atlantic University, 2007), 264–304.
19. Linda Lyons, "Today's Teens Keeping the Faith," http://www.gallup.com/poll/12928/todays-teens-keeping-faith.aspx, September 7, 2004, accessed March 24, 2017. Also see Heather Hendershot, *Shaking the World for Jesus: Media and Conservative Evangelical Culture* (Chicago: University of Chicago Press, 2004), 59; and Rebecca Leung, "Rocking for Christ: Christian Music Becoming Big Hits on Mainstream Radio

Stations," http://www.cbsnews.com/news/rocking-for-christ/, December 1, 2004, accessed March 24, 2017. For a more skeptical view about the influence of Christian rock, see Alan Wolfe, *The Transformation of American Religion: How We Actually Live Our Faith* (Chicago: University of Chicago Press, 2005), 210–213.

20. "Pat Boone Minus Those White Bucks," *New York Times*, May 4, 1997, H20.
21. "The State of the Art Was Often Weird," *Washington Post*, December 28, 1997, G10; Bill Broadway, "The Christian People's Choice Awards," *Washington Post*, January 31, 1998, B8; "Pat Boone on 'The American Music Awards' - EMMYTVLEGENDS.ORG," YouTube video, 8:55, posted by "FoundationINTERVIEWS," January 8, 2016, https://www.youtube.com/watch?v=GXGcxLiyoao; Richard Harrington, "Boone to Be Wild: Mr. Milquetoast Sheds His Image with 'No More Mr. Nice Guy,'" *Washington Post*, February 1, 1997, C1; Richard Harrington, "Bad to the Boone: After Complaints, Network Cancels Gospel Show," *Washington Post*, February 22, 1997, H1.
22. Edward Gilbreath, "Why Pat Boone Went 'Bad,'" http://www.christianitytoday.com/ct/1999/october4/9tb056.html, October 4, 1999, accessed July 3, 2017.
23. Larry B. Stammer, "Heavy Metal Spoof Sinks Pat Boone's Show," http://articles.latimes.com/1997-02-20/news/mn-30649_1_heavy-metal, February 20, 1997, accessed July 3, 2017.
24. Harrington, "Bad to the Boone," H1; David Haldane and Renee Tawa, "Pat Boone Apologizes for Metal Shock," http://articles.latimes.com/1997-04-16/news/mn-49203_1_singer-pat-boone, April 16, 1997, accessed July 3, 2017.
25. Jeff Wright, "Christian Music Fair Canceled," *Register-Guard* (Eugene, OR), 1A. Also see Audrey Martin, "Cancellation Was a Cop-Out," comment on Ignite Your Faith, "Speak Up!" http://www.christianitytoday.com/iyf/1998/janfeb/8c1007.html, January–February 1998, accessed March 18, 2017; and Steve Rabey, "Christian Singer Appeals to Fans of Secular Music: Is Amy Grant Sending Mixed Messages?" *Christianity Today* (Carol Stream, IL), November 8, 1985, 62.
26. Jonathan Merritt, "Is the Christian Music Industry Liberalizing on Gay Marriage?" http://theweek.com/articles/444405/christian-music-industry-liberalizing-gay-marriage, August 21, 2014, accessed March 20, 2017.
27. Mark Moring, "Jennifer Knapp Comes Out," http://www.christianitytoday.com/ct/2010/aprilweb-only/jenniferknapp-apr10.html, April 13, 2010, accessed March 20, 2017.
28. Phil Crawley and Andy Higgs, "Bill Mallonee: Sex & the Married Man," http://www.crossrhythms.co.uk/articles/music/Bill_Mallonee_Sex__the_Married_Man/8263/p1/, October 30, 2003, accessed March 20, 2017.
29. Jay R. Howard and John M. Streck, *Apostles of Rock: The Splintered World of Contemporary Christian Music* (Louisville: University Press of Kentucky, 2004), 202.
30. Brian Steensland and Philip Goff, *The New Evangelical Social Engagement* (New York: Oxford University Press, 2014).
31. Jon Huang, Samuel Jacoby, Michael Strickland, and K. K. Rebecca Lai, "Election 2016: Exit Polls," https://www.nytimes.com/interactive/2016/11/08/us/politics/election-exit-polls.html?mcubz=0&_r=0, November 8, 2016, accessed October 1, 2017; Ruby Lott-Lavigna, "What Does It Mean for a Leader When Their Entire Country's Music Culture Rejects Them?" http://www.newstatesman.com/world/north-america/2017/01/what-does-it-mean-leader-when-their-entire-country-s-music-culture, January 20, 2017, accessed March 20, 2017.
32. "Deep Generational Divides in Views of Homosexuality and Same-Sex Marriage," http://www.pewforum.org/2015/11/03/u-s-public-becoming-less-religious/pf_15-10

-27_secondrls_overview_gendivide640px/, October 23, 2015, accessed March 20, 2017; "Religion Among the Millennials: Introduction and Overview," http://www.pewforum.org/2010/02/17/religion-among-the-millennials/, February 17, 2010, accessed March 20, 2017.Walbert Castillo and Michael Schramm, "How We Voted—By Age, Education, Race and Sexual Orientation," http://college.usatoday.com/2016/11/09/how-we-voted-by-age-education-race-and-sexual-orientation/, November 9, 2016, accessed March 20, 2017; Gregory A. Smith and Alan Cooperman, "The Factors Driving the Growth of Religious 'Nones' in the U.S.," http://www.pewresearch.org/fact-tank/2016/09/14/the-factors-driving-the-growth-of-religious-nones-in-the-u-s/, September 14, 2016, accessed March 24, 2017. The shift in musical tastes and theological focus coincided with another major change. The Pew Research Center's polling data showed that by 2015 millennials were far less likely to affiliate with a religion than those in previous generations had. They made up the largest part of the growing category of religious "nones," and 35 percent of millennials were "religiously unaffiliated." That compared to "those who identify as evangelical Protestants (21%), Catholics (16%) or mainline Protestants (11%)." Michael Lipka, "Millennials Increasingly Are Driving Growth of 'Nones,'" http://www.pewresearch.org/fact-tank/2015/05/12/millennials-increasingly-are-driving-growth-of-nones/, May 12, 2015, accessed March 24, 2017.

33. David Stowe, *No Sympathy for the Devil: Christian Pop Music and the Transformation of American Evangelicalism* (Chapel Hill: University of North Carolina Press, 2011), 248–249.
34. John Jeremiah Sullivan, "Upon This Rock: Rock Music Used to Be a Safe Haven for Degenerates and Rebels. Until It Found Jesus," http://www.gq.com/entertainment/music/200401/rock-music-jesus?printable=true, January 24, 2004, accessed April 3, 2012.
35. Beaujon, *Body Piercing Saved My Life*, 6.
36. Mark Allan Powell, "Jesus Climbs the Charts: The Business of Contemporary Christian Music," *Christian Century* (Chicago), December 18–31, 2002, 26.
37. "The Burning," *Seinfeld*, season 9 (Culver City, CA: Sony Pictures Home Entertainment, 2013), DVD. See also Nicholas Dawidoff, "No Sex. No Drugs. But Rock 'n' Roll (Kind Of)," *New York Times Magazine*, February 5, 1995, 40–44, 66, 68–69, 72. The award-winning HBO series *The Sopranos* also took a shot at the genre in a 2001 episode. Mob boss Tony Soprano's sister, Janice, and her feckless boyfriend are fans of Christian rock. The two of them make a humorous attempt at composing songs together. "To Save Us All from Satan's Power," *The Sopranos*, season 3 (New York: HBO Home Video, 2015), DVD.
38. Michael Lipka, "Evangelicals Increasingly Say It's Becoming Harder for Them in America," http://www.pewresearch.org/fact-tank/2016/07/14/evangelicals-increasingly-say-its-becoming-harder-for-them-in-america/, July 14, 2016, accessed March 21, 2017.
39. Giagnoni, "Christian Rock Goes Mainstream," 61, 80–81; Anna E. Nekola, "US Evangelicals and the Redefinition of Worship Music," in *Mediating Faiths: Religion and Socio-Cultural Change in the Twenty-First Century*, ed. Michael Bailey and Guy Redden (London: Routledge, 2016), 133; Donald Miller quoted in "Moved by the Spirit: Pentecostal Power & Politics after 100 Years," http://www.pewforum.org/2006/04/24/moved-by-the-spirit-pentecostal-power-and-politics-after-100-years2/, April 24, 2006, accessed March 20, 2017.
40. Paul Taylor and Rich Morin, "IV. Rock's Rise," http://www.pewsocialtrends.org/2009/08/12/iv-rocks-rise/, August 12, 2009, accessed March 20, 2017. See also Kira Dault,

"The Pews Are Alive: U.S. Catholic Readers on Parish Music," *U.S. Catholic* 79, no. 3 (March 2014): 26–29.

41. Ed Stetzer, "Worship Leaders Are Not Rock Stars," http://www.christianitytoday.com/edstetzer/2015/march/worship-leaders-are-not-rock-stars.html, March 31, 2015, accessed March 20, 2017.
42. Steven P. Miller, *The Age of Evangelicalism: America's Born-Again Years* (New York: Oxford University Press, 2014), 103. See also Anna Nekola, "'I'll Take You There': The Promise of Transformation in the Marketing of Worship," in *Christian Congregational Music: Performance, Identity and Experience*, ed. Monique Ingalls, Carolyn Landau, and Tom Wagner (New York: Routledge, 2016), 120–121.
43. Frank Church Brown, *Good Taste, Bad Taste, and Christian Taste: Aesthetics in Religious Life* (New York: Oxford University Press, 2000), 232.
44. Eddie Gibbs and Ryan Bolger, *Emerging Churches: Creating Christian Community in Postmodern Cultures* (Grand Rapids, MI: Baker Academic, 2005), 44–45.
45. Quote from Brett McCracken, "A New Kind of Hipster," https://relevantmagazine.com/culture/music/features/3181-a-new-kind-of-hipster, September 2, 2005, accessed October 1, 2017. See also Scot McKnight, "Five Streams of the Emerging Church," http://www.christianitytoday.com/ct/2007/february/11.35.html, January 19, 2007, accessed March 20, 2017; Bill J. Leonard, "Emerging Church Movement," in *Encyclopedia of Religious Controversies in the United States*, ed. Bill J. Leonard and Jill Y. Crainshaw (Santa Barbara, CA: ABC-CLIO, 2013), 1:270–272; and Brett McCracken, "Hipster Faith," http://www.christianitytoday.com/ct/2010/september/9.24.html, September 3, 2010, accessed March 20, 2017.
46. Frank Newport, "Who Are the Evangelicals?" http://news.gallup.com/poll/17041/who-evangelicals.aspx, June 24 2005, accessed March 24, 2017; Albert L. Winseman, "U.S. Evangelicals: How Many Walk the Walk?" http://news.gallup.com/poll/16519/us-evangelicals-how-many-walk-walk.aspx, May 31, 2005, accessed March 29, 2017); "We Poll the Pollster: An Interview with George Gallup, Jr.," and "The Christianity Today–Gallup Poll: An Overview," *Christianity Today* (Carol Stream, IL), December 21, 1979, 10–12, 12–15; Allan Parachini, "The New Jesus Music: Gimme That Big-Time Religion," *Los Angeles Times*, November 23, 1980, X3. A mid-1970s extensive study of U.S. seminarians' views on music tracked some new openness to contemporary music in church services. Jack Wayne Schwarz, "The State of Church Music Education for Ministerial Students in Protestant Seminaries in the United States" (DMA diss., University of Southern California, 1975), 56–65, 76–77, 111–114. See also Charles Brown, "Selling Faith: Marketing Christian Popular Culture to Christian and Non-Christian Audiences," *Journal of Religion and Popular Culture* 24, no. 1 (Spring 2012): 113–129.
47. Dawidoff, "No Sex," 40. Howard and Streck, *Apostles of Rock*, 150, 199. For an early journalistic treatment, see Wayne King, "'Jesus Rock' Now a New Musical Industry," *New York Times*, June 10, 1977, 16.
48. "Contemporary Christian Music," in *Encyclopedia of Evangelicalism*, ed. Randall Balmer (Waco, TX: Baylor University Press, 2006), 185–187; Powell, "Jesus Climbs the Charts," 20.
49. Leung, "Rocking for Christ." See also Jackie Sheckler Finch, *Insiders' Guide to Nashville* (Guilford, CT: Globe Pequot, 2011), 37.
50. Stephen D. Perry, "The Meaning of Contemporary Christian Music in the Lives of Evangelicals," in *Evangelical Christians and Popular Culture: Pop Goes the Gospel*, ed. Robert H. Woods Jr. (Santa Barbara, CA: Praeger, 2013), 1:119.

51. Lorraine Ali, "The Glorious Rise of Christian Pop," http://www.newsweek.com/glorious-rise-christian-pop-154551, July 15, 2001, accessed March 24, 2017.
52. Miller, *The Age of Evangelicalism*, 103.
53. Powell, "Jesus Climbs the Charts," 26.

Acknowledgments

1. "Irish Impressions," in *The Collected Works of G. K. Chesterton*, ed. James V. Schall (San Francisco: Ignatius Press, 2001), 20:92.

ACKNOWLEDGMENTS

"I have often done the little I could to correct the stale trick of taking things for granted," wrote G. K. Chesterton a century ago. "All the more," he went on, "because it is not even taking them for granted. It is taking them without gratitude."[1] This project, of course, owes a great debt to friends, family, colleagues, and many others. I hope I have not taken that for granted or taken that without gratitude.

I first started working on the book when I was chair of the history department at Eastern Nazarene College in Quincy, Massachusetts, and an editor of *Historically Speaking* at Boston University. Colleagues like Don Yerxa, Bill McCoy, Karl Giberson, Del Case, Joe Lucas, and Scott Hovey were excellent conversation partners. I spent a good many late afternoons with Scott and Joe, discussing the wonderful worlds of bubblegum rock, garage pop, punk rock, yacht rock, and city rock over a pint of ale at Cornwall's in Kenmore Square. Back in Quincy, Austin Steelman and Katie Brinegar, student research assistants, skillfully tracked down scholarly articles, interviews, and more.

At Northumbria University in Newcastle upon Tyne my new Americanist colleagues Mike Cullinane, Sylvia Ellis, David Gleeson, Joe Steet, Brian Ward, and Henry Knight Lozano listened to me yammer on about the manuscript. They read sections and offered helpful advice.

One of the best things about this project has been that it's given me the chance to present my research in the United States, Germany, the United Kingdom, and Norway. I'm particularly grateful to the U.S.–Norway Fulbright Foundation and the friendship and assistance of Rena Levin, Petter Næss, Kevin McGuiness, and Kelly McKowen. It was while I was a Roving Scholar in Norway in 2012 that the book began to take definite shape. In seminars across the Atlantic, colleagues, friends, and mentors were superb hosts and lent me their advice and guidance. These included Dan Scroop and Andrew Hook at the University of Glasgow; Tony Badger at Claire College, Cambridge University; John Schmalzbauer at Missouri State University; Christopher Cantwell at the University of Missouri-Kansas City; Doug Thompson and Sarah Gardner at Mercer University; John Turner and the staff and students at Heidelberg University's Center for American Studies; Deborah Kitchen-Doderlein and Mia Brunelle Jønnum at the University of Oslo; Alex Goodall and Patrick Doyle at the Institute of Historical Research in London; Bevan Sewell and Richard King at the University of Nottingham; Peggy Bendroth at the Congregational Library and Archives in Boston; Brian Kelly and Crawford Gribben at Queens University Belfast; Uta Balbier at Kings College London; Tonia M. Compton at Columbia College; Peter Kuryla at Belmont University; Joe Crespino, Gary Laderman, Mike Camp, and Patrick Allitt at Emory University; Philip Goff and Ray Haberski at Indiana University–Purdue University Indianapolis; Emma Long at the University of East Anglia; Andrew Moore at Saint Anselm College; and Daniel Silliman, Jonathan Riddle, Suzanna Krivulskaya, Thomas Tweed, and Darren Dochuk at the University of Notre Dame.

I benefited much from the wisdom, conversations, and suggestions of other friends and colleagues like Vernon Burton, Becky Goetz, Barton Price, Rick Kennedy, Greg Markov, JoAnne Markov, Mike Lynn, Alice Tachney, Ted Ownby, Darren Grem, Kate Carte Engel, David Hempton, Hugh McLeod, Kathryn Lofton, Eddie Couchenour, Mark Hayse, Jared Miller, Amy Stortz Miller, Bobby Cave, Jeff Teel, John Ringhofer, Ronny Tveite-Strand, and Grant Wacker.

A summer 2015 fellowship at the Wesleyan Center at Point Loma Nazarene University in San Diego provided plenty of time and space to research and write. Beth Bollinger and director Mark Mann at the center were wonderfully helpful. The view of the Pacific was inspirational. I'm grateful for the insights gained at a 2016 National Endowment for the Humanities seminar on "Problems in the Study of Religion" at the University of Virginia. Leaders Chuck Mathewes and Kurtis Schaeffer, along with the participants, were encouraging and lively interlocutors. Other funding from the Congregational Library in Boston and the Southern Baptist Historical Library and Archives in Nashville provided much needed travel support.

Joyce Seltzer, my editor at Harvard University Press, offered up indispensable advice and gave her critical attention to the project. Kathi Drummy at the press provided great assistance along the way. Mary Ann Short, a diligent copy editor, saved me from making numerous mistakes and had a sharp eye for detail. Portions of Chapter 1 were originally published in "'Where else did they copy their styles but from church groups?': Rock 'n' Roll and Pentecostalism in the 1950s South," in *Church History: Studies in Christianity and Culture* Vol. 85, No. 1 (March 2016): 97-131. They are reprinted with the permission of Cambridge University Press.

My research and writing would not have been possible without tremendous help from librarians and archivists. They responded to my e-mail follow-up questions and pointed me to valuable sources that I often didn't even know existed. Their assistance throughout was critical. Among those are Darrin Rodgers and Glenn Gohr at the Flower Pentecostal Heritage Center; Taffey Hall and Bill Sumners at the Southern Baptist Historical Library and Archives; Patrick Robbins at Bob Jones University's Fundamentalism File; Glenda Seifert, at MidAmerica Nazarene University's Mabee Library, who tracked down scores of obscure articles; Adam Gossman at the Fuller Theological Seminary Archives and Special Collections Department; and Lucinda Cockrell, Dale Cockrell, and Grover Baker at the Center for Popular Music at Middle Tennessee State University. Every chapter benefited from the perceptive and careful reading of critics. In that regard I'm indebted to John Turner, Daniel Williams, Steven Miller, Paul Harvey, Larry Eskridge, and Charles Reagan Wilson. Matthew Sutton and David Stowe read the manuscript in its entirety, provided ample feedback, and saved me from a host of embarrassments.

My family in Kansas, Colorado, California, and Norway are deeply appreciated, among them Janice Stephens, Phil and Nicole White, Dave and Nicole Stephens, Kjerstin Løvdal and Kjetil Midtbø, Hanne and Atle Lofstad-Haug, and Øystein and Ragnhild Løvdal. Thanks are due to them for their sympathetic attention, kindness, and encouragement. Playtime breaks with Hans and Camilo Lofstad-Haug and Johnny and Harry White were a fun respite.

Finally, Hilde Løvdal Stephens was a constant source of ideas and a wonderful companion through it all. She read the manuscript, pointed out infelicities, and gave me excellent suggestions. Our research projects took us on trips from coast to coast, as well as to Oslo, Edinburgh, and London. She was an insightful critic and a voice of reason when I was in the valley of the shadow of writer's block. Thanks especially to her for her reassurance, friendship, and love.

INDEX